'CENTURIES WILL NOT SUFFICE'

I0895971

ABOUT THE AUTHOR

Pritpal ('Prit') Buttar was educated at St John's College Oxford where he gained a BA in physiological sciences. From Oxford he went on to King's College Hospital School of Medicine and Dentistry, London, where he obtained his MBBS, followed by the Royal College of General Practitioners, London, where he received his MRCGP. From 1987 to 1992 he was a Medical Officer in the Royal Army Medical Corps. On leaving the army he worked as a GP.

Prit has written a number of books on the Eastern Front in both the First and Second World Wars. His works have been translated into Polish, Lithuanian, Estonian, Finnish, Hungarian, Italian and Chinese. He has played a leading role in battlefield tours in Lithuania with NATO units and has appeared in a National Geographic Channel documentary on the International Military Tribunal at Nuremburg, speaking on the events on the Eastern Front.

'CENTURIES WILL NOT SUFFICE'

A HISTORY OF THE LITHUANIAN HOLOCAUST

PRIT BUTTAR

AMBERLEY

This edition published 2025

Amberley Publishing
The Hill, Stroud
Gloucestershire, GL5 4EP

www.amberley-books.com

Copyright © Prit Buttar, 2023, 2025

The right of Prit Buttar to be identified as the Author
of this work has been asserted in accordance with the
Copyright, Designs and Patents Act 1988.

All rights reserved. No part of this book may be reprinted
or reproduced or utilised in any form or by any electronic,
mechanical or other means, now known or hereafter invented,
including photocopying and recording, or in any information
storage or retrieval system, without the permission in writing
from the Publishers.

British Library Cataloguing in Publication Data.
A catalogue record for this book is available from the British Library.

ISBN 978 1 3981 2545 2 (paperback)
ISBN 978 1 3981 1516 3 (ebook)

1 2 3 4 5 6 7 8 9 10

Typeset in 10.5pt on 13.5pt Sabon.
Typesetting by SJmagic DESIGN SERVICES, India.
Printed and bound in India.

Appointed GPSR EU Representative: Easy Access System Europe Oü, 16879218
Address: Mustamäe tee 50, 10621, Tallinn, Estonia
Contact Details: gpsr.requests@easproject.com, +358 40 500 3575

Contents

Dramatis Personae

Adler, Anita	wife of Hermann Adler
Adler, Hermann	a Jew in Vilnius, originally from Nuremberg
Asmus, Friedrich	Wehrmacht officer, effectively Plagge's deputy in *HKP 562*
Behrens, Hans	company commander in *Polizeibataillon 309*
Best, Werner	head of the German Security Police until September 1939
Borkowska, Anna	mother superior of the Dominican convent in Pavilnys
Bradfisch, Otto	commander of *Einsatzkommando 8*, later head of Gestapo in Łódź
Čartokaitė, Joheved	a Jewish girl in the Kaunas ghetto
Daleuge, Kurt	head of the German uniformed police; Heydrich's replacement as Protector of Bohemia and Moravia
Deschwanden, Alfons von	German soldier in *HKP 562*
Ditfurth, Wolfgang	commander of 403rd Security Division
Eichmann, Adolf	head of the Jewish Affairs division of the SD
Elkes, Elkahan	head of the *Judenrat* in the Kaunas ghetto

Emaitisaite, Luisa	a Jew in Vilnius
Esterowicz, Perella	a young Jewish girl in Vilnius, daughter of Samuel Esterowicz
Esterowicz, Samuel	a Jew in Vilnius
Fried, Anatol	head of the *Judenrat* in the Vilnius ghetto
Genkind, Solomon (Solly)	a young Jewish boy in Kaunas
Gens, Jacob	head of the Jewish ghetto police in the Vilnius ghetto
Gdowski, Andrzej	the Catholic priest of the Church of St Teresa of Avila in Vilnius
Göcke, Wilhelm	commandant of Kaunas concentration camp
Gollub, Avraham	a Jew in the Kaunas ghetto, member of the *Judenrat* and diarist
Grauer, Gustav	deputy commander of *Einsatzkommando 3*
Grossman, Haika	Jewish resistance fighter
Goebbels, Joseph	German propaganda minister
Halder, Franz	chief of the German general staff until September 1942
Hamann, Joachim	subunit commander in *Einsatzkommando 3*
Heydrich, Lina, formerly Lina von Osten	wife of Reinhard Heydrich
Heydrich, Reinhard	head of the SD, Protector of Bohemia and Moravia
Himmler, Heinrich	head of the SS
Hingst, Hans Christian	*Gebietskommissar* in Vilnius
Jäger, Emma, formerly Emma Weber	first wife of Karl Jäger
Jäger, Karl	commander of *Einsatzkommando 3* until August 1943

Jeckeln, Friedrich	higher SS and police commander, Ostland
Jordan, Fritz	effectively the commandant of the Kaunas ghetto
Jost, Heinz	commander *Einzatzgruppe A* from March 1942 to September 1942
Kittel, Bruno	member of the SS, responsible for the liquidation of the ghettos and the *Kinderaktion*
Koppelman, Moisei	head of the Jewish ghetto police in the Kaunas ghetto
Kortkampf, Gerhard	subunit commander in *Einsatzkommando 3*
Kruk, Herman	Polish Jew in the Vilnius ghetto, librarian and diarist
Kučinskienė, Fruma	Jewish child in the Kaunas ghetto
Leeb, Wilhelm Ritter von	commander of Army Group North until January 1942
Lohse, Hinrich	Reichskommissar for Ostland
Molotov, Vyacheslav Michailovich	Soviet foreign minister
Müller, Heinrich	head of the Gestapo
Murer, Franz	director of the food and agriculture department in Vilnius, effectively responsible for food supply to the ghetto
Neugebauer, Rudolf	head of the Vilnius Security Police and SS, February 1942 October 1943
Paukštys, Bronius	a Catholic priest in Kaunas
Paulavičius, Jonas	a Lithuanian farmer near Kaunas
Pflugbeil, Johann	commander of 221st Security Division
Piłsudski, Józef	first Polish head of state after the First World War
Plagge, Karl	major in the German Army, commander of *Heereskraftfahrpark 562*

Rauca, Helmut	member of *Einsatzkommando 3*, Gestapo representative for Jewish affairs in Kaunas
Ribbentrop, Joachim von	German foreign minister
Rolnikaite, Mascha	a young Jewish girl in Vilnius
Rondholz, Friedrich	member of *Polizeibataillon 309*
Roques, Franz von	commander of rear area units behind Army Group North until April 1943
Sakowicz, Kazimierz	Polish Lithuanian journalist living in Ponary, who kept a diary of the killings
Salinger, Max	a Jew in Vilnius
Sandberger, Martin	commander of *Sonderkommando 1a* and head of security police and SS in Estonia
Schauschutz, Franz	commander of *Einsatzkommando 9*
Schmid, Anton	NCO in the German Army, head of the *Versprengten-Sammelstelle* in Vilnius
Schneider, Heinrich ('Pipo')	platoon commander in *Polizeibataillon 309*
Schönbrunner, Oskar	Wehrmacht officer in charge of a tailoring workshop in Vilnius
Schweinberger, Horst	SS NCO responsible for the shootings at Ponary
Stahlecker, Franz Walter	commander of *Einsatzgruppe A* until March 1942
Sugihara, Chiune	Japanese consul in Kaunas until September 1940
Tenenbaum, Mordechai	Jewish resistance fighter
Wagner, Eduard	Quartermaster-General of the German Army until July 1944
Weiss, Martin	SS NCO in *Einsatzkommando 3*
Żeligowski, Lucjan	Polish officer, founder of the Republic of Central Lithuania
Zwartendijk, Jan	executive of Philips electronics company, Dutch honorary consul-general in Kaunas until August 1940

Glossary of Terms

AK	Armia Krajova ('Home Army'), Polish resistance army created around the former units of the Polish Army
Anschluss	'Union', the annexation of Austria into the German Reich
Barbarossa	codename for the German invasion of the Soviet Union in June 1941
Einsatzkommando	'Task Command', subunit of an Einsatzgruppe
Einsatzgruppe	'Task Group', unit organised from SS, SD and police personnel to ensure security immediately behind the front line
FPO	Fareinikte Partisaner Organizatzie ('United Partisan Organisation'), amalgamated Jewish resistance group
Freikorps	German military units created from formations of the German Army at the end of the First World War, used mainly to suppress Bolshevik groups within Germany and in the Baltic Wars of Independence
Gebietskommissar	subordinate of a Reichskommissar, responsible for a specific district

Gestapo	Geheime Staatspolizei ('Secret State Police'), German secret police
GFP	Geheime Feldpolizei ('Secret Field Police'), military equivalent of the Gestapo
Grossaktion Warschau	'Major Action Warsaw', the operation by the SS to liquidate the Warsaw Ghetto
Hilfswillige	'Volunteer helpers' or Hiwis, voluntary auxiliary forces made up of recruits indigenous to the territories of Eastern Europe, mostly former Soviet prisoners of war who volunteered to help the German military in a variety of roles, often in order to escape the harsh conditions in the prison camps
HKP	Heereskraftfahrpark ('Army Motor Vehicle Park'), engineer unit for repair of wheeled army motor vehicles
HSSPF	Höherer SS und Polizeiführer ('Higher SS and Police Leader'), head of SS and police units in an occupied area
Judenrat	'Jewish council', representative body of Jews in the ghettos
LAF	Lietuvių Aktyvistų Frontas ('Lithuanian Activist Front'), pro-German and anti-Soviet Lithuanian paramilitary group
Maline	hiding place constructed by the Jews in ghettos and camps
NKVD	Narodnyy Komissariat Vnutrennikh Del, the People's Commissariat for Internal Affairs, effectively the interior ministry of the Soviet Union and the forerunner of the KGB.

Omakaitse	Estonian 'Home Guard', pro-German and anti-Soviet paramilitary group
Operation Reinhard	codename for the accelerated killing of Jews through 1942
Orpo	'Ordnungspolizei' ('Order police'), the regular uniformed police force of Germany
Reichskommissar	head of a Reichskommissariat
Reichskommissariat Ostland	the German civilian administration in the Baltic States and the western parts of Belarus
Reichsministerium für die besetzten Ostgebiete	'Reich Ministry for the Occupied Eastern Territories' or Ostministerium, German government department technically responsible for occupied territories across Eastern Europe
Rollkommando	'Mobile command', specialised mobile subunit of an Einsatzgruppe
RSHA	Reich Sicherheitshauptamt ('Reich Main Security Office'), created by combining the German Security Police and the SD
SD	Sicherheitsdienst ('Security Administration'), effectively the intelligence service of the Nazi Party
Selbstschutz	'Self-defence' paramilitary formations organised by ethnic Germans and others in support of the German Army
Sicherheitspolizei	'Security Police' or 'Sipo', created by combining the Gestapo and the civilian criminal police (Kriminalpolizei)
Sonderkommando	'Special command', subunit of an Einsatzgruppe

SS	Schutz Staffeln ('Protection Squads'), paramilitary organisation of the Nazi Party, consisting of the Allgemeine SS ('General SS'), responsible for policing and other non-military duties, the Waffen-SS ('Armed SS'), which formed front-line combat formations, and SS-Totenkopfverbände ('SS Death's Head Units'), which manned the concentration camps, death camps etc.
Versprengten-Sammelstelle	'Stragglers Collection Point', rear area unit responsible for returning men to their units from hospitals, leave, or those left behind for other reasons
Wehrmacht	German armed forces

'What these scum perpetrate here in the name of the German people – centuries will not suffice for us to cleanse ourselves!'

Feldwebel Berger

Introduction

There is something about large numbers that numbs the human brain. Intellectually, we can understand calculations involving huge figures, but at a different, more subjective and personal level, these numbers defeat our emotional comprehension.

On 23 August 1923, the German newspaper *Vossische Zeitung* published an article by Kurt Tucholsky entitled *Französischer Witz* ('French wit'). This article quoted a French diplomat: 'The death of one man: that is a catastrophe. A hundred thousand deaths: that is a statistic!' Perhaps recalling this article, or the words of the French diplomat, Josef Stalin made a similar comment in January 1947 which was reported by the *Washington Post*: 'If only one man dies of hunger, that is a tragedy. If millions die, that's only statistics.' A fundamental truth about our comprehension of such numbers underlies the words both of the French diplomat and Stalin.

Most people have little difficulty in empathising with bereavement. After all, everyone will suffer one or more bereavements during their lives. We can comprehend the despair and emotional turmoil of others who deal with loss. We can even contemplate the pain when someone suffers multiple bereavements, such as the loss of their family. But as the numbers grow, the scale of our empathy struggles to keep up. When we hear of an aircraft crash with perhaps a hundred people killed and we see pictures of distraught relatives desperate for news, we don't scale up our concept of grief a hundred-fold. And as the numbers climb higher, we are utterly incapable of imagining bereavement and loss on such a scale. The impact of the deaths of a thousand people feels little different from one or two hundred deaths. Even comparing these numbers to the population of a nearby town or city, or the number of people who could fill a football stadium, does little to help our imagination cope.

As a consequence of this, when we consider some of the terrible death tolls of the past – or indeed in recent times with hundreds of thousands dying in a worldwide pandemic – the numbers pass through our brains as little more than intellectual facts. We can condemn the mass murder of six million Jews during the Second World War, but do we really think of these deaths as individual people, each of whom had a past full of triumphs and failures, a future full of hopes and fears, a life that was suddenly cut short? Six million futures destroyed, each with connections to dozens of other people – many of whom were also victims of the Holocaust. Perhaps if our brains were able to grasp the emotional scale of such terrible events, there would be fewer of them.

When people think of the Holocaust, the mental pictures are of trains bringing thousands of victims to the death camps, where they were gassed and then cremated, or in many cases worked to death. But before the industrialised mass murder of these camps was designed and deployed, huge numbers had already perished. Operation *Barbarossa*, the German invasion of the Soviet Union on 22 June 1941, resulted in a rapid advance across the western parts of Ukraine and Belarus and the swift occupation of the Baltic States, which had been forcibly annexed by Stalin just a few months previously. Hundreds of thousands of Jews – many of whom had fled previous German advances into Poland – didn't have time to escape before the area was overrun, and they found themselves under German control. By 25 November 1941, just five months after the German invasion, a report produced for the SS listed in detail the killing of 137,346 people in Lithuania alone; nearly all of them had been shot in mass executions. The precision of this report is in itself horrifying, breaking down the killings by daily locations and dividing them into men, women and children, with further categorisation as Jews, communists, or other groups listed for extermination.

The huge scale of killing by gunshot had serious implications. Numerous options had been considered in preceding years regarding the removal of Jews from Germany and other parts of Europe, ranging from transporting them to a remote island like Madagascar to persuading the Soviet Union to move them to Siberia. A Jewish 'colony' in southeast Poland was briefly considered before another plan was formed: Jews would be sent east into the territories that were to be seized from the Soviet Union and would then be worked to death building new roads and railways. The mass killing of Jews in Lithuania and Latvia was at least partly intended as a means of creating space for Jews from Germany and elsewhere to be held prior to their transfer further east.

When the German invasion stalled outside Moscow in late 1941, there was a need to reconsider. The war was clearly going to last longer than originally thought, and with so many Germans serving in the armed forces there was sudden recognition of workforce shortages. Consequently, the policy of starving tens of thousands of Soviet prisoners of war to death was reconsidered, with the intention to use the men as forced labour instead. Similarly, the Jews who had been confined to ghettos across Eastern Europe would provide a labour force and would have to be 'eliminated' at a later stage in other ways than those originally planned.

Many within the SS and elsewhere were concerned about the financial cost of the operation to kill the Jews of the Baltic States and similar operations in Belarus and Ukraine, especially as it was now seen as a potential model for the mass murder of Jews from other parts of Europe. The impact of such mass executions on the men involved was also a concern. Senior German officials were troubled by the effect on their men of being involved in such crimes, whilst simultaneously showing no sympathy for their victims. Some of the soldiers and paramilitary personnel resorted to alcohol; others took refuge in the numbing quality of large numbers, painstakingly recording the killings as a balance sheet of death to distance themselves from the appalling reality of what was happening. These factors, together with others, contributed to the decision to switch to killing by the use of poison gas.

The apparatus required for murder on such a scale, whether by shooting or gassing, was huge. Much of it grew in an ad-hoc manner; but much of it was planned in detail. Many accounts place responsibility for the murders – or at least the physical act of murder – on the SS, but the reality is that almost all parts of the German military, and other occupation bodies, were involved. After the war, many German military veterans attempted to portray the role of German combat forces as being distinctly different from those involved in the killings carried out behind their front lines; even the combat divisions of the SS were seen as purely military formations, with no involvement in the terrible crimes being carried out elsewhere. But the reality is very different. Almost every German military unit that served on the Eastern Front contributed in some way to the slaughter of Jews and others in the occupied parts of the Soviet Union, either directly or indirectly, and thousands of men from the occupied regions – Ukrainians, Lithuanians, Latvians, Estonians, Belarusians, even Russians – took part in the killings. Indeed, these local recruits were responsible – under direct orders of German officers – for most of the shootings that took place in 1941.

The men who entered the Soviet Union as part of the German invasion of 1941 had been widely briefed, both in general and specific terms. This was to be a different war from previous campaigns – it was explicitly a *Rassenkrieg* or 'racial war', and many of the normal conventions of the conduct of armies were to be ignored. In the case of the units specifically tasked with implementing the murder of Jews, communists and other 'undesirables', the briefings were more detailed, making clear that their role would involve the destruction of tens of thousands of civilians of all ages. Nevertheless, many who found themselves involved in the machinery of mass murder were horrified by what they saw and experienced. Some refused to take part – contrary to widespread belief, both at the time and in the years that followed, there were often few sanctions against such individuals, particularly if they were from the 'mainstream' military. A few took extraordinary risks to prevent killings.

It is perhaps easier to comprehend the killings, and the men involved in carrying them out, if they are considered in detail. A small number of individuals, both before and during the German occupation, showed great moral integrity and did what they could to save innocent victims; others either embraced the Nazi plans to reshape the ethnic makeup of Europe with enthusiasm, or doggedly followed orders. This is the story of how the Holocaust unfolded in Lithuania, and the roles played by these people.

Some, like Jan Zwartendijk and Chiune Sugihara, were foreign diplomats who defied the instructions of their governments to rescue Jews; others, like Andrzej Gdowski, were Lithuanian civilians who took enormous personal risks to defy the occupation authorities; and many, both those responsible for the slaughter and those who tried to prevent it, were German soldiers. Karl Jäger was a senior officer in the SS, sent to the region with his men specifically to carry out mass killing. Karl Plagge and Anton Schmid were soldiers who found themselves in Vilnius as part of the occupation forces and rebelled against the horror of what they saw. All three were veterans of the First World War and were shaped by the events of the years between the wars, but with very different outcomes.

Jäger and his colleagues represent the machinery of murder that was deployed with such calculation by Nazi Germany; Plagge and Schmid were ordinary men who found extraordinary courage to stand up against such crimes. In one of the darkest episodes of European history, they stand out as shining examples of courage

1

The Birth of the *Einsatzgruppen*

The border between what was East Prussia and Lithuania is roughly at the same latitude as the border between England and Scotland. From about the beginning of June, the nights aren't properly dark – it's perfectly possible to walk around even in the middle of the night without the aid of lights. On the morning of 22 June 1941, shortly before the waning thin crescent of the moon rose in the eastern sky, the German side of the frontier was the scene of great activity. Troops had been gathering in the area for weeks, but the great moment, delayed due to the weather and the need to send German troops into Yugoslavia, was now at hand: *Barbarossa*, the German invasion of the Soviet Union, was about to commence.

Hitler had made no secret of his ultimate intention to attack the Soviet Union. In the first volume of *Mein Kampf*, written in 1924 while he was imprisoned in the Bavarian city of Landsberg following the failed 'Beer Hall Putsch' of 1923, he described the need for Germany to acquire colonies that would permit the German population to increase, and the natural direction for such territorial expansion was to the east:

> [New territories] could be acquired primarily at the expense of Russia. The new empire must once again march the road of the ancient knights of the German Orders and use the sword to provide land for the German plough, which can then provide our daily bread.[1]

The revelation of the non-aggression pact (often referred to as the Molotov-Ribbentrop Pact after the two foreign ministers who negotiated it) between Germany and the Soviet Union on 23 August 1939, just days before the German invasion of Poland, came as a great shock to many people, both within the two nations involved and elsewhere. There was widespread hostility towards Bolshevism in Germany, both within the ranks of the Nazi Party and amongst conservative circles that were suspicious of, or even hostile to, Hitler's regime, and the sudden proclamation of the new treaty was utterly unexpected. Similarly, the Soviet authorities had made no secret of their portrayal of Nazi Germany as a fundamental enemy of Bolshevism. But neither side had any intention of adhering to the new treaty for longer than was necessary. Even as Molotov and Ribbentrop were signing the pact, Stalin was hunting ducks with his inner circle of associates and told them: 'Of course it's all a game to see who can fool whom. I know what Hitler's up to. He thinks he's outsmarted me but actually it's I who's tricked him.'[2]

Nonetheless, the German invasion on 22 June 1941 took Stalin by surprise. There had been plenty of warnings to the Soviet leadership that a German invasion was imminent, with information arriving from other nations, Soviet agents abroad, and from the Red Army's observers along the frontier, but Stalin appears to have ignored all the reports. Before the sun rose, German artillery began to bombard Soviet border positions and the Luftwaffe ranged deep into Soviet airspace, striking at airfields, bridges, railways and other targets. At first, Moscow forbade any Soviet military response that might involve shelling or air attacks into German territory, thinking – or perhaps hoping – that the reports of fighting were mistakes, or merely represented local unofficial actions.

It wasn't the first time that German troops had invaded the lands that lay to the east of Germany. A long campaign was fought across Eastern Europe and the western parts of what was then the Russian Empire in the First World War, placing such a strain on Russia that it brought about the fall of the Romanov dynasty and subsequently the October Revolution that put the Bolsheviks in power. But the invasion of 1941, like the attack on Poland in 1939, was significantly different. It is one of the bitter ironies of history that when the Germans and their Austro-Hungarian allies drove the armies of Tsarist Russia from the territories that the Russians had seized at the beginning of the First World War, the people who were most enthusiastic in their welcome were the Jews of what is now eastern Poland – the anti-Semitic conduct of the Russian forces was notorious before the war, and their behaviour in these territories more than confirmed the fears of the Jewish communities.

The Germans had entered these lands in the First World War with the intention of establishing a series of client states from the western provinces of the Russian Empire, but the territorial ambitions of the Third Reich were significantly different. On the eve of the invasion of Poland in 1939, Hitler made clear his intentions, as General Franz Halder, the chief of the German general staff, noted in his diary:

> Goal: annihilation of Poland, that is, destruction of active power. We are not setting out just to reach a specific line or establish a new frontier, but rather we seek the annihilation of the enemy, which we must pursue in ever new ways ...
>
> Means to this end: it does not matter what they are. *The victor is never called upon to vindicate his actions. The question is not one of the justice of our cause, but exclusively of achieving victory* [emphasis in original] ...
>
> Execution: Harsh and remorseless. We must steel ourselves against humanitarian reasoning![3]

Whilst the intention of Nazi Germany – as outlined in *Mein Kampf* – was to establish new colonies in Eastern Europe from which Germany would be able to get sufficient agricultural, mineral and industrial resources to make it invulnerable to coastal blockades, the German concept of colonisation was significantly different from the policies followed by the British, French and others during the 19th century. The Germans had no intention of simply controlling their new colonies with a relatively small occupation force and even smaller body of administrators. Their intention was the 'Germanisation' of the new territories, with most of the population being replaced by ethnic Germans.

A foretaste of this occurred in the late 19th century in what is now Namibia, where the Germans responded to local unrest by attempting the wholesale extermination of the Namaqua and Herrero people of the region, with the intention of providing space for German settlers.[4] The plans for the new German colonies in Eastern Europe were, from the outset, based upon the expectation that millions of men, women and children in the existing populations would have to die to create space for the ethnically superior Germans to replace them. A minority of the Slavs of Poland and the European parts of the Soviet Union would be permitted to survive as labourers for their new masters, but most would be killed.

The armies that entered the Soviet Union on that June morning were closely followed by special SS formations that were to play a leading role in the mass murder that was to come. From the start of Germany's expansionist entries into neighbouring countries, such groups of SS personnel had been deployed, but with mixed results. Over time, their structure and their orders had therefore evolved.

The first entry into a foreign country by Hitler's armies for the purpose of annexation was in 1938. With growing pressure both within Austria and in Germany for Austria to seek union with Germany, the Austrian chancellor, Kurt Schuschnigg, announced his intention of holding a referendum on the issue. His intention was to secure a large vote in favour of an independent Austria and in order to forestall this, Hitler ordered his army to cross the border early on 12 March. Many Austrians greeted the German soldiers with enthusiasm, but others – particularly the large Jewish community in Vienna – had good reason to fear the new developments.

Even as the columns of the German Eighth Army threaded their way along the roads of Austria, an aircraft landed in Vienna and two men disembarked. One was Heinrich Himmler, head of the SS. The other was Reinhard Heydrich, who would play a huge role in the mass killings of the coming years.[5]

Heydrich was in many respects the physical embodiment of the Nazi Aryan dream. He was tall, blond, blue-eyed and athletic, and totally convinced of the need to establish German hegemony over a racially homogeneous Europe. He was born in 1904 in the German city of Halle; his father Bruno was an accomplished musician and his mother Elizabeth was the daughter of Professor Eugen Krantz, director of the Dresden Conservatory. Bruno Heydrich's father died when Bruno was just 11 years old, and his impoverished mother married a locksmith named Gustav Süss; although Süss was a Lutheran Christian, the surname was common in the Jewish community, and this was the source of later rumours that Heydrich was 'tainted' with Jewish ancestry.

Too young to serve in the First World War, Heydrich joined the navy in 1922. It seems that he was a competent naval officer, but he soon acquired a reputation for arrogance. In late 1930, Heydrich – who had, until this time, shown little interest in political matters – met Lina von Osten, who was a committed supporter of the Nazi family, at a ball in the city of Kiel. It seems that he was captivated by her almost from their first encounter and within a few weeks they were engaged to be married. This proved to be disastrous for Heydrich's naval career. He was already involved with another woman, whose father – either a senior naval officer, or someone with influential contacts within the navy – made a formal complaint to the naval staff. Heydrich was summoned to a Court of Honour to explain himself. Had he adopted a suitably penitent tone, it is likely that he would have escaped with little more than a stern reprimand, but his growing arrogance was his undoing. His conduct during the hearing was such that the presiding officers recommended his dismissal on the grounds that he was not a suitable person to be a naval officer. He was duly discharged in April 1931.

Had he not met Lina von Osten, Heydrich's life would probably have taken a very different path. Suddenly unemployed – though the terms of his dismissal permitted him a small severance salary for the next two years – Heydrich was hugely downcast by the turn of events. Through family contacts, he was encouraged to apply for a post in the SS. Himmler, the head of the SS, wished to create an intelligence service for his organisation, to gather information on potential opponents both within the Nazi movement and in Germany as a whole. Heydrich had no experience whatever of intelligence affairs, but one of the references provided for him on his departure from the navy mentioned that he had served as a signals and intelligence officer. The former was correct, but the latter was entirely false. Nonetheless, when Himmler interviewed Heydrich for the post in the summer of 1931, he asked him to describe how he would organise the new intelligence service. Heydrich's knowledge of such matters was almost exclusively derived from a longstanding interest in works of fiction dealing with espionage, but he managed to impress Himmler through a combination of imaginative improvisation and the liberal use of military terms that he had learned during his time in the navy. He was awarded the post of head of the new SS Intelligence Service, which was soon given the name of the *Sicherheitsdienst* or SD (Security Service).

Despite having avoided any involvement in the turbulent politics in Germany during the preceding decade, Heydrich rapidly made up for lost time. The bullying he experienced as a schoolboy with regard to his alleged Jewish ancestry may have played a part, but he rapidly became completely committed to Nazi concepts of racial hierarchy. For Heydrich and many other Nazis, the linkage between Jews and Bolshevism was a completely natural one and even if he hadn't willingly embraced the Nazi dogma regarding Jews as a parasitic infestation of European culture, the elimination of the Communists, sworn enemies of the Nazis, inevitably meant the elimination of the Jews. Like most figures in the Nazi Party, he took every opportunity he could to increase his personal power. The SD grew in size and scope throughout the 1930s and following the *Anschluss* or annexation of Austria, its personnel, together with men from the Gestapo, were rapidly deployed to round up those opposed to the new regime.

The purpose of the deployment was to ensure that security was maintained until more formal arrangements could be put in place; Heydrich repeatedly painted a picture of Germany being beset by hidden enemies, both inside and outside its borders, and these enemies would have to be destroyed, or they would destroy Germany. It isn't clear how strongly he personally believed this, or whether he used it as a means of persuading others to allow him to increase his powers, but the narrative that he created fitted well with the paranoid view of the Nazis that human affairs were the ultimate demonstration of social Darwinism – the strongest would survive and prosper, but only if they showed no weakness and dealt with their enemies swiftly and thoroughly.

The deployment of SD personnel in Austria proved to be something of a disaster in some respects. On the first night of the occupation, Heydrich's men rounded up about 21,000 individuals. Many of Austria's Jews were from wealthy families in Vienna and the temptation to indulge in looting proved irresistible. The property seized from Jews was meant to be registered and carefully stored as it now belonged to the German state, but just four days after the arrests and confiscations began, Heydrich had to issue an order threatening 'merciless' action against those who were taking advantage of the situation to enrich themselves.[6]

Looting wasn't the only problem; one of the SD officers, Horst Böhme, was meant to arrest Wilhelm Freiherr von Ketteler, a German diplomat who had been working in Vienna but was rightly suspected of plotting to assassinate Hitler. Ketteler disappeared on the first night after the German arrival and his body was found floating in the Danube a few weeks later. Analysis showed that Ketteler had been subdued with chloroform prior to being dumped in the river. Many of Ketteler's high-ranking associates demanded an investigation, which – at least in public – proved fruitless. Nonetheless, Joseph Goebbels, the German propaganda minister, noted in his diary that this killing and other similar murders had resulted in outrage in senior Nazi circles, and these were likely to cause trouble for Heydrich. A post-war investigation later concluded that Ketteler had been arrested by Böhme, who then tried to interrogate the diplomat. When he refused to cooperate, Böhme administered chloroform and drowned him in a bath, and then dumped the body in the Danube.

Heydrich was able to restore order in the ranks of his men and tried to pass off many of their excesses as the acts of Communists who had disguised themselves as Germans. Many of the attacks and thefts had been carried out by members of the Nazi Party who were not under Heydrich's direct control, and he wrote to Josef Bürckel, who had been appointed as *Reichskommissar für die Wiedervereinigung Österreichs mit dem Deutschen Reich* ('Reich Commissar for the Reunification of Austria with the German Reich'), who had overall control of Nazi Party members in Vienna:

> Unfortunately, Party members have participated in large-scale, completely unjustified attacks in recent days. I have today published a press statement stating that Communist supporters, dressed in

> Nazi Party uniforms, have been conducting illegal property seizures, house searches and arrests. I must point out that these comments were in fact not directed primarily at Communist supporters but rather at our own Party comrades. It would be regrettable if the Gestapo was forced to arrest our own Party comrades on a large scale. I therefore urgently request that you issue appropriate instructions to all Party agencies.[7]

It took two further threats before Heydrich was able to bring his men and other Nazi workers to heel. For a man who deliberately cultivated an image of the ruthless pursuit of Nazi ideological aims with efficiency and energy, the indiscipline of the SD and others was an embarrassment. Nevertheless, the operation was largely a success, with almost all potential sources of resistance to Nazi rule swiftly eliminated.

Later in 1938, Hitler's attention centred on Czechoslovakia and Heydrich and his SD began preparations for what was to come. Once again, it was his intention to eliminate actual and potential opponents as quickly as possible; perhaps influenced by his penchant for espionage novels, Heydrich repeatedly conjured the image of shadowy forces that plotted against Nazi Germany, with the Jews consistently playing a leading role in such conspiracies. During September, two *Einsatzgruppen* of 'task groups' were formed, made up of a total of 11 sub-formations or *Einsatzkommandos* and totalling about 850 men. When the Sudetenland was annexed in October, the *Einsatzgruppen* went to work immediately and – with the help of Sudeten German paramilitary volunteers – within a few short weeks they had arrested between 10,000 and 20,000 people. Most were released in subsequent months, but many remained in captivity.

In March of the following year, Germany occupied what is now the Czech Republic, creating the Protectorate of Bohemia and Moravia. Once again, Heydrich's *Einsatzgruppen* were sent into the newly acquired territories on the heels of the occupying troops. Many German exiles had made their homes in Prague. Some fled before the arrival of the Germans, but others were arrested. As had been the case in Austria, there were episodes of apparently random violence and looting, but whilst these left Heydrich feeling angered and exasperated, the incidents were at least on a lesser scale. The deployment of the *Einsatzgruppen* in the Sudetenland and during the occupation of the Czech lands managed to avoid most of the indiscipline and excesses that followed the entry into Austria.

As war with Poland grew increasingly likely during the summer of 1939, Heydrich planned another, much larger security operation; Hitler issued orders for him to commence preparations as early as March. The successful model of the *Einsatzgruppen* would be employed again in what became known as Operation *Tannenberg*. The SD compiled lists of those who were to be arrested, with a total of over 60,000 names – on this occasion, the intention was not just to arrest actual and potential opponents of the Reich. Hitler intended to destroy Poland as a nation, and in order to help achieve this he intended to eliminate the Polish intelligentsia. The arrests would go far beyond politicians and military figures. Teachers, business figures, aristocrats, and clergy, who might form the focus of Polish nationalist sentiment, were also to be detained. And, of course, there was the question of Poland's large Jewish population.

For *Tannenberg*, Heydrich deployed five *Einsatzgruppen*, later increased to seven. As he built up the SD during the 1930s, Heydrich was careful with his choice of recruits. Most of the senior personnel were committed Nazis, who personally embodied the Nazi ideal of the future German: they were often highly educated, physically fit, and completely unflinching in their loyalty to Nazi policies and to Heydrich. Perhaps in an attempt to avoid the problems that had arisen in Austria, the leaders of the *Einsatzgruppen* were selected from men who had proved themselves over the preceding years. Many had been involved in operations in Austria and the Czech lands, but others were deliberately moved from administrative posts to take part in field operations as an opportunity for them to prove their value as senior SS officers.

Their orders were uncompromising. A document entitled *Richtlinien für den Auswärtigen Einsatz der Sicherheitspolizei und des SD* ('Guidelines for the overseas deployment of the security police and SD') was issued on the eve of the invasion of Poland to the commanders of the *Einsatzgruppen*. The SS personnel were to tackle the 'leading stratum of the population in Poland and render them impotent'; in addition, the document continued, 'The task of the security police *Einsatzkommandos* is the fight against all elements in foreign countries in the rear of the combat troops that are hostile to the Reich and the German people.' Unlike previous operations, the orders on this occasion included sections intended to ensure better discipline. Sexual relations with women of non-German origin would be punished severely, and the personnel of the *Einsatzkommandos* were warned against excessive violence: 'The mistreatment or killing of detained persons is strictly prohibited and, if it is undertaken by other persons, it is to be prevented. Force may only be used to break up resistance.'[8]

The trouble that had occurred in Austria – and to a lesser extent in and around Prague the following year – resulted in the German

Army feeling uneasy about the future involvement of the SS in military operations. In an attempt to address this, Heydrich and Werner Best – the head of the German Security Police and effectively Heydrich's deputy – had a meeting with General Eduard Wagner, the chief of staff of the department of the army's quartermaster-general in late August. The outcome was to the satisfaction of all concerned. The *Einsatzkommandos* were instructed to ensure that they had liaison officers attached to local military headquarters in order to ensure close cooperation.

It is difficult to know how strictly Heydrich intended his subordinates to interpret these orders. It was characteristic of his policy that the instructions to the *Einsatzgruppen* used imprecise language, such as ‘neutralise’ or ‘render impotent’, without defining what this actually meant. This was part of a deliberate policy to encourage initiative amongst his men. This would, it was hoped, result in healthy competition to achieve the aims of Heydrich and would lead to innovation that could be used in future – again, this was part of the Nazi belief in competition as part of Darwinism and the survival of the fittest.

Despite the instructions to avoid mistreatment of those under arrest, the additional orders issued at a conference two weeks before the invasion of Poland hinted at a liberal interpretation of what might constitute resistance and would thus justify violence. The officers present were told by Heydrich that Poles were responsible for numerous atrocities against ethnic Germans in Poland and that severe punishment of anyone responsible for such crimes would be part of the task of the *Einsatzgruppen*. In later years, some of those present remembered clearly that Heydrich informed them that in their mission to ‘liquidate’ thousands of those regarded as the Polish leadership and those responsible for the wildly exaggerated alleged atrocities, saying that ‘anything is permissible.’[9] Hostages were to be seized, and executed at the slightest sign of any resistance.

From the outset, the *Einsatzgruppen* showed particular energy in attacking Jews. Heydrich was aware that Poland was about to be partitioned between Germany and the Soviet Union and he wished to drive as many Jews as possible into the Soviet zone. Hundreds were shot, many were burned alive after being herded into synagogues and other buildings that were then set alight. Some of the personnel of the German Army were horrified by the events unfolding behind their front line, and many raised official protests. These reached Halder, the chief of the general staff, who was of course well aware of Hitler's intentions and of the orders issued to the *Einsatzgruppen*. Others complained to Generaloberst Wilhelm Keitel, head of the Wehrmacht high command, but his response was that such decisions had been made by Hitler and could not be questioned.

Others within the army approved of what they saw as harsh but necessary measures to ensure the rapid pacification of conquered territory. Many army units were themselves involved in arbitrary executions, while others handed over suspected individuals to the *Einsatzgruppen* in the certain knowledge that the prisoners would be executed.

Further help for the *Einsatzgruppen* came from the *Selbstschutz* ('Self-Defence') paramilitary units that were created by ethnic Germans in Poland. These men showed great energy in killing Poles with little or no provocation. Whilst he was in favour of widespread executions, Heydrich was less enthusiastic about much of the violence perpetrated by the *Selbstschutz*, particularly in connection with non-Jewish Poles.

Tensions between the SS and the army escalated steadily throughout the campaign and there was a further meeting between Heydrich and Wagner to clarify matters. Wagner was able to extract agreement from Heydrich for one unit – *Einsatzgruppe zur Besondere Verfügung* ('Special Purpose *Einsatzgruppe*'), commanded by Obergruppenführer Udo von Woyrsch and responsible for some of the worst atrocities – to be withdrawn from Poland. Heydrich also agreed to keep the army better informed about the activities and orders of his men. After Wagner refused to comply with Heydrich's demand that military tribunals dealing with detained Poles work faster, Heydrich responded by issuing secret orders to the *Einsatzgruppe* commanders to overburden the military tribunals with so many cases that they would simply collapse.

By the end of 1939, after just four months of operations in occupied Poland, the *Einsatzgruppen* had killed 65,000 civilians. Although Heydrich was able to prevent much of the looting and disorder that had marked the activities of his men on previous campaigns, the vastly greater brutality displayed created lasting distrust between the army and the SS. During the campaigns in the west that resulted in the occupation of parts of Scandinavia, the Low Countries and France, the *Einsatzgruppen* were no longer present. To the disappointment and frustration of Heydrich and Himmler, Hitler agreed with the army that the campaigns in the west were against people who were racially different from the 'inferior' Slavs of the east. Occupation of the new territories in the west would be under more traditional military control.

Nonetheless, as plans began to be drawn up in early 1941 for an invasion of the Soviet Union, the organisation of Heydrich's units continued to evolve. In late 1939, his SD was combined with the German Security Police – which was itself a combination of the Gestapo and the *Kriminalpolizei* – to form the *Reich Sicherheitshauptamt* ('Reich Main Security Office' or RSHA). Heydrich was thus now in charge of a powerful body with both intelligence capabilities and responsibilities, and the personnel to enforce policies in occupied regions. With a new war against a Slav nation being planned, the *Einsatzgruppen* were once more prepared for action. Every deployment of Heydrich's teams, from Austria to Poland, had seen an escalation in the scope of their targets and a growth in their violence. The invasion of the Soviet Union would follow this trend.

As had been the case with the invasion of Poland, Hitler spelled out his intentions before the start of the campaign. Halder made a note of the briefing given by Hitler in his diary on 30 March 1941 when the Führer outlined his plans for *Barbarossa*:

> [This will be] a clash of two ideologies. Crushing denunciation of Bolshevism, identified with a social criminality. Communism is an enormous danger for our future. We must forget the concept of comradeship between soldiers. A Communist is no comrade before or after the battle. This is a war of extermination. If we do not grasp this ... thirty years later we shall again have to fight the Communist foe ...
>
> This war will be very different from the war in the west. In the east, harshness today means lenience in the future. Commanders must make the sacrifice of overcoming their personal scruples.[10]

The invasion of the Soviet Union would involve three army groups, and Heydrich organised a total of four *Einsatzgruppen* to accompany them – two such groups would follow Army Group South into Ukraine and Crimea, while the other two army groups were assigned a single *Einsatzgruppe* each. The *Einsatzgruppen* would have *Einsatzkommandos* numbering a little more than 120 men each, but in addition had *Sonderkommandos* ('Special Commands') of similar size who were to follow the advancing Wehrmacht units more closely. In most cases, these *Sonderkommandos* had instructions to establish early contact with local anti-Bolshevik groups, many of which were in contact with Germany before the invasion began.

During the invasion of Poland, the *Einsatzgruppen* had been nominally subordinated to their associated Wehrmacht armies, but *Barbarossa* would be different. From the outset, it was made clear that Heydrich's formations would be answerable ultimately to Heinrich Himmler, who was given a free hand to ensure security behind the front line. Once again, Heydrich and Wagner met to discuss the precise arrangements, and it seems that Wagner was very content to pass responsibility for the potentially messy task of pacifying the rear areas to the SS.

Nonetheless, the Wehrmacht would have to provide logistic support for the *Einsatzgruppen* – ammunition, fuel, etc. – and had been given clear instructions of its own with regard to the conduct of the war.

The infamous *Richtlinien für die Behandlung Politischer Kommissare* ('Guidelines for the treatment of political commissars', often abbreviated to *Kommissarbefehl* or 'Commissar Order') was formally issued less than a month before the invasion began. The Bolshevik enemy could not be expected to adhere to any principles of humanity or international law, and it was therefore appropriate for the Germans, too, to pay no regard to such matters. As the 'originators of barbaric Asiatic methods of warfare' the Soviet Union's political commissars were to be shot as soon as they were captured; any individuals who were clearly commissars but had not taken part in any actions against the Germans were to be handed over to the *Sonderkommandos* who would assess their culpability.

Many of the documents that circulated in the Wehrmacht and SS prior to the invasion routinely made the links between Jews and Bolshevism, deliberately blurring any boundary between the two: if Bolshevism was the enemy, then logically the Jews were also the enemy, as Bolshevism was seen as a largely Jewish project intended to undermine and destroy non-Jewish nations.

Army Group North, which would strike across the Baltic region towards the city of Leningrad, was under the command of Field Marshal Wilhelm Ritter von Leeb. The forces at his disposal were substantial – Sixteenth and Eighteenth Armies, and Fourth Panzer Group (renamed Fourth Panzer Army at the end of the year). Units of the neighbouring Army Group Centre would advance towards Moscow and would capture the Vilnius region. Both Army Group North and Army Group Centre had an associated *Einsatzgruppe*, but it was expected that once the advance towards Moscow developed, responsibility for the rear zone around Vilnius would be removed from *Einsatzgruppe B*, attached to Army Group Centre, and would be assigned to *Einsatzgruppe A*, operating with Army Group North.

The leadership of the *Einsatzgruppen* was carefully selected from the personnel of the SD. Whilst Heydrich was aware of the need to keep his men under control and thus avoid the friction of previous campaigns, the orders issued both to the SS and the Wehrmacht gave far greater leeway for the manner in which they would operate. Nonetheless, the commanders of the *Einsatzgruppen* were all educated technocrats who had proved their worth.

The commander of *Einsatzgruppe A* was Franz Walter Stahlecker. Born in 1900, he – like Heydrich – experienced the end of the First World War within Germany and witnessed the disorder as the 'home front' collapsed; it wasn't difficult for Germans of this generation to see the end of the conflict as a betrayal of the brave soldiers in the front line. Stahlecker joined the *Deutschvölkischer Schutz- und Trutzbund* ('German Nationalist Protection and Defiance Federation') in 1919, where he was immersed in a strongly anti-Semitic society. The group increased rapidly in size in the following few years and its constitution gave a clear picture of its beliefs: 'The Federation fights for the moral rebirth of the German people ... It considers the insidious and destructive influence of Jews to be the primary reason for the defeat [of Germany] and [believes that] the removal of this influence is vital for the political and economic recovery of Germany, and the salvation of German culture.'[11]

Probably in an attempt to improve his credibility when he first joined the Nazi Party and the SS, Heydrich claimed that he too had been a member of the Federation, but there is no documentary evidence to confirm this. Following the assassination of the German foreign minister Walther Rathenau in 1922, the Federation and many similar groups were banned.

With funding from his wealthy parents, Stahlecker studied law at Tübingen University and graduated with a doctorate in 1927. Prior to Hitler's accession of power, the German police services were organised at the level of individual German states and having joined both the Nazi Party and the SS in 1932, Stahlecker took up a senior post in the Württemberg State Police. By 1934, he was head of the state's internal security police and shortly after he was recruited by Heydrich into the ranks of the SD, after the individual state police forces were merged. After serving as head of the Gestapo in the city of Breslau, he became head of the security police in Vienna following the *Anschluss*. He held a variety of posts in both Austria and the Protectorate of Bohemia and Moravia and was the nominal head of the *Zentralstelle für Jüdische Auswanderung in Wien* ('Central Agency for Jewish Emigration in Vienna').

The main figure in this department was Adolf Eichmann, who – with only a modest amount of knowledge of Jewish matters – had succeeded in positioning himself as a leading expert in the SS with regard to the Jews. At the time, the policy of the Nazis was to drive the Jews from Germany through a mixture of forced and voluntary emigration, but the bureaucratic machinery for emigration resulted in constant delays – by the time an applicant had secured one particular document, other documents had passed their expiry date. Acting largely independently of his nominal superior Stahlecker, Eichmann streamlined the process with the result that the rate of emigration of Jews from Vienna was greatly accelerated. This model was then adopted elsewhere in the Reich.

The commencement of the Second World War made resolution of the 'Jewish problem' much more difficult. Emigration was no longer so straightforward, and the conquest of Poland greatly increased the number of Jews in German-controlled territories. But if emigration to other countries was no longer an option, there remained the possibility of creating a Jewish 'colony' in Eastern Europe. The Polish city of Lublin was designated as a possible centre for such a colony and in October 1939 Stahlecker and Eichmann travelled from Warsaw into the eastern part of Poland to identify a suitable 'transit camp' where the Jews could be held prior to their transfer further east. A few days later, Eichmann submitted a report to Berlin stating that a location had been identified near the San River around the small town of Nisko.

In what was effectively a trial run of a planned larger forced transfer, trains were organised to take Jews from Ostrava, Vienna, and Katowice to the new colony. Within days, nearly 5,000 Jews arrived in Nisko. The selection of the region by Eichmann and Stahlecker was more due to the convenience of railway connections than anything else and the new arrivals found themselves driven into a swampy region just outside Nisko on the banks of the San – no camp or other accommodation actually existed at the time. Hastily, work parties were organised; able-bodied Jews were set to work constructing basic barracks, while the rest were driven away to the east and the Soviet-occupied parts of Poland. Further transfers of Jews were halted.

After these experiences with the 'Jewish problem', Stahlecker was sent to take command of security police and SD personnel in occupied Norway. In late 1940, he returned to Berlin and the headquarters of the RSHA. He was in every respect an ideal candidate for command of one of the *Einsatzgruppen* that would be deployed in the Soviet Union. He had worked both as head of police and security agencies, and in a department trying to expel Jews from occupied areas. His radical anti-Semitic credentials and his loyalty to the Nazi Party and its policies were impeccable. It was therefore unsurprising that he was selected by Heydrich.

The rigorous selection policies of Heydrich and Himmler ensured that the senior personnel of the SS were, as far as possible, committed Nazis who would set the best personal and professional examples to their subordinates. Most of the senior personnel of the *Einsatzgruppen* that were to be deployed in the Soviet Union were highly educated men, the majority aged 40 or less; 11 out of the 17 officers of Stahlecker's *Einsatzgruppe A* were lawyers, and nine had doctorates. Their political reliability was another factor that influenced selection – 13 out of 17 had been members of the Nazi Party (or one of the right-wing groups that it absorbed) before 1933, and the rest had proved their dedication to Nazi policies in the following years. Several training establishments were created, including one in the castle in the town of Pretzsch near Leipzig. A series of conferences took place in the castle in the weeks prior to the commencement of *Barbarossa*, as the officers of the *Einsatzgruppen* were selected and informed about their coming mission.

That mission was gradually defined by Himmler and Heydrich in meetings that took place throughout the first half of 1941. As part of the overall planning, two figures in the RSHA – Standartenführer Hans Ehlich and Oberführer Konrad Meyer – drew up a set of documents known as *Generalplan Ost*, which went through several permutations. Part of this plan was entitled *Wirtschaftspolitischen Richtlinien* ('Economic Policy Guidelines'), and first circulated in May 1941. It was the first document explicitly to make an estimate of the expected deaths required for the success of German policies:

> As many as ten million people in this region will be surplus and will either need to die or be driven into Siberia. Attempts to save the population there from starving to death by the shipment of food surpluses from the Black Earth Zone [i.e. southern European USSR] can only be at the expense of supplies to Europe. This will reduce the strength of Germany during wartime, and will undermine the ability of Germany and Europe to withstand the [British] blockade.[12]

Further details of the plans being drawn up by Himmler and Heydrich appeared at a conference on 11 June chaired by Himmler in Wewelsburg Castle in Westphalia, where Himmler had established what he saw as a 'Nordic academy' for the SS. Almost all of the SS leadership and the men who had been designated as future heads of police and security in the occupied parts of the Soviet Union were present. They were told that the intention was to change the ethnic makeup of all of Eastern Europe. In addition to the 'elimination' of Jews from German-controlled Europe, millions of others – the Roma people, Slavs, and other 'inferior' people – would have to make way for future German settlers. The population of the European Soviet Union had grown substantially since the First World War, particularly in cities, and the attendees were told that it would not be possible to feed this population if food was to be appropriated for the Reich. The number of people expected to die as a result of the Nazi occupation policies had now increased to 30 million.[13]

Two days after the Wewelsburg conference, Heydrich addressed the officers who would command the *Einsatzgruppen* and expanded upon their coming duties. In two meetings – one in Berlin and one in Pretzsch Castle, where many of the personnel of the *Einsatzgruppen* had been assembled – he made clear that the coming weeks would see actions of unprecedented severity. The details of what was discussed, and precisely when, are controversial. No written records have survived, and most of the information that is available was gained from interrogations and the trials of *Einsatzgruppen* personnel at a later date – some of the statements that they gave have been proved to be incorrect, which casts doubt on much of their testimony. It is possible that Bruno Streckenbach, head of the Personnel Officer of the RSHA, told the men at the conference that Hitler had ordered the liquidation of Jews in the Soviet Union, though Streckenbach later denied this. During the conference in Pretzsch, Heydrich spoke in a manner that made clear that for him at least, Bolsheviks and Jews were essentially the same individuals.

Heydrich addressed his field commanders again on 17 June, this time in Berlin, less than a week before the commencement of *Barbarossa*. Again, there are no surviving documents that can give clear information on what was said. Walter Blume, one of the men who would command an *Einsatzkommando* in the Soviet Union allegedly asked Heydrich for clarification: 'Are we supposed to shoot the Jews?' The reply was a simple assurance that the answer to that question was self-evident. A similar reply was given to Blume's question of whether he and his men were to shoot Jewish women and children.[14] This conference was followed by written instructions sent by telegram on 29 June, after the invasion had commenced, to the four commanders of the *Einsatzgruppen*:

> With reference to my oral instructions on 17 June in Berlin, I wish to call your attention once more to the following:
> 1. The attempts by local anti-Communist or anti-Jewish groups to engage in cleansing activities within the territories now to be occupied should not be hindered in any way. On the contrary, they must be implemented, and intensified where necessary, though without leaving any trace [of German involvement] and directed onto the right paths. But this should be done in such a way that the local self-defence groups cannot later refer to any orders or political assurances given [by Germany].
>
> Since such a course of action is obviously possible within the initial period of military occupation, the *Einsatzgruppen* ... must strive to move in as quickly as possible ... with an advance party so that they can carry out what is required.[15]

This was followed by a second telegram to the men appointed as higher SS and police commanders in each sector.

> All the following are to be executed:
> Officials of the Comintern (together with professional Communist politicians in general);
> Top- and medium-level officials and radical lower-level officials of the Party, Central committee and district and sub-district committees;
> People's commissars;
> Jews in Party and State employment, and other radical elements (saboteurs, propagandists, snipers, assassins, inciters etc.)[16]

Heydrich deliberately left the judgement of which Jews were to be regarded as Party and State employees to his subordinates; he would, of course, have been aware that within the Communist system, this category would include all Jews working for the enormous state sector.

The personnel who were selected as subordinates to Stahlecker and the other *Einsatzgruppe* commanders were chosen with the same care. They, too, were highly motivated members of the Party and SS who had demonstrated their willingness to take radical action, often at their own initiative. Like Stahlecker and his peers, these men were also highly educated or trained, and were in the main in their twenties or thirties. The commander of *Einsatzkommando 3*, which would be part of Stahlecker's *Einsatzgruppe A*, was unusual, but only in one respect: he was far older than the men around him, and older than his subordinates.

Unlike Heydrich, Stahlecker and so many of the other men preparing to carry out the genocidal policies of Nazi Germany, Karl Jäger was a veteran of the First World War. He was born in the Swiss German town of Schaffhausen in 1888 and he and his family moved to the Black Forest town of Waldkirch shortly after. His father was a professional musician and Jäger became an accomplished pianist and violinist. The town was the location of several companies that specialised in the manufacture of musical instruments and after he left school, Jäger was employed by one such firm, Musikwerkfabrik Gebrüder Weber, which made orchestrions – the large musical devices found in fairground rides. Shortly after, he met and married Emma Weber, the daughter of the owner of the firm.

When the First World War began, Jäger became an artilleryman on the Western Front. He served in a variety of roles, including time in the trenches as a forward artillery spotter and as a gun commander, and like many of his comrades he returned to Germany embittered by the apparently sudden collapse of his nation. After several years in uniform in the most stressful circumstances imaginable, the transition to civilian life was almost impossible and he drifted into the right-wing paramilitary groups that were springing up throughout Germany, and it is probably through the membership of one such group that he first became aware of the new National Socialist Party, which he joined in 1923.

He was able to resume his previous work in the orchestrion factory but in an era of economic turmoil, the Weber company was just one of many that found it increasingly difficult to survive. In 1931, the factory closed and Jäger joined the millions of unemployed men in Germany. Whilst many relied on government for unemployment relief payments, Jäger refused to accept any such money due to his political hostility to the Weimar Republic. The limited savings of the family rapidly evaporated, and a marriage that had been under slowly increasing strain, ever since the angry, embittered Jäger returned home at Christmas 1919, broke down completely. Jäger and Emma separated, though it would be several years before their divorce was finalised.

Jäger spent increasing time on Nazi Party activities, rapidly organising local groups around Waldkirch. His energy earned him the nickname of the 'Waldkirch Hitler', but despite his political views he was happy to take up work in a local clothing factory run by a Jewish family. Many who knew him in those days remembered Jäger and other SS officers with approval and respect. The description given by an elderly woman in a radio interview in 1990 is typical:

> For me, he was a man of exemplary and strong character, punctilious in his correctness, as was the leadership of the SS in peacetime … They played a lot of sports, and played music – they were an elite … And I should say that there were many gentlemen who were obliged to join the SA or SS or the Party for professional reasons, as their career prospects would otherwise be hindered.[17]

Despite his obvious organisational talents with the local Party and SS, Jäger might have languished in the provincial backwater of Waldkirch but for a decision by senior Nazi Party members to offer preferential employment to longstanding members of the Party. Even once this policy began, he might have been overlooked; although he joined the Party at a very early stage, this was before the Nazis were briefly banned after Hitler's failed 'Beer Hall Putsch' in 1923. During this period of proscription, many Party records were lost or destroyed, including documents concerning Jäger's Party membership. Re-establishing his credentials was not straightforward but in 1936 he was given the SS rank of Hauptsturmführer – equivalent to Hauptmann or captain in the regular army – and placed in command of the SS in Ludwigsburg, a little to the north of Stuttgart. Further posts followed and in 1938, with the rank of Sturmbannführer (major), he was posted to the SD in Berlin. He made a good impression on his superiors, as can be seen from his personal assessments: 'slim, with a strong physique and a Nordic appearance … open, honourable, honest, and reliable, and of a modest nature'.[18]

He was, therefore, in many respects the epitome of the sort of individual that Himmler and Heydrich regarded as the ideal SS officer, but with two notable exceptions. Firstly, he was much older than most of his fellow SS officers. Secondly, he had no higher education qualifications or police experience.

Despite these two exceptions, Jäger continued to rise through the ranks and in 1940 he was promoted – at the personal recommendation of Heydrich – to Standartenführer (colonel). During this time, he helped draw up the lists of Polish intelligentsia who were targeted by the SS and SD after the conquest of Poland and in 1940 he was in command of SD counter-espionage activities in the Netherlands. Throughout his time in the SD, he was periodically sent on training courses for SD personnel at various establishments. Whilst the subject matter of these courses varied, it was standard policy for all such establishments to develop an underlying theme for the men that Himmler and Heydrich expected to be the leaders of huge change across Europe. Although Jäger seems to have shown few if any signs of anti-Semitism in his earlier years, he was now immersed in the SS dogma that equated Jews with Bolsheviks and portrayed both Bolshevism and western capitalism as attempts by the Jews to subjugate all other races. Werner Best, who was in charge of the personnel section of the administrative and legal affairs section of the Gestapo and effectively Heydrich's deputy in the SD, gave a typical address to senior Gestapo officers 1935:

> It is one of the most foremost tasks of the Gestapo to ensure that the principles of the NSDAP for the life of the German people for all time remain its guiding principle. This task can only be fulfilled if these principles are first recognised by all persons working in the Gestapo as binding for them. Failure to comply must therefore have serious consequences for the official position of officers, employees and other workers of the Gestapo. One of the most important principles of the NSDAP finds its expression in its position on the race question, especially in its attitude towards Judaism. The guidelines of the NSDAP regarding shopping in Jewish shops and the use of Jewish doctors, lawyers, etc. are therefore binding for all Gestapo members.[19]

Jäger was one of the SS officers summoned to Pretzsch early in the summer of 1941. On the first day of the conference, Jäger met Heydrich, who informed him that he was to take command of *Einsatzkommando 3*, part of Stahlecker's *Einsatzgruppe A*. His mission was to secure Lithuania in the wake of the advancing Wehrmacht, and thereafter he would become commander of the security police and SD throughout Lithuania. Once it was deployed, *Einsatzkommando 3* would function as three 'platoons', commanded by Sturmbannführer Gustav Grauer, Untersturmführer Joachim Hamann, and Hauptsturmführer Gerhart Kortkampf.

Grauer, born in December 1909, joined the hard-line right-wing *Adler und Falke* ('Eagle and Falcon') youth movement in 1922 before he finished his schooling and subsequently attended universities in Heidelberg, Freiburg, Kiel, Munich and Berlin. He had a degree in economics and a doctorate in law, and was a regular police officer before the war, serving in the *Kriminalpolizei*, often abbreviated to *Kripo* – roughly equivalent to the British CID – and held posts in the public prosecution service. In addition to commanding a platoon of *Einsatzkommando 3* he was to act as Jäger's deputy.

Joachim Hamann was the son of Adolf Hamann, a Baltic German who moved to Kiel shortly before the First World War. He was just five years old at the end of the First World War. He studied chemistry and pharmacy but struggled to find employment during the Great Depression. He joined the SA in 1931, the Nazi Party the following year, and subsequently the SS. When the Second World War commenced, he volunteered for front-line service and saw action as a paratrooper in Poland and France before being assigned to the security police in Berlin in the summer of 1940; the Wehrmacht was happy to release him, as there had been complaints from men under his command that he had mistreated them and he even spent a brief period under arrest while investigations were carried out, but no charges were laid against him. In Berlin, he worked within the ranks of the Gestapo and became known amongst his peers for his 'fanatical hatred of Jews'.[20] He also put his spare time to good use, studying law in evening school and then the University of Berlin. When he was assigned to *Einsatzkommando 3*, his experience as a paratrooper was put to use and he was made responsible for the military training of all personnel.

Kortkampf was also a child at the end of the First World War, living in the city of Emden. After he left school he worked as a bookseller before joining the SA and subsequently the SS, in 1933. Two years later, he was recruited into the growing ranks of the SD by Heydrich and sent to Stettin, where he continued to work until he was summoned to Pretzsch in the summer of 1941. Whilst he lacked the higher education of Grauer and Hamann, his service in the activities of the SD meant that he was thoroughly versed in what would be expected of him in his forthcoming role.

It is worth noting that the training provided by Hamann and a few others was almost all of the 'militarisation' that was provided for the police officers and others who made up the bulk of the *Einsatzgruppen*. Much like the SD teams deployed in Austria at the time of the *Anschluss*, these units were intended primarily to establish a strong security presence and to eliminate security threats. It was the definition of such threats that had widened, and as German military operations moved into countries where such threats were likely to be greater and more diverse, the role of the *Einsatzgruppen* would also widen.

Stahlecker, Jäger, Grauer, Hamann, Kortkampf – these were the men selected by Heydrich to lead the SD and SS in Lithuania. He expected them to implement the security policies of Nazi Germany without hesitation, and deliberately left them considerable leeway to interpret their instructions as they saw fit; this, it was expected, would result in innovation and healthy competition as they sought to prove their value to their superiors. In total, *Einsatzkommando A* numbered just a few hundred men, yet within days they would be involved in mass killings that would continue for the rest of 1941. It would not be possible for them to carry out their tasks without aid. Some of this would come from regular army units, which had explicit orders to cooperate with the SS, but much of their help would come from local people in the Baltic region. The background to the animosity of Lithuanians towards Communists, Jews and others played an important part in the horror that followed the arrival of the Wehrmacht.

2

Lithuania, the Jews, and the Poles

The coming of war across the borders of Poland, Denmark, Norway, the Netherlands, Belgium and France – and through the air and sea to Britain – was generally met with trepidation and fear. By contrast, as the Wehrmacht columns marched through the heat and dust of midsummer into the Baltic region, they were greeted almost everywhere by local crowds who showered the invaders with flowers, food and other gifts. One Lithuanian later wrote: 'It fell like a clap of thunder on Lithuania: WAR [emphasis in original text]. What a joy, WAR. People meet and congratulate each other with tears of joy in their eyes. Everyone thinks that the hour of liberation is at hand.'[1]

The enthusiasm of the greeting deserves closer inspection. Of the three nations that make up the Baltic States, only Lithuania had a history of independent nationhood prior to the First World War. For many centuries, Lithuania – often in conjunction with Poland – controlled large swathes of territory, sometimes stretching deep into what is now Belarus and Ukraine. At the time of the Crusades, the entire region was controlled by pagan tribes, and the desire to impose Christianity on the region – in conjunction with establishing trading posts and other financial interests – ultimately brought the attention of the Christian states to the eastern Baltic.

The crusading Order of Brothers of the German House of Saint Mary in Jerusalem, usually known as the Teutonic Order or the Teutonic Knights and largely made up of men from the German states and cities, was established in 1191 during the siege of Acre by crusader forces.[2] The leaders of the Third Crusade – the French King Philip II and the English King Richard I – showed little interest in the welfare of the German knights in their forces, and in an attempt to improve conditions for their countrymen who were sick or wounded, a group of crusaders from Bremen and Lübeck established a new monastic warrior order. This new order purchased land close to Acre and became a dominant force in the locality but was ultimately driven out of the region in 1291.

By this date, the knights were also firmly established in Eastern Europe. A contingent of the Teutonic Order's knights accompanied by German settlers moved to southern Hungary in the second decade of the 13th century to fight against Moslem forces in Transylvania. The knights were swiftly successful, causing friction with the local Hungarian nobility – at first, the Hungarians had been grateful for foreign aid against the Moslems, but the victories of the knights persuaded them that their enemy wasn't as powerful as they feared. In addition, the refusal of the knights to accept Hungarian authority led to their expulsion from Hungary in 1222.

Not long after, the order joined a campaign by Duke Conrad of Masovia to subjugate the pagan tribes along the Baltic coast. Over time, the Teutonic Knights came to control much of what would become East Prussia and Lithuania and refused to acknowledge Polish rule, seeing themselves as answerable directly to the Pope. The mission of the knights to spread Christianity, if necessary by force, through the region effectively became redundant when Lithuania embraced Christianity in 1387, by which time the wealth of the order was considerable. Continuing friction between the knights, the Poles to the south and the Lithuanians to the east ultimately led to the Battle of Grunwald or Tannenberg in 1410, against the combined forces of Poland and Lithuania. The knights suffered a decisive defeat and much of their territory passed into the hands of the Polish-Lithuanian alliance, and in 1435, the neighbouring Livonian Order, which controlled much of what is now Latvia, lost its grand master and many of its senior figures in battle against an army made up of Lithuanians, Poles and local warriors.

Over the following years, the region remained home to large numbers of German settlers, and it was during this period that the German concept of *Ostsiedlung* ('Settlement in the East') originated. Ultimately, this in turn gave rise to the concept of *Drang nach Osten* ('The Drive towards the East'), an expression that was coined in the 19th century. Most of the German settlers in the region embraced Lutheran Christianity, and when the entire eastern Baltic coastline – and the eastern parts of Poland – became part of the Russian Empire after the First Partition of Poland in 1772, there were distinct differences in the populations. The northern area was home to people who spoke a language related to Finnish, in what would ultimately become Estonia. The population of the central and southern regions spoke what were originally similar languages, but the area around Riga was largely Lutheran while the people of the former Lithuanian territory remained staunchly Catholic owing to their historic close links with Poland. Throughout the region, many of the original German settlers – some of them able to trace family links to the knightly orders that had first established German control of the area – formed much of the local aristocracy. The Russians granted them numerous privileges in return for their support, creating the basis of later distrust and enmity between ethnic Germans and other inhabitants.

Although nationalist movements began to appear throughout the region in the 19th century, many ordinary people in the Baltic region showed little enthusiasm. A person living in Lithuania was more likely to identify as a Catholic than as a Lithuanian or as a citizen of the Russian Empire. But in addition to people of Estonian, Latvian, Lithuanian, Polish and German heritage, the Baltic region increasingly became the home of large numbers of ethnic Russians, often as a result of deliberate official policy. And for centuries, the region was home to another growing population that saw itself neither as Christian, Baltic, German nor Russian.

Anti-Semitism has of course been a recurring problem in European history – attacks on Jewish communities occurred in ancient times and Christian Europe saw frequent episodes of mass expulsions, seizure of property from Jews, and massacres. In 1543, Martin Luther published a pamphlet entitled *Von den Juden und ihren Lügen* ('On the Jews and their lies'), an ironic title in that Luther must have known that his pamphlet contained many falsehoods about the Jews. His earlier suggestions that Jews should be encouraged to convert to Lutheran Christianity were replaced by a much harder line, using the words of Jewish prophets to justify violence against the Jews. The pamphlet repeats many of the commonly believed untruths that were spoken about Jews, and it uses language that would not be out of place several centuries later. Amongst the measures demanded by Luther were calls for synagogues, Jewish homes, and Jewish schools to be razed and for Jews to be denied the right of safe conduct on highways. The fabled wealth of the Jews should be seized and whenever Jews sincerely converted to Christianity, they should receive payment from the seized assets. Jews should be forbidden to lend money and young Jews should be required to take up physical labour. Luther concluded with the words:

> When you lay eyes on or think of a Jew you must say to yourself: Alas, that mouth which I there behold has cursed and execrated and maligned every Saturday my dear Lord Jesus Christ ... in addition, it prayed and pleased before God that I, my wife and children,

> and all Christians must be stabbed to death and die miserably ... Perhaps he has spat on the ground many times this very day over the name of Jesus, as is their custom.[3]

Many Jews who fled from repeated persecution made their way to the eastern parts of Europe, resulting in large numbers living in Poland, Lithuania, Latvia and European Russia. The Partition of Poland resulted in a significant increase in the number of Jews living in Russia and Catherine the Great passed a law in 1791 that restricted Jews to the western parts of the Russian Empire in a region known as the Pale of Settlement. There were repeated attacks on Jews throughout this region, often with official encouragement.

An episode in the Ukrainian city of Kiev in 1911 showed clearly just how widespread anti-Semitism was in Imperial Russia and how it was sanctioned at the highest level. Andrei Yushchinsky, a 13-year-old boy, disappeared on his way to school and his mutilated body was found shortly after in a cave near a brick factory. The investigating police officer was Nikolai Krasovsky, and from an early stage senior officials wanted him to arrest and prosecute Menahem Mendel Beilis, a Jew who worked in the brick factory. Beilis's son was a friend of the dead boy, and a city lamplighter came forward to claim that he had seen a Jew abducting Yushchinsky. Beilis was arrested that summer and became the centre of a virulent anti-Semitic campaign in local and national newspapers, which repeated many of the recurring lies about Jews kidnapping and killing Christian children in religious rituals. Tsar Nicholas, who made no secret of his anti-Semitic views, took a personal interest in the case and insisted on regular updates.

Krasovsky was certain that Beilis was not the child's killer and continued to investigate the case, ignoring both threats and inducements from superiors, resulting in his dismissal. He discovered that Yushchinsky had been friendly with a Ukrainian boy, whose parents stored stolen property for a gang of thieves; Yushchinsky had been killed after he fell out with his friend and threatened to tell the police about the stolen goods. The official investigation continued to insist that Beilis was the killer and he was brought to court late in 1913, having spent much of the intervening time in prison. Despite a high-profile campaign in the press, which published lurid tales of alleged confessions in which Beilis admitted the killing and involvement in occult Jewish rituals, the court found that there was actually no substantial evidence against Beilis and he was acquitted. In later years, documents emerged that showed that Tsar Nicholas and the Justice Minister were both aware that the case against Beilis was completely fabricated, but nonetheless were in favour of continuing with the prosecution in the hope that a conviction would establish in a court of law the concept of Jews carrying out ritual murders of Christian children. On the eve of the trial, the Justice Ministry ordered the arrest and exile to Siberia of several key defence witnesses, and the judge was given a personal audience with the tsar. Nicholas even presented him with a gold watch and promised him even larger rewards in the event of a successful prosecution.

Given their treatment at the hands of the Russian Empire's authorities, it is unremarkable that so many Russian Jews joined the ranks of the Bolsheviks when new revolutions broke out in 1917.

Being the closest of the Baltic provinces of the Russian Empire to Germany, Lithuania was the first part of the region that came under German control in the First World War, and in 1918 the new Bolshevik government that had come to power in what had been the Russian Empire was forced to sign a humiliating treaty with Germany in the city of Brest-Litovsk. Under the terms of this treaty, large territories in the west would become quasi-independent states under the hegemony of Germany. Before the Germans could create these states, the advance of the French, British and American forces in the west, combined with growing turmoil within Germany itself, brought the war to an end. By this stage, the entire Baltic region was under German occupation, but the great bulk of the German soldiers in the three Baltic States were simply anxious to go home as soon as they could.

At the same time, the Bolsheviks were eager to recover the territories that they had conceded to Germany and were quick to invade the region from the east, even as nationalist movements attempted to establish new states. In the north, Estonia was able to repel a Bolshevik invasion with the aid of British light cruisers deployed in the area and Finnish volunteers. Latvia endured a Bolshevik occupation of all but a small region on the coast and ultimately succeeded in achieving independence through the services of German 'volunteers' and locally raised troops.

The Germans fighting against the Bolsheviks were part of what was known as the *Freikorps*, made up of units from the former German Army that were deployed both domestically and abroad against left-wing groups, and whilst they fought against the Bolsheviks in Latvia, this was not really for the benefit of helping the Latvians gain independence. Rather, it was part of a lingering attempt by some parts of the German government and military to create the client states that had been intended for the area as a result of the treaty with Bolshevik Russia. These *Freikorps* formations showed some reluctance to leave and it was only after the intervention of Estonian forces from the north and increasing pressure from the Western Powers that they were persuaded to return home. For many of the German soldiers, there was a huge sense of betrayal: they believed that they had been promised land in the new Latvian state in return for their service and had been cheated of their rewards.

But if Estonia and Latvia achieved independence and largely secured all of the territory that they claimed as theirs, the same wasn't true of Lithuania. During the 19th century, Imperial Russia attempted to 'Russify' the entire Baltic region, imposing the Russian language on many institutions, banning publications in other languages and placing restrictions on non-Orthodox clergy. When the Germans occupied Lithuania in 1915, heavy-handed Russian policies were replaced by equally heavy-handed German rule. Catholic schoolteachers were replaced by Germans, in some cases soldiers in uniform. Food was requisitioned with little compensation in a manner that showed almost no understanding of the need to leave sufficient grain in the hands of farmers both for seed for the following year and for the farmers to have an incentive to continue producing food.

By the end of the war, a provisional Lithuanian government was in place, but the country was badly threatened by its neighbours and as yet had no armed forces of its own. German troops remained within Lithuania but were weary of war and merely wished to return to their homes in Germany; to the east, Bolshevik Russia was desperate to discard the humiliating Treaty of Brest-Litovsk and reclaim all the territory of the old Russian Empire; and to the south, the new state of Poland was rapidly rearming with the help and encouragement of western nations. For many Poles, including Józef Piłsudski, the head of state, Lithuania should be part of a new Polish-Lithuanian commonwealth – it is a measure of the past close relationship between the two countries that Piłsudski was actually born in Lithuania.

To complicate matters still further, the ethnic makeup of the different regions was potentially explosive. The eastern borders of the new Polish state were poorly defined and a large disputed area existed with a mixture of Polish, Ukrainian, Belarusian and Russian citizens. Whilst the precise mix varied from one area to another, one thing was almost constant: the further east the location, the greater the likelihood that the Poles were a minority. The population of the southeast parts of Lithuania was equally heterogeneous, consisting of Lithuanians, Poles, Belarusians and Russians. In the midst of this part of Lithuania was the city on which all sides made claims and was also home to a very substantial Jewish population. The number of Jews in Vilnius grew over centuries, and the city was sometimes known as the 'Jerusalem of Lithuania'; Napoleon Bonaparte is often attributed with giving it the name of the 'Jerusalem of the North'. With such a mixture of residents, Vilnius was known by a multitude of different names. To the Jews it was Wilne, the Poles called it Wilno, the Belarusians knew it as Vilnia, while the Russian name, Vilna, was the one most widely used by other nations. But to the Lithuanians, it was Vilnius, their ancient capital.

According to a census carried out by the Russian authorities in 1897, Vilnius had a population that was 40% Jewish, 31% Polish, 20% Russian, 4% Belarusian and only 2% Lithuanian. In some circles, there was even talk of creating a Jewish state around it. At that time, Vilnius boasted several Jewish newspapers, though the edict that banned Lithuanian newspapers and books applied equally to anything printed in Hebrew, resulting in a drastic drop in publications shortly after the census. There were over 100 synagogues and Jewish study halls in the city as well as hundreds of Jewish schools. From 1905, the Lithuanian population began to grow relatively quickly at a time when unrest swept through Imperial Russia, followed by repression by pro-tsarist groups that took the opportunity to unleash pogroms against Jewish communities. There were episodes of anti-Jewish violence in Lithuania, too, leading to many Jews emigrating, predominantly to the USA. Despite this the Jewish community, centred around Kaunas and Vilnius but also present in smaller towns throughout both Lithuania and Latvia and in the Latvian capital Riga, had good reason to consider their relative affluence and safety a blessing.

As German troops withdrew from the region in late 1918, the Lithuanians were still only the third largest group in the city of Vilnius, outnumbered by the Poles and Jews, with the former now comprising the largest part of the population. The new state of Lithuania had declared that Vilnius was its capital, but the Germans handed over the city to local Polish forces that were in the process of being incorporated into the new Polish Army. The tiny Lithuanian forces in the area, together with Lithuanian politicians, could do little more than protest and depart for Kaunas, some distance to the west, but Polish control lasted just a few days. Bolshevik forces were approaching rapidly from the east, led by units that contained large numbers of Polish and Lithuanian Communists and these formations now took control of the region.

With Germany engulfed in post-war confusion and chaos, the Lithuanians attempted to recruit *Freikorps* elements to their cause. A substantial loan had been agreed between the Lithuanian government and the new administration in Berlin to pay for German 'volunteers' to fight on behalf of Lithuania, but initial attempts to recruit veterans of the German Tenth Army, which was retreating through Lithuania, proved disappointing. However, demobilised soldiers in Saxony proved more willing to join the cause and these men began to arrive in Lithuania in the first days of 1919. They were just in time. Organised into the German 46th Saxon Volunteer Division and cooperating with a newly formed Lithuanian division, they succeeded in preventing the Red Army from continuing its triumphant advance to and beyond Kaunas. At the same time, the new Polish government began to flex its muscles and authorised its forces to advance northeast into the eastern parts of Lithuania. Arming his men with weapons discarded by the Germans – either abandoned, or deliberately left behind after negotiations with Polish representatives – Piłsudski attempted to secure as much land as possible to the east before the final borders of Poland were decided. In April 1919, as the weather slowly grew warmer, a Polish force of just 2,500 infantry and 800 cavalry launched an attack towards Vilnius.

Thwarted in their initial intention to conquer the entire Baltic region, the Bolsheviks had declared the creation of a new state just a few weeks earlier; combining the occupied eastern territories of Lithuania with Belarus, the Lithuanian-Belarusian Soviet Socialist Republic, usually abbreviated to Lit-Bel, was to be part of the new family of Bolshevik states. One of the divisions of the Red Army was renamed the Lithuanian Rifle Division but most of its personnel were Russian – there was widespread hostility towards Bolshevik rule and the new authorities were reluctant to recruit from the 'liberated' areas of Lithuania, believing that providing weapons for men who may prove to be less than entirely trustworthy would be a serious mistake. Consequently, it was mainly the poorly organised – and even more poorly supported – units of the Red Army that had originally invaded Lithuania who found themselves facing the Poles.

The Polish thrust to Vilnius was led by the cavalry group, which rapidly swept into the city. It seems that this swift advance took the Bolsheviks by surprise. The railway station was swiftly captured, and a train was immediately dispatched towards Poland so that the infantry following the cavalry group could move forward faster. By 21 April, all of Vilnius was in Polish hands.

When the Bolsheviks had arrived in the city, there had been a wave of arrests and executions. Many of the Bolsheviks were Jewish – the organised anti-Semitism of the old Russian regime ensured that Jews joined the Bolsheviks in large numbers – and inevitably, many of the Poles and Lithuanians living in Vilnius were quick to label Jews as the perpetrators of the arrests and executions. But a similar wave of killings followed the arrival of the Polish forces as suspected Bolsheviks and sympathisers were rounded up. The Poles, who formed the largest group of civilians in the city, rejoiced at the arrival of their fellow countrymen;

the Jews, who formed the second largest group, were also broadly in favour, given the historic hostility towards Jews from the Russian Empire. Despite the allegations that Jews had assisted the Bolsheviks during their occupation, the reality was that the wave of arrests and executions had resulted in the detention and deaths of proportionately more Jews than Poles – these arrests were targeted at the intelligentsia and the wealthy, categories in which the well-educated Jewish population was disproportionately represented. The government of Lit-Bel, which had been based in Vilnius, succeeded in escaping before the Poles were able to take complete control of the city, and moved to Minsk.

The Lithuanians were also moving their forces forward. The Lithuanian element suffered from poor training and limited equipment, but the combined force of Lithuanians and Saxons advanced on the northern flank of the Polish drive towards the northeast. By the end of June, all of Lithuania had been liberated from Bolshevik control. The Saxon volunteers were demobilised; many went home, but others joined *Freikorps* units in Latvia. Negotiations between the Poles and Lithuanians began in earnest to decide the fate of the regions that they had collectively liberated. From the outset, Piłsudski was reluctant to recognise Lithuania as an independent state, still hoping for the re-creation of the historic Polish-Lithuanian Commonwealth (though of course with Poland being the senior partner in this arrangement), and there was little agreement on how the nations should reconcile their differences.

The Vilnius region became a major bone of contention. Whilst the Poles could claim to have the largest population in the city, the surrounding countryside was predominantly Lithuanian. Attempts by the Lithuanians to gain support from the former Entente powers were hindered by the fact that US President Woodrow Wilson's famous 'Fourteen Points' – a list of demands to be met for the restoration of peace in Europe – included an explicit requirement for the re-establishment of the Polish state, but there was no mention of the status of Lithuania.

In late July, the French proposed a new, albeit temporary, boundary between Lithuania and Poland, passing control of the Vilnius and Suwałki regions to Poland; the militarily weak Lithuanian government had no choice but to accept. However, Piłsudski was unwilling to accept this arrangement, which was far more favourable to Poland than to Lithuania – he continued to press for the two states to combine. In the late summer of 1919, he and a colleague travelled to Vilnius and the surrounding area, seeking support from pro-Polish Lithuanians for a coup to topple the current Lithuanian government in Kaunas. The coup was planned to take place on the night of 28 to 29 August but was postponed for two days at the last moment; the news of the postponement didn't reach all participants and when some moved early to cut telephone lines, Lithuanian intelligence became aware of developments and began to take countermeasures.

Large numbers of Poles and their sympathisers were rounded up in Kaunas and the Poles promptly abandoned their planned coup and attempted to portray the Lithuanian actions as an anti-Polish measure. Throughout this period, most of the Jews of Vilnius continued to live their lives quietly, attempting to avoid entanglement in the politics of the region. Although some, particularly younger adults, had cooperated with the Bolsheviks, most simply wished to be left in peace.

In 1920, a resurgent Red Army once more advanced towards the west. Vilnius changed hands again as the Polish Army, heavily committed along Poland's entire eastern frontier against the Bolsheviks, fell back. Ultimately, the war would end with victory for Poland, but before the decisive Battle of Warsaw, Lithuania and Bolshevik Russia signed a peace treaty. Critically, this treaty included the return of Vilnius to Lithuania, with the result that the city was securely in Lithuanian hands by the time that Polish troops pursuing the defeated Red Army approached the region.

This was unacceptable to Poland, and hostilities between Lithuania and Poland broke out almost immediately after the defeat of the Bolshevik forces. The new League of Nations attempted to intervene with the creation of a demarcation line but Piłsudski suspected this arrangement as being a precursor to the Vilnius region passing permanently into Lithuanian control, and he initiated an elaborate plan. In October 1920, Lucjan Żeligowski, commander of a Polish infantry division, told his officers that he intended to march on Vilnius to create a new, Polish-dominated Republic of Central Lithuania. Despite the unwillingness of many of his men to take part in this venture, he pressed ahead with his plan and when he crossed the frontier and advanced towards Vilnius he encountered no meaningful opposition. His arrival in the city was greeted with enthusiasm by the Polish majority, and after a few attempts by the very limited military forces of Lithuania to intervene, a ceasefire came into force between Poland and Lithuania a few weeks later.

Żeligowski declared the creation of a new civilian government in his Central Lithuanian state early in 1921; the following year, this government voted to unite with Poland. It was several years before the truth emerged: far from being an independent act, Żeligowski's invasion, followed by the creation of the Republic of Central Lithuania and its union with Poland, had all been carried out with the prior knowledge, approval and support of Piłsudski. The Lithuanians were left with their government in the temporary capital of Kaunas, but despite official nomenclature that stressed this temporary status, most of the administrative apparatus of the Lithuanian state became centred on Kaunas as the years passed.

Despite having the second largest population in Vilnius, the Jews had almost no say in the events that unfolded in the city as it was first handed over to the Poles by the retreating Germans, then came under Bolshevik control before being captured by the Polish Army, and then was taken once again by the Red Army and handed to Lithuania, only to be seized by Żeligowski and subsequently reunited with Poland. The Lithuanian inhabitants in the city – and the large numbers of Lithuanians in the surrounding towns and villages – were deeply resentful of the manner in which they felt they had been forced to join Poland, while the Poles were determined to keep control of the region, regarding with suspicion anyone who thought otherwise.

Cautiously, the Jews of Vilnius began to re-establish their cultural and social life. The entire region suffered badly during the Great Depression and as little more than a regional city in Poland, Vilnius experienced a steady decline in its fortunes. Historically, the city had traded extensively with towns and cities in Lithuania, but the hostility of the Lithuanians to Poland effectively cut off most of that trade. Many workers, regardless of whether they were Polish, Jewish or Lithuanian, struggled to earn enough to survive; the historical tendency of Jewish families to encourage educational attainment by their children resulted in a disproportionate number of Jews earning more than many Polish and Lithuanian citizens, attracting envy and dislike. In response to the complaints of the Polish population of the city, the government created new taxes on Jewish companies, and arranged the forcible nationalisation of textile and timber industries, both of which were dominated by Jewish owners, added to the growing hardship of the Jewish population.

Just as anti-Semitism grew elsewhere in Europe in the 1930s, Poland saw a steady increase in attacks, both verbal and physical, on Jews. For centuries, Poland had been a relatively safe region for Jews – one estimate suggests that during the 16th century, the region was home to up to 80% of the world's Jewish population. During the 17th and 18th centuries, there was a growing tide of anti-Jewish sentiment throughout Poland, often instigated by the Catholic Church; leaflets circulated with language that was almost indistinguishable from later Nazi publications, describing Jews as 'social parasites', 'insects eating Poland from within', and as 'God's plague'.[4]

The Polish National Democratic Party was a leading proponent of policies that favoured 'ethnic Poles' during the closing years of the

19th century when Poland was divided between Germany, Russia and the Austro-Hungarian Empire, and it was explicitly in favour of the expulsion of Jews from Poland. Roman Dmowski, the co-founder of the party, wrote that 'All Poland's troubles are the result of centuries of Jewish invasion. If we want to be a great nation, we must get rid of the Jews.'[5]

It would be wrong to characterise all Poles as anti-Semitic, but Poland was not immune from the general rise of anti-Semitism across Europe in the 1920s and 1930s. The National Democratic Party declared Jews as 'the enemies of ordinary citizens' and accused them of attempting to control trade, industry, the professions, and the media. Openly anti-Semitic newspapers began to circulate and there were occasional violent clashes in the streets of Vilnius, resulting in the death and wounding of many people. Jewish students at the city's university faced discrimination, being banned from eating their meals in the same halls as Polish and Lithuanian students.

At least partly in response to the growing hostility towards Jews, a number of bodies grew up in Vilnius amongst the Jewish population. Many of these were particularly popular amongst younger Jews and actively promoted Zionism, often associated with socialism. The Polish authorities had banned the Communist Party, but inevitably a party existed in secret; many of its members were Jewish, accepting without question the frankly false assertions of the Soviet Union that under Soviet socialism, anti-Semitism and other forms of racism were irrelevant and had been abolished.

The people of Vilnius were thus deeply divided as the 1930s passed and the clouds of war began to gather. The Poles resented the continuing wealth of many Jews and sought every opportunity to reduce what they saw as unacceptable disparities; the Jews were fearful that the pogroms of the past would return, and a small but steady trickle of émigrés continued to leave the region. The Lithuanians watched both the Poles *and* Jews with resentment, longing for the restoration of Lithuanian rule to the region. Worse was to come.

When Germany and the Soviet Union announced their Non-Aggression Pact in August 1939, a protocol attached to the pact was not publicised and remained secret throughout the war – indeed, the Soviet Union continued to deny its existence long after. This protocol effectively divided Eastern Europe into zones of influence. In addition to partitioning Poland between the two powers, the protocol specified that the Soviet Union would be able to control Estonia and Latvia, while Germany would gain Lithuania. By the time that the defeat of Poland was complete, the Wehrmacht had occupied rather more of southeast Poland than had originally been intended, and as a result the protocol was modified – to compensate the Soviet Union for the loss of this Polish territory, Lithuania would now become part of the Soviet sphere of influence, with the exception of a strip along the Baltic coast that had been part of East Prussia before the end of the First World War, and the southwest corner of the country. In accordance with the protocol, the Red Army entered Polish territory from the east on 17 September and faced almost no opposition, with the great bulk of the Polish Army fully committed against Germany. The Vilnius region, which was part of Poland at the time, saw a large influx of refugees from Poland, particularly Jews fleeing the approach of the Germans; the city and the surrounding area swiftly came under Soviet control as the Red Army advanced.

What followed was a brutal demonstration of *Realpolitik* and the application of pressure on small countries by a larger neighbour.[6] All three Baltic States were forced to accept Soviet forces stationed on their territory. Estonia had given shelter to a Polish submarine during September and Stalin declared this a violation of neutrality; Estonia would have to accept Soviet troops on its soil to ensure there were no such lapses in future. Latvia then came under pressure to comply with what had been forced upon Estonia – but Lithuania was a more complex matter. The Germans had not yet seized the southwest part of Lithuania and Stalin ruthlessly exploited this, informing the Lithuanian foreign minister that he had three choices. The first was to accept the presence of Soviet troops on his territory, as was the case with Estonia and Latvia. The second, which could be combined with the first, was the return of the Vilnius region to Lithuanian control. The third was for southwest Lithuania to be seized by Germany.

The Lithuanian city of Klaipėda on the Baltic coast was once the German city of Memel, the most northern part of East Prussia, and Germany had already secured the return of Memel and the coastal strip to its south. The thought of even more territory in the area being seized by Germany horrified the Lithuanians, and Stalin accentuated the difference between the Soviet Union and Germany: the former was prepared to return the Vilnius region to Lithuania, while Germany wished to tear away Lithuanian territory. When it became clear to the Lithuanians that they could only secure the return of Vilnius by accepting Soviet garrisons in Lithuania, the government gave in.

With the Red Army now deployed in all three Baltic States, the Soviet Union moved on to the next stage in the spring of 1940. In the case of Lithuania, allegations were made that Soviet soldiers stationed in Lithuania were being lured into criminality by Lithuanians. The Soviet government in Moscow refused to provide any details but demanded a full investigation by the Lithuanians. Blocked from speaking to any of the Soviet soldiers involved – they had apparently been transferred back to the Soviet Union to recover from their experiences – the Lithuanian government found itself in a Kafkaesque world in which it stood accused of unspecified crimes and, completely unable to ascertain the nature of the alleged wrongdoing, could do nothing to comply with the demands for rigorous investigations. Matters steadily escalated with Moscow demanding the dismissal of the entire Lithuanian government and its replacement with figures who were more friendly to Moscow. The size of the Red Army garrisons in Lithuania was also to be increased.

The Baltic States were isolated from any potential help – Sweden to the west was carefully neutral, Germany was seen as a potential predator, and the Western Powers faced a peculiar difficulty with respect to Lithuania. Vilnius had been part of Poland before the war, and having declared war on Germany in support of Poland, neither Britain nor France showed any desire to recognise the removal of the Vilnius region from their ally; consequently, both countries did nothing to support Lithuania. The three Baltic States had brief discussions early in 1940 about how they might coordinate their resistance to increasing Soviet pressure, and Stalin now used this as a lever against them. In June, Latvia and Estonia were given an ultimatum: they, too, had to appoint new, Soviet-friendly governments. Without the means to resist and lacking powerful allies abroad, the three countries had to agree to the Soviet demands.

With pro-Soviet governments in place, the final stage of annexation began. New elections were held with predictable results: all of the countries returned overwhelming majorities of Communist Party candidates. In some cases, local officials triumphantly announced that the total number of votes cast – only pro-Soviet candidates were permitted to stand for election – exceeded 100% of the registered voters. The first item of business for all three new governments was to apply to join the Union of Soviet Socialist Republics.

If the governments of the Baltic States – and Lithuania in particular – were forced to choose between two hostile neighbours, the Jewish population had no real choice. Many – perhaps most – of the Jews of the Baltic region, and the Jewish refugees from Poland, might have preferred to pursue a strictly neutral line and avoid entanglement with the Soviet Union, but such a policy was impossible to follow. Many Jews actively embraced the arrival of Soviet rule, not least because they saw the Red Army as the only protection they could get from German persecution. Consequently, large numbers of Jews secured work from the new authorities. This resulted in them being identified by the non-Jewish population with the unwelcome Soviet occupiers. It is estimated that between 20% and 40% of the membership of the Polish Communist Party was made up of Jews, though these actually represented a small minority of the region's Jewish population.[7]

Whenever new regions came under Soviet control as a result of the Molotov-Ribbentrop Pact, one of the first consequences was a wave of arrests. Large numbers of intelligentsia, politicians, industrialists, businessmen, and any others perceived to be hostile to rule from Moscow were rounded up and imprisoned. In the eyes of the Soviet authorities, the Poles were regarded as particularly untrustworthy, and the large numbers of Poles who were dismissed from their posts in government agencies, as well as those who were arrested, greatly increased the hostility of the Polish population to the Soviet Union. By the end of 1940, arrests in Lithuania alone exceeded 200 per week and included those who were suspected of having ties with foreign powers – it is a measure of the extremes to which this was taken that completely apolitical philatelists were included in this latter category. The pace of arrests continued to accelerate in early 1941 and shortly before the German invasion in June, a report submitted to Stalin showed that over 40,000 people had been arrested in the Baltic States. Most were deported to Siberia, and few would ever return to their homelands.

The involvement of many Jews with the new authorities inevitably resulted in many non-Jews associating them with the arrests and deportations. The fact that the Jewish community suffered proportionately more arrests than the non-Jewish population was either not noticed or ignored. In Vilnius, tensions between the three ethnicities in the city were particularly pronounced, as they had been throughout the 1930s. The Polish population bitterly resented not only the defeat of Poland but also the assignment of the region to Lithuania; the Lithuanians associated the Jews with the new Communist rulers and became increasingly hostile; and many of the Jews in Lithuania began to seek ways to escape. The main obstacle faced by the Jews was the insistence of the Soviet authorities that they would only permit people with valid passports and entry visas to other countries to leave Lithuania, and obtaining such documentation was almost impossible. For many Jews in Lithuania, help in obtaining these papers came from unlikely sources.

Most foreign diplomats in Lithuania did little or nothing to help the Jews. The US State Department had taken a particularly hard line, insisting that anyone seeking a visa for travel to the USA had to have a sponsor there; in addition, the traveller needed a certificate from the local police to prove that they were of good moral standing and had no significant convictions. Obtaining both of these proved almost impossible for most of the Jews who wished to travel to the United States, but other diplomats proved to be far more helpful.

In 1939, the Dutch businessman Jan Zwartendijk, who worked for the Philips electronics company, travelled to Kaunas in order to establish an office in the city. He became friendly with several Jews there, not least because the city was home to several highly regarded Talmudic schools, or *Yeshivot*, and Dutch Jews travelled to the region to study in these establishments; through these Dutch Jews, Zwartendijk met many local Jews. He remained in the city as war broke out. The Dutch government had an ambassador in Riga with consuls in both Estonia and Lithuania, and when Germany invaded the Netherlands in 1940 the ambassador de Dekker dismissed the consul in Kaunas on the grounds that he and his wife were Nazi sympathisers. Zwartendijk had made no secret of his anti-Nazi views and when he learned of this, the ambassador asked him to become the Dutch honorary consul-general in Kaunas. At first, Zwartendijk was unwilling to take up the post, but he allowed himself to be persuaded. Within days, he found himself in a country under the control of the Soviet Union.

One of the consequences of the Soviet takeover was that commercial activity in the country almost ground to a halt. In a telegram to the Philips headquarters in Eindhoven, Zwartendijk outlined the situation:

> The banks are closed ... The general mood is rather nervous ... The coming weeks look rather sombre. What is going to happen exactly is not entirely clear yet, but I'm convinced that there will no longer be an independent Lithuania ... Commercially we are finished here, whatever the further developments may be. It can only become bad or still worse.[8]

This assessment meant that both of Zwartendikjk's roles – as the head of Philips in Lithuania and as honorary consul-general – were likely to come to an end in the near future.

While Zwartendijk was awaiting instructions from both his commercial and diplomatic superiors, events continued to unfold in Lithuania. Pessia Lewin was a Jewish woman who had originally been a Dutch citizen before she married a Polish Jewish political figure and became a Polish citizen. Together with her husband, her young son, and her mother and brother who had been visiting the family in Łódź when Germany invaded Poland in September 1939, Lewin fled to Kaunas and in the summer of 1940 she attempted to secure visas permitting travel to the Dutch territory of Curaçao. Zwartendijk sympathised with her but pointed out that as she was no longer a Dutch citizen, he was unable to help her.

Lewin persisted with her efforts, writing to Dekker in Riga. The ambassador was also sympathetic but responded that he was unable to help as the issuing of visas had been suspended. After further correspondence, he conceded that Lewin's brother and mother would be able to travel to Curaçao without a visa, though this would require the assent of the Dutch governor of the colony. The determined Lewin wrote back once more, asking if the ambassador would be happy to write a statement in her Polish passport stating that no visa would be required to enter either Curaçao or Suriname, but leaving out the qualifier regarding the permission of the local governor. She must have been at least mildly surprised when Dekker returned her passport with the following endorsement: 'The Royal Dutch Legation in Riga hereby declares that no visa is required for entry by foreigners to Suriname, Curaçao and the other Dutch possessions in America. Riga, 11 July 1940.'[9]

Armed with this endorsement in her passport, Lewin returned to Zwartendijk's office in Kaunas and asked him to endorse her husband's travel documents with the same words. Zwartendijk agreed, and the family moved one step closer to escaping from Lithuania.

Coincidentally, another person had also approached Zwartendijk seeking similar documentation. Nathan Gutwirth was a Dutch Jew who had been in one of the Jewish schools in the city and he had been introduced to Zwartendijk via mutual friends in the Jewish community. Gutwirth also managed to obtain an entry in his passport from Zwartendijk identical to that obtained by Lewin. Word began to spread in the tight-knit Jewish community. Zerach Warhaftig, a lawyer, was a Polish Jew who had fled to Lithuania as the Germans approached Warsaw in 1939 and asked Gutwirth to enquire whether Zwartendijk was prepared to issue similar documentation to other Jews. Without consulting Dekker in Riga, Zwartendijk agreed to do so, adding that he had been ordered by the Soviet authorities to close his office and would therefore be departing from Lithuania in the next few days.

Warhaftig lost no time in informing other members of the Jewish community of Zwartendijk's willingness to issue what had become known as 'Curaçao visas'. A steady stream of Jews visited the office from where Zwartendijk had been conducting consular business – the Soviet authorities had insisted that he place a large picture of Stalin prominently in the window facing the street – and over four days in the last full week of July, he issued over 1.300 such documents. Many, perhaps most of those he helped had no idea of his name, and he was known to them as 'Mr Philips Radio'. When the consular office re-opened on Monday 29 July, Zwartendijk and two aides resumed their task. The consulate finally closed on 1 August, and the total of visas issued in that time was over 3,500.

Two days later, Zwartendijk closed his Philips office too and moved out of Kaunas. He had to wait for permission from the Soviet authorities to travel to the Netherlands, and finally returned to Eindhoven in mid-September. He remained an employee of Philips through the war and had a brief moment of anxiety when Gestapo officers summoned him to their office for questioning. Fortunately, it proved to be a false alarm: a man who was being pursued by the Gestapo had been shot and killed, and a piece of paper was found in his pocket bearing Zwartendijk's name. The matter proved to be completely unrelated to Zwartendijk's activities in Lithuania and resulted in no further investigations.

Many of the Jews who tried to get visas lacked any travel documentation at all, and given the short timescale, there was no opportunity for them to apply for passports, even if the Soviet authorities had been willing to issue them. Some were able to obtain counterfeit passports; about 30 men ended up with identical fake documents identifying them as 'Jakub Goldberg'. But securing the entry visas for the Dutch colonies was merely a first step. In order to be permitted to leave Lithuania, the Jews who were fortunate enough to have been helped by Zwartendijk would need further documentation to demonstrate that they would be able to reach their ultimate destinations. None would have been able to escape from Kaunas had it not been for the intervention of a second diplomat.

Chiune Sugihara was born in 1900 in central Japan, the son of a tax collector. His father wished him to become a doctor, but he refused to sit the medical school entrance examination and instead joined a government-sponsored international student programme. During this time he became fluent in Russian and also studied English, Chinese, French and German while living in the city of Harbin in China in the 1920s. He met and married a White Russian woman, Claudia Semenovna Apollonova. The marriage lasted 11 years before ending in divorce, and while he was still in Harbin he was approached by White Russian exiles who attempted unsuccessfully to recruit him as a spy.

Sugihara returned to Japan and was almost immediately sent to Manchuria, where he met and married Yukiko Kikuchi. In 1937 he was told that he would be posted to Moscow, but having learned of the approach made to him by the White Russian exiles, the Soviet authorities refused to recognise him as a diplomat. Instead, he was sent to Helsinki as chargé d'affaires the following year.

When Germany and the Soviet Union announced the signing of the Molotov-Ribbentrop Pact in August 1939, some within the Japanese government and military began to doubt the commitment of Germany to its treaty obligations to Japan. The two countries had signed the Anti-Comintern Pact in 1936 (extended to include Italy the following year) that committed them to cooperate to restrict the international spread of Communism, and many in the Japanese government saw the new German-Soviet treaty as a clear breach of the 1936 agreement. It was decided to establish a consulate in Kaunas, operating independently from the main Baltic region embassy in Riga, from which it was hoped that Japanese diplomats and agents would be able to monitor military activity by the Soviet Union and Germany and thus detect any signs of preparations for war by either side. In particular, German preparations for war would enable the Japanese to transfer forces from the Soviet-Manchurian border to the Pacific. Partly because of his fluency in Russian, Sugihara was given the post.

Throughout the summer of 1940, crowds of Jews and others who were desperate to leave Lithuania gathered around the various foreign diplomatic residences in Kaunas. Sugihara and his wife had become acquainted with some of the local Jews shortly after they arrived in the city the previous winter and heard harrowing stories of the persecution of Jews that was taking place in German-occupied Poland. The sequence of events that followed isn't clear, but it is likely that after large crowds of Jews gathered outside the building where Sugihara lived with his family and from where he conducted consular affairs, he met five Jewish representatives and Zwartendijk. At this meeting, he learned that Zwartendijk was prepared to issue 'Curaçao visas' – an alternative account of events is that he was already issuing the visas at this point – but the Jews requested entry visas to Japan as they wished to travel across the Soviet Union to the Pacific, from where they could seek passage aboard ships to the Japanese city of Kobe, home to a substantial Jewish community.

In response to the requests for visas to Japan, Sugihara sent a telegram to the Japanese Foreign Minister in Tokyo:

> I request permission to issue visas to hundreds of Jewish people who have come to the consulate here in Kaunas seeking transit visas. They are suffering badly. As a fellow human being, I cannot refuse their requests. Please permit me to issue visas to them. This request is a humanitarian plea. The refugees' request for visas should not be denied.[10]

A reply from Tokyo informed Sugihara that he could not issue any visas to persons who did not have a 'firm end visa' – the Japanese Foreign Minister wanted at all costs to prevent the arrival in Japan of refugees who would not be able to travel onwards. When Sugihara asked for clarification and again requested permission to issue visas, he was given clear instructions not to do so.

After discussing the matter with his wife, Sugihara decided that he would issue visas anyway. He drove to the Soviet embassy in Kaunas – despite the recent takeover, there was still a Soviet diplomatic presence in the city – and spoke to the Soviet consul. Aided by his fluent Russian, he was able to secure agreement with the Soviet authorities that they would permit the refugees to travel across the Soviet Union to Vladivostok. He then returned to his office and began the work of producing hundreds of visas. Members of staff were organised to help him draw up the documentation. When a German Jew, Moshe Zupnik, reached the front of the waiting queue, he told Sugihara's staff that he had 300 passports with him and wished to get visas for them all. Sugihara agreed to provide visas in return for Zupnik's help in processing the applications.

In an attempt to continue issuing visas, Sugihara ignored a further telegram from Tokyo ordering him to close the consulate and asked the Soviet authorities for a small extension on their deadline for closure. In the meantime, he and his helpers wrote hundreds of visas every day, starting early in the morning and working late into the night. After the first few days, the checks that they had been making on the documentation of each applicant ceased – they simply issued visas regardless of whether the passports were valid or expired. The Soviet authorities permitted him to continue consular functions until 28 August and the small team worked until the last moment. When he and his family finally left the building and moved to the Hotel Metropolis before travelling onward by train to Berlin, Sugihara continued to handwrite visas on headed consular notepaper and stamped them with the official consular stamp. Even when they reached the railway station a few days later, he continued to produce visas with the applicant's name left blank, handing them out in bundles to the hundreds who continued to wait in hope.

For those lucky enough to secure visas from Sugihara and Zwartendijk, the next step was to get tickets for rail travel to Vladivostok. They were fortunate in that the Soviet government saw them as a source of much-needed foreign currency. Most had to pay several times the normal price of a ticket, but thousands set off on the long journey across Siberia. When they reached the port of Vladivostok, they found themselves in further difficulties. On the one hand, the Soviet authorities were anxious for their immediate departure; on the other hand, Japanese officialdom had caught up with events and issued strict instructions that the documentation of every individual had to be checked carefully before they would be permitted to travel onward. Purely by chance, the acting Consul-General of Japan in Vladivostok was Saburo Nei, who was an old acquaintance of Sugihara from their time in Harbin where they had studied foreign languages together. Both as a gesture of solidarity towards his friend and out of a sense of obligation to honour the promises made by his diplomatic counterpart in Kaunas, Nei permitted the Jews to travel on to Japan.

None of the Jews who received travel documents from Zwartendijk actually travelled to Curaçao. Had they done so, they would almost certainly have been refused entry as they lacked the necessary certification from the governor of the colony, which was an important centre of crude oil production. Instead, most of the refugees travelled to Japan, China, Canada, the USA, and Palestine. Many of the Jews who reached Kobe received help from the local Jewish community and from aid organisations overseas, and large numbers were able to travel onwards to the USA, Canada and elsewhere; as many were originally Polish citizens, they were also aided by Tadeusz Romer, the Polish ambassador in Japan who represented the Polish government-in-exile in London. Several of the Jews who were left in Kobe were then transferred by the Japanese authorities to Shanghai, home to another Jewish community.

At one stage, the group of men who had identical documentation in the name of Jakub Goldberg were placed aboard a ship leaving the Soviet port of Nakhodka, near Vladivostok, but were refused entry into Japan by the authorities. Eventually, Romer was able to persuade the authorities to allow them to come ashore in the Japanese port of Tsuruga on condition that they left Japan within three weeks, something that Romer was able to organise.[11]

Zwartendijk issued over 2,000 passports, and between 4,500 and 6,000 Jews were able to travel to Japan using Sugihara's visas – some accounts give numbers as high as 10,000. At a time when most of the other diplomats in the region did little to help the Jews, these two men took it upon themselves to do all they could to help the refugees escape. But despite the humanitarian efforts of these two men – in the case of Sugihara, acting in direct contravention of the orders he had received from Tokyo – the great majority of Jews were unable to leave, including many who had obtained documentation from either or both men.

The Jewish community now comprised the original substantial population of Lithuanian Jews swollen by refugees who arrived from Germany before 1939 and Poland thereafter. They had little choice but to trust that the Red Army would be able to defend the region if war with Germany were to come.

3

The First Days of German Occupation

The advance of the Wehrmacht into the Soviet Union has often been portrayed as an irresistible armoured onslaught. Whilst this was not entirely true in some sectors, it is a reasonable description of the invasion of Lithuania. There was brief fighting around the town of Raseiniai where a Red Army counterattack with two mechanised corps briefly stopped the German advance, but the outcome was the near-complete destruction of the Soviet armoured force that was thrown into the attack, leaving the rest of the Soviet units in the region badly weakened. With the Red Army in full retreat everywhere, anti-Soviet groups briefly seized control of Kaunas on 23 June; many of their personnel were made up of Lithuanians who had been drafted into the Red Army but had deserted.

In villages, towns and cities, crowds of Lithuanians gathered after the departure of Soviet troops to await the arrival of their 'liberators'. In the town of Dusetos, to the northeast of Vilnius, a local anti-Soviet partisan wrote in his diary: 'What joy! The Germans are covered with flowers (and characteristically, not a single red bloom – they're all as white as snow).'[1]

The Germans entered Kaunas a day after the Red Army had left and were met by thousands of Lithuanian residents applauding and cheering, but other residents were filled with trepidation. Dov Levin was one of many thousands of Jews whose worst nightmares were about to be realised: 'Although crowds of Lithuanians greeted the Germans with flowers, it was no surprise that we closed our shutters, lowered our curtains, and locked ourselves up in our homes.'[2]

On the same day, German armoured columns took control of Vilnius; here, too, they received an enthusiastic reception from the Lithuanians in the city, but it should be remembered that although the region was now officially part of Lithuania, the Lithuanians formed a minority of the population of Vilnius. Briefly, Radio Kaunas transmitted the Lithuanian national anthem together with a proud proclamation: 'This is Kaunas calling, this is the free and independent Lithuania.'[3] But whilst the Germans were delighted with their reception and the support they received from so many Lithuanians, they had no intention of permitting an independent government to establish control over the region.

Many Jews, particularly those who had been working for the Soviet authorities, attempted to leave as the Red Army pulled out towards the east. The sheer speed of the German advance overtook many as they struggled along roads heading east and northeast that were choked with refugees and the detritus of the defeated Red Army. German fighter aircraft roared past overhead, often machine-gunning the tangle of vehicles and people on foot. Some turned back to their homes even before the German ground troops reached them.

Joheved Čartokaitė was a 17-year-old girl living in Kaunas with her mother and sister; her father was a teacher who had worked in a private Jewish school in the city, but this was closed down by the Soviet authorities and he was sent to be the director of a school in Alytus, returning home at weekends. When the arrival of German troops in Kaunas was imminent, the family decided to try to flee north in the hope of reaching Latvia, believing that the Red Army would eventually bring the Germans to a halt. After two days of walking towards Daugavpils, they ran into German troops who had outpaced them and were ordered to turn back. Mrs Čartokaitė had injured her foot during their long march and the family sought shelter in a nearby farmhouse; the Lithuanian family gave them shelter and helped treat her foot, and they continued back to Kaunas. Here, they moved in with Mrs Čartokaitė's parents – their own apartment had been requisitioned by the Germans. A week later, Mr Čartokas, Joheved Čartokaitė's father, rejoined the family. Together with other Jews, he had made the hazardous journey from Alytus – about 30 miles (50km) – travelling mainly at night to avoid German and Lithuanian patrols.

Solomon Genkind – Solly to those who knew him – was a young Jewish boy living with his brother, sister and parents in Kaunas. When he was born in 1928, his family lived in the town of Heydekrug in southwest Lithuania. Before the First World War, this region on the northern banks of the Niemen River had been part of the German province of East Prussia but was occupied by Lithuanian troops in the chaotic years that followed the end of the conflict. Although most of the rural population was Lithuanian, the towns had predominantly German populations and the first language that he learned was German. In 1934, as the local ethnic Germans began to grow increasingly hostile towards their Jewish neighbours, the family moved to Kaunas. Late in 1939, when the Jewish community was celebrating the festival of Hanukkah, Genkind went to see his aunt in the hope of getting some money from her so that he could go to see a new Laurel and Hardy movie. At her home, he met Chiune Sugihara, who gave him a few coins for his cinema ticket. On impulse, Genkind invited the Japanese consul to his family's Hanukkah party; he and his aunt were astonished when Sugihara gracefully accepted the invitation. One of the other guests at the party was a Jewish refugee from Warsaw who described the terrible treatment of Jews in Poland, at the hands of both the Poles and especially the Germans. Genkind's father Chaim told Sugihara that he had visas for travel to the United States but was waiting to sell his business interests. Sugihara quietly advised him that he shouldn't worry too much about his business interests, but Chaim Genkind chose not to follow this advice.

During 1940, the Genkind family had been amongst the many Jews who acquired visas from Chiune Sugihara but stayed in Lithuania because they were unable to obtain the forged Polish passports that they had been promised. Solly's older brother Herman had been working for the Soviet authorities because he spoke Russian, Lithuanian and German fluently, and discovered that Chaim Genkind was on a list of people to be deported to Siberia, but the German invasion intervened. When they learned of the German invasion, the family attempted to leave Kaunas:

> The narrow road leading toward Ukmerge and the Latvian border was jammed with refugees and retreating Soviet troops. An endless variety of vehicles, horse-drawn wagons, motorcycles, and bicycles threaded their way through a huge swarm of people on foot. Although ragged columns of Soviet soldiers mingled among them, most of those on foot were civilians, and most of them were Jews.
>
> Almost as soon as we got out of Kaunas, the Luftwaffe attacked the road, apparently intent on machine-gunning everything that moved. Everyone dove for the ditches. I lay face down in the dirt, trembling as bullets thudded around us, raising clouds of dust …
>
> Late in the afternoon, as a column of Soviet tanks and ammunition trucks made their way past us, we heard again the shrill whistle of diving Stukas. Again the screaming civilians ran in all directions, while a few Russians took shots at the aircraft with their rifles.
>
> 'Into the ditch!' my father shouted, waving us toward a gully by the road.
>
> In the distance the first bombs exploded sending flames and pillars of earth spurting into the sky. I remember watching the

> bombs advance in a neat pattern, like a tailor taking stitches, when suddenly I was lifted off my feet. A tremendous explosion shook the earth, sucking the air out of my lungs. I found myself up in the air, my feet flying up behind me and my eyes, strangely, wide open. It must have taken a mere second or two, yet time seemed suspended. I saw a truck exploding in flames and a body rising into the air in pieces, the severed head flying past me, its eyes bulging.[4]

Shortly after, the Genkind family watched in horror as a group of Lithuanian partisans executed several Jews in a nearby field. Soon they were overtaken by the advancing German forces and decided to return to their apartment; a Lithuanian agreed to take them on his wagon, and it took them four days to reach the city. At one point, they were stopped by Lithuanian partisans who clearly intended to kill them, but a car carrying two SS officers appeared. To the astonishment of the Genkind family, Solly's brother Herman climbed the embankment and had a long conversation with the Germans, as a result of which one of the SS officers brusquely ordered the Lithuanians to release the family. The family watched helplessly as Herman climbed into the car with the two Germans and was driven away.

Many of the Jews in Vilnius also tried to flee before the Germans arrived. Mascha Rolnikaite was a Jewish girl of 14, and in some respects her father fitted the stereotype of the Soviet-supporting Jew – he was a lawyer who had defended Communists in court before the Soviet takeover and subsequently obtained employment with the new Soviet authorities. As the Red Army units began their hasty withdrawal from Vilnius, Mr Rolnikas left his family and went out to secure either train tickets or motor transport. In the meantime, his family watched the Soviet troops leaving the city from their apartment. When the last of the Soviet soldiers had left, Mrs Rolnikaite decided she couldn't wait any longer and with her four children she set off for the railway station, hoping in vain that she would find her husband there, giving each child a small bundle of clothes while she carried the largest bundle herself. Next, she led the children out of the city along the main highway running east, as Mascha Rolnikaite later wrote:

> Together with other people we set off down the road. The sun shone. We were covered in dust. We walked along the first stretch of road, and the city was still in sight.
>
> Ruwele [Mascha's brother, the youngest child] wanted to stop and rest. Mama took his bundle from him but it didn't help – he continued to whine. And it wasn't easy to carry a five-year-old.

Rajele [the second youngest child] wasn't any braver than him, even though she was two years older – she started to cry. I really wanted to stop and rest too, but I remained silent.

Then we stopped for a while. Others who had more energy overtook us. Mama persuaded the little ones to go on. But they soon began to ask if we could stop again. We rested. This time we weren't the only ones: other families sat near us.

We all went on together. Heavily loaded cars drove past us. They couldn't take us with them; but they urged us to hurry, the Germans were close behind. But how could we hurry?

What to do? Some wanted to press on – they would rather die of exhaustion and hunger than at the hands of the Germans. Others suggested that the Germans wouldn't be as bestial as people said. You didn't have to get involved with politics. You could just keep quiet and wait to be liberated. We weren't going to be able to get to Minsk on foot, particularly with small children.

The little ones wanted to go home. Mira [the second oldest child] said we should press on. I remained silent. The little ones cried. Mama turned back. We weren't the only ones who went back to the city.

The apartment manager told us that Papa had come home shortly after we left. He left a message that he was going to find a car for us.[5]

Like tens of thousands of other Jews, the family could only wait in trepidation to see if their worst fears were going to be realised.

The Lithuanians who took advantage of the departure of the Red Army in Kaunas included members of the *Lietuvių Aktyvistų Frontas* ('Lithuanian Activist Front' or LAF), which was created in 1940. Its founder was Kazys Škirpa, who had been the Lithuanian military attaché in Germany. He had served in the Imperial Russian Army in the First World War and commanded a small Lithuanian force during the Lithuanian War of Independence before entering politics. When the Soviet Union annexed his nation, he founded his resistance movement while in Berlin with the encouragement of the Germans. He believed that he would be able to secure complete independence for Lithuania, but the Germans had different ideas from the outset. They cooperated with Škirpa with the intention of using the LAF as an auxiliary force to assist their occupation plans, making deliberately vague comments about the future of Lithuania and deferring such discussions until the area was under German control. The *Einsatzgruppe* units intended for operation in the Baltic region numbered fewer than 1,000 men – if they were to carry out their task of killing large numbers of Communists, Jews, and others deemed to be undesirable, they would require considerable help, and the LAF was an obvious potential source of such aid.

In the summer of 1940, Škirpa met Peter Kleist, a German diplomat with special responsibility for Eastern Europe. The two men agreed to draw up leaflets that would be dropped by air over Lithuania urging people to join the LAF and inviting Germany to save Lithuania from 'Jewish Communism'. The linkage of Jews to the hated Communists, already an established part of Nazi thinking, became part of the ideology of the LAF. Whilst the overall plans for resolving the 'Jewish Problem' still involved the mass displacements of Jews to the east where they would either be worked to death building roads and railways across the conquered Soviet Union or would be expelled into the barren plains of Siberia, Heydrich and Himmler wished to take advantage of the immediate aftermath of the invasion to kill as many Jews as possible. This would serve several purposes. Firstly, it would help eliminate a significant number of adult men who might form the nucleus of resistance against the Germans. Secondly, it would terrorise the surviving Jews and make them more compliant. And thirdly, it would help to create sufficient space to accommodate the Jews of Germany and elsewhere who could then be sent east.

Prior to the German invasion, there were meetings between senior SS figures and members of the LAF. It was the intention of the Germans for action to commence as soon as possible against Jews and others, and almost as soon as the Red Army had departed, Lithuanian mobs began to attack Jews and those suspected of having collaborated with the Soviet occupation. Many of those involved were members of the LAF, but large numbers were ordinary civilians. Jews and suspected Communists were pursued through the streets of cities, towns and villages and beaten or killed in open view. Elena Kutorgiene, a woman living in Kaunas, saw what happened:

> A large number of armed people wearing armbands in national colours surged through the streets. Hostile, uncouth individuals ran back and forth with rifles with fixed bayonets. Jews were led away singly and in groups and I looked at them with great sorrow … A large, elegant, somewhat older man passed me, his face white but still calm and collected, and then came a group of women and elderly … The crowds gathered in Laisvės Alėja mocked those who passed and rejoiced in their suffering, smirking and laughing … All that I saw left me shocked and devastated. A woman … came up to me with tears in here eyes and said, 'How terrible, that people can be happy about something like this!'[6]

A Wehrmacht staff officer from the headquarters of Army Group North had been ordered to proceed to Kaunas on 27 June to locate suitable accommodation for Leeb and his staff. His route led him through Gedimino Gatvė, a street in the centre of the city:

> During the drive through the city I came to a fuel station where a large crowd had gathered. In the crowd there were also several women who held their children high or, in order to be able to see better, stood on stools or boxes. The repeated surges of applause – shouts of 'Bravo', clapping, and laughter – at first led me to think it was a victory celebration or some form of sporting event. But in response to my questions, I received the answer that the *Totschläger von Kowno* ['the Kaunas killers'] were at work here. Collaborators and traitors were finally getting their just desserts here! But coming closer I was witness to the most dreadful scene that I saw during the course of two world wars.
>
> On the concrete forecourt of the fuel station there was a middle-sized, blond man of about 25, who was leaning on a wooden pole as thick as an arm and that was as high as his chest. At his feet lay between 15 and 20 dead or dying people. Water poured constantly from a hose, washing the shed blood into a drainage ditch. Just a few steps behind this man were about 20 men – watched by a few armed civilians – standing in mute acceptance as they awaited their grim execution. After a slight beckoning, the next came forward silently and was beaten to death in the most bestial manner with the wooden pole, and every blow was accompanied by the enthusiastic calls of those watching.[7]

When he reached the headquarters of Sixteenth Army, the staff officer reported what he had seen. Many of his colleagues shared his shock and anger, but he was informed that this was apparently a spontaneous reaction by the Lithuanian population as a result of the Soviet occupation, and that orders had been issued 'from above' that the Wehrmacht was not to intervene. Gunshots echoed through the city streets all night, and the following morning the staff officer ventured out once more:

> I didn't see any more executions taking place in the streets as I had the previous day. Instead though there were long columns of 40 to 50 men, women and children who had been driven from their homes and were being herded through the streets by armed men. From one of these columns a woman broke away and fell to her knees before me and pleaded with me with her hands raised for

> mercy and to help her, before she was thrust back in the roughest of manners. I was told that these people were being taken to the city prison. But I suspect that they were taken directly to a place of execution.[8]

An official photographer accompanying the German Sixteenth Army as it passed through Kaunas also witnessed the events on Gedimino Gatvė:

> In the afternoon, I found a gathering of people near my chosen quarters in the courtyard of a fuel station, enclosed on three sides and cut off from the road by the crowd. I found this scene there: in the left corner of the courtyard, there was a group of men aged between 30 and 50. There must have been about 40 or 50 people who had been rounded up by some civilians and were being held together. The civilians were armed with rifles and wore armbands, as can be seen in the photographs I took at the time. A young man, who must have been a Lithuanian ... with rolled-up sleeves was armed with a long iron bar. He pulled one man at a time from the group and then dealt one or more blows to the back of the head with his iron bar. In this manner, he slew the entire group of 40 or 50 people in three quarters of an hour. I took a series of photographs of these executions ...
>
> After they had all been slain, the young man put down his iron bar, produced a harmonica, stood on the heap of corpses and played the Lithuanian national anthem ... The behaviour of the civilians who were present (including women and children) was remarkable, as they began to applaud after each killing and then commenced to sing and clap when the national anthem began. There were women in the foremost ranks with small children in their arms who witnessed all of the events from beginning to end. I asked a German-speaker what had happened here and was told the following: The parents of the young man who had killed the others had been dragged from their bed two days before and promptly shot because they were suspected of being nationalists and this was now the young man's revenge. Nearby there lay a row of dead people who according to the civilians had been killed by the retreating Commissars and Communists.
>
> While I was still talking to the civilians, an SS officer spoke to me and demanded that I hand over my camera. I was able to refuse as firstly it was an official camera and secondly I had special orders from Sixteenth Army Headquarters to photograph everything.[9]

A military bakery unit was also passing through the city. When he encountered a large crowd, the Wehrmacht Gefreiter (corporal) driving one of the trucks stopped and clambered onto the roof of the cab to see over the heads of the civilians and witnessed another slaughter taking place:

> I saw how Lithuanians armed with a variety of striking implements were raining down blows on other civilians until they showed no more signs of life. As I didn't know why these people were being killed in such a gruesome manner, I asked a nearby medical Feldwebel [sergeant] whom I didn't know personally. He told me that the people who were being killed were all Jews who had been seized by Lithuanians in the city and were being brought to this square. I didn't find out why these Jews were being killed. At that time I had no personal experience of the persecution of Jews, and had heard nothing about it. Almost all of those watching were German soldiers, who stared at the grim scenes with fascination.
>
> When I reached the square where the Jews were being killed about 15 corpses or badly wounded were laid out on the square. There were about five Lithuanian convicts nearby who had been released and were ready to kill more Jews … As I was an amateur photographer, I took two photographs of this singular scene that I could see by standing on my vehicle. As the film was then finished I took it from the camera in order to load a fresh roll. At that moment a Wehrmacht officer, probably a paymaster, approached me and told me that we weren't to take any photographs of such events. I had to give him my personal and unit details and he confiscated my camera. I could only save the photographs that were on the film that I had already removed … [In these photos] five Lithuanian convicts can be seen clearly, holding implements in their hands and striking right at the bodies of the Jews lying before them. Members of the Lithuanian 'freedom fighters' can also be seen, with armbands on their left arms. They constantly brought more Jews to the square where they too were killed by the convicts. The Jews lying in the square weren't all killed at once. After they were brought to the square, they were struck quite indiscriminately on the head or face until they were stunned and collapsed on the ground. Then they were struck by the convicts until there were no more signs of life. Then more Jews were brought into the square and killed in the same manner. I remained at the spot where this grim scene took place for about ten minutes. While I was watching the square, I witnessed between ten and fifteen Jews being killed …

> Before they were killed, the Jews prayed and muttered to themselves. Some of the badly wounded Jews lying on the ground also murmured amongst themselves.[10]

The Gefreiter reported what he had seen to his superior, a Hauptfeldwebel (staff sergeant) in the bakery company. The Hauptfeldwebel decided to see for himself:

> I made my way to the square that had been described, where as far as I can remember there were other members of our unit, who had gone there with me. It was a paved square about 20m across. One side of the square opened directly onto the street, two sides were lined with houses. The rear of the square faced open land, perhaps a park.
>
> I saw that civilians, some with armbands and some wearing overalls, armed with iron bars, were killing other civilians. Whether their victims were Jews I couldn't tell. But comments were made that they were Jews who had cheated Lithuanians in business dealings. From the soldiers I found nearest me I heard that the victims were being killed as personal acts of revenge. I estimate that there were 15 to 20 bodies lying in the square when I reached it. They were then dragged away by the Lithuanians and the square was washed clean of blood with a hose. When I asked where the bodies were being taken I was told that they were going to the graveyard. I saw how the Lithuanians grabbed the hands and legs of the corpses and dragged them away. Subsequently, another group of delinquents was pushed and shoved into the square and simply beaten to death by the civilians armed with iron bars without any ceremony. I watched one group of delinquents being killed and then had to walk away as I didn't want to see any more. This process seemed to me the grimmest and most brutal thing. As long as these people continued to be killed, many German soldiers and also civilians continued to watch. The soldiers didn't take part in the proceedings, neither approving nor disapproving. We could hear shouts of approval and advice from the Lithuanian civilians.[11]

The widespread attacks on Jews and Communists lasted for three days, and it is estimated that about 6,000 individuals were killed. Undoubtedly, many of the attacks were spontaneous, often acts of revenge against those believed to be either Communists who had been involved in the deportations and repression of the Soviet occupation or had collaborated with the Soviet authorities; but even if some of the perpetrators of the violence described above were themselves victims, the indiscriminate manner in which Jews were herded into the designated killing areas and then beaten to death far exceeds the amount of retaliation that might have been expected. The recollections of the witnesses above is consistent in that anyone who raised the matter with higher commands was told that these attacks were purely an internal Lithuanian matter that occurred spontaneously, with the implication that the conduct of the Soviet authorities – and their Jewish collaborators – justified the attacks. But there were also other forces at work. Most of the members of the LAF who carried out the attacks were armed with weapons captured from the retreating Red Army, and in many cases these weapons were supplied by the Germans. Walther Stahlecker and the staff of *Einsatzgruppe A* entered Lithuania on 23 June, and in a report that he wrote the following autumn, he recalled the beginning of the German invasion:

> Taking into account consideration that the population of the Baltic States had suffered most severely while under the rule of Bolshevism and Jewry when they were incorporated into the USSR, it was expected that after liberation from this foreign rule they would to a large extent eradicate those elements of the enemy left behind after the retreat of the Red Army. It was the task of the *Sicherheitspolizei* to instigate these self-cleansing activities and to direct them into the appropriate channels in order to achieve the aim of the cleansing as rapidly as possible. It was equally important to establish for the future, incontrovertibly and beyond doubt, that it was the liberated population itself that took the severest measures on its own initiative against the Bolshevik and Jewish enemy, without obvious German instructions. In Lithuania this was achieved in the first instance in Kauen [Kaunas]. To our surprise, it was not easy at first to instigate any major anti-Jewish pogrom there. Klimatis, the leader of this partisan group, was the first to be recruited for this purpose and succeeded in starting a pogrom, helped by instructions given to him by the small advance detachment operating in Kauen, in such a way that no German orders or instructions were seen by outsiders. In the course of the first pogrom on 25-26 June, the Lithuanian partisans eliminated more than 1,500 Jews, setting fire to several synagogues or destroying them by other means, and burned down an area where there were about sixty Jewish houses. During the following nights, another 2,500 Jews were eradicated in the same way. …
>
> These self-cleansing actions were carried out smoothly because the Wehrmacht authorities, informed in advance, showed their understanding of events …

> Both in Kauen and Riga, evidence was gathered on film and by photographs to establish as far as possible that the first spontaneous executions of Jews and Communists were carried out by Lithuanians and Latvians.[12]

In other words, Stahlecker claimed that the activities seen by the German photographer and other such attacks were actually being orchestrated by the men of the *Einsatzgruppen*. It is difficult to know for certain whether some or all of the attacks were actually instigated by the Germans; it was routine for the *Einsatzgruppen* to submit reports that exaggerated the numbers of 'enemies' that they had killed, and whilst some of the violence may have been orchestrated by the Germans, it was too widespread for this to be universally true and Stahlecker may have been attempting to claim credit for killings that were not instigated by his men. Prior to the invasion, senior figures in Heydrich's RSHA held meetings with exiled Lithuanian, Latvian and Estonian anti-Communist groups as well as similar figures from Ukraine, and the leaflets circulated by members of the LAF prior to the German invasion repeatedly and deliberately blurred the boundary between Jews and Communists – both were regarded as enemies and were to be liquidated. The polarisation of Lithuanian society provided fertile ground for the Germans to promote their calls for the extermination of such 'enemies', and members of the LAF were willing allies.

It would be wrong to label all Lithuanian civilians as being hostile both to Jews and suspected Communists. Most were horrified by the wanton brutality that erupted. Some sheltered Jews and other potential victims, but many were too scared of drawing the attention of the violent perpetrators of the pogroms on themselves and did little. Whilst many might have cheered and applauded the activities of men like the iron bar-wielding young man seen in Kaunas, most watched in horrified silence.

Obtaining food became a dangerous activity for the Jews of Kaunas, who were in constant fear of being seized by the Lithuanian paramilitaries. Solly Genkind and his sister Fanny ventured out every few days to see what they could buy for the family. Usually, they escaped with no more than a few curses or blows, but on one occasion they were less fortunate:

> One day Fanny and I split up as usual. I had no luck and was glumly returning home when I spotted my sister being led into a side street by a gang of Lithuanians. One of them had a thick rope around her neck and pulled her along like an animal. Her dress was torn and she was bleeding from the nose. They were drinking and

laughing and boasting about how they were going to rape her one by one, and how she was going to enjoy it.

Without giving myself time to think I ran at the Lithuanian pulling the rope and rammed my head into his stomach with all my strength. He gasped and dropped the rope. I scooped it up and shouted, 'Ready, set, GO!'

We took off in a burst of speed, leaving the startled Lithuanians momentarily confused. Thank God they were too drunk to run very far. Fanny pulled off the rope after a couple of blocks, and once we reached a quiet side street we were able to slow down a bit. I covered her with my jacket and we made it home safely, but the incident seemed to rob her of all her spirit. The next day she refused to leave the apartment and she wouldn't even eat.[13]

Although the killings were concentrated in and around Kaunas, similar events unfolded elsewhere, but in the initial phase of German occupation Vilnius was run by a joint Lithuanian-German administration and during this period there were no mass pogroms; about 50 Jews and Soviet prisoners of war were massacred on 24 June in the grounds of the Franciscan church in the city, but this was an exception.[14] Jewish men were rounded up in parts of Vilnius and ordered to gather on the streets outside their houses with just a small wash kit – they were told that they were being taken away for a few days of forced labour, after which they would be permitted to return home. In most cases, at least in the first days of the occupation, this proved to be true, but some Jews met a different fate, particularly after the first few days of the German occupation had passed. A column of Wehrmacht trucks was moving forward to Vilnius in early July and passed through Ponary, close to the city. One of the drivers recalled what he saw:

While we were carrying out vehicle maintenance, we suddenly saw a column of about 400 men coming from the direction of Vilnius on the road through the pine forest. The column, which was made up exclusively of men aged between 25 and 60, was led through the forest under the guard of Lithuanian civilians. The Lithuanians were equipped with rifles. The people were fully clothed and had only the most essential baggage with them. As far as I can recall, the escorting men wore armbands, but I can't remember what the colours were. I do remember that Hamann and probably Hechinger followed this column. After about an hour Hamann returned to our accommodation. He was white-faced and told me in an agitated manner what he had seen in the forest. He said: 'You saw the Jews marching past earlier, but none of them are alive now.' I replied to him that this wasn't possible, and he replied that all the men had been gunned down. Those who hadn't been killed by the gunfire were then dealt a coup de grace ...

The following day, I think, around midday, we saw a group of 400 Jews on the same road coming from Vilnius and going into the same forest. They, too, were escorted by armed civilians. The prisoners were very quiet. I didn't see any women or children either in the first or the second group.

This group was now followed by several of my comrades from the truck column. As far as I remember, this included Unteroffizier Riedl, Dietrich, Schroff, Hamann, Locher, Ammann, Greule and perhaps others whose names I can't recall. After we had followed this group about 800-1000m, we came across two large pits in the sand. The pits weren't connected but were separated by the road and a strip of land. Just before the pits we overtook the column and then stood by the entrance to the right-hand pit. I was about 6-8m from the entrance to the pit. On either side of the entrance was an armed civilian. The escorting party then led people to the right-hand pit in small groups. At the edge of the pit was a trench into which the Jews had to go. The trench formed the shape of a cross.

The trenches were about 1.5m deep and wide. As this was a dry, sandy area, the trenches were reinforced with wooden boards. When the Jews were led into the pit in groups, an older man stood for a moment at the entrance and asked in good German: 'What do you want of me? I'm just a poor composer.' Then the two civilians standing at the entrance struck the man several times and he fell into the pit. After a short time all the Jews had been herded into the cruciform trench. My comrades and I had moved to the entrance to the pit. From here, we could clearly see that the men in the trench were being beaten by the guards who stood around the trench. They were then led forward ten men at a time into the pit. They had already been stripped of their upper clothes and their heads were covered with a piece of cloth ...

I should add that the offenders had to grab hold of each other around the upper body as they were led to the execution site. About 6-8m from the group there was a firing party of ten men at the edge of the road. As far as I can remember, the firing squad then shot the group when commanded. The shots were fired in salvoes so that the men fell into the pit together. The 400 Jews were thus killed in the same manner over about an hour. The shooting proceeded very quickly. Anyone who was still moving in the pit after being shot

> was finished off by a single shot. The pit into which the executed men fell was about 15-20m across and about 5-6m deep.
>
> From our position we could see into the pit and thus determined that about 400 Jews who had been shot the previous day were lying in the same pit. They were lightly covered with sand. Right on top of the layer of sand there were three men and a woman who had been shot earlier in the morning. Body parts were protruding through the layer of sand. After about 100 Jews had been shot, other Jews had to scatter sand over those who had been executed. After shooting all the group, the firing squad laid their weapons on one side.
>
> At this point I had the opportunity to speak to these men. I asked one how he could do this so easily and pointed out that the Jews hadn't done anything against him. He replied: 'Yes, after what we have experienced under the rule of the Jewish Russian commissars, after the Russians entered Lithuania ... it's not difficult for us.' During our conversation he explained to me that he had been suspected by the Russians of being a spy. He was imprisoned and taken to several GPU ['*Gosudarstvennoye Politicheskoye Upravlenie*' or 'State Political Directorate'] prisons, even though he was innocent. He was just a simple truck driver and had done no harm to anyone. Amongst other things, they had torn away his fingernails to extract a confession. All of the guards or their relatives had been forced to endure similar severe tribulations. He continued that a Jewish commissar had burst into a home, tied up the man and raped his wife in front of his eyes. Then he had literally slaughtered the woman, torn out her heart, cooked it in a pan and eaten it. In addition, my comrades told me that a German soldier had been shot from a church tower. As a consequence, another 300-400 Jews had been shot in the pit. I should add that the following day roughly the same number of Jews was led along the road. Apart from that one day I didn't visit the execution site ...
>
> I can only say that the mass shooting in Ponary was a scene of horror. I said to myself at the time: 'Dear God, please don't let us lose the war, as it'll go badly for us if they seek vengeance on us.'[15]

Other Germans from the same unit saw Lithuanians lining up their victims by the side of the pit and then machine-gunning them. Some of the soldiers returned to the execution site a few days later when they could no longer hear any gunfire:

> When I reached the execution site a man in grey uniform was standing on the road between the two pits and waving us away.

> Nevertheless, we went on and I said to him that he didn't need to do that as we had already seen everything. When I approached him I saw that he had a dark band around his left arm with the letters 'SD'. I also saw that somewhat to one side was a small wagon with two horses. Another SD man sat on the wagon ... In the wagon were two very well-dressed older Jews ... The two Jews were forced to climb out and I saw that both were trembling terribly. They seemed to know what was intended. The SS soldier who had wanted to wave us away had a machine-pistol. He let the two Jews go to the edge of the pit and shot them both in the back of the head so that they fell into the pit. I can still remember that one had a towel and soapbox, which also fell into the pit...
>
> I should add that we all wondered what would happen if we lost the war and had to atone for all this.[16]

It is impossible to know how many of the atrocities described by the Lithuanian guard actually took place, but the episode with the raped wife and the act of cannibalism seems too far-fetched to be true. Nonetheless, such tales clearly circulated and even if people doubted their veracity, they served as excuses for further bloodshed. The Germans rapidly adopted the seizure of hostages to ensure good behaviour as a standard practice; it was also normal to use Jews and Poles as hostages, as these were the communities from which the Germans most expected resistance. For example, Oberstleutnant Eberhard von Ostmann, who was appointed commandant of Vilnius after its capture by the Wehrmacht, issued orders as soon as he took up his post on 25 June that 80 hostages were to be seized; of these, 60 were to be Jews and 20 were to be Poles.[17] It seems that the inclusion of Poles was at the insistence of the Lithuanian authorities; the Lithuanians remained in a minority in the Vilnius region, and this appears to have been an attempt to influence the Germans into treating the Poles less favourably than themselves.[18]

Jews were often attacked at random in the streets of Vilnius and Kaunas, or arrested on the slightest pretext. Samuel Esterowicz was a Lithuanian Jew who had studied law in Petrograd during the Russian Revolution and subsequently in Berlin, where he studied politics and economics. In the years before the war he was a sales representative for an electronic components manufacturer in the city, and his desire to be fair to everyone allowed him to establish a strong relationship with some of his customers:

> Boleslaw Poddany was a car dealer, the exclusive representative of Ford, Opel, and Buick cars. Poddany purchased replacement car

batteries and light bulbs as well as some other products from me. When my relatives, friends and acquaintances learned that in me they had a primary wholesale source of car batteries, they demanded that I should sell directly to them. This put me in a difficult position, since if I sold batteries from the factory storehouse directly to the customers, who would buy from my clients, the retail merchants? On the other hand, if I should refuse the requests of people close to me, I would antagonise them – an unacceptable alternative for me.

I finally found a solution to this difficulty – I sold them batteries somewhat higher than wholesale, and then every month I sent the difference … to Poddany, my largest customer.

My action made a memorable, almost stupefying impression on Poddany, who had a completely different concept of the honesty of Jewish business people – he became a faithful client.[19]

The relationship between Esterowicz and Poddany, established in this manner, would have far-reaching consequences.

Shortly after the German occupation, Esterowicz experienced the precarious state of the Jewish population. He had sheltered a man named Sushinski, a Communist, in his apartment for a few days until he could flee, as Perela, his daughter, who was aged twelve at the time, later recalled:

On the night of Sunday 29th June, we were awakened by thundering knocks of rifle butts on our front door and a bayonet-armed Lithuanian patrol led by a German officer stormed in when my father, terrified and pale, opened the door. The German yelled: 'Did you signal the Russians?'

Father assured him with trembling lips that we couldn't have, we even took the fuses out so as not to turn on a light by mistake. A civilian Lithuanian broke into Sushinski's room and triumphantly produced a Soviet emblem he found there. The civilian, named Labanauskas, occupied the apartment across the landing from ours. Apparently he was drunk and put on a light, and when challenged by the patrol he assured them it wasn't him but the Jews across the landing who were signalling the Russians. Father, Kaplanski and his son Shelik [who also lived in the apartment] were taken to the police station …

At the police station a miracle happened: one of the Lithuanian soldiers declared that the light was not in the Jews' apartment but in Lananauskas' window – Father and the Kaplanskis were free to go but had to stay in the station because of the curfew. They saw Jews being cruelly beaten ... Suddenly: horror! A group of ultra-Nazi SS came into the station and after hearing that they were Jews, lunged rabidly at Father and the Kaplanskis, placing them face to the wall, searching them and threatening to kill them right there after they found some newspaper pieces in Shelik's pocket. Then another miracle happened. Father was trying to translate the innocuous newspaper pieces into German ... when one of the SS men asked: 'How do you speak such good German?'

Father answered that he was a graduate of the Berlin Business School. The SS man asked whether he remembered the Kranzler coffee house in Berlin, and Father with his photographic memory said that of course he remembered, he quoted its location and described all its delights. The SS man said: 'I was the Kranzler violinist!' and then he said repeatedly, 'You are not a Jew, you are not a Jew!' He let them go at dawn.[20]

Vova Gdud was a 17-year-old boy who tried to flee from Vilnius to Minsk but was one of those who turned back after being overtaken by the German Army. He was then caught up in one of the round-ups of Jews:

They took us to the Bernardynka public park and told us that we would be taken to Molodeczno, a town in Belarus, to clean up the ruins of the bombardment ... Instead in the morning we were taken to Ponary ...

When we came to Ponary there was a huge mass grave excavated, ready for us. There were two machine-guns standing in front of the truck. The first thing they told us was we couldn't talk, scream or move – if there was any commotion when we got out of the truck the two machine-guns would go off. They took us one at a time from the truck to the grave, shooting each one in the back of the head. I was standing on the truck looking at it – nobody said a word, nobody moved. When my turn came I went off the truck towards the grave like everybody else, and just a few feet from the grave, I fell. At the same time, synchronous with my falling, the Lithuanian executioner shot me with his handgun. I happened to fall not as a consequence of his shooting – I just fell and he fired in the same second and he believed that he got me and that was why I fell.

There was not a scratch on me, but he didn't question this. The next victim they killed just about where I was fell on top of me and soaked me with his blood. They brought all the trucks, took off everybody (perhaps 30 people in each truck) and killed all the people from the Bernardynka park. After everything was finished the machine-guns sprayed the bodies in the grave and around the grave because not everybody was dead, a lot of people were still moaning. There was a lot of shooting for several minutes. I don't know what happened to me at that time, but I have no exact recollection of when the shooting stopped – I have a blank, I may have passed out.

When I opened my eyes, saw nothing, moved my head and saw nobody around, I got up and started to walk towards the gate ... There were two guards at the gate who saw me and one of them took a shot at me but it was hilly terrain and I dropped down and he didn't hit me. I ran back to the grave, which was next to the barbed wire. That was the most horrible moment of my life – here I was, young and healthy but terrified because I couldn't get out. It was daytime and if I tried to climb over the barbed wire the guard would probably see me from far away and shoot me. My only chance of getting out was to dig under the barbed wire. I dug with my bare hands, scared that if I wasn't fast enough they would catch me ... I don't know how long it took me, but I squeezed through and ran away.

I was all bloody and in tatters from the barbed wire. On the road I stumbled into the hut of a Polish peasant I didn't know and told them my story. They were kind to me. I washed up, they gave me some clothes, and I went home.

None of the Jews who lived in our apartment building believed me when I told my story – they said I was crazy, I must have had a nervous breakdown after having my friend killed on the way to Minsk.[21]

With the resistance of the Red Army overcome, the Wehrmacht pushed on into Latvia and Estonia. The city of Riga, the largest urban area in the Baltic States, was first established as a fishing and trading port during the Viking era, but at the beginning of the 13th century the newly appointed Bishop Albert of Livonia arrived and established the crusading Order of Livonian Brothers of the Sword as part of a drive to convert the local tribes to Christianity. This order was dominated by German knights and they were followed by German settlers and traders, thus starting the longstanding connections between Riga and German cities on the Baltic coast.

On 29 June, just a week after the invasion of the Soviet Union began, German troops occupied all of the city on the left bank of the Daugava

River and proceeded to capture the rest over the following two days; as had been the case elsewhere, there was little attempt by the Red Army to stop the Germans and most of the fighting was against Soviet units attempting to escape to the north. A rapid advance across the rest of Latvia and all of Estonia followed and with all of the Baltic region in German hands by the end of the summer of 1941, the area was handed over by the Wehrmacht to the civilian occupation authorities as the *Reichskommissariat Ostland*. It was natural that the administrative centre of this territory should be Riga, and this was where Stahlecker established his headquarters for *Einsatzgruppe A* for the moment; when the Wehrmacht crossed into Russia proper and began what was meant to be its final advance on Leningrad, he and his headquarters followed closely behind. His various units were now deployed across Ostland. As it was the last part of the Baltic States to be occupied – and in any case had the smallest Jewish population – Estonia had relatively few Jews remaining when the Germans took control, and *Einsatzkommando 2* and *Einsatzkommando 3* were accordingly assigned to what had been Latvia and Lithuania respectively. Of the other units of *Einsatzgruppe A*, *Sonderkommando 1a* was deployed first in Riga and then in Estonia, while *Sonderkommando 1b*, having been the first major unit to enter Kaunas, was redeployed further east in Belarus.

This period also saw the end of joint Lithuanian-German administration of the cities and regions of Lithuania. Many of the Lithuanian paramilitary groups that had begun to organise themselves along the lines of a national army were disarmed and disbanded, while others were converted into police auxiliaries to serve under German control; they were ordered to expel any Poles in their ranks, and one of the first tasks given to the Vilnius police was to draw up comprehensive lists of the names of the city's Jewish population.

The Lithuanian authorities were told that all future proclamations would be issued exclusively by the Germans and the role of the various municipal administrations that had been set up by the Lithuanians would be restricted to carrying out the instructions of the Germans. Throughout Vilnius, Lithuanians had proudly flown the national flag, but the Germans now ordered that this cease, on the grounds that sufficient time had passed for the Lithuanians to celebrate their liberation from Soviet control. Within days, restrictions on the movement of Jews were announced, with the requirement to wear Stars of David, curfews, and orders that only a restricted number of shops would be permitted to sell goods to Jews.

The intention of Heydrich and Himmler was for the use of SS and police units in the newly occupied regions to take place in three distinct phases. The first phase was effectively complete, with the *Sonderkommandos* having instigated 'spontaneous' actions against Jews and Communists by the local population. The second phase could now begin, with the deployment of the *Einsatzkommandos*. They would be aided by battalions of police from Germany made up of men drafted from the ranks of the *Ordnungspolizei* ('Order Police' or *Orpo*, effectively the bulk of the green-uniformed regular police of the Reich). This would ultimately be followed by a third phase once the areas were completely subjugated and were under civilian control, with the *Einsatzkommandos* moving on to other tasks and being replaced by SS brigades that would be organised and deployed in a flexible manner in keeping with the tasks that remained to be carried out.

Whilst many of the men in the *Orpo* battalions were regular police officers, others were recruited from the ethnic German communities of Eastern Europe who had already formed themselves into paramilitary *Selbstschutz* groups. A total of 23 *Orpo* battalions were raised in early 1941, increasing to 26 by the end of the year, and some of these were attached to army units. As part of its preparations for the occupation of the Soviet Union, the Wehrmacht mobilised several security divisions; these consisted of three security regiments, each with three or four battalions, often with one or more *Orpo* battalions attached to them. The personnel of the security divisions consisted mainly of conscripts who were thought to be too old for service in the front line but would be able to cope with rear area duties, though they included a number of younger men. Ultimately, many of these security divisions were inserted into the front line as the tide of war turned against Germany, but for the moment the divisions were sent into the newly occupied territories to 'pacify' them and prevent any disorder behind the advancing troops.

One man who was drafted into the ranks of a security division was a Viennese soldier named Anton Schmid. He was born in 1900 and served in the army of the Austro-Hungarian Empire on the Italian Front, where he experienced its total defeat; shortly before the end of 1918, he was able to return to Vienna where he resumed work in the post office where he had been employed as a youth. Not long after, he left the post office and by the mid-1920s he had established a small but profitable shop selling and repairing domestic electrical goods. As his shop developed, Schmid moved into larger premises and took on three employees, two of whom were Jews.

Hermann Adler, who he would encounter in Vilnius during the war, later said that Schmid had been in love with a Jewish girl and had a good relationship with her entire family, but this came to an end when the girl and her family moved to Palestine; there is no documentary evidence to support this, but as is described later, Adler spent considerable time with Schmid in Vilnius and it is quite possible that Schmid shared this story with him.[22] Regardless of the truth of this account, it is beyond question that Schmid was consistently on the most friendly terms with the Jewish community in his working-class suburb of Vienna. An elderly resident of Vienna who was interviewed in the 1990s recalled an incident from shortly before Hitler's annexation of Austria:

> There was a baker's shop on the corner of Pappenheimgasse and Klosterneuburger Strasse that was owned by a Jewish woman by the name of Tobor. When Hitler was active, someone – a typical Nazi thug – came and smashed the window. Schmid came past and saw what was happening and dealt him a couple of slaps. At that point a police patrolman appeared – on horseback, at that time many of the police were still mounted – and was about to attack Schmid with his sabre, but Schmid took it from him and bent it … And then they led him down Pappenheimgasse to the police station.[23]

The outcome of this incident isn't known, but given that Schmid continued to run his shop without interruption, it seems that little or no action was taken against him by the police. On several occasions Schmid volunteered to help out his Jewish acquaintances and friends by joining them at their Saturday prayers so that they could have the required quorum of people present – a remarkable gesture for a devout Catholic at a time when persecution of Jews was gathering pace. After the *Anschluss*, he drove several times to the border with Czechoslovakia with Jewish families so that they could leave Austria for what at that time they believed was a safe destination, ignoring the pleas of his wife to avoid drawing the attention of the Nazi authorities to himself. Whilst such activity would not have led to any prosecution, it would certainly have resulted in unwelcome scrutiny and questioning, and at a time when so many in Germany and Austria preferred to look the other way and ignore what was happening to the Jews living nearby, Schmid showed a resolute commitment to helping those he believed to be in need of help.

When the Second World War commenced, Schmid was nearly 40 years old. As he was too old for front line service, he was assigned to a reserve battalion that was deployed in southeast Poland before being sent to a garrison town to the south of Vienna. In 1941, he joined the ranks of the newly created 221st Security Division, which was deployed in the central sector of the long frontier with the Soviet Union. Once *Barbarossa* commenced, Schmid's battalion was used to guard railway lines and bridges near the city of Białystok. Assigned to the security division was a regiment of *Orpo* personnel, including *Polizeibataillon 309*, which entered Białystok on 27 June. Like many such police battalions, this unit had previously been deployed in occupied Poland where it had already taken part in actions against 'enemy' elements of the population; this was often a graded process, in which men were asked to carry out increasingly repressive tasks over a period of time so that they gradually became accustomed to such work. Prior to deployment in the Soviet Union, Major Ernst Weis, the battalion commander, addressed the company commanders, as a court proceeding after the war stated:

> Weis informed his officers of the Führer order concerning the newly commenced campaign in Belarus. These orders included the declaration that the war was directed against Bolshevism and the Jews. Weis wanted them to understand that his battalion should proceed against the Jews without remorse. In his opinion the Führer order was to be interpreted that the Jews were to be exterminated with no regard for age.[24]

The events that followed the arrival of *Polizeibataillon 309* in Białystok demonstrate the degree to which individual units – and particularly their commanders – were frequently left to take matters into their own hands.

Amongst the personnel of *Polizeibataillon 309* was Heinrich Schneider, a platoon commander often known to his comrades as 'Pipo'. He was widely regarded as a fanatical anti-Semite:

> [He] saw red even when only a single Jew was involved ... [He] not only gunned down or permitted his platoon to kill many Jews without cause, but also on one occasion even put the lives of several of his men at risk with his wild behaviour when he fired a burst from his machine-pistol at an innocent and defenceless Jew.[25]

'Pipo' Schneider and his platoon were allowed to attack Jews with little attempt to restrain them; throughout the company, it was common knowledge that Schneider and his men regarded Hauptmann Hans Behrens, the company commander, as a 'cowardly weakling'.

One of the first tasks given to the men of the police battalion in Białystok was to search for Red Army stragglers. There were occasional exchanges of fire with groups of Soviet soldiers, and in one search of houses a platoon of policemen found four Red Army soldiers hiding in a cellar. They promptly surrendered and were led out of the building and made to stand facing a wall. Their hands were tied behind their backs while the search of the houses continued. Meanwhile, Friedrich Rondholz, a platoon commander who had no official business in the area, arrived on the scene. He was described by men who had served with him as 'domineering, robust, stubborn, headstrong, ruthless and cold-tempered'; he strode up to the prisoners, drew his pistol, and executed them with a single bullet to the back of each head. When the commander of the search platoon remonstrated with him, Rondholz apparently shrugged and replied, 'It's war.'

Shortly after they arrived in Białystok, many of the battalion's personnel looted shops and houses and seized a considerable quantity of alcohol; they were soon intoxicated and randomly shot several Jews. At midday on 27 June, Weis, the battalion commander, issued orders that the area of the city around the main synagogue was to be searched for men of military age, who were to be detained; it is characteristic of the manner in which both *Orpo* and *Einsatzgruppe* units operated that the order did not specify what was to be done with those who were rounded up. The search rapidly became disorderly. Anyone who resisted was at risk of being shot out of hand; doors that were slow to open were knocked down and hand grenades were thrown in; some elderly Jews were dragged into the streets, their beards set on fire, and forced to dance. At least 50 Jews were killed during the search.

Johannes Otto, a non-commissioned officer, saw a member of the battalion fire on a Jew who was running from him. When he asked him why he was firing, the man replied: 'Button your lips, you probably haven't learned enough ideology yet.' At one point, Schneider sent one of his men into a house to drive out the occupants. As the policeman returned followed by a solitary Jew, Schneider waved him to one side and then shot the Jew with his machine-pistol before turning to the rest of the platoon and remarking, 'That's how it's done.' By the end of the search, Schneider had killed at least five people. An elderly Jew accompanied by a younger helper managed to reach the headquarters of 221st Security Division and pleaded with Generalleutnant Johann Pflugbeil, the division commander, for mercy. He turned his back on them, while one of the officers undid his trousers and urinated on the kneeling Jews.[26]

Schneider and his men may have regarded Behrens as a coward, but the company commander showed little hesitation in getting involved in the mistreatment and killing of the Jews. At one point, he handed over a Jew to Midecke, one of his men, with the words, 'Take him away, I'll shoot him myself.' The Jew pleaded with Midecke to let him go as he had three young children; concluding that one Jew would make little difference, Midecke released him. A little later, Rondholz came across

Behrens standing next to a group of about 30 Jews – men, women and children. Behrens told him to shoot the Jews; he justified this by saying that the Jews had been captured with weapons in their possession. Rondholz pointed out that the women and children were hardly guilty of having weapons, but although Behrens repeated his order, Rondholz pushed the women and children to one side; the rest were marched a short distance, put up against a wall, and shot.[27]

The Jews who were rounded up were taken to a marketplace where Behrens separated Orthodox Jews from the other prisoners; he then ordered his men to execute Orthodox Jews on the spot. The rest, including many women and children who had either been herded into the marketplace with their menfolk or who had followed of their own volition, were pushed into the main synagogue. A senior Wehrmacht officer then appeared on the scene and told Behrens that the defenceless civilians should be released – regardless of who he was, such events shouldn't be permitted and if Behrens wanted to let off steam, he should volunteer for front-line service. Behrens replied sharply that it was none of the Wehrmacht's business and he had his orders to follow. The Wehrmacht officer then left.

Behrens now ordered the company personnel to nail shut the doors of the synagogue. Fuel was poured onto the building and it was set alight, and several hand grenades were thrown into the interior. A group of Jews managed to break down the main door from the inside but were gunned down when they tried to run out to safety. Some of those inside held infants from the windows, begging the Germans to save their children; the response was more gunfire. It is estimated that as many as 700 people perished within the building, and many more were killed when the flames spread to neighbouring buildings. In addition, at least another 1,000 were executed in the marketplace and elsewhere. Pflugbeil raised objections only when some of the shootings were carried out in a park right next to his headquarters.

As darkness gathered, Weis and most of his battalion continued to roam the streets, many of the men heavily intoxicated; overcome with alcohol, Schneider collapsed in a street, where he was run over by a Wehrmacht truck. Belatedly, Pflugbeil demanded a report from Weis, who replied that he had been drunk on the day and had no recollection of events. His company commanders, including Behrens, then submitted a report that bore little relation to the actual events.[28] In the days that followed, the personnel of *Polizeibataillon 309* and its sister formation *Polizeibataillon 322* carried out the executions of hundreds more Jews in the nearby forests.

Although Schmid's battalion did not take part in the massacre that involved the burning of the synagogue, he and his comrades would undoubtedly have heard about it; in any event, Pflugbeil had issued orders for much of his division – including Schmid's battalion – to seize hostages, 'particularly Jews', and to shoot them at the slightest sign of resistance.[29] Like all Wehrmacht personnel on the Eastern Front, the men of the division would have been made aware of the various orders issued before the invasion relating to how the war was to be conducted. On 11 July, the police battalions of the division were issued a fresh order:

> All male Jews between the ages of 17 and 45 convicted as looters are to be shot according to martial law. The shootings are to take place away from cities, villages and major roads.
>
> The graves are to be levelled in such a way that no pilgrimage site can arise. Photography and allowing spectators at the executions is forbidden. Execution sites and grave locations are not to be made known.
>
> In particular, battalion and company commanders are to ensure the spiritual care of men who take part in this action. The memories of the day are to be obliterated by holding social events in the evenings.
>
> Furthermore, the men are to receive continuous instruction about the political necessity of these measures.[30]

The terrible inferences are plain. If the intention was purely to shoot looters, there was surely no need to organise evening events to erase the memories of what had happened. The order deliberately left the judgement of what constituted looting to the men carrying out the operation. The day after the order was issued, Jewish men were rounded up indiscriminately and taken to the city stadium. Throughout the day, trucks took small groups of Jews away to a nearby forest where the Red Army had dug a series of anti-tank ditches, where *Orpo* firing squads killed them. The slaughter continued until nightfall and stopped only when it was impossible to continue by the light of the truck headlamps. The following day, the last of the Jews in the stadium were taken to the ditches and shot. At least 3,000 were killed.[31]

A few days later, as 221st Security Division moved east behind the advancing Wehrmacht, it reached the area around the town of Slonim. Here, it was preceded by *Einsatzkommando 9*, which was part of *Einsatzgruppe B*, operating with the German Army Group Centre. This *Einsatzkommando* had already moved through Vilnius before handing over the city to *Einsatzkommando 7b*, and near Slonim it was responsible for a massacre of 1,255 Jews on 14 July. Further massacres followed, with another 1,153 Jews being killed on 6 August; by this time, personnel from Schmid's battalion – perhaps including Schmid himself – were tasked with supporting the *Einsatzkommando* action with transport, guards, and ammunition. Events in Białystok and Slonim were far from isolated incidents; such killings were repeated throughout the western parts of the Soviet Union as the Germans advanced. On 24 August, Schmid must have been relieved when his battalion was detached from 221st Security Division and ordered to proceed to Vilnius, where it was to take up garrison duties.

While the first wave of 'spontaneous' pogroms and actions such as those carried out by *Polizeibataillon 309* claimed thousands of victims across Lithuania and elsewhere, the personnel of *Einsatzkommando 3* moved from Pretzsch to the East Prussian town of Eydtkuhnen. It was a typical railway town on the borders of the old Reich. The only fine buildings were around the railway station, where wealthy travellers had whiled away some time in one of the well-appointed waiting rooms until a broad-gauge train arrived to take them onwards to the great cities of Imperial Russia, Saint Petersburg and Moscow; it was deliberate policy on the part of Imperial Russia to use a different railway gauge from Germany, so that in the event of war, it would not be straightforward for the Germans to use Russian railways to transport supplies.

The unit remained in Eydtkuhnen for a week, and the men found various ways of amusing themselves while off duty. As he watched his men – and in particular his immediate subordinates, Grauer, Hamann and Kortkampf – Jäger must have been acutely aware, not for the first time, that there was a considerable gulf in age between him and his men. But what he lacked in age – or specialist education and experience – he intended to remedy through determination to carry out his mission.

The briefing given by Heydrich in Pretzsch had been restricted to senior officers only, and it was deliberately verbal – both Heydrich and Himmler were careful not to leave written records of the instructions that they issued to the *Einsatzgruppen*. Stahlecker, Jäger and other senior officers were instructed to make their subordinates aware of their mission with regard to the Jews of the Soviet territories only when they were about to cross the border, but as most of Jäger's immediate subordinates had been present at Pretzsch earlier in the year, it is likely that they had at least some idea of what was expected of them. Again, instructions were passed on verbally. The few accounts of what was said were obtained from SS personnel who were present and were later prosecuted, and the reliability of these accounts is open to question, as many of their statements formed part of the defence of these men; but Alfred Filbert, commander of *Einsatzkommando 9*, was reported to have told his men that they were carrying out their mission in accordance with the requirements of National Socialist racial policy – no military or security justification was given for the killings.[32]

A week after the invasion began, Karl Jäger and his men crossed into Lithuania in a column of vehicles. One truck struck a landmine and was destroyed, without any of its occupants being injured; with that exception, the journey to Kaunas was without major incident. Jäger established his headquarters in a building already requisitioned for the purpose by *Sonderkommando 1b* in Kaunas – although the Lithuanian authorities had been keen to return their seat of government to their ancient capital of Vilnius as soon as possible, such plans had been effectively abandoned in the turmoil of the Soviet takeover and Kaunas remained the main administrative hub of the country. The Germans swiftly established themselves in the city and got down to work. The 'spontaneous' pogroms of the first days of occupation were over. The serious business of implementing the full range of duties of *Einsatzgruppe A* could now commence in earnest.

4

The Gathering Darkness

Despite the first wave of killings of Jews across Lithuania, Stahlecker and his staff at the headquarters of *Einsatzgruppe A* concluded at the beginning of July that it would not be possible for such actions to continue – 'spontaneous' acts of revenge and 'self-cleansing' by the Lithuanian population were not consistent with the restoration of law and order in the region. Nonetheless, Stahlecker had good reason to be satisfied with how events had unfolded. He later wrote that from the beginning of the campaign, he enjoyed a good working relationship with the Wehrmacht. As soon as *Einsatzgruppe A* crossed the border,

> ... it was a question of establishing personal contact with the army commanders as well as the rear area commanders. From the outset it should be stressed that cooperation with the Wehrmacht was generally good, and in some cases, for example with regard to Fourth Panzer Group under Generaloberst Hoepner, very close, indeed almost cordial. The few misunderstandings that arose on the first days in a few locations were resolved by personal discussion.[1]

Other reports also showed the close manner in which the *Einsatzgruppen* worked with the military. In a report written on behalf of Heydrich on 4 July 1941 summarising the activities of the German security police and SD, Gruppenführer Heinrich Müller – chief of the Gestapo – wrote about Stahlecker's arrival in Riga:

> Group leader Brigadeführer Stahlecker entered Riga with the combat troops. *Einsatzkommando 1a* and elements of *Einsatzkommando 2* were with him. Cooperation with the army command was excellent. It was possible to achieve frictionless incorporation [of the SS

> personnel] into the leading units. Together with the Wehrmacht, steps were taken to ensure security against remaining Russians and armed Communists.[2]

The area around Vilnius was overrun by the divisions of Third Panzer Group, part of Army Group Centre, but as the front line moved deeper into the Soviet Union, the region was handed over to the units operating behind Army Group North. Generaloberst Hermann Hoth, commander of this panzer group, felt obliged to reinforce orders that had been issued before the invasion. On 28 June, he rebuked his subordinate commanders about their 'excessive negligence in dealing with the long-recognised Asiatic methods, murder, treachery and wickedness' of the enemy. Soldiers who permitted Communist officials to remain alive, contrary to the infamous Commissar Order, were threatened with court martial.[3]

Prior to the invasion, Hoth – like almost all of the commanders of the German armies on the Eastern Front – had made clear the linkage between the Jews and the Communists. Later, in November 1941, he reinforced this with a fresh order in which he once more emphasised that any resistance or 'machinations' by Jewish-Bolshevik agitators were to be eliminated without mercy: 'It is the same Jewish class of beings who have done so much damage to our own Fatherland by virtue of their activities against the nation and civilisation, and who promote anti-German tendencies throughout the world, and who will be the harbingers of revenge. Their extermination is a dictate of our own survival.'[4]

Many German officers would attempt to claim after the war that the atrocities on the Eastern Front were exclusively carried out by elements of the SS, and that the regular army was largely blameless, but Stahlecker's comments and the orders issued by Hoth and others paint a very different picture. Even the actions of the Germans against so-called partisans reveal the manner in which the suppression of 'enemy activity' was often merely a cipher for further anti-Jewish measures, as the report produced by Müller on 6 July 1941 shows:

> From Tilsit [on the pre-war border between East Prussia and Lithuania, now the Russian town of Sovetsk] three large-scale cleansing actions were carried out and in fact 201 people in Garsden [Gargždiai], 414 people in Krottingen [Kretinga], and 111 people in Polangen [Palanga] were shot. In Garsden, the Jewish population supported the Russian border guards in their defence against German attacks. During the first night of occupation, an

> officer and two quartermasters were insidiously killed. In Polangen, in a similar manner an officer was shot stealthily by the population the day after occupation. In all three large actions, predominantly Jews were liquidised.[5]

After the war, Hoth was prosecuted for issuing orders to persecute Jews and suspected Communists. He attempted to defend himself on the grounds that this was merely an instruction for his men to remain vigilant; he told the court that 'The German soldier in his good nature … easily forgot that he was still in enemy territory.' He denied that any of the civilian hostages that were taken came to any harm, and when challenged on the number of Jews who were arrested and subsequently killed, he replied that 'It was a matter of common knowledge in Russia that it was the Jew in particular who participated to a very large extent in sabotage, espionage etc.'[6] This ignores the manner in which the Germans operated in the occupied territories. People were arrested largely on suspicion – and given the manner in which Jews had been demonised in the eyes of German soldiers before the invasion it was inevitable that they would be particularly suspicious of Jews. There was little or no legal process after arrest to determine the guilt or innocence of those detained, so that the treatment of Jews as suspected enemy insurgents became a given.

As had been the case in occupied Poland, the Jewish communities in Kaunas and Vilnius were ordered to form representative committees. In Kaunas, the Jewish leaders were summoned to the headquarters of the occupation forces and told that the Germans regarded the pogroms of late June as 'internal disputes between Lithuanians and Jews'.[7] However, in order to prevent further disturbances, the Jews were told that they were to be moved into a designated area of Kaunas where they could be protected from future attacks.

The reality was that it was difficult to continue instigating and justifying such attacks, as the area around Kaunas was now 'pacified'. Müller's daily report for 11 July recorded:

> In general, the situation in the Kaunas area is quiet. Only very occasionally are units of troops fired on from concealed positions by the Red Army. Severe actions by the Wehrmacht and police in response to these are not carried out … The Lithuanian population is for the time being consistently friendly to the Germans and in every respect helps German soldiers, police bodies and the other organisations active in the area. Their help is mainly in finding and handing over Lithuanian Communists, Red Army stragglers and Jews …

> In Kaunas a total of 7,880 Jews have been killed to date, partly through pogroms and partly through mass shootings by Lithuanian groups.[8]

The military commander of the rear area behind the advancing armies of Army Group North was General Franz von Roques. Coincidentally, his brother held a similar post in the rear area behind Army Group South in Ukraine. His orders included the setting up of ghettos in major towns and cities, but he showed little inclination to implement these instructions, concentrating on other rear area duties. It would be incorrect to assume that this was in any way a rejection of the ghetto policy; it seems to have been dictated by his assessment that he lacked the resources for the creation of the ghetto. He also claimed after the war that he had refused to implement the Commissar Order, but testimony from his subordinates contradicted this. His intelligence officer recorded in the official military diary at the end of June that there was little difficulty in identifying Soviet commissars, who could then be 'rendered harmless' quickly. When Jäger and the personnel of *Einsatzkommando 3* arrived in the city, Roques informed him that there were several fortifications around the edge of the city that were suitable for the detention of large numbers of prisoners. Jäger's first impression of Kaunas was not especially encouraging. He later recorded: 'When *Einsatzkommando 3* entered Kaunas, the Jews were still walking freely in the main streets. As a first measure, identification of the Jews was carried out and the construction of a ghetto in Kaunas was organised.'[9]

The ghetto would be in the Vilijampolė section of the city, an area that had been home to about 5,000 relatively poor Jews until the pogroms that followed the arrival of the Germans. At first, the area was enclosed with barbed wire, but more substantial enclosures would follow at a later date. It was frequent practice for the Germans to establish the ghetto with two parts, and this model was followed in Kaunas, with a small ghetto separated from the main ghetto by Panerių Gatvė; the two were connected by a wooden footbridge across the street. The value of this arrangement was that it permitted the Germans to close the connection between the two ghettos whenever they wished; they could then clear the more manageable number of residents of the smaller ghetto and take them away for execution, and subsequently redistribute the population of the larger ghetto between the two.

A total of 30,000 Jews from Kaunas and the immediate surrounding area were moved to the ghetto. Up to ten people had to share a single room, and the water supply to the area was completely inadequate for such a large population. The Jewish Council that had already been created was given nominal control of the ghetto and had an unarmed Jewish Police force at its disposal, but in reality, all of the rules and regulations of the ghetto were imposed by Hans Cramer, the German civilian administrator of Kaunas.

Solly Genkind and his family, who had tried unsuccessfully to flee from Kaunas before the arrival of the Germans, were amongst those who moved into the ghetto. All Jews had been ordered to move to the ghetto by 15 August, but Solly's parents decided to move a week earlier. They were fortunate: shortly after they left their home, several hundred Jews in the neighbourhood were rounded up and taken to one of the nearby forts, where they were shot. At first, the Genkind family lived in two rooms, but as more Jews arrived in the ghetto, other members of the extended Genkind family moved in with them.

Two Germans were placed in overall control of the ghetto. Hauptsturmführer Fritz Jordan was attached to the new civil authority in Kaunas. He took on the role of commandant of the ghetto and was both feared and detested by the Jews. He was known to have fits of rage and arbitrarily issued demands for items to be handed over, ranging from clothing and art objects to the most bizarre items – on one occasion, he demanded that the Jews provide him with two palm trees for his office. Hauptscharführer Helmut Rauca was a member of *Einsatzkommando 3* and worked closely with Hamann, one of Jäger's subordinates. He was formerly a Gestapo officer and was appointed as the Gestapo representative for Jewish affairs in the city.

Jäger and the personnel of *Einsatzkommando 3* wasted no time in commencing their primary task of eliminating the 'enemies of the Reich'. The ring of forts around Kaunas had been built in the 19th century and the substantial buildings were of little military value by 1941, but they were now put to a new use. Several of the forts were conveniently close to the ghetto and Jäger's men established a presence in Fort VII where many Jews had already been executed by Lithuanians during the first days of the German occupation. On 4 July, 463 Jews – most of them men – were taken from the ghetto to the fort and executed by gunshot. Two days later, another 2,514 were killed there. In addition to the personnel of *Einsatzkommando 3*, men from a police battalion helped guard the perimeter of the fort, and Lithuanian volunteers from the ranks of the partisan paramilitaries that had surfaced with the departure of the Red Army were also involved. Indeed, the Lithuanians carried out the bulk of the shootings.

Jäger's first personal experience of mass executions left him profoundly shocked. He visited Fort VII and saw thousands of corpses lying in the fort courtyard, victims of the Lithuanian paramilitaries: 'That was the first execution place that I had seen. It was so shocking for me that I couldn't cope with it for a considerable time.'[10]

Despite the widespread anti-Semitism throughout Europe, particularly in Nazi Germany, and the indoctrination of the German army and police, such a reaction was common amongst those who were suddenly confronted with the reality of what was happening. In some cases, exposure to such events was carefully managed. For example, police reservists who were deployed in Poland were first tasked with overseeing forcible relocations of Jews to ghettos, and on occasion those who were too infirm to be relocated were shot on the spot. The exposure of the men to violence was then gradually increased and encouraged. As a senior officer, Jäger had no such induction. He later recalled that he met Stahlecker shortly after he first visited Fort VII. Jäger later described what he was told: 'The Jews are the bearers of Communism. In addition they instigate acts of sabotage and thus endanger the front line. In defence against this, in the rear areas as well as the homeland, they must be destroyed. Furthermore, he reminded me that I was now a soldier and must therefore be aware what an order in wartime entailed.'[11]

Neutralisation of the intelligentsia at an early stage of the occupation was now standard German policy. As soon as the ghetto was established, Rauca ordered that about 500 well-educated Jews – doctors, engineers, lawyers, university lecturers, etc. – were to form a special work party that would be given clerical tasks in the town hall. In preparation for this move, Jäger made use of an informer in the ghetto. Josef Kaspi-Serebrowicz was a Jewish journalist who had been critical of the Soviet authorities during their time in Kaunas and had been imprisoned, and he was released by the Wehrmacht after their arrival in the city. Jäger was quick to realise that Serebrowicz could be put to good use and he was persuaded to cooperate with the Germans. As soon as the ghetto was formed, Rauca passed on to Serebrowicz Jäger's instructions to draw up a list of Jewish intelligentsia, and the names that he passed to Rauca were compared with the Jews who came forward.

Despite their knowledge of massacres that had already taken place, the men gathered willingly, believing that by providing their services to the occupation authorities they would be reducing the risk of further killing. On 18 August, a total of 534 individuals were led through the ghetto gate. But instead of being taken to the Town Hall, they were marched to Fort IV where they were all shot. The teacher Mauša Čartokas, Joheved Čartokaitė's father, avoided this fate by hiding in his sister's cramped room in the ghetto.

The murder of the Jewish intelligentsia became known as the *Intelligenz-Aktion*; Jäger later gave a figure of 711 killed, but this is either an exaggeration – and many of those involved in the killing of Jews across the occupied parts of the Soviet Union routinely exaggerated the total of people killed in the hope of impressing their superiors – or it includes additional victims who were also slaughtered at Fort IV. By 10 August, the daily reports recorded that about 29,000 persons had been 'liquidated' since the Germans overran the Kaunas area.[12] Nor were all the killings purely in the various forts and other locations used for mass murder. Joheved Čartokaitė witnessed the random manner in which any Jew in the Kaunas ghetto might encounter death:

> Hauptsturmführer Alfred Tornbaum [commander of a company from *Polizei-Battailon 11*] appeared in our room with his pistol drawn. He ordered the wardrobe doors to be opened and the drawer under the sofa to be pulled out, where our winter coats were stored, and he told the Jews accompanying him to take the winter clothing and two suits that belonged to my father to the truck standing in the courtyard. I wanted to get some money out of my father's jacket pocket – his wages and holiday money for two months – but Tornbaum threatened me with his pistol and ordered that the money be left there … I argued with him and tried to persuade him that without the money we wouldn't be able to buy any food. His eyes bored into me, as if he wanted to strip me naked. Then he said that if I went to work, we would have enough to eat and get by. And once more, his piercing stare, to which I responded fiercely that I would rather starve than work for him. My parents and grandparents, overcome with fear, waited for his reaction. But nothing happened. He continued on his looting spree.
>
> Through the window I saw how our belongings were taken to the truck and suddenly I heard Tornbaum shout, 'Jump, Jew!' The Jew, an elderly man who was taking our belongings to the truck without haste, stood still with surprise, and as he was unable to understand the shouted German words, he began to hop from one leg to another. Tornbaum took aim and shot him several times.[13]

With the Baltic States no longer seen as a combat area, the entire region was handed over to the civil administration of what became known as *Reichskommissariat Ostland*. The head of this administration was Hinrich Lohse, who was simultaneously *Gauleiter* (local party leader) in Schleswig-Holstein; it was entirely characteristic of the Nazi hierarchy that senior figures attempted to hold several powerful positions at the same time. Such an acquisitive attitude to power also meant that like many other senior Nazis, Lohse was unwilling to delegate effectively, resulting in an administration that was often clumsy and controlled by a series of contradictory decrees issued from above.

The manner in which the Nazis ran the occupied territories was chaotic. Lohse's *Reichskommissariat Ostland* was technically subordinate to the *Reichsministerium für die besetzten Ostgebiete* ('Reich Ministry for the Occupied Eastern Territories', often known as the *Ostministerium*) under the control of Alfred Rosenberg. When this new ministry was created in July 1941, other agencies were ordered to assign personnel to it, but many of those agencies had ambitions of their own for the occupied regions. Consequently, they often sent their poorest members of staff to the *Ostministerium*, or men who would then spy on the *Ostministerium* for their former agencies or would even undermine the work of Rosenberg's ministry. Hitler deliberately allowed overlapping spheres of interest and authority in order to encourage competition – the Darwinian theorising mentioned earlier – resulting in wasteful turf wars. The SS and the *Ostministerium* competed to demonstrate their commitment to Hitler's desire to rid Germany of its Jews; to make matters even more confusing, many of the personnel of the *Ostministerium* and its subordinate agencies like *Reichskommissariat Ostland* were members of the SS, but their loyalties were often not straightforward.

In addition, Hermann Goering, who held a plethora of different roles, had overseen Germany's Four-Year Plan for economic measures from 1936 to 1940 and in the process created the industrial conglomerate known as the *Reichswerke*. Even though the plan technically came to an end a year before the conflict with the Soviet Union, many of its officials remained in post and Goering continued to have huge influence on German industry, including exploitation of the occupied territories. This put him in direct competition with the *Ostministerium*, resulting in further friction and inefficiency. The Wehrmacht, too, had an interest in the labour available in Lithuania and elsewhere. Satisfying the desire of the SS for a rapid extermination of all Jews whilst also permitting the smooth functioning of the other agencies involved was certain to cause difficulties.

After he arrived in Riga on 27 July, Lohse issued instructions for the confinement of Jews in ghettos; in some cases, such work had already begun, while in others it was barely at a planning stage. The instructions covered numerous matters, including the supply of rations – this was not to exceed the minimum level needed to keep the inmates alive. After intervention from Stahlecker, he added an amendment that specified that his new regulations were not to be interpreted in any way as restricting the activities of the Security Police. The following month, Lohse issued a more detailed document regarding the management of the Jewish population. All *Gebietskommissars* – the local representatives of *Reichskommissariat Ostland* – were to ensure the compulsory registration of all Jews; Jewish physicians were permitted only to treat Jewish patients, and Jews were banned from working in a variety of professions. Jews were to be cleared from the rural areas and from 'places that are important from the economic, military, or ideological point of view, or are resorts and spas'. Limits were specified not only on rations for ghetto inmates but also payment for forced work:

> The remuneration is not to correspond to the work performed, it has only to serve for the bare subsistence of the forced labourer and his non-working family members, taking into account his other ready money ... The private enterprises and persons for whose benefit the forced labour is performed pay an adequate sum of money at the pay-office of the *Gebietskommissar*, which in its turn pays out an adequate remuneration to the forced labourers.[14]

It is relevant that Lohse stressed the importance of ensuring that the non-Jewish citizens of the Baltic region received adequate remuneration to remain motivated to help the Germans; he clearly excluded Jews from this thinking. In this context, his directive explicitly stated that it was provisional, 'only for so long as extensive measures for the ultimate solution of the Jewish problem are impossible'.

By the end of August, Jäger's jurisdiction would extend to almost all of Lithuania – the town of Šiauliai was passed to *Einsatzkommando 3* in October. As had been the case in Belarus, German security divisions were deployed throughout Lithuania – 207th Security Division was based in Šiauliai, 281st Security Division was in Kaunas, and 285th Security Division was a little to the east. The Vilnius area came under the control of 403rd Security Division. Like the division in which Schmid had served near Białystok, these units had *Orpo* battalions attached to them. The commanders of the divisions interpreted their orders in different ways. Generalleutnant Karl von Tiedemann and Generalleutnant Friedrich Bayer, of 207th and 281st Security Divisions respectively, issued orders explicitly forbidding the shooting of 'parts of the population purely on the grounds that they were members of the Communist Party or its followers, i.e. Jews'.[15] They also showed reluctance to hand over civilian hostages to the security police as the latter often executed them for little or no reason.

By contrast, Generalmajor Wolfgang von Ditfurth, commander of 403rd Security Division near Vilnius, regarded the local rear area commander as too old and unwilling to take firm measures. Shortly after, this commander was replaced by Oberstleutnant Max Zehnpfenning, and he and Ditfurth cooperated smoothly, allocating their men to work alongside the SD.

The killing of Jews in Vilnius escalated immediately after the arrival of *Einsatzkommando 9* in the city on 2 July; in addition to the slaughter witnessed by Wehrmacht soldiers at Ponary, there were shootings within the city itself. The total rose steadily and by 19 July *Einsatzkommando 9* reported that it had killed 7,629 people – Jews, Communists, criminals, and others. Ditfurth cooperated fully, with the proviso that the involvement of his men was limited to logistic support and guard duties. He requested that the killings take place as inconspicuously as possible and ideally out of sight from his soldiers. A few days later, the SD in Vilnius claimed that their accommodation had come under fire from partisans and immediately executed 300 Jews in retaliation. Ditfurth made no objection, though he noted that the evidence for the alleged attack on the accommodation was almost non-existent.[16]

The process followed by *Einsatzkommando 9* was to take Jews to Lukiškės Prison, where they were held pending transfer to Ponary. Jewish women congregated outside the prison, desperate to obtain information about family members who had been detained. Some of those held in the prison were ultimately released, but most were transferred to Ponary after a wait of several days or months. On occasion, Jews were simply marched directly to Ponary and executed immediately.

The execution of Jews at Ponary was the slowest part of the extermination process. The commander of *Einsatzkommando 9* was Obersturmführer Franz Schauschutz, and he was swift to make changes in order to improve efficiency. He banned the use of machine-guns for mass execution, as had been used by the Lithuanians prior to his arrival, on the grounds that this was wasteful of ammunition. Instead, aimed shots were to be fired with rifles at individual victims. In addition to saving ammunition, this was more likely to ensure that the victims were killed with a single shot rather than being wounded. He also made changes to the overall organisation of the killings. From 8 July, he was able to report that his improvements had raised the number of daily killings to 500.

Although most of the killings were carried out by Lithuanian auxiliaries, instructions had been issued – again, verbally – to ensure that all personnel in the *Einsatzkommandos* took part. Each man, even those in administrative posts, was required to take part in at least one execution, firing at the victim with his personal weapon. The incident in which the SD killed 300 Jews in retaliation for the alleged shots fired at their accommodation was a case in point; most of the killings were carried out by *Einsatzkommando* personnel, with Filbert, the unit commander, personally carrying out some of the shootings.[17]

Kazimierz Sakowicz was a Polish journalist who lived in the village of Ponary. He could hear gunfire from his house during the massacres and kept a secret diary of the killings. He was a supporter of the Polish resistance groups but via his neighbours he sometimes received information about Lithuanian forces that were cooperating with the Germans. One of his entries records the terrible scenes that recurred throughout the late summer and autumn:

> There were about 4,000 people ... mainly women and babies. As they followed the route into the forest, they realised what awaited them and cried out 'Save us!' [There were] infants in prams, carried in their arms etc.
>
> The people were beaten before they were shot ... The men were shot separately and the women had to strip to their underwear. [There were] many items, furs and valuables that they thought they would take with them to a ghetto ... During the executions they were moved forward so that the group had to stand on the bodies of those already killed. They went on and on over the corpses! The graves were then closed the following day.[18]

In addition to the security divisions and the *Einsatzgruppen*, other German military units that would operate in the rear areas of the front line were also moving into the region. Some were part of the occupation forces and were there to control, subjugate or exploit the newly acquired territories, but others operated in support of the combat formations that were continuing their advance into the depths of the Soviet Union. The commander of one of these military support units would play a major role in the fate of many of the Jews of Vilnius.

Karl Plagge was born in the city of Darmstadt in 1897, the second of two children. His father was the last in a line of family members who had served in the armies of Prussia and Germany as doctors; he died when his son was seven years old, but true to the family tradition, the young Plagge intended to follow in his father's footsteps. He was too young to join the German Army at the beginning of the First World War but was drafted into the ranks of the infantry in 1916 at the end of his school years. He served on the Western Front as a junior officer, fighting in the battles on the Somme and around Verdun, and was taken prisoner by the British in the closing weeks of the conflict. He remained in captivity for three years, during which there was an outbreak of polio in his prison camp; many of the inmates and guards were affected, and Plagge was left with a marked limp.

When he returned to Darmstadt in 1921, Plagge became a student in the local university. His ambition to become a doctor was not fulfilled – having had to raise her children alone after her husband's death, his mother did not have the financial resources to fund medical studies. Instead, he took courses in chemical and mechanical engineering. He married Anke Madsen in 1924, the year that he graduated, and the couple took up residence with Plagge's mother. In the years that followed, Plagge took a number of engineering jobs, but became unemployed as the German economy floundered in 1930. Resuming his interest in medical matters, he took a course in medical chemistry in Frankfurt-am-Main, a short distance to the north of Darmstadt, and he and his wife then opened a small medical laboratory in the basement of his mother's house, providing laboratory services to local doctors. It was sufficient for the family to survive, but in a nation convulsed with economic turmoil and increasing political violence, Plagge and many others searched for leadership that would restore both stability and pride. In early 1932, he joined the Nazi Party, believing that it was the only political group that had the strength to save Germany from complete chaos; like many Germans at that time, he had little insight into the manner in which the Nazis and their supporters were actually responsible for much of that growing chaos. He later wrote:

> Influenced by the constant growth of unemployment in 1931 and the ever greater general crisis I joined the Nazi Party in about January 1932, as their statements (elimination of unemployment, state employment schemes, limits on highest wages etc.) seemed to offer hope of an improvement of the crisis. Personally, I hoped for nothing other than taking part in the general economic revival, and even later at no point did I seek a salaried post or appointment, even though it would have benefited me, but instead I refused to gain any financial benefits from my Party membership. At that time, I believed Hitler's social promises and affirmations of peace, and believed that I was working for a good cause, particularly as at that time one was free to join or leave a party.[19]

Almost from the start of his time as a member of the Nazi Party, Plagge struggled with much of the ideology that he was expected to embrace. He found the boorish conduct of many Nazi figures deeply distasteful and hoped that the racial theories of the Party would prove to be no more than a passing phase. As the German economy recovered, he secured work in a business run by Kurt Hesse, manufacturing small electrical appliances. Hesse's wife, Erika, was half-Jewish, and before long Plagge was being warned by senior members of the local Nazi Party about his friendship with his employer. As an educated man with technical skills, he was expected to take part in Party activities and he volunteered to give technical lectures, but he pointedly refused to attend training courses on ideology and racial theory.

In 1936, Plagge was asked to give lectures at an educational institution set up by the Nazi Party organisation *Kraft Durch Freude* ('Strength Through Joy'). This was a body intended to provide recreational and sporting facilities for working-class Germans in an attempt to promote National Socialism and Plagge was hesitant about involvement, fearing that once again he would be expected to promote the Party's racial theories. Despite these concerns, he attempted to organise a series of talks on subjects that he regarded as entirely technical and scientific; but once more he found himself at odds with Party officials:

> My relationship with the Party broke down when speakers were sent whom I had to reject entirely due to their dogmatic ideology. There was a serious clash with the district educational leader who accused me of 'diluting ideology'. During this interview he accused me of associating almost exclusively with Jewish people and Freemasons, and with treating Jews in my laboratory. He downgraded my position [in the educational institution] and threatened to bring me before a Party court ... I accepted the consequences of this clash and from then on (1938) I not only completely withdrew from any Party activity, but also held more closely to my path of human compromise and openly condemned any inflammatory agitation.[20]

Plagge had joined the Nazi Party believing that its racial policies were little more than populist exploitation to allow it to come to power, and that it would build a strong but peaceful Germany. Any remaining allegiance to the Party disappeared when he attended an engineering conference in Stuttgart in early 1939. One of the speakers was Robert Ley, the head of the *Deutsche Arbeitsfront* ('German Labour Front' or DAF, a Nazi Party organisation intended to replace independent trade unions). Ley told the conference that within three years, the German flag would be flying over Warsaw; Plagge came away from the conference convinced that the Nazis were planning a war of conquest. With the steady increase in restrictions on Jewish and part-Jewish people in Germany, Plagge did what he could to help his friend and employer. He was designated as a senior engineer in the firm partly to avoid the danger of the firm being seized due to the ethnicity of Hesse's wife, and when Kurt and Erika Hesse had a baby boy, Plagge became the child's godfather.

When war broke out, Plagge was conscripted into the army with the rank of Hauptmann (captain). His disability from his days as a British prisoner, combined with his age, made him unsuitable for front-line service; instead, he was tasked with organising a vehicle repair workshop. This unit was first formed in Plagge's home city of Darmstadt before being sent to Poland, and from there it entered Lithuania in the wake of the Wehrmacht. Designated *Heereskraftfahrpark 562* ('Army Motor Vehicle Park 562' or *HKP 562*) it was responsible for carrying out repairs on wheeled motor vehicles that couldn't be repaired by the engineer units in the front line, and took up residence in Vilnius at the beginning of autumn in 1941. Its total strength was 13 officers, 41 NCOs and 148 lower ranks, which was clearly too small a workforce to provide vehicle repair support for all of Army Group North – once it had deployed, *HKP 562* was expected to recruit workers from the local population.

As they drove into the city, the personnel of *HKP 562* would have passed military checkpoints on the outskirts of Vilnius. The main purpose of these checkpoints was to identify and detain suspected Red Army personnel and Jews who were attempting to leave the city. In their first week of activity in the second half of July, these checkpoints had already detained 104 people, more than half of them Jews. In some respects, the persecution of Jews in Vilnius proceeded at a slower tempo, at least at first, than in Kaunas, and a ghetto wasn't established until September 1941; however, Jewish men were forcibly rounded up and dispatched as work parties prior to this date, and many were marched to Ponary where they were shot. It is estimated that prior to the creation of the ghetto, about 21,000 Jews had already been killed.

Plagge and his men found a large collection of damaged vehicles awaiting their attention and set about creating a network of workshops. Several Poles and Lithuanians were recruited, including Boleslaw Poddany, the Polish garage-owner who had been a customer of Samuel Esterowicz. During the Soviet occupation, his garage had been nationalised, but it was now back in his control and it was absorbed into Plagge's *HKP 562*. The German workshop still didn't have enough personnel to deal with its workload and Poddany made contact with Esterowicz, offering him work with the Germans as a store man. It proved to be a fortunate turn of events; Esterowicz and others who worked for the German military units received special identity cards, which provided them with a degree of protection against random arrests.

After their abortive attempt to escape from Vilnius, Mascha Rolnikaite's family – without their father, who didn't return from his attempt to secure transport out of the city – spent the rest of the summer in a state of increasing fear. Signs appeared in restaurants forbidding entry to Jews, and when Mascha and her sister attempted to go to school, a Lithuanian boy named Kaukorius tried to turn them away. Fortunately, the two girls encountered Henrikas Jonaitis, a Lithuanian teacher, who was less hostile. He escorted them home and promised to visit the family that evening. He continued to drop by from time to time, bringing small amounts of food. The family was left wondering at the kindness of this man who barely knew them.

Soon, German soldiers and police began to move through Jewish areas of Vilnius, confiscating radios, typewriters, and even bicycles. Despite Heydrich's stern orders about looting, many of the police personnel – and perhaps their Lithuanian helpers – took advantage of these raids to seize furniture and other belongings. Jews were now required to wear yellow stars on their clothing and a strict curfew was imposed upon them. In addition, they were not permitted to walk on pavements or to travel in cars or buses. Towards the end of August, Mascha was watching from the window of the family apartment:

> A group of drunken Germans were striking a young Jew. They dragged him to the town hall, made him stand with his face to the wall, and abused him. The poor man must have thought that they were going to shoot him, and trembled terribly.
>
> A crowd gathered. A red-haired German officer with bulging eyes and a crumpled hat proclaimed that the 'damned Jew' had opened fire on a German soldier in Gedimino Prospektas. Consequently, all Jews would have to pay. A soldier of the Greater German Reich was worth more than a thousand of the likes of this individual. He called for this offender to be struck down as a contribution to the destruction of the enemies of the German people.
>
> Some grinned with pleasure while others went further and openly showed their rage.[21]

The *Gebietskommissar* or head of the German civilian administration in the Vilnius municipality was Hans Christian Hingst, who had joined the Nazi Party in 1930. He had been a manager of a law firm prior to the war and was dispatched to the occupied territories to put his expertise to use in running affairs in Vilnius. His deputy, with responsibility for 'Jewish Affairs', was one of the worst figures in the bloody history of the Lithuanian Holocaust: Franz Murer.

Born in 1912 in the Austrian province of Styria, Murer spent his teenage years living away from home for much of the year. He was the seventh of eight children in a family with a modest farm, and after the collapse of the Austro-Hungarian Empire the financial situation in Austria deteriorated sharply, placing considerable pressure on the farm. Hoping that Franz, their cleverest child, would benefit from the best possible education and would thus be able to offer financial support for the rest of the family, his parents sent him to a school some distance from home. Murer thus experienced the turmoil of the 1920s without his parents and family and was exposed to radical politics at an early age; Styria had proudly maintained a status of banning Jewish settlement until the mid-19th century and the Jewish population remained very small, but nonetheless was the focus of growing anti-Semitism – many of the Jews in Styria were involved in banking and other financial affairs, and they were an easy target for a rural population that was forced to take out ever larger loans.

In 1932, Dr Josef Wurzinger, co-leader of the *Katholischen Bauernbund für Steiermark* ('Catholic Farmers' Union of Styria') wrote a letter to the Austrian government, making three demands. Two of the demands – a ban on imports of food that could be produced locally unless there were reciprocal arrangements for Austrian exports, and better policies to help those who were out of work to find employment, were unremarkable; but alongside these was a call to 'free the people from bondage to the Jews'.[22]

After leaving school, Murer, took a number of agricultural posts. He wasn't an active member of any political group, but like many Austrians he was aware of the stark differences between Germany and Austria, especially after Hitler's accession to power: the Nazis lauded the farmers of Germany as hard-working sons and daughters of the nation who established a bond between the German people and the physical land of Germany, whereas Austrian farmers faced endless financial worries. This was one of the main factors behind the widespread support within Austria for union with Germany.

Not long after the *Anschluss*, Murer applied to become a candidate at the *NS-Ordensburg Krössinsee*. This institution, near the German town of Falkenburg – now the Polish town of Złocieniec – was one of a number created by Heinrich Himmler, emulating the network of castles built by the Crusader knightly orders, but Himmler's intention was to use these 'castles' as centres where the future leadership of Germany could be trained and prepared. Murer joined a class in the institution in Pomerania in late 1938, where he and others identified as potential leaders of the Nazi Party had daily lectures and physical training for five months. Thereafter, he was assigned to the Luftwaffe as a member of an anti-aircraft regiment – in the German military, anti-aircraft units were part of the air force rather than the army. In August 1939, he was sent home before the start of the Polish campaign and was not recalled to the ranks until the following year, when he took part in the invasion of France. He left behind in Styria his new bride Elizabeth, who was expecting their first child.

Murer remained with his anti-aircraft regiment, deployed on the northern coast of France, until July 1941 when he was ordered to go to Berlin. Here, he was sent to the new headquarters of the *Ostministerium*, and thence back to the *Ordensburg* in Krössinsee. Here he joined a group entitled *Führerkorps Ost* ('Leadership Corps East') where he and others were prepared for their tasks in the east, with a clearly stated long-term aim: through a mixture of settlement by Germans and expulsion of 'unwanted elements', the region was to become part of the Greater German Reich. Removed from the ranks of the Luftwaffe, Murer – and the others in *Führerkorps Ost* – were issued with new golden-brown uniforms that distinguished them from other uniformed services. It seems that Rosenberg originally intended for all of the personnel deployed as part of the *Ostministerium* to wear uniforms of the same field grey as the army, but there happened to be a surplus supply of brown material and he was ordered to use this instead. These uniforms would eventually earn the men a derogatory nickname from the soldiers of the Wehrmacht – they were *Goldfasane* ('golden pheasants'), strutting around the rear areas and avoiding front-line duty.

Murer was then assigned to Hingst's team in Vilnius as director of the food and agriculture department and price supervision section of the local administration, but effectively functioning as Hingst's adjutant. In this role, he was responsible for many aspects of Jewish affairs, particularly the food supply for the ghetto. In later years, he would claim that his work had been entirely administrative and office-based, but the reality was that it was far wider. Almost as soon as he arrived in Vilnius, he was involved in a singular episode.

On 6 August, Murer summoned the elderly Jews who had been organised into the *Judenrat* to represent the Jewish community. He met them outside his office in a small street and subjected them to a tirade of abuse, blaming the Jews of Vilnius for the suffering of the Lithuanian people as well as being part of a larger worldwide conspiracy to subjugate the world. As recompense for these crimes, he demanded the payment of a sum of five million roubles by 9am the following day. As a gracious concession, he issued a fresh proclamation later in the day stating that jewellery and precious metals would be an acceptable alternative. Failure to make payment would result in the immediate execution of 5,000 Jews.

There was widespread consternation. With a strict curfew in force for Jews, there was little time to organise collection of this sum and there was a scramble to gather together as much money as possible, with the population of most streets and districts organising small subcommittees to oversee the process. The following morning, the *Judenrat* handed over a little less than 700,000 roubles and about a pound of gold and jewellery. Murer demanded payment in full with further threats, and the *Judenrat* decided to contact Hingst to ask for clemency. When they attended the *Giebetskommissariat* offices, they were met once more by Murer, who moderated his tone, giving the Jews permission to continue collecting money over the following days. Ultimately, Murer received nearly 1.5 million roubles, 33 pounds of gold and jewellery, and nearly 200 wristwatches. It isn't clear whether Murer and Hingst paid all or even part of it into official coffers, and it is noteworthy that no other Jewish communities in Lithuania were subjected to such demands for a single mass payment, though Jewish houses were frequently searched for valuables.

Whilst it is possible that this particular episode was entirely at the instigation of Murer, it is more likely that the recently arrived adjutant would not have initiated it on his own initiative and that the probable originator was Hingst. Given his previous irritation at looting activities in Austria and elsewhere, it is likely that Heydrich would have taken stern measures had he been aware of what was happening.

Nor were Murer and Hingst alone in taking advantage of their positions to secure personal gain. Arbitrary confiscation of money and valuables was technically not permitted, but enforcing this in a region with different agencies competing against each other was almost impossible. Lohse wrote to Obergruppenführer Hans-Adolf Prützmann, who was *Höherer SS und Polizeiführer* ('Higher SS and Police Leader', usually abbreviated to *HSSPF*) for the region known as Russia-North, reiterating the existing regulations and stating that he would personally be held responsible for the disposal of any looted goods. The letter had no discernible effect, and shortly after the *Gebietskommissar* for the town and district of Siauliai in Lithuania wrote to Lohse to complain about the activities of *Einsatzkommando 3*: 'Standartenführer Jäger sends his men through the area to confiscate Jewish property, for which I as the *Gebietskommissar* am responsible for proper registration and disposal.'[23]

This complaint relates to the activity of *Rollkommando Hamann*, whose activities are described in more detail below. In addition to killing rural communities of Jews, Hamann took advantage of the situation to gather considerable wealth. On one occasion in the town of Panevezys, his men seized a quantity of cash from local Lithuanian police officers who had in turn taken it from the Jews, and he was reported to have accumulated several chests of gold bullion and valuables during his activities in the countryside.[24] There were also complaints that Hamann threatened to execute local representatives of the *Gebietskommissar* in Raseiniai unless valuables that had been confiscated from the Jews were handed over to the SS. Nor was such behaviour limited to gold, money and jewellery. Lucian Wysocki, the SS and police leader for Lithuania, organised shipments of large quantities of confiscated furniture from Lithuania to Germany. About 2.5 million roubles that had been confiscated from Jews in Vilnius was appropriated by the SS in contravention of the rules regarding the disposal of such items. Much of this loot was handed over to higher SS authorities, but much of it vanished into the pockets of those involved.

Despite the payment of the 'ransom' demanded by Murer, random beatings and killings of Jews continued. A few days later, the 86-year-old Dr Yakow Wygodski, a highly respected member of the Jewish community and a former member of the Polish Sejm (the parliament of Poland) called on Murer and asked him to intervene to stop the attacks on Jews. Murer assaulted the man and threw him down the stairs from his office; Wygodski was then taken to Lukiškės Prison where he died shortly after.

At the end of August, Murer instigated an event that became known to the Jewish community as the 'Great Provocation'. He took two Lithuanian paramilitaries to a Jewish apartment in the Old Town. From this apartment, the two men fired at a group of German soldiers some distance away without hitting anyone and fled, returning with a group of SS personnel from *Einsatzkommando 9* who had been waiting for them. Two Jewish men who lived in the building were seized, accused of carrying out the shooting, and beaten and shot to death on the spot. A day later, a proclamation signed by Hingst appeared on placards around Vilnius:

> Yesterday afternoon, German soldiers in the city of Vilnius were ambushed and shots were fired.
>
> Two of the cowardly bandits were captured. They were Jews.
>
> The perpetrators have forfeited their lives. They were shot immediately.
>
> To prevent such hostile acts, the severest countermeasures have already been taken. Responsibility rests with all of the Jews.
>
> With immediate effect, all Jews of either sex are forbidden to leave their residence between 1500 and 1000. Only Jews and

> Jewesses who have been expressly ordered to carry out work are exempted.
>
> These orders are issued for the safety of the population and to safeguard their lives. It is the duty of every decent citizen to cooperate so that peace and order can prevail.[25]

Throughout the following night, German troops – from *Einsatzkommando 9* and *Orpo* battalions – and Lithuanian paramilitaries swept through the Jewish quarter of the Old Town, driving out the Jewish population as a prelude to establishing a ghetto. It was an unusually hot day for September, and the Jews of Vilnius were driven remorselessly through the streets by Lithuanian police, as one Jew later described:

> We dragged along, a group of Jews with parcels. The street was full of Jews ... People walked along harnessed to bundles they dragged after them on the road. People fell, packages broke open. Before me a woman was bowed under a bundle from which rice trickled endlessly like a necklace on to the roadway. I walked laden down, angry. The Lithuanians egged us on, not allowing us to pause.[26]

As the number of Jews being driven to the ghetto exceeded the ability of the Lithuanian and German personnel manning the gates to process them all, many were herded into Lukiškės Prison while others were marched to Ponary. Groups of Jews were taken at regular intervals from the prison to Ponary, where they were executed; in a report written shortly after, Jäger listed these deaths as amounting to 864 men, 2,019 women and 817 children.[27]

Herman Kruk was a Polish Jew, born in Płock in 1897. He was not a particularly observant Jew, but he detested the widespread persecution of Jews in the dying Russian Empire and then in Poland. After working as a photographer, he helped develop a substantial Jewish library in Warsaw and fled to Vilnius when the Germans invaded Poland. Here, he worked in the Jewish library and managed to secure a visa to emigrate to the United States; as his wife was still trying to obtain a visa, he postponed his departure until it was too late, and he later turned down an offer from the Soviet Union to travel to the west on condition that he acted as a spy. He kept a diary of his experiences and observations, and on 4 September he described the first clear news that reached the Jews about what was happening in Ponary; six Jews had survived the killings and had managed to return to Vilnius. The first was a young girl called Yudis Trojak, who told Kruk how she and most of her family – one brother had fled with the Red Army and her father was working in a peat camp outside the city – were rounded up by Lithuanian paramilitaries and taken to Lukiškės Prison:

> On Tuesday morning [3 September] they led us all out into the jail yard, and all were sure that we would be released. But an order came to leave all our belongings and get into the waiting trucks. Travelling in the covered trucks, a woman saw that we were riding through a forest. Later we heard shooting. A wailing arose. We didn't understand what was happening with the men because they were led away on foot.
>
> When we got out of the trucks, we were taken to a forest, among sand hills, and there we waited …
>
> Not until 5 in the afternoon did they take ten of us. From there we walked about five minutes. They blindfolded us and stood us in front of a pit … I adjusted the cloth so I could see … There in the pit lay a lot of dead bodies, whole mountains of them.[28]

When the paramilitaries opened fire, Yudis was hit but not killed and fell into the pit. Together with a few other wounded women she managed to crawl from the pit that evening. They reached an isolated Lithuanian house where they were sheltered for the night; the following day, the Lithuanian woman who lived in the house managed to bring them to Vilnius. A similar story was told by a girl named Pesye Schloss who was shot in the arm by a bullet that passed through her mother before hitting her. Not long after, she managed to extricate herself from her dead mother's embrace and was also able to return to the city with a group of others who had survived. Kruk was utterly horrified by what he heard from the girls:

> I don't know if I will ever live to see these lines, but if anyone anywhere comes upon them, I want him to know that this is my last wish: let the words someday reach the living world and let people know about it from eyewitness accounts …
>
> The hand trembles, the ink is bloody. Is it possible that all those taken out of here have been murdered, shot in Ponary?[29]

Many Jews simply refused to believe these stories. It seemed inconceivable that such massacres were taking place. Instead, they clung to their hope that there were other work camps, and most of their missing friends and relatives had been taken there. Jakob Gens, a Jewish man who had served in the Lithuanian Army before the war, was to become a leading figure in the Vilnius ghetto. He was married to a Catholic Lithuanian and was director of the Jewish Hospital in Vilnius before the creation of the ghetto. His daughter Ada, who was 17 at the time, later described the part played by her father in the events when the wounded reached the hospital: 'When they came into the hospital, my father took them to a separate area and started to question them. They were all bleeding, so he sent his personnel with hot water to wash the blood from the sidewalks so that if the Germans [came] there wouldn't be a trail ... My father isolated these people in a separate part of the hospital because he was afraid of a general panic.'[30]

Those waiting in Lukiškės Prison were systematically searched for valuables. After a few days, the SS personnel in the prison demanded that any Jews with professional or other qualifications should come forward. They – and their immediate families – were issued with special passes, as were others whose names were already on lists of skilled workers. These Jews were driven into the area of the Old Town that had been cleared and was now designated as the ghetto, while the rest were marched to Ponary. As was the case in Kaunas, the ghetto consisted of a larger main ghetto and a small ghetto that neighboured it. The large ghetto became home to about 29,000 people; the smaller ghetto accommodated a further 9,600.

During their move to the ghetto, Mascha Rolnikaite and the rest of her family became separated. Mascha was forced into the larger ghetto where she was unable to find the rest of her family. Believing that they had been sent to the small ghetto, she begged the Lithuanians guarding the gate to let her pass; one of them struck her, but the other turned out to be Kaukorius, the Lithuanian boy who had refused to permit her to return to her school, and he now allowed her to leave the large ghetto, taking her at gunpoint to the small ghetto. To her despair, she was unable to find her family there either. The following day, under heavy guard, she and a group of other Jews were permitted to march to the large ghetto, where she was reunited with her mother and siblings.[31]

The Esterowicz family also moved into the ghetto, as Perela later recalled:

> Since we were one of the early arrivals in the ghetto, we and the Zlatin family were able to occupy a room on the second floor ... Standing in the street, Father finally spotted Grandmother, Aunt Anya and her daughter Shela and Aunt Emma with her daughter Eva and son-in-law Lolek. They all squeezed into our room with their packs ... The number of people who lived in our modest-sized, narrow, elongated room of about 6 feet by 24 feet grew to 26 by evening.[32]

Elsewhere in Lithuania, Jäger's men were beginning the task of eliminating the Jewish non-urban population, in keeping with Lohse's instructions. Compared to other regions of Europe, Lithuania's economy was comparatively rural, with Vilnius and Kaunas as the only major cities. In order to deal with the Jewish population elsewhere in the countryside, Stahlecker, Jäger and Hamann held discussions before they entered Lithuania. Hamann was to establish a mobile killing unit designated *Rollkommando Hamann*, which was tasked with carrying out a series of massacres around rural Lithuania. In a report at the end of 1941 Jäger described its functioning in detail. The language of his report is chilling:

> The conduct of such actions is primarily a question of organisation. The decision systematically to render each area free of Jews requires thorough preparation of every individual *Aktion* and knowledge of the prevailing circumstances in each area concerned. The Jews had to be gathered at one or more locations. Depending on the number, a place for the required graves had to be located and dug. The approach road from the assembly area to the grave should be 4-5km. The Jews were transported to the execution site in groups of 500, separated by at least 2km. This arbitrary example shows the difficulties and nerve-wracking work involved:
>
> In Rokiškis, 3,202 people had to be transported 4.5km before they could be liquidated. In order to carry out this work within 24 hours, 60 of the 80 available Lithuanian partisans had to be assigned to transportation and barriers. The remainder, who were constantly replaced, carried out the work together with my men. Trucks were only rarely available for transportation. Attempts to escape, which occurred from time to time, were exclusively prevented by my men at risk to their lives. Thus, for example, three men of the *Rollkommando* shot down 38 Jews and Communist officials on a forested road, without anyone escaping. The journey to and from individual actions was 160-200km. Only by careful use of time was it possible to conduct up to five actions per week whilst at the same time continuing the work that accrued in Kaunas, thus ensuring that there was no holdup in service operations.[33]

Information from witnesses and other sources helps to give a more complete picture of the killings at Rokiškis, and the manner in which *Rollkommando Hamann* operated. The town lies 98 miles (158km) to the northeast of Kaunas, and on 15 August 1941, Jäger's headquarters in Kaunas informed the Lithuanian police in Rokiškis that an operation against the local Jewish population was imminent. The Jews of Rokiškis numbered about 3,500, which at the time constituted nearly half of the population. The warning order advised the local police that only volunteers who wished to take part in the operation would be required and that the rest of the police could take on guard duties. Immediately, the local police – largely made up of men who had surfaced as nationalist partisans as the Red Army withdrew – rounded up about 500 Jews and took them to nearby woodland. The victims were ordered to undress in groups of between 30 and 40 and were ordered into a pit that had been dug. They were then gunned down. The following day, the killings continued at a higher tempo. Throughout the days of the shootings, large quantities of vodka were available for the men carrying out the killings, and there were reports that many of them were completely intoxicated by sunset.[34]

Preparation of the pits that were to receive the corpses of the Jews was carried out usually by non-Jewish labour; whilst it would have been possible to use Jewish work parties, it seems that Hamann and others decided that the allocation of Jewish workers to such labour gangs might alert the local Jewish community to what was about to happen. In many cases, existing excavations were used, such as anti-tank barriers dug by the Red Army, old quarries, or natural land features. On other occasions, digging was carried out by Red Army prisoners of war, and on a few occasions by Lithuanian labourers.

When they were marched to the execution sites, the Jews were forced to hand over their valuables, usually to German personnel. Any attempt to retain items such as wedding rings resulted in violence or death. The victims were then required to strip and place their clothes, shoes etc. in separate piles. On some occasions, individual Jewish women were raped by Lithuanian or German guards, sometimes in full view of the rest of the Jews, before being executed. The guards forced the Jews into the pits where they were made to lie or kneel, packed tightly together, often on top of those who had already been executed. The killing was carried out by men standing at the edges of the pits, armed usually with rifles and only rarely with automatic weapons. On only a few occasions was any concerted attempt made to ensure that all of the Jews had been killed by the volley of shots; sometimes, a German would climb into the pit and finish off any wounded Jews with a single pistol shot, but on many occasions the next group of Jews would find themselves forced to kneel on bodies that were still groaning or crying out. The pits were then covered over with lime and earth, usually by the same prisoners of war who had dug them.

The relationship between Hamann and Jäger was as complex and confusing as so many other parts of Nazi organisation. Although Hamann was Jäger's subordinate within *Einsatzkommando 3*, he seems to have behaved as if he was directly under Stahlecker's command. Much of the confusion lies in the sources of information regarding the structure and organisation of the *Einsatzgruppen*; in many cases, including the precise command and control arrangements for *Rollkommando Hamann*, information has come from the post-war court testimony of men who were involved in SS operations against the Jews, and who may have wished to persuade the authorities that they personally were not involved in these command structures. In many cases, SS officers who were anxious during the war to claim that killings were carried out under their orders and command were just as anxious to claim quite the opposite once the war was over.

In most cases, *Rollkommando Hamann* made little attempt to spare Jews capable of work. When the unit went to Siauliai on 10 September, Hans Gewecke, the local *Gebietskommissar* protested that many of the Jews were needed for essential work; Hamann replied that his orders were to liquidate all of the Jews regardless of economic considerations. Gewecke took his protests directly to Lohse, who then applied pressure on Jäger to restrain Hamann's activities.[35]

In early October, *Rollkommando Hamann* was disbanded. The Jewish population of the rural areas of Lithuania had been almost completely exterminated. Hamann returned to Berlin, proud to have played his part in ridding the German people of their greatest foes – it is estimated that his *Rollkommando* killed about 60,000 Jews, and he personally claimed that the number was as high as 77,000.[36]

At a time when most of the slaughter of Jews in the Baltic States was directed either at the intelligentsia or those considered unfit for work, Hamann was by contrast driven by a desire to eliminate all Jews, regardless of gender or age. He was accompanied on his journey to Berlin by Grauer and Kortkampf, who were also no longer required in Lithuania. All three were sent to a training establishment to teach future SS officers, but Hamann soon moved on to other duties. The role of teacher didn't appeal to him and he was assigned to an operation codenamed *Zeppelin*; this attempted to create units from Russian émigrés and deserters, and also from volunteers from the hundreds of thousands of Red Army prisoners of war – many of these volunteers were motivated by a desperate desire to escape the appalling conditions in the prison camps rather than any ideological issues. These units were then to be parachuted behind enemy lines to carry out similar activities to those being performed by pro-Soviet partisans behind German lines.

Hamann was sent to organise units that would be deployed by Army Group North, and his training regime was harsh. Men who failed to reach the required standard were either executed or dispatched to concentration camps. The efficacy of the *Zeppelin* units was almost zero. Most either deserted back to the Soviet side or ran away to join anti-German partisans even before they were deployed.

Jäger's personal involvement in the killings in Kaunas and elsewhere is difficult to determine. In his orders to his subordinate commanders, he stressed the need for officers to lead by example and the manner in which he led *Einsatzkommando 3* demonstrates his drive and determination to make up for any perceived disadvantage that his age might have given him, but there are few confirmed witness statements that show him present when mass killings were taking place. He has been tentatively identified in a photograph showing a Jew being executed by a shot to the back of the head at Ponary, but this identification has been disputed.[37] Nonetheless, it is likely that he was present on some occasions – he was certainly identified as being in the Kaunas ghetto during one of the 'actions' – and given his style of command and leadership, it is also likely that he personally participated in the killings. The scale of the operation was so great, and the number of SS personnel was so limited – *Rollkommando Hamann*, for example, had between eight and ten German troops, including Hamann himself – that there was no room for any inefficiency, and one of the verbal orders that was passed down by Heydrich was that all personnel of the *Einsatzgruppen* – including their officers – were to be involved personally with at least one killing.

Whilst Hamann and his small team faced organisational challenges in their operations, the killings in Kaunas and Vilnius were far easier to organise and sustain. After *Einsatzkommando 9* moved out of Vilnius and the city came under Jäger's control, he dispatched Peter Eisenbarth and Erich Wolff to oversee operations. Both had the rank of Obersturmführer; Eisenbarth had been recruited from the ranks of the Gestapo, while Wolff had previously served in the SD. They were fresh out of SS leadership training in Berlin and like so many of their peers, they were anxious to impress their superiors and undertook their duties with energy and efficiency. They had under their command Oberscharführer Horst Schweinberger, who had played a role in Murer's staging of the attack on German soldiers that was used as a pretext for the creation of the Vilnius ghetto.

The conduct of the Jews being taken to the execution grounds was generally passive. One of the Jews in the Vilnius ghetto later wrote: 'The people went to the slaughter in despair, utterly listless, like a herd of sheep. Nobody made even the slightest protest, and right to the last minute they all clung to the false hope that they would somehow remain alive, that a miracle would happen and they would be spared from death.'[38]

Not all the Jews went to their deaths so meekly. Near the end of August, *Rollkommando Hamann* went to the town of Kėdainiai, a little to the north of Kaunas. They killed 2,076 Jews, including 767 women and 599 children; one Jewish man grabbed two of the Lithuanian paramilitaries and dragged them into the pit where the executions were taking place and succeeded in strangling one of them before he was shot.[39] In October, one of Jäger's regular reports mentioned an event that took place in the small town of Žagarė in northern Lithuania:

> On 2 October, 50 Jews escaped from the ghetto there. The large manhunt that was promptly organised resulted in many being caught and shot. During the planned execution of all the Jews of Žagarė, the Jews attacked the guards and personnel of the *Einsatzkommando* security police on a prearranged signal during their transportation. Some of the Jews, who had not been searched thoroughly enough by the Lithuanian guards, had knives and pistols and leaped on the guards with shouts of 'Long live Stalin!' and 'Down with Hitler!' and wounded seven of them. After 150 Jews were shot on the spot, the transport of the remaining Jews to the execution site proceeded smoothly.[40]

By the end of the day, the Jewish community of Žagarė had been completely eliminated. A total of 2,236 people – 633 men, 1,107 women, and 496 children were shot. The figures that Jäger sent to Stahlecker show that the initial wave of killings in late June and the first half of July involved mainly Jewish men, as anyone thought capable of organising resistance was eliminated; thereafter, the numbers of women and children increased significantly. There was another reason why men were targeted in the first killings. Some of the junior officers in the *Einsatzgruppen* had expressed concerns about exposing their younger personnel, particularly those with families, to the slaughter of Jewish women and children. By focusing on male Jews in the first wave of killings, it was possible to harden attitudes before moving onto more widespread extermination.

Jäger's reports, meticulously listing the numbers and categories of those killed – Jewish men, women and children, suspected Communists, the mentally or physically infirm, Roma, and other undesirable groups – were then compiled with other reports and passed on to Heydrich, who wrote regular reports for circulation in the higher ranks of the

Nazi leadership. Within an often chaotic system whose members were expected to compete for Hitler's approval and to show their dedication to the cause, Heydrich and Himmler had quickly realised that by encouraging their men to slaughter the Jews of the Soviet Union before the war was actually over, they could demonstrate beyond question their primacy through their determination and efficiency, and therefore needed to ensure that the rest of the hierarchy was aware of their achievements.

The elimination of Jews outside the big cities was sometimes carried out by units other than *Rollkommando Hamann*. Vova Gdud, who had returned to Vilnius from Ponary after his lucky escape from death, was living in the town of Niemenczyn (now known as Nemenčinė), where his father owned a turpentine factory. In order to avoid the attention of the Germans, Gdud's father appointed a young Lithuanian, Stepanas Nera, as director, and Nera and Gdud became good friends. In late September a Polish woman warned the Gduds that graves were being dug nearby in preparation for mass executions and the four members of the Gdud family immediately hid in a large pile of timber near the turpentine factory, where they had already prepared a shelter. Leaving Vova Gdud's mother and brother in the hiding place, he and his father slept in the forest, and the following day he set off to seek out a man named Gasperowicz, a Polish friend who had offered help in the past:

> I walked out of the huge forest, came to a field, and here from the other end of the field walked out Stepanas with a rifle on his shoulder – I saw him and instinctively ran back into the forest, but he had seen me too and I felt embarrassed to run away from him ... if I went back to the forest now, and I could as he was still quite distant, that would mean that I didn't trust him. But we were friends, I couldn't do that! So I marched right out and said, 'Stepanas, where are you going so early in the morning with a rifle?'
>
> He answered, 'Just hunting.' I saw that he had a handgun sticking out and didn't quite know what to think. He acted very normal and asked me, 'Where are you going?' I said that my father had sent me to Gasperowicz to hire him to transport some turpentine to the city. 'Well,' he said, 'let's go together.' So we went on with some small talk and came to Gasperowicz. He [Stepanas Nera] said, 'Why don't you wait here a minute and I'll go in and talk to him.' I waited, wondering why he was going to talk to him, After two minutes he came out with his rifle pointed at me and said, 'Get in!'[41]

Inside the house, Nera told Wincent, the son of the Gasperowicz family, that he was to ensure that Vova Gdud remained inside and disappeared. Nera returned a few minutes later and when he opened the door, Gdud made a dash for freedom. Nera fired at him several times but missed and Gdud was able to escape. His father was rounded up with about 700 other local Jews but managed to flee when their Lithuanian captors lined them up and opened fire on them. His mother and brother were arrested by Lithuanian police and executed.

The Jews who were now confined to ghettos were available to the different occupation agencies as labour; in return, each agency paid the SS a small fee per prisoner. A very small fraction of that payment was passed to the Jews, whose daily rations were far below the minimum that Lohse had described in his orders. Ration cards were issued to the residents of the Vilnius ghetto, as Mascha Rolnikaite described. The rations

> … were completely inadequate, very much in line with the motto: too little for life, too much for death. Bread – 135g per day; the other rations were calculated per week: 80g pearl barley, 50g sugar, 50g oil and 30g salt. That's what it said on the cards. But we never saw any oil or sugar. And instead of pearl barley they gave us bread and black peas.[42]

Many of the families in the ghettos had succeeded in bringing small amounts of cash or valuables with them and tried to trade with the local population for food whenever an opportunity arose, but work parties that returned to the ghetto were searched and anyone found carrying concealed food was severely punished. Leon Schmigel, who had fled from Warsaw with his son Abraham, worked at the airfield on the edge of Vilnius and on one occasion they succeeded in trading some bed-linen for food. They divided this between them and attempted to smuggle it back into the ghetto. Schmigel later described what happened:

> My son and I were in a column, my son four places in front of me. When we reached the gate … the Lithuanians found my son had meat and butter. Murer had arrived at the gate. The Lithuanians led my son to Murer and also gave him the meat. Murer said to my son that he should kneel down and put his hands up. My son did this. Murer took out his pistol and aimed at his neck. He then fired, and my son was dead …
>
> After my son there was a man, a woman and then another man. They were allowed through. The woman had some potatoes and

> firewood, which she had to give to the Lithuanians. They found some firewood and potatoes on me too, and I was also led away by the Lithuanians. The woman was given ten lashes and I received 25.
>
> Then Murer arrived and had me lower my trousers, raised his stick and gave me first ten, then 15 lashes.[43]

The multiple German organisations in Vilnius often clashed, sometimes unintentionally. In September, Hingst and Murer ordered all Jewish workers to register in a Labour Office, from which they regulated the use of Jewish labour and the wages that were to be paid to Jews – 20 pfennigs per hour to men, 15 pfennigs per hour to women, and 10 pfennigs per hour to those aged under 16. Shortly after, Schweinberger demanded that the *Judenrat* give him 1,500 people for work at an unspecified location, almost certainly a pretext to take away another group of Jews for execution. The *Judenrat* responded by obtaining a letter from Hingst stating that Jewish workers could only be assigned by the new office that had been set up. Schweinberger lost his temper: 'What is this? You shit Jews want to tell me what I can do? The Labour Office is shit! And the *Gebietskommissar*, all of it's shit! The Gestapo and I give the orders here!'[44]

On this occasion, Schweinberger had no choice but to back down. The ghetto was under the control of Hingst's civil administration, and he had to resort to other means of securing victims. In the Vilnius ghetto, those capable of skilled work were ordered to live in the large ghetto while the remainder of the population was moved to the small ghetto. Groups of those in the small ghetto were then taken to Ponary every day for execution. The detailed management of each ghetto was in the hands of the *Judenrat*, who in practical terms did little more than pass on the instructions they received from the SS.

In September, Jacob Gens, the superintendent of the Jewish Hospital in Vilnius, was nominated as chief of the Jewish ghetto police, the main instrument through which the SS controlled the ghetto. The head of the ghetto *Judenrat*, Anatol Fried, was relatively unknown in the Jewish community, but he was one of the few survivors of the *Judenrat* that had first been created after the Germans arrived in Vilnius; aware that the rest had been killed on Murer's orders, Fried was not a man who was likely to cause difficulties for the Germans.

The head of the *Judenrat* in Kaunas was Elkhanan Elkes, who had been a physician before the war. He had good contacts within the diplomatic community and had played a major part in negotiating the departure of Jews who had 'Curaçao visas' with the Soviet authorities. He was extremely reluctant to take up the post and only did so after several other people had refused and Rabbi Yakov Shmukler personally beseeched him to accept the role.[45] The head of the ghetto police was Moisei Koppelman, who had been the Lithuanian representative of the London-based Lloyd's insurance group.

At the beginning of September, Feldwebel Anton Schmid arrived in Vilnius. His battalion commander was now the local commandant, and he assigned Schmid a new role. An office had been established in the railway station in the city – the *Versprengten-Sammelstelle* ('Stragglers Collection Point'). Soldiers who had become separated from their units were directed there, and it was Schmid's task to find them transport to the railhead nearest to their units. When he arrived at his new place of work, where he would also have his accommodation, he found that the office employed several Jewish clerks.

From the moment that he arrived in Vilnius, Schmid would have been aware of the persecution and killing of the Jewish population. He later wrote to his wife that Jewish children being taken to Ponary were sometimes beaten to death, often by having their heads swung against tree-trunks. Regardless of the instructions issued to the SS and *Orpo* battalions about killing their victims out of sight, the killings were clearly common knowledge amongst the numerous military units in Vilnius; in any case, many of the victims were taken to Ponary from Vilnius by train, and Schmid could watch them being loaded into cattle trucks from his office.

It isn't clear at what point Schmid realised three important facts. Firstly, the Jews working for him had the special Wehrmacht-accredited identity cards, which gave them some protection from arrest. Secondly, as they were classed as working for the military, they received additional rations. For many families in the ghetto, this made the difference between slow starvation and survival. And thirdly, Schmid discovered that he was largely left to his own devices and could function without close supervision. In particular, he could issue further work permits and identity cards to Jewish workers as he saw fit. Slowly, he began to increase the number of people working for the *Versprengten-Sammelstelle*.

Not long after he arrived in Vilnius, Schmid encountered a Jew in the street. The man was Max Salinger, who came from the city of Bielsko-Biala in southwest Poland and was fluent in Polish and German. He fled Poland to escape the German invasion before being trapped in Lithuania after the onset of *Barbarossa*; he avoided being rounded up and sent to the ghetto, but if he were to be discovered, he faced certain death. Why he chose to approach the stocky moustached Schmid in his Wehrmacht uniform is unknown. Perhaps he saw Schmid looking on with horror as a work-party of Jews was led past, on its way to or from the ghetto, or possibly he had heard from other Jews that Schmid had taken on additional workers in his office without any clear need for more staff. In any event, Schmid agreed to help him and the two men returned to the office near the railway station.

In addition to helping stragglers back to their units, the office was also meant to notify units if men in hospital succumbed to their wounds or to illness, and one such individual was a Gefreiter (corporal) by the name of Max Huppert. Perhaps inspired by the fact that this dead soldier had the same first name as Salinger, Schmid arranged for Salinger to adopt the identity of Max Huppert; he gave him a Wehrmacht uniform and a full set of documents, and then notified Huppert's unit that the soldier was being retained in Vilnius to help run the *Versprengten-Sammelstelle*.

A few days later, Schmid was returning to his accommodation in the rooms adjacent to his office from the nearby *Soldatenheim*, one of many such 'soldiers' clubs' that were set up by the Wehrmacht to provide dining and recreation facilities for soldiers. It was dark and past curfew, and he must have been startled when a young woman stepped out of the shadow of a doorway and asked him for help. Her name was Luisa Emaitisaite; she was a 23-year-old Jew who had evaded one of the random raids by Lithuanian police when she was out of the ghetto with a work party but had then missed the deadline for returning to the ghetto before the gates were closed. Cautiously, she asked the uniformed soldier in front of her if he knew of a cheap hotel where she could stay the night.

Schmid replied that such a plan was risky, as she would have to show identity documents at the hotel; he had clearly realised that she was Jewish. Instead, he suggested that she return with him to his accommodation where she could shelter for the night. It was a remarkable turn of events – that the young woman should speak to a soldier in the uniform of her persecutors, that that this soldier should offer help. Even more remarkably, she agreed to accompany him. She told her rescuer that her family had been taken to Ponary, and she had heard no more. Aware of the stories brought back to Vilnius by the small number of survivors, she had to assume that her family were all dead.

Schmid allowed Emaitisaite to stay in a spare room in his accommodation, and a few days later suggested to her that like Max Salinger, she should work for his office, as she was fluent in German, Polish and Lithuanian and was a skilled typist. In order for her to do so, Schmid would have to help her obtain a new non-Jewish identity, and to secure this he turned to a Catholic priest. As a devout Catholic, Schmid had taken to attending a nearby church every Sunday, the Church of St Teresa of Avila. The priest in the church was Andrzej Gdowski, who had lived in Austria for many years before the war and instantly recognised Schmid as having a pronounced Viennese accent. Schmid took Emaitisaite to the chapel and explained to the priest that she was a Jew, and that in order to obtain documentation for her, he needed a letter from the priest stating that she was a Catholic who attended the chapel. Schmid had clearly thought the entire business through and added that the letter from the priest should explain that her parents had been deported by the Soviet authorities, and all of her documents had gone with them. After a moment's thought, Father Gdowski agreed to help. To the amazement of Emaitisaite, he told his visitors: 'An old man like me can no longer be fearful of men, and I can answer to God for such a deception.'[46]

This was only the first hurdle. Armed with the letter confirming Emaitisaite's new identity, Schmid and Emaitisaite still had to negotiate their way through five different offices of the city administration. The agency that proved least cooperative was the Lithuanian official who issued work permits; without directly threatening the man, Schmid made a fuss about removing his pistol from its holster and placing it ominously on the desk while he searched for one of the forms that another office had already issued, and the official conceded the point. Schmid was even able to secure accommodation for Emaitisaite with a female paediatrician. Three hours after they had left the office by the railway station, the process was complete.

The manner in which Salinger and Emaitisaite were saved from probable death is remarkable. Both took an extraordinary risk in approaching a uniformed Wehrmacht soldier whom they almost certainly didn't know. In addition, Emaitisaite chose to accompany him back to his accommodation, placing herself entirely at his mercy. There must have been something about Schmid that attracted such faith and confidence. His conduct is also remarkable. At a time when the Jews were regarded by the German authorities as almost indistinguishable from Communists, and the two groups were collectively seen as the mortal enemies of the German people, Schmid was giving aid and succour to the enemy in a time of war; regardless of the other rules he broke in disguising Salinger as a German soldier and in obtaining false documentation for Emaitisaite, he faced execution if he was caught, and he must have been aware of this. Yet on both occasions, he showed no hesitancy in risking his life to save these two strangers he encountered on the streets of Vilnius. It was one thing to help Jews in Austria during the months and years before the war, but quite another to do so in an occupied country in wartime. But for a man who had shown such kindness towards the Jews of Vienna, the events he either experienced personally or heard about while his battalion was in Białystok seem to have hardened his opinions and brought him to the point where he was prepared to take great risks.

Whilst many in the Catholic Church throughout Europe showed hostility towards the Jews, Father Gdowski and many others put aside historical distrust and enmity in the name of humanity. Even in Poland, where anti-Semitism was rife in almost all parts of Polish society, several priests called on their parishioners to bury their prejudices and to offer aid to the Jews who were being persecuted so cruelly by the Germans. When some clergy moved beyond such exhortation and offered material aid, they faced severe punishment at the hands of the Germans, and several were imprisoned and executed.

Father Gdowski helped several other Jews who were attempting to escape, sometimes in collaboration with Schmid and on other occasions independently. He sheltered small groups of Jews within the cloisters of the Carmelite monastery of which he was the superior and put aside a room in his church for them to use as a synagogue. The Carmelite monks ran a small boarding school in Vilnius and Michael Stołowicki, a Jewish boy from Warsaw, arrived in Vilnius in late 1939 with his mother and Catholic nanny. His mother died shortly after their arrival and his nanny told everyone that Michael was her child. When the Germans occupied the city, she feared that her subterfuge would be discovered, and she took Michael to Father Gdowski's church. She explained to the priest that Michael wasn't her child and that he was a Jew; Father Gdowski sprinkled a few drops of holy water on Michael, declared him a Catholic, and enrolled him into the school. He survived the war, and he and his nanny – who had promised his mother that she would care for Michael – then travelled to Palestine.

Father Gdowski was not the only member of the Catholic clergy who helped Jews in the Vilnius region. Just to the east of Vilnius there was a Dominican convent in Pavilnys, where Sister Anna Borkowska was the Mother Superior to nine other nuns. Shortly after the German occupation began, she offered shelter to a group of 17 young adult Jews who had fled from the city. Within the walls of the convent, the group became the centre of a resistance cell that planned – unsuccessfully – for the residents of the Vilnius ghetto to rise up against the Germans. It would have been almost impossible to keep such a large group completely hidden, so Sister Borkowska provided them with nuns' habits and they took turns to work in the convent gardens and fields. Sister Maria Mikulska of the Benedictine convent in Vilnius, with the approval of Archbishop Romuald Jałbrzykowski, sheltered several Jews from the Germans; such activities took place at numerous locations across the city, and were fairly straightforward to organise in 1941 as the Germans and their Lithuanian helpers were too busy dealing with the substantial Jewish population at their mercy in the ghetto to search too closely for hidden Jews.

Another catholic priest who gave aid to the Jews was Father Bronius Paukštys, who was rector of the Church of St Michael the Archangel in Kaunas. He deplored the unwillingness of other members of the clergy to take a stand – for example, Archbishop Vincentas Brizgyz, the head of the Catholic Church in Lithuania, refused to intervene on behalf of Jews out of fear that the Germans might respond by widespread suppression of the church. Father Paukštys forged birth certificates and baptismal records, mainly for children, and hid many Jews in his church, providing aid for those who attempted to flee from the ghetto. His activities drew the attention of his church superiors who reprimanded him and ordered him to desist. He ignored such threats and continued to do what he could, helped by his brother Juozas, who was a professor of agriculture in Kaunas.

Major Plagge's workshops continued to recruit more Jews into their staff. It seems that Plagge deliberately stretched the terms of who he could employ as much as possible, as Alfred Stumpff, who served in *HKP 562* with the rank of Oberleutnant, recalled:

> Plagge employed Jewish workers in large numbers in his workshop … This included a large number of Jews who were neither usable by nor necessary for the actual work of the *HKP*. For example, Jews were employed as barbers, cobblers, tailors and cooks and even cleaners, Jewish women and girls worked as gardeners and there was even a Jewish doctor who took care of the health of the civilian workers. To outsiders, these people were classified as skilled workers for vehicle repairs. From personal discussions with Plagge, I knew that he deliberately hired or retained a large number of these Jews only in order to keep them away from the extermination activities of the SD and Party officers.
>
> Plagge himself treated the Jews in the most decent manner and ensured that this was also done by his subordinates.[47]

Although Plagge was consistently careful to adopt an aloof attitude towards the Jews and not to discuss his views about the Jews and German occupation policy with his men, they had little doubt about his views. Friedrich Asmus was an officer in *HKP 562*, effectively acting as Plagge's deputy:

> He never revealed his political views or made any politically provocative statements [but] it was known in our unit that those

> comrades amongst us who were opponents of National Socialism found a ready ear with Plagge and suffered no disadvantages. Big Nazis, 'Jew-eaters' and bullies were swiftly sidelined, transferred, or removed from the unit under some pretext. I remember people, including those of senior rank, who displayed excessive National Socialist behaviour and who then left the unit. Harsh methods were not tolerated ... Plagge worked tirelessly against the growing poverty of the Polish civilians, a considerable number of whom, apart from our soldiers, worked in the repair workshops. He provided clothing, firewood, additional food, and tobacco. I had the impression that Plagge was constantly thinking about how he could counteract the growing plight of the population. Characteristic of this attitude on Plagge's part is something that a Polish master craftsman said to me when we left: 'As long as you were here, every day was a Sunday for us.'[48]

One of the men in Plagge's *HKP 562* who was remembered by many of the Jews for his kindness was a Feldwebel (sergeant) from the city of Chemnitz in Saxony, named Berger – unfortunately, his first name is not known and it has proved impossible to discover his fate. He was standing with a group of Plagge's Jewish workers when another group of Jews was marched past, on their way to Ponary. Berger exclaimed while watching the Jews being driven to their deaths: 'What these scum perpetrate here in the name of the German people – centuries will not suffice for us to cleanse ourselves!'[49]

Despite the small increase in rations for Jews who worked for the Wehrmacht, starvation was never far away, not least because many of Plagge's workers felt obliged to share their food with less fortunate occupants of the ghetto. Hans Zeuner, the quartermaster of *HKP 562*, was ordered to obtain sufficient vegetables to provide all the workers with a daily meal while they were in their workplace. Some of the Polish workers had family contacts who could obtain additional food from local farms, and Plagge permitted a market in the workshop where the Jews could exchange some of their dwindling stocks of money and valuables for food; in addition, he organised a small fund that was administered to those in particular need. The overall food supply of the workforce was hardly generous, but it was sufficient to keep the workers and their families reasonably healthy. But the workers had to show great care when returning to the ghetto at the end of the working day. With a determination that bordered on obsession, Murer had instigated regular searches and anyone caught bringing food into the ghetto was punished severely. The German plan for the Jews was to use them as forced labour, but to work them to exhaustion and death, or kill them by other means; consequently, men like Murer regarded it as a waste of resources to give them more than the most minimum food, even if the consequence was that they grew steadily weaker.

Those who were caught smuggling food were badly beaten, and several were killed on the spot, but food continued to enter the ghetto by a variety of routes, not just by individuals smuggling in small quantities. From time to time, wagons delivered firewood, and the Jewish labourers assigned to this task tried to obtain sacks of potatoes and other food that could be hidden in the wagons.

Although the Wehrmacht work permits were largely respected by Security Police and SD patrols, the Lithuanian police in Vilnius often ignored them and continued to round up Jews at regular intervals. On occasion, some of Plagge's workers were caught and taken to Lukiškės Prison. As soon as he became aware of any arrests, Plagge intervened immediately. On other occasions, he even stepped in when he became aware of prisoners who weren't actually workers at *HKP 562*. Georg Raab, who had the rank of Oberfeldwebel (staff sergeant), later recalled several such occasions. A Polish engineer who had been a teacher at the technical college in Vilnius was arrested and spent several weeks in Lukiškės Prison; one of his friends contacted Plagge, who immediately drove to the SD headquarters and requested the files relating to the man. He then negotiated his release on the grounds that he had skills that were useful to *HKP 562*. A Jewish doctor was one of several Jews arrested as a reprisal for shots being fired at a Lithuanian policeman, and he and a Polish accountant who had also been seized as a hostage were released after Plagge's intervention.

When the SD arrested another Jewish doctor and his elderly father, Plagge drew up work permits for both of them, even though they had never worked for *HKP 562*, and thus secured their release.[50] On other occasions, Plagge permitted workers and their families to stay in the workshops overnight if there were rumours of arrests. For example, during the immediate aftermath of the alleged sniping attack on German soldiers that was organised by Murer, Samuel Esterowicz and his daughter Perela spent a night in the workshops to avoid being rounded up.

Schmid, too, was steadily increasing the number of people under his care. In addition to running the *Versprengten-Sammelstelle*, he was also responsible for a workshop in the neighbouring building where upholstery for motor vehicles and railway carriages was repaired, and this gave him the opportunity to increase his workforce considerably. The workforce of the upholstery workshop included several Red Army prisoners of war, and Schmid ensured that they received the same care as his other workers. In addition, several German soldiers joined the workforce; when stragglers reported to the office, he interviewed them and found that many were desperate not to return to the front line. In an era where post-traumatic stress disorder was not recognised and their conduct would be treated a cowardice, he simply added them to his workers.

The Jews working for Schmid would eventually number about 150. As Wehrmacht workers, they all received the invaluable identity cards that were known amongst the Jewish community as *Todesurlaubsscheine* ('holiday from death cards'). These identity cards served a double function. Firstly, those not in receipt of identity cards that confirmed their usefulness to the occupation forces were at far higher risk of arrest; and secondly, by changing the rules when passes were reissued, the number of Jews employed by the occupation forces could be reduced at a rate that was commensurate with the ability of Jäger's men to kill the rest.

The alacrity with which both Plagge and Schmid took steps to protect Jews and Poles is remarkable. To a large extent, they were aided by the manner in which the Germans were implementing their occupation policies. The many competing occupation agencies in Lithuania often seemed to be motivated more by the desire to establish their own dominance than in cooperating for the benefit of the occupation policy as a whole. Consequently, relatively junior ranked figures like Schmid found themselves with plenty of leeway to make their own decisions with little requirement for permission from others. But such leeway worked for others, too. Men like Murer were of comparatively low rank, yet they were in positions of great power.

Despite having protective identity cards, the Jews working for Plagge and Schmid were still in danger of arrest by random sweeps. On many occasions, both Plagge and Schmid were able to intervene with the SD or Lithuanian police and secure the release of those detained, but on other occasions the arrested individuals disappeared down the road to Ponary. As the end of 1941 approached, the danger of such a fate steadily increased as Jäger, Murer and others took further steps towards the 'liquidation' of the Jews of Lithuania.

5

The First Winter

In mid-September, the daily report from Müller at the headquarters of the Security Police and SD in Berlin recorded approvingly that the elimination of Jews in Lithuania was proceeding at a fast pace; Karl Jäger's determination to execute his orders with exemplary efficiency was having the desired result. But even if Lithuania was now a singularly bad place for Jews, worse was to come.

After Rauca conducted the *Intelligenz-Aktion* in the Kaunas ghetto, there was a period of several weeks when there were no organised mass killings – instead, there were random attacks and searches, which left the population both increasingly impoverished and on edge for fear of further such raids. Jews returning to the ghetto were regularly searched and faced severe beatings if they were found to be trying to smuggle extra food or any other item into the ghetto. When a Jew named Sholom Rabinovich was caught attempting to buy vegetables in a local market, he was brought before Jordan, the German commandant of the ghetto; Jordan personally executed him on the spot. On another occasion, Rauca was overseeing the search of Jews at the ghetto entrance and discovered that one of the Jews had a silver spoon hidden in his clothing, presumably an item that he had hoped to trade for food whilst outside the ghetto. Rauca beat the man severely with a wooden club before drawing his pistol and killing him with a single shot to the back of the head. This period was merely a lull before the Germans once more stepped up their efforts.

On 15 September, Jordan visited the ghetto and handed the *Judenrat* 5,000 work permits, which became known as *Jordan-Scheine*. These were to be distributed to skilled workers only. After much acrimonious debate, the *Judenrat* decided that it had no choice but to comply and handed out the permits as ordered. Those who received the permits were left wondering whether they would actually provide any protection, while those who failed to obtain a permit were left in fear that they might be killed.

In the days that followed, those with *Jordan-Scheine* were regularly marched from the ghetto to places of work, such as at Aleksotas, just outside the city, where the Germans were rebuilding and expanding an airfield that the Luftwaffe had bombed during the invasion. The airfield was widely regarded as an undesirable labour assignment. As it was some distance from the ghetto, workers faced a long march often in poor weather, followed by a gruelling day of hard labour under the supervision of guards and overseers who often beat them for the slightest infringement. In addition, the location of the airfield meant that there was less opportunity for the Jews to try to trade with local civilians for food, but many still found opportunities to evade the restrictions. Despite her defiant words to Tornbaum, Joheved Čartokaitė had no choice but to work in order to survive and was assigned to the airfield:

> The Jews were marched to the airfield via the Aleksotas Bridge in columns. Here the columns broke up as the bridge over the Nemunas had been blown up and there was only a small wooden stage between the two ends. We therefore crossed the bridge in single file; right next to us passed the free inhabitants of Kaunas. After crossing the bridge we were once more put in rows and columns. The same thing happened on our return. I had stitched the obligatory yellow star, which should have been on my chest and back, on my headscarf, so that if I took the scarf off, I had no markings.
>
> When returning from the airfield it was the simplest thing to slip away from the work brigade. When such an opportunity arose, I quickly put my marked headscarf in my pocket while crossing the bridge and continued not with the column but along the pavement just like other normal people. I then waited, hidden in the grounds of the Jesuit school, until the entire column had passed.
>
> On my first trip into the city I called on my friend Bronius Elijošaitis. While the barbed wire fencing wasn't complete, he had come into the ghetto a few times to visit my classmate Freda Karnovski and me and to bring us food. Bronius suggested that I should seek out his family after dark so that the neighbours wouldn't notice. One of them served in the militia and who knew how many Jews he had taken to their deaths in Fort VII before the ghetto was established?[1]

Bronius Elijošaitis's mother gave Joheved Čartokaitė useful advice. If she was going to be on the run, she should avoid staying in any place for more than three days to avoid detection. In this manner, she was able to spend several nights outside the ghetto, rejoining a work party on its way back and using the opportunity to smuggle food for her family. She found that many Lithuanians were hostile both to the German occupation and their fellow Lithuanians who collaborated with the Germans and asked one such acquaintance if he could put her in touch with the resistance movement. He replied that the repression of dissent was so great that any such move was unwise for the moment.

The *Jordan-Scheine* that had been issued in Kaunas in September proved to have some protective value. On 4 October, the Germans and Lithuanians carried out an 'action' against the small ghetto, allegedly in response to shots being fired at a German police officer. Those who had *Jordan-Scheine* were largely spared, but the rest of the population of the ghetto was taken to the nearby Fort IX. The Jews had set up a small hospital for contagious diseases in the ghetto, and the Germans decided to deal with this in a predictably appalling manner. Jehoshua Rosenfeld, who was a member of the ghetto police, recalled the terrible event: 'After the doors and windows on the ground floor had been nailed shut, the hospital and all the ill patients together with the nurses and the duty doctor, Dr Davidovich, were set ablaze. People who attempted to climb out of the windows on the upper floors were shot as soon as they appeared at the windows by police who were dealing with the hospital.'[2]

Solly Genkind had just witnessed his uncle Jacob being shot by a German guard and had helped his aunt Leena and his father carry the unconscious man into the hospital. He and his father watched in horror:

> Even as the Germans poured can after can of gasoline along the foundation of the building, I was telling myself that this wasn't really happening.
>
> Several torches were lit and thrown before our horrified eyes, the gasoline exploding with loud thumps. Blue flames began to shoot up along the building's dry timbers.
>
> At first all we heard was the roar of the flames as they ate their way through the wood. Then we began to hear the terrible shrieks and almost inhuman cries of those inside. That blood-curdling sound will remain branded in my soul forever.
>
> Several of the doctors and nurses tried to break out through the windows but were cut down by a hail of fire from the machine-guns. They were the lucky ones.
>
> At some point I thought I saw a figure in a white dress through one of the upper windows. I was sure that it was Aunt Leena, but she soon disappeared from view as other windows shattered and

> a thick black smoke poured out of every opening, enveloping the whole building …
>
> I thought I was inured by the murders I had already seen, but this act of barbarism shattered me completely. I covered my ears, unable to shut out the horrible screams emanating from the building, and fell to the bottom of the trench sobbing …
>
> Even the Germans and Lithuanians stood in silence. No one was laughing or talking. Many of them pulled out handkerchiefs and covered their noses. Perhaps even they realised the enormity of what they had done.[3]

Joheved Čartokaitė attempted to slip through the fence around the ghetto on the day that the Germans moved against the small ghetto, but as she crawled under the barbed wire she was confronted by a Lithuanian guard. When she started speaking to him, they realised that one of her schoolmates was the sister of the guard; he let her through the barbed wire and even gave her the address of his parents, who proved to be friendly. Later that evening, the guard returned to his parents' residence intoxicated and blackened with soot. He had taken part in the attack on the small ghetto, and she was horrified that on the one hand he had helped her through the barbed wire and had even directed her to his parents' residence, but on the other hand he took part in the destruction of the small ghetto, including setting fire to buildings when Jews were still inside.

With meticulous attention to detail, Jäger recorded the number of Jews who were executed at Fort IX after the destruction of the hospital: 315 Jewish men, 712 women, and 818 children, a total of 1,845 people. This 'action' accounted for about half of the population of the small ghetto, merely a prelude.

A few days later, Joheved Čartokaitė tried once again to slip through the barbed wire in order to trade with local people, taking with her a shirt that belonged to her father. She saw an elderly Lithuanian woman who agreed to exchange the shirt for a large piece of cheese but when a guard became suspicious, the elderly woman summoned him with a shout. Čartokaitė was taken to a guard post where several Lithuanians beat her and then handed her over to another guard:

> He dragged me into an empty room and fiddled with his army belt. Now, I thought, he'll rape me, and during those brief seconds the most varied thoughts passed through my head about how I should defend myself or cry out. The soldier, a young guy of my age and wearing glasses, placed a chair in the middle of the room and holding his belt, ordered me to sit. He caught hold of my hand

> and hit me with the belt buckle to force me to sit. We dragged each other in a circle – he held my hand tightly and I tried to keep my distance, but I couldn't ward off his blows. My head and shoulders were particularly badly hit. He didn't curse, but struck me with all his strength. During this an armed Gestapo man saw us through the door, which was still ajar, and broke into peals of laughter. In a flash, I had the impression: whoever laughs like that has no malice. So I complained to this man, demanding to know why he was laughing and that it might be better if he ordered the beating to stop. He paused but nonetheless gave the soldier the order to stop hitting me: 'That's enough, it'll do!' he said. The bespectacled guard refastened his belt and clutching my cheese I slipped through the small door into the ghetto. My shoulders, head, back and arms were swollen and bruised but at the time I was so angry I felt no pain and didn't shed a single tear in the guard post.[4]

The first assault on the small ghetto was followed by a much larger clearance, which became known as the *Grosse Aktion*. On 27 October, Rauca ordered the *Judenrat* to arrange for all of the Jews in the ghetto to assemble in a central square. He told them that the intention was to determine which Jews were capable of heavy work, but fearing that this would result in more killings, many in the *Judenrat* didn't want to cooperate. After another bitter and prolonged debate, the *Judenrat* complied. That evening, Jews who did not have *Jordan-Scheine* tried desperately to obtain one, or some other form of work permit. The following morning, Rauca and Jordan personally oversaw the filtering of the gathered Jews. With no regard to the possession of *Jordan-Scheine* or other documents, the two men sorted the Jews on what seemed arbitrary criteria into two groups. According to some witnesses, Jäger was present for perhaps an hour of this selection process. Forced to stand in lines all day without food or water, even the Jews who were ultimately classified as being capable of work suffered considerably, and about 50 collapsed; many of them were elderly or unwell, and died shortly afterwards.

Joheved Čartokaitė was still recovering from her beating when Rauca and Jordan carried out their selection:

> My family – father, mother, sister and my father's mother – were sent to the 'wrong group' during the selection. I saw an acquaintance of my parents, the former director of the Jewish academy in Virbalis, Dr Bramsonas, and I shouted out his name and asked him to find out where we were being taken. He had been a volunteer in the fighting for Lithuanian independence after the First World War and was now

> deputy commander of the Jewish police. For shouting out, I was struck on my back with a rifle butt. Dr Bramsonas ran over to the notorious Hauptscharführer Rauca, who was indicating with his index finger to which side the Jews were to go, left or right, and then came up to the soldier guarding us and whispered something to him and then ordered us to change group. We then crossed to the other column but our grandmother hadn't noticed and went further with the 'wrong group'. I pushed forward to try to pull her back. That earned me more blows from the guard and I was pushed back towards my parents.
>
> My grandmother was a 90-year-old woman; she lived in the ghetto with her daughter, my father's sister. She had a lightweight folding chair with her and could at least sit down, but it was very cold. [Earlier,] I had run from the square to the ghetto, which was forbidden, and fetched my grandmother a cushion. She settled on the cushion and was at least a little warmer. Thanks to the intercession of Dr Bramsonas we had been directed to the 'good side' and I saw from a distance how she tucked the pillow under her arm and with the little chair in one hand, moved away from us. I don't know if she was able to make the journey on foot to fort IX. One can only guess her sad fate.[5]

Avraham Gollub, who was 32 years old at the time, described the contrasting fortunes of those who were 'vetted' by Jordan and Rauca, and the manner in which the ghetto police attempted to help the Jews:

> Except for an occasional sarcastic smile, Rauca's face did not betray any emotion, whereas Jordan stood with a frozen, sullen expression on his face and watched with fear-inspiring eyes the Jews passing in front of him. At first he was a little hesitant, lest he transfer to the good side those 'not deserving' it, but he regained his composure quickly and followed Rauca's example by motioning families and whole columns either to the left or to the right without hesitation.
>
> There was, nevertheless, some difference between Jordan and Rauca. The former did not motion to the bad side anyone holding a Jordan certificate, not even family members of the permit holder, without taking into consideration their age and physical condition …

On that day the Jewish policemen displayed initiative, daring, and resourcefulness – they cheered up the dispirited, they lent a hand to those who collapsed on the ground or fainted, and gave them water. They even worked wonders: while lining up the survivors in a new column, they seized every opportunity of transferring individuals – and even whole families still waiting for their turn – over to the good side. They did this with cunning and deftness. They would signal by a wink, or a movement of the hand, to slip away, to jump quickly, or to crouch and crawl toward them without drawing the attention of the guards. Whenever such a person drew near them, the Jewish policemen would set upon them screaming and push them brutally to the good side, pretending that they were forcing him back to his correct place. But whenever they did not succeed in deceiving the guards, a hail of curses and blows would pour on the unfortunate policeman caught in the act.[6]

The Jews who were classified as not suitable for work were herded into the small ghetto. Solly Genkind and his sister Fanny witnessed the events that unfolded the following day:

> I woke up in the morning to the terrible screaming of my sister Fanny. I sat up in bed just in time to see her clutching at the windowsill before her knees buckled and she fell to the floor.
>
> We all rushed to the window, Mother and Anushka [his aunt] kneeling and lifting Fanny up, trying to revive her. The rest of us stared through the glass. In the grey light of early morning an endless column of people moved up a distant hill towards Fort IX. Miles and miles of people. It wasn't as gory as many scenes I had witnessed, yet it was a thousand times worse. In my imagination I could see these unfortunate thousands being shoved into huge graves, layer upon layer of the dead being covered with freshly dug earth.
>
> Driven by an inexplicable force, we threw on our coats and together with thousands of others we rushed to the ghetto fence. Armed Lithuanians lined both sides of the street as far as the eye could see, ready to shoot anyone who tried to escape. It is impossible to describe the cries of people on both sides of the fence as they recognised friends and relatives, sometimes parents, brothers, and sisters. How could the heart take it in without breaking to pieces? How could the mind remain sane?
>
> I kept trying to see if I recognised anyone on the other side. The numbers were so great that the death march lasted from dawn to noon, but we weren't able to bear it so long and stumbled away, shocked to the bone ...
>
> Although Fort IX was several kilometres away, we could hear the faint but unmistakable chatter of machine-guns.[7]

A few days later, Genkind was astonished when a boy named Kuki Kopelman, who had been marched away with the other Jews, turned up in the ghetto dressed in a large overcoat. He told Genkind and his family what had happened at Fort IX. Even after all they had endured, the account must have been devastating to hear:

> German and Lithuanian guards stood at the entrance with several large dogs straining at their leashes, barking and snarling furiously. We were pushed through the gates.
>
> Several trucks were standing inside the courtyard, their engines running. They often backfired and it sounded like shots.
>
> A young German officer addressed us: 'In spite of the ridiculous rumours, you're going to be transported to working camps in the east. You will shower and then be issued working clothes. Undress and leave your clothing here.' He spoke in civil tones, and in spite of all we knew about this death factory he almost sounded convincing.
>
> Whatever spark of hope we felt was extinguished when we heard a long burst of machine-gun fire and distant screams. The Germans had heard it too, for they raised their guns and pointed them at us.
>
> 'Quickly, you Jews! Undress and into the showers! You're just hearing the backfire of some trucks,' the officer shouted. They wanted to dispatch us at maximum speed and efficiency, I suppose. Resistance on our part might have delayed their tight schedule.
>
> But no one moved, no one seemed able to move a muscle. The officer calmly walked up to an elderly man who was standing near the front, drew his pistol and shot him in the face. When he fell to the ground his head opened up and his brains poured out into the mud.
>
> Suddenly everyone was undressing. When you're about to die, even a few minutes seem precious, as if another second might bring a reprieve. Finally we all stood naked, covering our private parts with our hands and shivering in the cold. These despicable men weren't satisfied with merely killing us, they had to humiliate us even at the end. Why didn't they allow us to die with our clothes on? Did they really need our ragged old clothes? …
>
> On the officer's signal the Germans and Lithuanians launched themselves at us. 'Run, run you Jew swine,' they shouted, lashing out at us with sticks and rifle butts, their dogs attacking the slow-moving ones, tearing pieces of flesh from their legs and buttocks. We started running in a wild panic with the guards and dogs after us … Then as we rounded a corner we saw dozens and dozens of machine-guns mounted around an open field. They were firing long bursts into a huge pit. I could hear screaming from inside and it drove me almost mad with fright.
>
> I wanted to run, to escape, but a mass of stampeding naked bodies crushed around me, encircling me like a straitjacket.

Lithuanians and Germans with rolled-up sleeves and red faces were loading and firing into the mob. You could see the yellow flashes from the barrels, and a veil of blue smoke drifting over the field.

It was a scene out of hell itself. There were hoarse shouts, the women's screams – shrill, and children and babies crying, and barking dogs. It stank of sweat and urine and excrement as terrified bodies just let go. I saw one bearded man standing by the pit, shaking his fists at the sky and screaming. 'Jews! There is no God! There is a devil sitting up there!' He looked a lot like my old Rabbi. Blood was streaming from him and they kept shooting at him, but he kept standing there, screaming at the sky.

Then we were at the pit. It looked like thousands of bodies, one on top of the other, screaming and writhing, begging the Germans to finish them off. A vision of hell. A vision of hell.[8]

Kuki Kopelman fell into the pit where he lay between two corpses and wasn't hit by gunfire. Amongst the victims who fell into the pit with him was a girl called Lena, Solly Genkind's childhood sweetheart, and Kopelman watched her bleed to death from a wound in her neck. Later, he climbed out of the pit; the guards were drinking alcohol and he was able to grab some clothes from the heaps of garments discarded by the Jews. With nowhere else to go, he made his way back to the ghetto and unobtrusively joined a work party that was about to enter through the gates.

In many – perhaps most – cases, the people taken away for execution had family members who survived. Fruma Kučinskienė was aged just eight when she and her family entered the ghetto. When Jordan and Rauca divided the Jews into those who would survive and those who were taken away, her grandparents and brother were put in the latter group but her father was able to persuade the Germans that her brother was capable of work; nonetheless, her grandparents were amongst those who were taken to the small ghetto and thence to Fort IX: 'That evening, when [everyone] returned to their homes, it was no longer so cramped. Everyone sat silently. Nobody spoke at our round table in the kitchen, and I didn't wish to go to bed.'[9]

In an entry with the caption of 'Clearance of the ghetto of redundant Jews', Jäger recorded the day's total of victims as 2,007 male Jews, 2,920 women, and 4,273 children: 9,200 individuals. The population of the Kaunas ghetto was reduced to about 17,000. For the moment, it was the last major killing. Although Jews continued to be beaten or killed in isolated cases, the civil and military authorities were now demanding a reliable source of labour and although Stahlecker had insisted that Lohse's civil administration should not be able to interfere with the work of *Einsatzgruppe A*, Jäger had no choice but to curtail his attempts to wipe out the population of the ghetto. It was the beginning of what became known to the ghetto inmates as the 'quiet time'.

Joheved Čartokaitė continued to break away from her work column to venture into Kaunas; after the death of her grandmother, she was more determined than ever to flee from the ghetto. Ona Mažeikienė, a Lithuanian woman who rented an apartment in the same building where Čartokaitė had lived, provided her with overnight shelter when she was unable to return to the ghetto. The following morning, as they parted, Mrs Mažeikienė said to Čartokaitė: 'If you ever don't know where you can stay, you can come here, child.' Others also sheltered her and gave her food to take back to the ghetto, but she couldn't find anyone who would put her in touch with the resistance. Instead, she began to try to obtain documentation that would classify her as a non-Jewish person. One night, she stayed with the widow of a Lithuanian Communist who had been executed by the Nazis. The woman told Čartokaitė that she bore a striking resemblance to the recently deceased daughter of her landlord. She agreed to ask the landlord for the girl's identity card, but unfortunately, he guessed that it was intended for a Jew – fearing the possible repercussions, he refused to give her the document.

An opportunity to escape came shortly after. An old schoolfriend, Jonas Adomavičius, and his sister Liudmila also sheltered Čartokaitė; they told an acquaintance, a landowner by the name of Jonas Saunoris, about her plight and asked him if he was willing to take her back to his farm. Although he didn't know her at all, he agreed to help Čartokaitė:

> As promised, Jonas Saunoris appeared at the brother and sister's residence on 15 January 1942, wrapped me in a huge sheepskin, put me on the sledge, covered me with a thick layer of straw, and we set off. As was fitting for a landowner, one of his farmers sat on the driving bench of the sledge. Jonas Saunoris and I shivered the whole way and not just from the cold but also from anxiety in case a police checkpoint might wish to see our documents. To make matters worse, we got lost and reached the estate in Monkiškis at dusk.[10]

Saunoris's parents had been deported to Siberia by the Soviet authorities during what was known as the 'Russian year'; he had been studying in the Polish city of Bydgoszcz and returned to Lithuania to find that his parents had disappeared. Despite the actions of the Soviet authorities, he regarded the Germans as no better and unlike many who had been badly treated by the Soviets, he showed no hostility towards the Jews or any others accused of collaborating with the enemy. He treated Čartokaitė like a sister and managed to get word to Čartokaitė's friends in Kaunas, who in turn informed her family in the ghetto that she was safe and well. She remained in the estate about 45 miles (73km) north of Kaunas for several months.

At about the same time that Jordan handed over the *Jordan-Scheine* in Kaunas, the Jews of the Vilnius ghetto were divided up, and those who did not already have work permits would have to move to the small ghetto. The German and Lithuanian forces commanded by Horst Schweinberger descended on the small ghetto on 1 October while the inmates were in the synagogue for Yom Kippur. By the end of the day, about 1,700 people had been rounded up and taken to Lukiškės Prison. Schweinberger also demanded of the *Judenrat* in the large ghetto that 1,000 Jews without work permits be handed over to his men. Fearful of German reprisals if they refused, the *Judenrat* agreed, but few Jews without official work permits were willing to come forward. As Schweinberger's men began to enter the ghetto and seize people at random, rapidly gathering far more than the originally specified 1,000, many Jews came forward in the belief that their permits would result in their swift release. Several hundred Jews were then marched out of the large ghetto. Only 600 were actually transferred to the small ghetto; the rest were taken in two batches to Ponary where they were executed. Again, Jäger submitted a detailed report on the number of victims: a total of 1,330 Jewish men, 2,357 women, and 1,018 children. In addition, four Lithuanian Communists were also executed.

This was merely the first stage of the planned reduction of the population of the Vilnius ghetto. Late on 3 October, the Germans and Lithuanians once more descended on the small ghetto and rounded up 2,000 inmates. They were told that they were being taken at dawn to a third ghetto at an undisclosed location where there was a shortage of workers. But the following morning, when the guards started to move the Jews towards Lukiškės Prison, many realised what was happening:

Moshe Frumkin, a youth of 18, cried out to the people who were being taken with him on the road to the prison: 'Don't let them take you! Escape into the streets!' Panic swept the column, women lay down on the road, the elderly stood petrified, and the youngsters ran away. Schweinberger ordered his men to fire. Dozens of people were killed, and the survivors were ordered to carry them. Nevertheless, many escaped, including Frumkin.[11] A total of 1,983 Jews were killed as a result of this 'action'. Another roundup took place late on 15 October, resulting in 1,146 people being shot the following day. The result was that the population of the small ghetto was reduced to fewer than 4,000.

Many of the heads of organisations in Vilnius that employed Jews became aware of the widespread sweeps, which often caught some of their workers. Both Plagge and Schmid attempted to secure the release of Jews who worked for them, as did many of the other agencies. As a result, several hundred people with work permits were able to return to the ghetto. But on 4 October, 432 Jewish men, 1,115 women and 436 children were taken to Ponary and executed. They included many who had been in possession of the precious work permits.

Early on 21 October, the final clearance of the small ghetto began. The Germans and Lithuanians methodically searched each building, trying to locate the Jews who were hiding. Even before the creation of the ghetto, the Jews of Vilnius had started constructing hiding places to avoid being rounded up and taken away either for forced labour or execution. These hiding places were known as *malines*, and were often of a substantial size, consisting of carefully boarded-up sections of loft spaces or even entire rooms with the doors sealed. The main problem with the *malines* was that food was in such short supply in the ghetto that it was impossible to stockpile sufficient for the occupants to remain hidden for long, and sooner or later some of the occupants would have to emerge to seek further supplies.

On 23 October, a total of 2,367 people were taken to Ponary for execution. Repeated searches took place in the days that followed, and in addition to the Jews who were found hiding, groups from the large ghetto were also seized. The result was that a further 1,328 men, 2,739 women and 1,247 children were taken away and killed. Several dozen others either remained hidden or escaped from the small ghetto; with nowhere else to go, most of them ended up slipping into the large ghetto with work parties who were returning at the end of the day.

The main attention of Murer, Schweinberger and the other Germans overseeing the killings had been on clearing the small ghetto, but preparations were being made for a major reduction in the population of the large ghetto. In the meantime, Murer continued to attempt to gain whatever personal financial benefit he could. Many of the Jews had given their valuables to trusted non-Jewish neighbours before they moved to the ghetto and tried from time to time to meet these neighbours so that they could then recover some of their valuables and use them to trade for food. This was not without risk to both the Jews and their neighbours, as Samuel Esterowicz described:

> Franz Murer came to the ghetto gate and summoned my childhood friend Victor Chelem. Victor and his sister Eugenia, the heirs of Isaac Chelem, were owners of a wholesale glass business and sizeable real estate in the commercial centre ... and were thought to have become very rich after the First World War.
>
> Murer demanded that Victor give up to him the gold that he had hidden outside the ghetto. Nothing would happen to Victor

> if he complied, Murer said, but if he refused he would be shot immediately.
>
> Victor could do nothing else but take Murer to his former apartment house and ask the caretaker, Nikolai Ordu, to give the gold to Murer.
>
> Murer kept his word and let Victor Chelem go – but he ordered Nikolai Ordu hanged. The body of Nikolai Ordu was left hanging in the cathedral square with a board fastened to him announcing that this was what awaited all those who hid Jewish property or who gave shelter to the Jews.[12]

Not long after the clearance of the small ghetto, the *Arbeitsamt* ('Office of Work') received new instructions regarding the total number of passes that were to be issued – the various agencies involved in the slaughter of Jews were determined to overcome the resistance of civil and military organisations that they felt were hindering attempts to 'liquidate' the Jewish population and were employing too many Jews instead of attempting to train Polish and Lithuanian workers to take their places. As the expiry date of existing identity cards approached, the Germans announced that 3,000 new yellow identity cards would be issued. Anyone who received a yellow pass could nominate a spouse and two children who would be covered by the pass – this concession came from the realisation that workers were likely to function better if they felt that their families were safe, and sparing these dependents was, after all, only a short-term expedient. All of the Jews were expected to be killed in the coming months. Implementation of these new rules would reduce the population of the ghetto to fewer than 12,000, as it was expected that some of the workers would not have a spouse and two dependents. At the time, the ghetto housed a little over 27,000 people.

The task of actually issuing the new passes was given to different agencies. Some employers of Jewish labour were given a set of passes, while the *Judenrat* in the ghetto was also assigned about 400, which were intended to cover the personnel employed within the ghetto, for example the ghetto police and the medical workers. There were far more than 400 such employees and Jacob Gens contacted Murer to request a larger allocation; Murer refused, saying that the total had been set by a higher authority.[13] Many Jews who had been deemed as unfit for work – the elderly and the infirm – had already been removed from the ghetto and although some Jews still hoped that they had been taken to an alternative location, most feared that they had been killed. Consequently, the new passes were widely seen as a further step in eliminating Jews regarded as unnecessary. Desperate people crowded into the offices of the *Judenrat*:

> Unspeakable, heart-rending scenes and tragedies were played out in the narrow corridors where people who didn't have yellow passes begged their more fortunate fellow residents to save them and to add them to their lists of relatives so that they could join the small group. The people were willing to give up everything they had. Not everyone behaved with appropriate humanity ... this nightmarish, chaotic registration, which can never be forgotten by those who experienced it, lasted all night. At dawn, those who hadn't been able to get a number, had to hide in *malines*, where many had already spent the night in fear of death, as they had no hope that anyone would nominate them as family members.[14]

As each worker assigned a yellow pass could register a spouse and two children, many of those who received the passes and didn't have a family added the names of other Jews; in some cases, they demanded money from those that they were adding to their families, but in most cases it was done for no payment. As the practice grew more widespread, the *Judenrat* demanded evidence that the nominated individuals were indeed family members. Documentary evidence was almost completely absent, and the *Judenrat* was forced to accept the verbal testimony of other Jews as to the veracity of the claimants.

Even before all of the yellow permits had been issued, the Germans began a series of sweeps to take away those who were no longer regarded as workers or relatives of workers, transferring them to the small ghetto from where they would then take them in groups to Ponary, and during such round-ups they regularly searched for *malines*; anyone found in such a hiding place was likely to be taken away for immediate execution, regardless of their yellow pass status. The sweeps often took place at night but might occur at any time, which caused disaster if Jewish workers were away from the ghetto and were thus unable to vouch for their dependents, as Mascha Rolnikaite described. Her mother worked as a seamstress outside the ghetto, leaving the children behind during the day:

> Around midday there was a loud turmoil – drunken soldiers had entered the ghetto. In an instant, the streets were deserted as if there were no people anywhere. The soldiers crossed the ghetto, shouting and shooting into the air. Mama, Mira and the other adults from our accommodation were away at work – what to do? Would they take us away? They could be expected to do anything. They didn't

need us as we weren't workers. The small children stared at me as if I knew what to do or how to save them. But what could I do? I was terrified myself. I just hid my feelings and calmed them to stop them crying. If only Mama would just come back!

The soldiers made themselves scarce. It became quiet. A little later Mama returned from work ...

[That night] I heard the noise of a vehicle driving past while I was sleeping. I got up, clambered past those who were sleeping and went to the window. Although it had a cover nailed over it, like all windows that faced the streets outside the ghetto, it was possible to see a small part of the forbidden street near the ghetto gate through a small gap.

Soldiers jumped from the trucks that had driven up. They took up positions. Should I wake the others or not? I thought it would be better not to scare them. The soldiers hadn't actually done anything. They stood like statues ...

More trucks rumbled up. Even more soldiers!

Alarmed, I woke the others. Panic broke out. Children cried, mothers shouted, nobody could find their things. I too was half-naked, shivering from fear and cold. Soon the soldiers were hammering on our door – they were already inside the gate! They came up the steps, knocked! Nobody opened the door. They hammered with their fists on the door. Soon they would break in!

A neighbour tiptoed to the door and said that everyone had been taken to the small ghetto from this accommodation. As a worker in the *Kailis* leather factory, he was the only one left here. Of course, they didn't believe him and wanted to see his work pass. Our neighbour opened the door a little and gave it to them. The killers looked at the pass and tore it up with derisive laughter and took him away.

But they went away and knocked on another door ...

I went back to the window. The gate [of the ghetto] was open. They drove people out of the ghetto and lined them up. They all had children and bundles with them. One man ran back. A shot rang out.[15]

During this phase of the history of the ghetto, Samuel Esterowicz was working for his Polish acquaintance Poddany, who informed him that he had been allocated only six yellow passes – at the time, Poddany's workshop employed 18 Jews. Esterowicz received a certificate but two members of his extended family, Mula Gerstein and Kuba Rotstein, were among those who were left seeking certificates elsewhere. Fortunately, they were both able to secure employment in other work parties that allocated them the precious passes. But even those who had certificates were often left with painful decisions on which family members they could protect. Because the family protection applied only to spouses and two children, elderly dependents could not be included. Esterowicz:

> My sister Emma received her yellow certificate from the *Judenrat* in recognition of her services to the community ...
>
> In addition to those who were killed previously – my brother Yefim, my two sisters' husbands Aaron and Alexander and my sister-in-law's husband Yermasha – the yellow certificates action condemned to death my mother, my sister Anya with her daughter Shela, my brother's wife Fanya and daughter Lila as well as Emma's daughter Eva and her husband Lolek. My wife was to suffer the loss of her mother with her sister, aunt Sara as well as her sister Vera with her husband Naum ...
>
> In those days [my sister] Emma remained steadfast to her own self. Even though realising that by this act she was condemning herself to death, Emma had insisted that the *Judenrat* should transfer her yellow life certificate to her son-in-law [Lolek], thus giving him the chance to save his wife – her daughter Eva.[16]

The last of the yellow permits were issued on 23 October and Gens ordered all of those with the new permits to assemble outside the *Judenrat* offices, together with their dependents. The dependents were then issued numbered blue cards, with the number being recorded on the back of the yellow permit belonging to the relevant worker. During the night, the Jews became aware that large numbers of Lithuanian and German police were taking up positions around the ghetto. The plight of those who didn't have either yellow permits or the accompanying blue cards became desperate. Some pleaded in vain with members of the ghetto police and *Judenrat*; some hid in *malines*; and several tried to escape the ghetto. Throughout the night, there were occasional gunshots as they were hunted down and killed.

In the grey morning light of 24 October, the ghetto police ordered all those with yellow permits to assemble for departure to their place of work. They were to take their dependents with them for the day. The staff of the *Judenrat* and their families were to gather near the *Judenrat* buildings. As they filed from the ghetto, the Jews with work permits and blue cards were carefully checked by teams overseen by Murer and an officer of the SD who was to play a major role in the extermination of the Jews of Vilnius: Martin Weiss.

Born in 1903, Weiss originally intended like his father to follow a career in plumbing and heating, but after acquiring the necessary basic qualifications he travelled to South America, where he helped his older brother manage a farm. He returned to Germany in 1927 and showed little interest in the politics of the era, concentrating on completing his qualifications as a plumbing and heating engineer. After his father's death he took on the business in 1928 and quietly prospered. During his time in South America he had become an accomplished horseman and when he joined the SS in 1934 he became part of a small SS cavalry group. When war broke out he was a member of a supply and support unit in the SS and took part in the 1940 campaign against France; thereafter he was demobilised and returned to his home near Karlsruhe. In early 1941 he recalled to the ranks of the SS and was sent to a training establishment close to Pretzch and accompanied *Einsatzkommando 3* into Lithuania, where he was assigned to duties with the SD. Despite his apparent lack of involvement in political matters – he joined the Nazi Party only in 1937 – he was to become one of the most energetic persecutors of the Jews. In 1946, Abram Suzkever, a Jew from Vilnius, gave testimony to the Nuremberg tribunals about Weiss's activities when the Jews left the ghetto for their workplaces:

> When I arrived at the ghetto I saw the following scene: Martin Weiss came in with a young Jewish girl. When we went in further, he took out his revolver and shot her on the spot.[17]
>
> As they inspected the documents of the Jews who had assembled, Murer and Weiss weeded out several who they regarded as not being of an appropriate age to be registered as spouses or children. The rest were permitted to leave for their workplaces, and the Germans and Lithuanians then began a methodical attempt to clear the ghetto. Many of the *malines* were discovered – in one, no fewer than 300 people had taken refuge. Some who attempted to resist were shot on the spot, but most were forced to assemble outside the main ghetto gate. They were told that they were being taken to a new place of work, and were marched away. Some were held briefly at Lukiškės Prison, but ultimately all were taken to Ponary. On 25 October alone, 2,578 were executed, and a further 1,203 two days later.

A Jewish locksmith, Ephraim Schuster, was unable to get a pass. He later described the events and the role played by Franz Murer:

> I tried to get out of the ghetto but wasn't successful. At about midday ... a group of Ukrainians marched in. At the time that this group arrived I was in Spitalgasse, hiding in the attic of a house. Murer and two others entered the house where I was hiding during this

> 'action'. Then I heard a great scream. I lifted some of the rafters and peered through, and saw that they were taking away a woman who was resisting them. The woman was pulled away by Lithuanian or Ukrainian soldiers. Murer wanted to help them take away this woman who fought against being deported. Then he drew his pistol and shot her. I couldn't tell whether she was killed or not ... [Three days later] I emerged from the attic and saw the woman ... lying in her blood.[18]

Many of those like Schuster who hid in *malines* survived the sweep, but the Germans were well aware that their 'action' had failed to capture all of those without permits. Through the ghetto police, Murer informed the Jews that anyone without a yellow permit or blue card should assemble for transfer to the small ghetto, where they would be assigned work and would receive permits. Several hundred individuals came forward; on 29 October, they were transferred to Lukiškės Prison. The killings continued until the end of the month. Despite this further 'action', it was clear from the number of those killed that many Jews without work permits were still in hiding in the ghetto. On 3 November, those with yellow permits or blue cards were ordered to move to the small ghetto for three days. Once more, documentation was scrutinised carefully and as before, the Germans removed anyone whose appearance did not seem consistent with their alleged status. Many of the Jews later recalled that Gens and other members of the ghetto police did what they could to protect people under the watchful eyes of the Germans:

> A line of five people is walking: husband, wife and three children ... Gens counts 'Father, mother, child, child.' The third child, a 12-year-old, he hits with a stick and removes from the line ... and ... marching in a line: a father, a mother and one child. Gens counts 'One: father, two: mother, three: child,' and suddenly he starts shouting a torrent of abuse at the father, 'You fool, how have you lost your second son?' And during the disturbance Gens places the crook of his staff around the neck of the 12-year-old, whom he had previously removed from the line, drags him and attaches him as a fourth member of the family. And again he raises his voice, 'You idiot, look after your son.'[19]

Mascha Rolnikaite and her family were amongst those who were moved to the small ghetto. She described what happened when the guards found a group of Jews taking refuge in a *maline*:

> There was a candlestick on the table, with an almost exhausted candle flickering in it. Rumpled beds, overturned chairs, a closet

that had been torn open. All the signs of the panic that had reigned here. The murderers had plundered everything, beating people with their rifle stocks, stuffing clothes into their uniform jackets. When they had gathered together everything, they opened up the cellars and leapt into them. They shone their flashlights on the damp, shimmering walls and the terrified faces. They, the overlords of Europe, ordered the people to kneel before them. Then they moved through the cowering people, mocked them, struck them across their backs with whips, laughing hoarsely. Once they were tired of their games, they drove the people from the cellar.

In the street, a young lad didn't want to be taken away. The rogues pulled his arms behind his back and dragged him over to the others while telling him that he needn't resist. He was only being taken to a work camp. But the young man kicked and bit them and finally succeeded in breaking free. A bullet struck him down.[20]

When they entered the small ghetto, the Jews found signs of hasty departure by those who had preceded them, as Samuel Esterowicz described: 'The lifeless streets of the small ghetto were horrifying – the room we entered was deathly quiet, there was an unfinished meal on the plates on a table, opened prayer books and prayer shawls spoke of a suddenly interrupted life, about people who were caught unawares when taken to their deaths.'[21]

In the days that followed, Jews went out to their workplaces as usual and then returned to the small ghetto, while police units carefully searched the large ghetto. On 5 November, the Jews were permitted to return to the large ghetto, where they found that many of the *malines* had been discovered. The 'action' accounted for a further 1,341 Jews, but a number of people who had successfully hidden in the small ghetto during the various clearances returned to the large ghetto with those who had been housed there temporarily during the searches, and several more had escaped detection during the three-day search. Not long thereafter, Murer reassigned the empty small ghetto to the Lithuanian civilian administration.

Despite giving up her yellow pass for the benefit of her daughter and son-in-law, Samuel Esterowicz's sister Emma was able to escape from Vilnius and the execution that awaited all those without yellow passes:

In our workshop I met a German soldier who, for some remuneration, delivered my sisters and Shelinka [Esterowicz's neice] to Voronovo [near the border with Belarus] in an armoured car …

My sister Emma must have had a foreboding of a sad fate awaiting them, she was sobbing bitterly as she was stepping into

> the car. To my great sorrow, Emma's forebodings turned out to be terrifyingly correct.
>
> The Lithuanian police came to Voronovo and arrested all the Jewish refugees from Vilnius, Emma, Anya and Shelinka among them, two weeks after their arrival. After keeping them locked in the local cinema for 24 hours, the Lithuanian police shot them all, numbering about 300 people, on 15 November 1941.[22]

A small number of Jews who were ordered to leave the ghetto were fortunate, at least in the short term. There were several fur and outer clothing factories in Vilnius before the German invasion, and these had been nationalised by the Soviet authorities; the Germans further consolidated them into a single large concern that became known as the *Kailis-Werke*. Shortly after the Germans occupied the city, production of winter clothing for the Wehrmacht was organised and several hundred Jews were employed. In early October, the *Kailis-Werke* was moved to the empty premises of the Elektrit radio factory, in order to centralise production at one site. The director of the factory was Oscar Glick, a Viennese Jew who fled to Vilnius before the German invasion. Shortly after the Germans occupied the city, he encountered a German soldier who was an old friend from Vienna; the soldier managed to get work for Glick. Using forged papers that categorised him as *Volksdeutsch* ('ethnic German' living outside the borders of Germany), Glick rapidly became a senior figure in *Kailis*. After securing yellow permits for all of the workers in the factory, he managed to get permission to move the workers and their families – nearly 1,000 people – from the ghetto to accommodation adjacent to the factory. The Jews who worked at *Kailis* were regarded with envy by many who had to work in far worse conditions, but for Glick and his wife Mina, luck was running out. There was a fire in the *Kailis* factory in January 1942; many attributed it to an accident, but others claimed that it was the work of Jewish resistance fighters. In the enquiry that followed, Glick's true identity was discovered. He and his wife were executed in February 1942.

In addition to the *Kailis* factory, another body that was responsible for manufacturing clothing – mainly shoes – was run by Oskar Schönbrunner, an officer from Bavaria. He was born in 1908 and joined the Reichswehr – the German armed forces prior to Hitler's assumption of power – in 1926. With the rank of Oberzahlmeister ('chief paymaster', equivalent to Oberleutnant in other branches of the Wehrmacht) he was deployed in Vilnius with the occupation forces within days of the arrival of German troops in a logistics role, with responsibility for clothing, accommodation, food and pay for the local military authority, and rapidly established a cluster of clubs for officers and other ranks.

Once this task was complete, he was assigned to set up a military tailoring service, which later expanded to other products, such as gloves and shoes. As the local Jewish community had been active in these fields, he was given permission to use Jewish labour and steadily increased his workforce to nearly 300 by early 1942. In addition, he took control of a local market garden that was to provide fresh produce for the military occupation staff, and once again employed Jewish labour. He was thus able to provide protection for a considerable number of Jewish workers; on one occasion, his superior officer intervened to prevent the SS from arresting several of the workers on the grounds that their work was essential for the war effort and must not be interrupted. Like Plagge, Schönbrunner could see that his Jewish workers were malnourished and took steps to improve matters.

In late 1941, Schönbrunner encountered an SS officer in the *Soldatenheim* where he was dining. Heavily intoxicated, the SS officer told him of the mass shootings that were taken place in Ponary and described in detail how children were often battered to death against trees. The revelations had a profound effect on Schönbrunner: 'An abyss opened up. What guilt had we brought upon ourselves!'[23]

Schönbrunner reported the conversation to his superiors, horrified that such events could be taking place. The response was a curt note that his report was untrue, but Schönbrunner was now aware of the extent of the mass killing of Jews. He noted that there seemed to be little sympathy for the Jews from any part of the population.

> The Lithuanian and Polish population said nothing against the shootings. I had the impression that they were of an anti-Semitic mindset. Whether this was the case from the outset or was caused by National Socialist influences, is beyond my knowledge. In any case the population looked on passively when the Jews were taken away for execution.[24]

As the elimination of 'surplus' Jews gathered pace, Isaak Glasman, a Jew who worked in the tailoring shop, reported to Schönbrunner that 150 Jews had been arrested by the SS and were being held in Lukiškės Prison prior to being taken to Ponary for execution. Many of these Jews, Glasman told Schönbrunner, were workers in the tailoring shop. Accompanied by Glasman, Schönbrunner immediately went to the prison and demanded the release of the Jews who worked for him. He had no authority for such an action, still less for the claim that he made in his argument with the SS personnel in the prison: he told them that he had been authorised to secure the release of 'his' Jews by the local head of the Security Police and SD. The SS officer on duty was of a lower rank than Schönbrunner and deciding not to argue the point, he asked Schönbrunner for the names of the relevant Jews. Glasman had already given Schönbrunner a list, and he now proceeded to read it out. As he did so, he could see that Glasman had added several Jews who were not workers in the tailoring shop, but read out the names nonetheless. Accompanied by about 150 released prisoners, Schönbrunner and Glasman returned to their workplace, where he tried to find employment for as many men as he could.[25]

Whilst the activities of Schmid and Plagge went largely unnoticed – at least for the time being – Schönbrunner's return to his tailoring workshop with such a large body of Jews attracted the attention of colleagues and superiors. Over the days that followed, he noticed other officers looking at him with embarrassed expressions and disapproval, but General Zehnpfennig, to whom Schönbrunner was answerable, seemed to behave as if nothing had happened – probably a pragmatic move, as any acknowledgement of Schönbrunner's actions would have required Zehnpfennig to take action against his subordinate and that in turn would have forced the authorities to take notice of Schönbrunner's complaints about the behaviour of the SS.

Despite issuing numerous yellow passes to his workers, Plagge was still faced with the loss of a significant number of the Jews that he had so far protected. He decided that the best way to proceed was to stress the value of these workers to the Germans and he contacted his military superiors, stressing that the ability of *HKP 562* to continue its vital work of repairing vehicles for combat units was being compromised. This led to discussions between the military authorities and Lohse's civilian administration in Riga. Lohse had already attempted to reduce the slaughter of Jews in order to protect the leather workshops in Siauliai, where almost all of the workers were Jews, but had been told that he should resolve the matter through local verbal discussions with the SS. However, he was also informed that 'in principle, economic considerations are not to be taken into account in the settlement of the problem.'[26]

Perhaps as a result of being blocked from using economic considerations, Lohse's administration was eager to take advantage of Plagge's complaint via military channels. Friedrich Trampedach, who was head of the Political Department of *Reichskommissariat Ostland*, wrote an order that was sent out on 12 November:

> The chief quartermaster of the Wehrmacht for Ostland complains that, in the course of the process of liquidation, Jewish skilled workers in armament factories and workshops, who cannot be replaced at present, are being taken away from the Wehrmacht.
>
> I unequivocally demand that the liquidation of Jews employed as skilled workers in the armament factories and workshops of the Wehrmacht be stopped, as there is no possibility of replacing them by other local workers at the present time. It should be determined with the *Gebietskommissare* which Jewish workers cannot be replaced by others.
>
> Arrangements should be made to train local workers as replacements as quickly as possible.
>
> This Order also refers to Jewish skilled workers in factories that do not serve the Wehrmacht directly, but perform important tasks for the war economy.[27]

As an employer of Jewish labour, Schmid also received a number of yellow passes. To the horror of those working in the *Versprengten-Sammelstelle* and the upholstery workshop, only 15 such passes were provided; after including family members, these would only give protection to 60 people. Amongst his workers who didn't receive a new yellow pass was Rachil, a sister of the wife of Samuel Esterowicz. Like several others, she was given permission by Schmid to remain in the *Versprengten-Sammelstelle* for the time being. Unless he could devise an alternative strategy, Schmid faced the almost certain death of many of those he had sheltered.

During this time, Schmid had made the acquaintance of several other prominent Jews, some of whom – briefly – became his closest friends. Hermann Adler was originally from Nuremberg where he had been a bookseller before he fled in 1938, travelling in stages to Vilnius where he met his wife Anita, a former opera singer from Vienna. Their intention to travel on to Palestine was thwarted by the political events of the following months and they joined the other Jews of Vilnius in the ghetto in September 1941. They worked with a group of Jews who were part of the *Dror* political youth movement to help needy ghetto residents and from one of their fellow workers they learned about Schmid's activities. They decided to seek work with him, as Hermann Adler later described:

> I knocked on the door and it was opened by a terrifying Gefreiter [it was Max Salinger, disguised as Gefreiter Huppert]. He asked, 'What do you want?' I replied, 'We would like to speak to the Feldwebel.' The Gefreiter: 'That's not possible. Civilians can't come in here! And in any case what do you want from the Feldwebel?'

> Then the Feldwebel walked past and asked, 'What's up?' The Gefreiter: 'It's two civilians who want to speak to you, Herr Feldwebel.' Schmid said, 'What do they want, then? I'd rather speak to civilians than with a German officer, no matter how high his rank. Let them come in!'[28]

The Adlers revealed to Schmid that they were Jews and that they had removed the obligatory yellow stars from their clothing – an offence punishable by death. Adler now suggested to Schmid that if Jews could escape from Vilnius to Białystok, they might be safer; at that time, the Jews living in the ghettoes of Belarus had a lower risk of being rounded up and taken away for execution. Schmid replied that he had a friend in Białystok who was also from Vienna, who would be able to help. Rather than send the Adlers back to the ghetto, he offered them a room in his accommodation next to his office.

In addition to running the *Versprengten-Sammelstelle* and overseeing the upholstery workshop, Schmid had also been tasked with driving a truckload of firewood into Belarus once a week, where it was used by a local military hospital. The German military had established a large clothing factory in Białystok where significant numbers of Jews were employed, and if the Jews fleeing from Vilnius could find work there, there was the possibility that – for the time being, at least – they would be safe. The identity of the NCO friend from Vienna who helped Schmid is unknown, but this was the area where Schmid's battalion had been deployed earlier in the year and it is likely that, just as he had been assigned to his various tasks, one of his comrades had been given similar duties in Białystok.

Another Jew Schmid encountered in the last weeks of 1941 was Mordechai Tenenbaum. He was born in Warsaw in 1916 and studied Turkish at the University of Warsaw's Institute of Orientalism. This proved to be hugely beneficial, as he was able to pass himself off as a Muslim Tatar under the name of Josef Tamaroff and thus wasn't classified by the Germans as a Jew. He moved around Lithuania, Poland and Belarus relatively freely. He, too, had contacts in Białystok, and after Adler told him about Schmid's activities, he asked Adler to arrange a meeting. At the end of October, Tenenbaum met Schmid in the office near the railway station, and together with Adler, they drew up arrangements for the transportation of Jews out of Vilnius.

The process that Schmid and his helpers adopted was later described by Hermann Adler. Jews who had fled the ghetto were taken first to the *Versprengten-Sammelstelle*, where Schmid provided them with a room. They often had to wait there for several days until the next truck journey to Białystok, Lida or Grodno. Schmid personally signed permits for the Jews in the truck in the event that they were stopped by German police units; the permits were not valid, but they were sufficient to pass a cursory inspection. In addition, his accomplice in Białystok provided him with a letter authorising the transfer of Jewish workers from Vilnius – again, the document wasn't a valid authorisation, but on at least one occasion Schmid was able to persuade a roadblock manned by personnel of the *Geheime Feldpolizei* ('Secret Field Police' or *GFP*, the military equivalent of the Gestapo) to allow him to pass.

It isn't known how many Jews were thus transported out of Vilnius. Adler later wrote that the total was as high as 350, which would have required Schmid to have made about 14 road journeys. In addition to those taken by truck to Belarus, Schmid issued an unknown number of permits and documents that permitted Jews of a sufficiently 'Aryan' appearance to travel from Vilnius by train. It is even more difficult to determine how many of the Jews who left Vilnius survived. At the time that Schmid was carrying out these measures, the ghetto in Białystok was going through a relatively quiet phase, having been 'purged' in September and October of over 4,000 inhabitants who were decreed to be unfit for work, but further executions took place in early 1942.

The steps that Schmid took to save Max Salinger and Luisa Emaitisaite were probably spontaneous acts of kindness and compassion, and thereafter his activity became progressively more at odds with his duties as a member of the Wehrmacht. However, his involvement with Tenenbaum and others in the Jewish resistance movement took him into completely new territory. In December 1941, Schmid received a visit from Tenenbaum, a Jewish woman named only as Esther, and Haika Grossman, a woman from Białystok who was also a member of the resistance movement. Grossman later described the meeting:

> Soon we were standing in Schmid's accommodation. It consisted of three rooms, none of them particularly large, one of which was his bedroom. [In it were] a bed, a cupboard, and a table. In the other rooms there was a hopeless mess. There were beds against the walls, with thin blankets lying on the mattresses. The floor was littered with leftover food. This was apparently where the refugees were sheltered. Schmid was well built, handsome, and had a nice face. His piercing gaze fell on me: 'You're from *HaShomer HaTzair*, aren't you? Mordechai told me. Oh yes, I well remember the Zionists from Vienna.'[29]

Grossman was in favour of armed resistance, but the tiny resistance groups in the Vilnius region lacked the organisation or weapons for any significant steps to be taken. Discussions on how the resistance movement should proceed were held in Schmid's accommodation, and Grossman was eager to try to use Schmid to obtain guns; Tenenbaum, by contrast, felt that the Jews should simply make use of Schmid's cooperation to move Jews to Białystok and elsewhere. He felt that the surviving Jewish population of the Vilnius ghetto was too small and downtrodden to be the centre of meaningful resistance, and that it would be far better to concentrate efforts in larger ghettoes, such as in Białystok or even Warsaw. Although there were suggestions later that Schmid provided a small number of weapons to the resistance fighters, there is no concrete record to confirm this. Schmid played host to these discussions, providing food and drink as well as shelter, but Adler was aware of the stress under which Schmid was now operating. He later recalled that after the others had left, Schmid would often drink heavily and lived in fear of being discovered. Nonetheless, he showed no inclination to curtail his activities. On one occasion, Adler asked him if he was risking his life too freely. Schmid replied: 'Everyone has to die. But if I can choose whether I should die as a murderer or a helper, then I choose death as a helper.'[30]

At the end of 1941, there was a small party to mark the New Year in Schmid's accommodation; Tenenbaum declared Schmid an honorary member of the Zionists, something that apparently delighted the Feldwebel from Vienna.

Whilst many Lithuanians were willing helpers of the Germans, at least at this stage of the war, the Poles remained generally hostile. Müller's daily report from the headquarters of the SD and Security Police in Berlin on 7 November commented on the mood and behaviour of the Poles around Vilnius:

> The Polish-Catholic clergy are, as before, the most active in anti-German propaganda ... The priest Jonas Gylis stated during his sermon: 'Just like executioners, they strike down innocent people, beating the elderly and pregnant women. Innocent people suffer like Christ before Judas ...' These words from the priest were apparently intended for those who were taking part in the liquidation of Jews. It is particularly significant for Gylis that, without securing permission, he went into the synagogue of the Jews to console them and to encourage them to be strong.[31]

For the moment, clergy like Gylis and Father Gdowski, who had helped Schmid, were safe. But their activities were clearly under close scrutiny and it was only a matter of time before the Germans turned their attention to them.

Despite being able to declare several parts of Lithuania *Judenfrei* ('free of Jews'), Jäger reported to Berlin that he encountered obstacles from other occupation authorities: 'There have even been repeated requests from some enterprises that Jews should be excused wearing Stars of David and they should be permitted to visit public restaurants etc. This mainly concerns Jews who are regarded as indispensable for those enterprises. All such requests are of course rejected by the offices of the Security Police.'[32]

It was a theme to which he returned in a report that he wrote on 1 December. This lengthy document, which has become known as the 'Jäger Report', was clearly intended to establish Jäger's credentials as the most successful of the officers tasked with the elimination of the Jews in the occupied parts of the Soviet Union. He listed the killings carried out both by 'Lithuanian partisans' before the arrival of *Einsatzkommando 3* and the slaughter that took place after. Jäger painstakingly recorded the totals of those killed by date and location – the overall numbers were 57,338 Jewish men, 48,592 Jewish women, 29.461 Jewish children, and 2,058 others (a mixture of suspected Communists, criminals, Roma, and the residents of mentally handicapped or psychiatric hospitals), giving a staggering total of 137,346 people shot or beaten to death in a little over five months. Whilst Jäger undoubtedly inflated some of the figures that he documented, it should be noted that the totals did not include those killed by the elements of *Einsatzgruppe B* in Vilnius before Jäger's men took over, and a few weeks later Jäger sent a handwritten note to Stahlecker increasing the total of those killed to 138,272. After listing the numbers of those killed, the report continued:

> Today I can confirm that *Einsatzkommando 3* has achieved the objective of solving the Jewish Problem in Lithuania. There are no longer any Jews in Lithuania apart from workers and their families. These are:
>
> In Siauliai – about 4,500
> In Kaunas – about 15,000
> In Vilnius – about 15,000
>
> I wanted to eliminate these worker Jews too, which led me into sharp conflict with the civil authority (the *Reichskommissar* [Lohse]) and the Wehrmacht and triggered a ban: these Jews and their families were not to be shot …
>
> I regard the *Judenaktionen* of *Einsatzkommando3* as mainly completed. The remaining worker Jews and Jewesses are urgently needed and I conclude that through the winter this workforce will be even more urgently needed. I am of the opinion that the sterilisation

> of male worker Jews should be commenced immediately to prevent reproduction. If a Jewess nevertheless becomes pregnant, she should be liquidated.[33]

After the departure of Hamann, Jäger's deputy was Hauptsturmführer Heinrich Schmitz, and he later told interrogators that many of Jäger's subordinate officers treated his obsession with numbers with derision. He added:

> Jäger only achieved his post due to shortages of personnel in wartime, and because aside from being a battery commander in the First World War and a revolutionary with the SA he had never held a significant command, he treated all men with regular official careers with mistrust and fear.[34]

On another occasion, Schmitz was equally dismissive: 'Jäger also suffered a lot from boredom, either reading or sitting by a listening device with which he could monitor all conversations in the office, or he made calculations in his 'shooting book'.'[35]

Regardless of Jäger's desire to impress his superiors, it seems that at least some of his men were unconvinced about his abilities. To an extent, this was due to the large degree of leeway that he gave his subordinates – for example, almost all of the killings in the Kaunas ghetto were either organised or overseen by Rauca. But the horrific figures that Jäger copied from his 'shooting book' into the report that he wrote on 1 December show without question that ultimately, these killings took place under his command.

Until December, the military campaign in the Soviet Union seemed to be progressing well. In the south, Kiev was captured in September in a huge encirclement battle that accounted for over 700,000 Red Army soldiers. In the north, the Germans reached the outskirts of Leningrad and almost completely encircled the city, and in the centre, the bulk of the Wehrmacht's armour was concentrated for one final push to capture Moscow before the winter. But operating at the end of long supply lines and far from their establishment strength, the German divisions that struggled forward through the steadily worsening snow ground to a halt just outside the Soviet capital; even if they had succeeded in pushing on to the city, the weakened infantry divisions probably lacked the strength to capture such a large urban area, and certainly lacked the strength to hold it. At the end of the first week of December, the Red Army launched a major counteroffensive that pushed back the German forces from Moscow. It was the first major setback the Germans had suffered, and it brought to an end the dream of a swift conclusion to the war.

The consequences of this were historic. As with almost every German military adventure to date, the invasion of the Soviet Union was a gamble. In order to create the army required for the assault, the German economy had been stripped of manpower, and Hitler had hoped that the resultant problems would only be temporary and would swiftly be alleviated by the rapid demobilisation of troops that were no longer needed in the east. Regardless of the views of Jäger and others who were determined to eliminate all the Jews, the killing of the remaining Jewish population of Lithuania and elsewhere would only make the workforce problems worse.

Similarly, the Germans had treated Soviet prisoners of war with a mixture of casual brutality and neglect, with hundreds of thousands being left to starve or to die of wounds and exposure in open-air compounds. There was now a sudden realisation that these men might be useful as workers, and although the conditions in which the Soviet prisoners were kept improved only marginally – the death rate remained many times greater than that of British or French prisoners of war – some of the prisoners were assigned to work parties in German factories and farms.

Another consequence of the failure to achieve a decisive victory against the Soviet Union in 1941 was that Heydrich's and Himmler's plans for the elimination of all of Europe's Jews were significantly affected. A number of different options had been considered over the years, all of which would have resulted in the deaths of millions of people; once the invasion of the Soviet Union began, the intention had been to move European Jews east where they would literally be worked to death constructing new roads and railways. One such project had already begun. Some ideologues in the Nazi Party had identified Crimea, on limited evidence, as being the original homeland of the Gothic tribes. As these crank ideologues saw the Goths as being the ancestors of modern Germans, there were plans to turn Crimea into a major cultural and leisure centre for the German Reich, and construction of a highway from Germany to Crimea was commenced, running through Ukraine. However, further construction projects would have to wait until the defeat of the Soviet Union, not least because of the burgeoning partisan movement across large areas that had been occupied by the Germans.

Heydrich and Himmler therefore moved on to other options to eliminate the Jews in German-held territory. The experience of the opening months of *Barbarossa* suggested that mass shootings were not a sustainable method. Aside from the considerable cost in terms of ammunition, there were repeated complaints that many German soldiers, particularly those with young families, found the task stressful and repellent. It is worth mentioning that the German officers who protested about the effect that the shootings had on their men did not express any sympathy for their victims. Himmler's main concern after personally attending a mass execution of Jews in Minsk in August 1941 was that such events might create large numbers of hardened, sadistic killers who would later be a problem for Germany.[36]

Nonetheless, in their determination to prove to Hitler that only the SS could be entrusted with the racial reshaping of the new territories of the east, Himmler and Heydrich remained determined to exterminate as many Jews as possible even before the end of the war. As early as mid-July, Rolf Heinz Höppner, a German official working in occupied Poland, suggested the use of poison gas to kill Jews not fit for work, and Gruppenführer Arthur Nebe, commander of *Einsatzgruppe B* in the central sector of the Eastern Front, made further suggestions about the use of gas a few weeks later. Acting on these suggestions, Heydrich ordered Walter Rauff, the head of technical services in the RSHA, to undertake detailed investigations.

Rauff's normal work included overseeing the substantial pool of motor vehicles used by the RSHA and he ordered experiments to be held at Sachsenhausen concentration camp in October 1941. A van was modified so that the exhaust was diverted into the cargo compartment, and the vehicle was loaded with 40 Soviet prisoners of war. The experiment was deemed to be a success and about 30 such vehicles were deployed, but they proved to be inefficient. Death through carbon monoxide poisoning was often slow, and the victims' struggles to get out of the vans caused as much distress to German personnel as shootings; moreover, the removal of gassed corpses from the vans was laborious and time-consuming.

As a result, there was greater interest in the use of *Zyklon B*, a cyanide-releasing agent. The first tests were carried out in Auschwitz in September and, like Rauff's experiments in Sachsenhausen, involved Soviet prisoners of war. It should be noted that these experiments occurred during the autumn, when it still seemed likely that the war in the Soviet Union would be over in a relatively short time – regardless of the plans to work the Jews to death in the east, Heydrich was keen to explore alternatives, even if only to deal with Jews who were deemed incapable of heavy work.

To date, mass killings of Jews had been restricted to the occupied parts of the Soviet Union, and Hitler had been unwilling to take such steps against the Jews of Germany and Western Europe. By the end of 1941, the mood changed. The entry of the USA into the war seemed to confirm Hitler's belief in a worldwide anti-German conspiracy of

Jews and he authorised the deportation of Jews from the Reich to the territories of the east, where they could be killed. Goebbels wrote in his diary about Hitler's views after a dinner in Berlin that was attended by senior Nazi Party members:

> The Führer has decided to make a clean sweep. He prophesied to the Jews that, if they ever started a world war again, it would result in their annihilation. This was no mere sophistry. The world war is upon us; the extermination of the Jews must be the necessary result. This question should be viewed without any sentimentality. We are not here to sympathise with the Jews but to sympathise with the German people. With the German people once more sacrificing 160,000 dead in the eastern campaign, the original instigators of this bloody conflict must pay for it with their lives.[37]

The reality was that with the actions of the *Einsatzgruppen* in the Baltic region, Belarus and Ukraine, the Nazi approach to the 'Jewish problem' had already moved on to mass extermination.

On 20 January 1942, as the Soviet counteroffensive to the west of Moscow ground to a halt and the war looked likely to drag on for an unforeseeable length of time, Heydrich held a meeting of 14 senior Nazi Party figures and SS personnel in a villa on the shores of Lake Wannsee. Although the meeting, later known as the Wannsee Conference, came to symbolise the adoption of mass gassing of Jews, the invitations for the meeting were actually issued the preceding November and given the extensive experimentation with poison gas in the last weeks of 1941, the conference was more the conclusion of the decision-making process than its starting point. It was also part of the process by which Heydrich tried to establish supremacy in dealing with the Jews of Europe, and he pointedly stressed that Goering had given him this task, regardless of geographical boundaries. He then outlined the history of Germany's attempts to deal with the 'Jewish problem'. He stressed that all of Europe contained about 11 million Jews, and that any solution had to be able to deal with this total – however effective the *Einsatzgruppen* might have been, their approach was completely inadequate compared to the scale of the task that lay ahead.

The proposal that Heydrich offered the conference was that the Jews would be moved east in stages, with many either dying during the process or ultimately being sent to the new extermination camps that were being built to use *Zyklon B*. Two of the men present, representing the civil administration of occupied Poland, pointed out that their territory contained large numbers of Jews who were unfit for work, and that preparatory measures – i.e. the construction of extermination camps – should proceed in this region immediately. These camps could then be used as other Jews were moved east, rather than moving them from one ghetto to another. Heydrich readily agreed, and after an inconclusive discussion about the status of people with mixed Jewish/Gentile parentage, the meeting came to a close after just 90 minutes.

Many further decisions remained ahead before the full-scale industrialised killing of Europe's Jews could begin, and it would be wrong to regard the Wannsee Conference as a decisive moment in the implementation of the Holocaust; but it was nonetheless another step. The murder of tens of thousands by gunshot was to be replaced by more economic means of slaughter, which would be less stressful for the perpetrators.

In Vilnius, Hermann Adler, Mordechai Tenenbaum and Schmid discussed a new suggestion: if the Jews could reach the Baltic coast, would it be possible for them to cross to safety in Sweden? The proposal was that Schmid would take a group of Jews to the Latvian port of Liepāja, where they would steal a fishing boat and would cross to the Swedish island of Gotland. This would involve a voyage of about 100 miles (162km) across the Baltic in winter; given that few if any Jews in Vilnius had any maritime experience, the scheme was dropped as too risky. Instead, the three men agreed to concentrate on the trips across the border into Belarus.

Throughout January 1942, Schmid continued to transport small groups of Jews to the nearby towns of Belarus, hoping that they stood a better chance of survival there. One of those who travelled to the town of Lida was a petty criminal who was arrested by the local security forces in Belarus and charged with attempting to break into a church to steal valuables. In an attempt to save himself, the would-be burglar revealed how he had been able to travel to Lida from Vilnius; despite this, he was executed shortly after. But the authorities were now aware of Schmid's activity, and at the end of January 1942, just a few days after Heydrich's conference in Wannsee, during one of his trips to Belarus, Schmid was arrested by the *Geheime Feldpolizei*.

6

The Prices to Be Paid

Schmid had taken precautions against being intercepted during his trips to Belarus and routinely used military telephones at his destination to call back to the *Versprengten-Sammelstelle* – to any German authorities who were listening, it would have seemed like an innocuous call to his office, but its purpose was to reassure Luisa Emaitisaite and the others that all was well. When no such call took place, the Jews in the *Versprengten-Sammelstelle* realised that something had happened. The Adlers joined a work party returning to the ghetto and passed a warning to Tenenbaum and others to stay away from Schmid's offices.

In the meantime, Emaitisaite and Salinger did what they could to destroy evidence in the *Versprengten-Sammelstelle*. There were numerous false identity documents and valuable items – the latter had been left there for safe keeping by some of the Jews that Schmid had helped – and at least some of these items were later discovered when the military authorities searched the building. Both Emaitisaite and Salinger used their false identities to good effect, disappearing almost completely in the days that followed.

The precise details of the circumstances in which Schmid was arrested are not clear. In addition to the story of the interrogation of the Jew who attempted to rob a church, Adler later heard that Schmid had been drunk whilst in Belarus and was overheard talking about his activities; another version of events was that two soldiers, Havel and Krause, who worked with Schmid, had informed the authorities of his actions. Unfortunately, the documentation relating to his arrest has not survived and the records from his court martial are also fragmentary, making reconstruction of events very difficult – some of these accounts that Adler discovered were probably little more than speculative gossip. He was held in military custody and would have faced interrogation at the hands of the *Geheime*

Feldpolizei. There is nothing to suggest that he betrayed the Adlers, Salinger, Emaitisaite or any of the others he had saved.

The court martial took place under the authority of the Wehrmacht field command in Vilnius. Many years later, Hermann Adler met a priest, Fritz Kropp, who saw Schmid at the time; this appears to be the only witness to the events of the trial to have been interviewed. From Kropp and other fragmentary sources, Adler was able to discover that the prosecutor in the court martial was Wolfgang Lotheisen, who Kropp described as being a sober, dutiful individual but not a fanatical Nazi. The military lawyer appointed to put forward Schmid's defence was, by contrast, a longstanding member of the Nazi Party. It seems that the defending lawyer attempted to justify Schmid's activities on the grounds that he had been acting to preserve the lives of valuable workers for the Wehrmacht, but during his court martial Schmid refused to accept this argument. He told the presiding officers that he had helped the Jews purely out of humanitarian motivation, and that he had loathed the manner in which the Jews were persecuted and killed.

Had Schmid accepted the defence that his lawyer wished to follow, it seems likely that he would have escaped with perhaps no more than a prison sentence; some soldiers were sent to penal battalions in the front line, but Schmid was too old for such an assignment, and he would probably have been released after a short period of detention. Instead, by rejecting this argument and declaring his hostility to the persecution of the Jews, Schmid must have known that he was placing himself in great danger. On 25 February, the court announced its verdict: he was guilty, and was sentenced to death. An appeal for clemency was rejected shortly after.

Two letters from Schmid to his wife Stefanie, written during his court martial, have survived, and from these it seems that when the court found him guilty and sentenced him to death, he was surprised by the outcome. They provide a small glimpse into his thoughts at the time. The letter of 9 April has survived only as an incomplete copy, and it is possible that there were errors in its transcription. Sections of it are difficult to unravel and understand:

> My dear Steffi
> Thank you for your two letters, which I received yesterday. It gladdens me that you, my love, are healthy and all is well with you.
>
> Today I can tell you of the fate that has been assigned to me, but I ask one thing: remain strong when you read on, as sadly I have been sentenced to death by a court martial in Vilnius, which I had never expected. But several of my comrades had already received

the same sentence and I wanted to spare you the news and didn't want either of you [referring to his daughter Gertha] to think that I didn't want to return to you, so I waited until it was too late and I can't be saved. It's war and in a nutshell, you'll hear more one day about how the court martial passed its verdict, but there's nothing that can be done to secure a pardon, which I did try to get, but was turned down.

But hold your head high, my love, I have come to terms with it and fate wishes it so. It is decided for us by our dear God above, and can't be altered. Today I feel more calm than I ever could have believed, but our dear God has willed it so and made me so strong, and I hope that He will make you as strong as me.

I want to tell you all that happened: there were many Jews here who were rounded up by the Lithuanian military and shot in a meadow outside the city, as many as 2,000 to 3,000 people. They smashed the children against trees along the road. Can you imagine? I had to take over the *Versprengten-Sammelstelle*, which I didn't want to do, where 140 Jews worked, and they asked me to take them away from there ... So I let myself be persuaded, you know already about me and my big heart – I couldn't think about it and helped them, which the court decided was wrong.

Believe me, my dear Steffi and Gertha, it is a severe blow for all of us, but please, please forgive me. I have only behaved like a human being and didn't want to do harm to anyone.

When you have this letter in your hands, my love, I will no longer be on this earth, and will not be able to write to you again, but it is certain that we will see each other once again in a better world with our dear God. I wrote an earlier letter on 1 April or perhaps earlier and enclosed the photograph of Gertha, which you will receive soon. I'm giving this to my priest. There are six men in my room, aged between 17 and 23, who face the same as me. Desertion and cowardice in the face of the enemy – those were their charges. And the Jews too are the enemy – so it seems ...[1]

Some aspects of this extraordinary letter are of particular historical interest. Schmid's reference to the 'Lithuanian military' is accurate in that most of the manpower used in the persecution and murder of the Jews was provided by local paramilitary and police units, but he would have been aware that German police battalions were also involved, and that the entire process was overseen by the Germans. Furthermore, his memories of the events in Białystok would still have been fresh – the killings that took place there were carried out entirely by the Germans themselves. It is possible, even likely, that his wording in the letter was deliberate, in that had he described the full degree of German involvement and oversight, the military censors would have deleted that part of his letter, or prevented it from being sent to his wife altogether. His description of the execution ground as an open meadow is also incorrect; Ponary was in a forested region. This suggests that he did not personally visit the killing ground. And whilst '2,000 to 3,000 people' may be a correct figure for a single day, the total of those executed was far higher. Again, the Jews he was helping – particularly Adler, Tenenbaum and others involved in the resistance – would have provided him with a more realistic estimate, but to include that in his letter would have risked the intervention of the censors.

On 13 April, Schmid wrote a final letter to Steffi:

> My dear Steffi
> Thinking of you in joy and sorrow, I will tell you everything – today judgement will be carried out on me and I must leave this world, and am sentenced to death. Please remain strong and believe in our dear God who decides the fate of everyone. I can't change anything now, or I would have spared you and Gertha everything. So I ask you to forgive me, I most certainly didn't mean to cause you this pain, but sadly there is no other choice. I am ready to die as God wills it so and his will be done. You have to come to terms with that. Please forget once more the pain that I am causing you, my dear ones, and say no more about it. All I did was save people, even if they were Jews, until my fate caught up with me, and that was my death. So just as I did everything for others during my life, so too I sacrificed everything for others. You will learn everything else when a comrade of mine visits you and explains how the court passed its judgement. Please also read the first four letters you have received and you will see that I wanted things to be different …
>
> Please forget me, my love, it's just how it is, fate has willed it so. Now I write my last lines to you and send my hugs and kisses to you both, my everything in this world and the next, where I will soon be by God's side, once again with my eternal love,
>
> Toni[2]

As the morning light spread across Vilnius on 13 April, Feldwebel Anton Schmid was taken from his cell and executed by firing squad. His body was allegedly interred in an unmarked grave in the military cemetery in the city, but its precise location has been impossible to determine. The six men with whom he had shared his cell were also executed the same day.

Fritz Kopp, the German Catholic priest who attended Schmid during his last days, wrote a letter to Steffi two days later:

> Dear Mrs Schmid
> I am fulfilling my sad duty by sending you the last words written by your dear man. On Monday 13 April, he had to depart from this world. I was with him in his last moments to offer him spiritual support. Once more, he accepted the Holy Sacrament and remained strong to the very end. His last words were the Lord's Prayer, which I spoke with him. His final concern and his last wish was that you too should remain strong and faithful. I too close with the hope that you trust in the hope of seeing him again before God and that you will travel your difficult road through life with strength and courage, believing in God's providence. Your husband's grave is in the 1914-1918 military cemetery in Vilnius, in the Anatol district.[3]

One can only wonder at the emotions that Steffi Schmid and her daughter must have experienced, receiving these letters several days after the execution had already taken place. Inevitably, news of the court martial, its verdict and the execution reached Vienna by a variety of routes, and several local people hurled stones at the Schmid residence, breaking several windows. Graffiti was daubed on the walls, but Steffi and Gertha Schmid remained in the apartment throughout the war and continued their lives. It is likely that other neighbours were more sympathetic to them, and they would have relied on that sympathy in the years that followed. As part of its judgement, the military court would have declared Schmid as being unworthy of military service, meaning that he was no longer regarded as a serving soldier. Consequently, his family would not have been entitled to any of the normal measures of financial support available to those who had lost loved ones in the war.

Anton Schmid was just 41 years old when he was executed. Throughout his life, he was a devout Catholic, but perhaps even more importantly in both peace and war he remained true to his immensely strong belief in his duty to his fellow human beings, regardless of their religion. From the testimony of Hermann Adler and others, it is clear that he knew that his actions would result in severe punishment, but he repeatedly took considerable risks to save Jews from persecution and death. His moral strength and integrity shine out in a time and location where there was so much suffering, persecution and death.

In Schmid's words, fate in the form of death caught up with him, but it was also catching up with others involved in the persecution of the Jews. After leading the headquarters of *Einsatzgruppe A* through Kaunas and on to Riga, Franz Walter Stahlecker and his men moved on to the north in the wake of the Wehrmacht. As early as 18 July, they crossed the old frontier between Estonia and Russia and reached Pskov; although the Red Army was reported to be making powerful counterattacks from the east against the flank of the German forces, the daily report from Müller stated that the capture of Leningrad – referred to in German documents of the time as Petersburg – might be imminent, perhaps in just three to five days:

> The deployment of the Security Police with Hoepner's panzer group, which is advancing on Petersburg, has been agreed in discussions between the Ic [general staff officer with responsibility for intelligence on enemy forces and intentions], the chief of staff and Generaloberst Hoepner. As a result, the leading elements of the spearhead division have been briefed according to a plan drawn up by the Security Police. As the leading elements of *Einsatzkommando 1a* and *Einsatzkommando 1b* can't be spared by Sixteenth and Eighteenth Armies, *Einsatzgruppe A* has moved all spare personnel from *Einsatzkommando 2* and *Einsatzkommando 3* in Kaunas and Riga to Pskov in preparation for the march on Petersburg. From here they are being assigned to the [leading] divisions.[4]

Five days later, Stahlecker and his headquarters moved on to Novoselye, about 28 miles (45km) to the northeast. It seems that there were discussions about replacing Stahlecker as commander of *Einsatzgruppe A*, for reasons that aren't clear; it is likely that Heydrich wished to assign him to new, higher commands rather than wanting to remove him for any perceived failure. At this stage of the war, *Einsatzgruppe A* was the most deadly of the *Einsatzgruppen* deployed on the Eastern Front, and its performance was unquestionable. Obergruppenführer Kurt Daleuge, head of the German uniformed police, sent a brief message to Heydrich on 24 July, recommending that Stahlecker should remain in post until Leningrad had been captured and 'cleansed', not least because he seemed to have such a good working relationship with the Wehrmacht.[5]

The swift capture of the former imperial Russian capital failed to happen as Müller and others had so confidently predicted, and Stahlecker remained near Pskov. By the second week of August, with Soviet resistance growing, the German Army Group North was struggling to concentrate sufficient troops to overrun the remaining Red Army units that continued to hold out in northern Estonia whilst pursuing its drive towards Leningrad to the east of Lake Peipus. There were also increasing problems with partisan activity in the rear of the Wehrmacht divisions, especially where they were operating within Russia itself rather than the Baltic States, which had only been incorporated into the Soviet Union a few months before the German invasion. The swampy and forested plains to the east of Lake Peipus, through which Army Group North was attempting to march, provided plenty of cover for Red Army stragglers and others who took up arms against the Germans. Müller's report of 10 August stressed the importance of the problem, and the measures that were being taken:

> It is completely impossible to comb through the forests with the troops available. Effective countermeasures can only be taken by extensive intelligence work and sharp terror tactics against the population of the countryside in which the partisans operate, so that as a consequence of this terror the population will denounce the partisans.
>
> For Army Group North, the war against the partisans as well as overall tactical command is particularly difficult because of the pronounced double nature of the front line to the north in Estonia and east of Lake Peipus ... The deployment of the Security Police is very difficult due to being dispersed on a front from Pernau [on the Baltic coast just north of the Latvian-Estonian frontier] to Sebezh [just within the old frontier of Russia, to the east of southern Latvia].[6]

Attempting to subdue the partisan movement by terrorising the local population was a policy that the Germans used consistently throughout the war and on most fronts. Whilst it may have resulted in some short-term gains, it also alienated many civilians who might otherwise have been inclined to amity towards the Germans. But confident of a swift victory, Stahlecker and his men carried out wide sweeps through the countryside, attacking and destroying villages that they suspected of harbouring partisans, Jews, Red Army stragglers, or any other opponents. At the same time, the partisans also put pressure on the local people to cooperate and to provide them with food and shelter. Some people may have helped either side willingly, but others did so out of fear.

In addition to killing partisans and terrorising civilians, *Einsatzgruppe A* was also responsible for dealing with groups of Soviet personnel who had deliberately been left behind by the retreating Red Army to carry out acts of sabotage, known to the Germans as *Vernichtungsbataillone* ('destruction battalions'). In the last days of July, the Wehrmacht captured about 250 of the personnel of these units in central Estonia and handed them over to Stahlecker's men; they promptly executed 210 of them. But despite all of Stahlecker's efforts, the partisan movement continued to increase its activity. On 16 August, a partisan group attacked German positions close to the headquarters of *Einsatzgruppe A*, killing two men.

As the Red Army was levered out of northern Estonia, many senior officers in the Wehrmacht began to consider what they should do when they reached Leningrad – it seems astonishing that such matters had not been discussed and concluded long before. On 9 September, Wagner – the quartermaster-general of the German Army – wrote to his wife: 'First we will have to let them stew in Petersburg, what can we do with a city of 3.5 million who will just be a drain on our food resources? There is no room for sentimentality.'[7]

Georg von Küchler, commander of Eighteenth Army, which was expected to take control of Leningrad, issued instructions that all of the Jewish population of the city was to be placed at the disposal of the SD, and informed his quartermaster that there was no need to take any measures for the supply of food to the civilian population. With the Wehrmacht increasingly stretched and the panzer divisions – without which rapid advances were almost impossible – being diverted to the south, it became increasingly clear that even if the capture of the city was a desirable objective, it was unlikely to happen in the near future. In October, Hitler issued new instructions: 'The Führer has decided that the surrender of Leningrad will not be accepted, even if offered by the other side … therefore no German soldier is to enter this city. Anyone who tries to leave the city towards our lines is to be driven back by gunfire.'[8]

The decision seems to have been driven by a wish not to take responsibility for feeding such a large population – the German plans for the conquered territories had always intended to eliminate most of the Soviet urban populations as 'useless mouths' in order to create the agricultural surpluses required to feed Germany. Slowly, the formations of Army Group North drew closer to Leningrad, but all talk of its swift conquest was gone. In early September, Stahlecker moved his headquarters to Kikerino, just 41 miles (66km) to the southwest of the centre of Leningrad.

The partisans continued to disrupt activity behind German lines; on 17 September, *Einsatzgruppe A* reported that many roads were attacked almost every night and that the constant disruption of rail traffic by the destruction of bridges or derailments of trains was causing severe supply difficulties. In order to try to suppress the partisans, Stahlecker and Ernst Busch, commander of Sixteenth Army, organised a major operation involving Stahlecker's *Sonderkommando 1b* and several companies of Wehrmacht troops. Stahlecker regarded the operation as a great success, with several partisans killed in combat and several more hanged in nearby towns and villages to deter others, but within days the partisans had resumed their operations. Just a week later, Stahlecker reported that there were constant battles between his teams and the partisans, in which the Germans usually emerged the winners, though at a cost. He added that as they moved through the area, they took the opportunity to 'cleanse fully' any towns of Jews as the opportunity arose.

In mid-October, *Einsatzgruppe A* moved its headquarters to the town of Gatchina, known at that time as Krasnogvardeisk, just 25 miles (42km) from central Leningrad. Instead of pressing on to capture the city, the Wehrmacht had taken up siege positions with the intention of starving the population and garrison; if the city were to fall to the Germans, the intention now was to drive any survivors away to the east rather than take on the burden of feeding them. The process of 'pacification' of the area behind the front line continued to rely on brutal measures: 'Unreliable elements [of the local population] who stand in the way of pacification of the area, were separated and taken to military or civilian prison camps, or by the *Einsatzkommando*. Between 2 and 12 October a total of 260 persons were executed.'[9]

Three weeks later, Stahlecker reported that following the capture of the town of Strelna, on the Baltic coast just outside Leningrad, his personnel arrested all local citizens who were deemed to be a danger to the German occupation; after 'partial confessions', they were all executed. Further repressive measures were reported on 21 November:

> In screening in Krasnoye Selo between 18 and 28 October, 70 suspects were detained and interrogated. Seven were identified as members of partisan groups and members of the Communist Party, and of being involved in acts of sabotage and were executed after confessing. The rest of the detained persons were released. The mayor and some of his helpers who had been appointed by the area commander were found to be politically unsuitable. After agreement with the area commander they were dismissed, and in view of their previous activity on behalf of the Communist Party, two were executed. In total between 24 October and 5 November 118 persons were executed, including 31 who were active enemy agents. Further executions took place after a few cases of unrest, refusal to work, and sabotage ... There was a major act of sabotage in Tosno where a sawmill, where construction material for five German divisions was being prepared, was burned down on 25 October ... Investigations revealed that it was due to arson, which was possible due to inadequate security. As a retaliatory measure, 13 hostages who had previously been specified as being held against acts of

sabotage were shot in the presence of community representatives at the scene of the sabotage.[10]

With the Leningrad front line now almost static, Stahlecker was able to release personnel for action elsewhere on the Eastern Front, but he continued to claim 'credit' for their activities. For example, in addition to the execution of a total of 855 people in a 'special action' in the Leningrad sector on 20 November, he also reported that *Sonderkommando 1b*, transferred to Minsk, killed 6,624 Jews between 7 and 11 November. As was almost always the case, these killings in Minsk might have been overseen by German personnel but were carried out mainly by their auxiliaries, on this occasion made up of Ukrainian nationalist volunteers. In a report sent to Heydrich at the end of January 1942, Stahlecker proudly summarised the activity of his *Einsatzgruppe A* since the beginning of the invasion of the Soviet Union. Its actions against the Jews were particularly highlighted, claiming 41,828 victims in Belarus, 136,421 in Lithuania, 35,238 in Latvia, 963 in Estonia – it had a far smaller Jewish population than its southern neighbours, and as it took the Germans longer to reach this area, there was more time for the Jews to flee to the east – and 3,600 in the territory between the Estonian frontier and Leningrad, a total of 218,050 men, women and children. Estonia, he informed Heydrich, was completely *Judenfrei* ('free of Jews'). In February, he declared the total of people killed by his men – Jews, Communists, partisans and others – as 240,410.

Despite the repeated actions to detain or kill all suspected partisans and their supporters, the level of activity against German forces in the rear zones continued to cause great difficulties. After each massacre that was carried out by Stahlecker's men – often with the assistance of the Wehrmacht – partisan attacks would decline in that area for a short time, only to rise again shortly after. It was fitting that partisan activity proved to be Stahlecker's nemesis. On 22 March 1942, a group of partisans opened fire on the headquarters of *Einsatzgruppe A* in Krasnogvardeisk. Stahlecker was hit in the thigh by a bullet and was immediately taken to a local field hospital, where it was confirmed that the femoral artery had been damaged. He was promptly transferred by plane to Riga, where he underwent surgery. He was thought to be out of danger and was put on a flight to Prague, where he could recover from his wound in the care of his family, but the bleeding from his femoral artery either restarted during the flight or hadn't been controlled properly before his departure from Riga, and he bled out before reaching his destination.

Stahlecker was in many respects the epitome of the senior SS figure that Himmler and Heydrich had wanted in their organisations. He was highly educated and politically dedicated to the Nazi Party, and showed great energy in executing its racial policies when his *Einsatzgruppe A* was unleashed on the people of the Baltic States and Soviet Union, but it would be wrong to describe him as a fanatic; he was a sober, purposeful, and efficient senior officer who used the considerable freedom assigned to him to carry out his orders with murderous thoroughness. Heydrich read a eulogy at his funeral, which was attended by numerous dignitaries, and both Hitler and Himmler sent wreaths. He was the most senior figure in the *Einsatzgruppen* to be killed to date and the manner of his death demonstrated the limitations of German policies with regard to partisans.

Stahlecker's replacement as commander of *Einsatzgruppe A* was Brigadeführer Heinz Jost. Like so many of the young men selected by Himmler and Heydrich, he was too young for service in the First World War and was involved in politics from a young age, becoming a prominent figure in the *Jungdeutsche Orden*, a nationalistic youth movement. He studied law and economics in Giessen and Munich and joined the Nazi Party in 1928, and in 1933, after Hitler came to power, he became director of police first in Worms, then in Giessen. At this stage in his career, he came to know Werner Best, who recruited him into the ranks of the SD. The two men worked closely together, and Jost was made responsible for creating a department within the SD to monitor foreign intelligence. He was formally appointed head of this department in 1936 and remained in post during the reorganisation of the SD into the overall structure of the RSHA.

Best and Heydrich had been close allies for many years, but in early 1939 a rift began to develop between them. While Heydrich wanted to reorganise the police and security services to ensure that they were under the tight control of politically suitable individuals who were committed to Nazi ideology, Best repeatedly proposed a reorganisation that would have given supremacy to the legally trained personnel who had always been at the top of the police hierarchy. Perhaps at least partly because of his association with Best, Jost became the focus of Heydrich's attention. After the war with the Soviet Union had started, Heydrich ordered Brigadeführer Walter Schellenberg, one of his close associates, to investigate the functioning of Jost's department with the intention of dismissing him. Schellenberg was an ambitious officer who had high hopes of replacing Jost and was unsparing in his criticism; he informed Heydrich that the department was inefficient, largely due to Jost's inability to control it. He portrayed Jost as lazy and lacking in motivation, putting in only short appearances in his office and largely leaving matters in the hands of his subordinates.[11] In August, Jost was dismissed. His replacement, inevitably, was Schellenberg.

This might have been the end of Jost's career in the SD, but a few months later he was appointed as Stahlecker's replacement. After the war, Jost would claim that this appointment was a punishment; Heydrich, Jost maintained, regarded him as having a soft disposition and assured him that he would have a purely administrative role as head of *Einsatzgruppe A* and could avoid any personal involvement in killings. Regardless of the truth of these assertions, Jost now found himself dispatched to the east.

Soon after taking up his new post, Jost met Karl Jäger. His assessment of Jäger is striking. Pre-war descriptions of Jäger repeatedly described him as a strong, handsome, impressive figure, but Jost's opinion was very different:

> [He was] an older, straightforward, simple personality, with the appearance of a bully but soft on the inside ... [Jäger said during a discussion one evening] he couldn't get to sleep and saw only dead women and children ... he couldn't face going home as he too had children and grandchildren. Overall he seemed a lost man, in need either of a rest home, or leave, as he couldn't find any peace.[12]

After a long separation from his first wife, Jäger finally secured a divorce in early 1940, and just two months later he married a second time. His second wife was Lotte Schlienkamp, who was 24 years younger than him. The experiences of commanding *Einsatzkommando 3* in Lithuania had a profound effect on Jäger and upon both his new marriage and his relationship with the children of his first marriage, as Jost further described on another occasion:

> During a meeting with Jäger in Riga at the beginning of my appointment he confessed his inner feelings and his troubled conscience. He told me that he couldn't sleep when he thought about the shootings in which he had taken part. He felt constantly haunted by ghosts and as a consequence he couldn't face his wife with a clean conscience, and found it impossible to sit his grandchildren on his lap.[13]

Whilst there had been concern in German circles about the psychological impact of the killings on German personnel, this was the first occasion that such a senior figure had expressed such feelings. With most of the personnel of *Einsatzkommando 3* now deployed elsewhere, Jäger's current post was as Commander of Security Police and SD in Lithuania, and the mass killings of 'surplus' Jews in 1941 meant that such activities were, for the moment, greatly reduced. It isn't clear at what stage Jäger began to experience such nightmares and disturbed sleep, but the assessment of some of his juniors – that he was obsessed with his reports and tallies of dead, and left much of the functioning of his unit to his subordinates – may suggest that he was troubled by what he had witnessed and ordered, but it is noteworthy that at no point did he take any steps to reduce the scale of killings. Rather, he continued to send detailed reports as if to prove to his superiors – and, perhaps, to himself – that he had the inner mental strength to carry out such tasks. The longstanding feeling that he was constantly being judged because of his age may also have played a part in his determination to see matters through, regardless of his nightmares and disturbed sleep.

In addition to Anton Schmid, fate caught up with several others who had been heavily involved in protecting the Jews of Lithuania. The SD had been monitoring the activities of the Catholic clergy with growing interest for several months and in March 1942 they carried out a series of arrests. Although this coincided with the period that Schmid was being held and presumably interrogated by the *Geheime Feldpolizei*, there is no evidence that he implicated any of those who had assisted him; rather, the arrests were based upon intelligence that the SD had obtained from its surveillance activities.

Andrzej Gdowski, who had helped Schmid secure identity documents for Luisa Emaitisaite and had helped many other Jews, was one of those who were arrested. Together with all of the other Carmelite monks in Ostra Brama, he was incarcerated in Lukiškės Prison, but the Germans were unable to bring him to trial – it seems that they had no firm evidence against him. Nonetheless, he remained in captivity for the duration of the war. After a period in Lukiškės Prison, the monks were moved to prison camps near Kaunas, from where they were eventually released by the Red Army in 1944. Father Gdowski returned to his church of St Teresa of Avila, but the monastery of Ostra Brama was converted into a hospital. Troubled by deteriorating health, Father Gdowski remained an active priest until he died in 1948, aged 78.

The nuns who had hidden a number of members of the Jewish resistance were also at risk of being arrested. Increasingly distressed and angered by what she saw and learned about the persecution and killing of the Jews, Mother Anna Borkowska moved from simply providing shelter and refuge to assisting the resistance. One of those sheltering in the convent was Abba Kovner. To date, Kovner had tried to instigate resistance amongst the Jews in the ghetto, and in early 1942 he – and perhaps others – authored a leaflet that was circulated amongst the inmates, entitled *Lamir Nisht Gefirt Vern vi Shaf tsu der Shkhith!* ('Let us not be led as sheep to the slaughter!'):

> Jewish youth, do not trust those who lead you astray. Of the 80,000 Jews of the 'Jerusalem of Lithuania', only 20,000 survive. Our parents, brothers, and sisters were torn away before our eyes.
>
> Where are the hundreds of men abducted for work by the Lithuanian kidnappers?
>
> Where are the naked women and children, who were taken from us on the night of the horror of provocation?
>
> Where are the Jews of Yom Kippur?
>
> Where are our brothers from the other ghetto?
>
> Everyone who was taken out of the ghetto gates never returned.
>
> All of the Gestapo's roads lead to Ponary, and Ponary is death!
>
> Those of you who hesitate, throw away any illusions you have. Your children, husbands, and wives are no more.
>
> Ponary is not a camp – everyone was shot there.
>
> Hitler plans to exterminate all the Jews of Europe. Lithuanian Jews were just the first in line.
>
> Do not go like sheep to the slaughter!
>
> It is true, we are weak and defenceless, but the only answer to the enemy is resistance!
>
> Brothers and sisters! It is better to fall as free warriors than to live at the mercy of murders!
>
> Defend yourselves to the last breath![14]

Whilst the manifesto was greeted with much scepticism in the ghetto – it is perhaps natural that many preferred to hope that their loved ones were still alive – this was the first occasion that an attempt was made to inform Jews that the Germans planned their extermination. But if resistance to the Germans was to become a reality, the Jews needed weapons, as Abraham Sutzkever, another of the Jews in the convent, knew:

> The fighters needed arms and the Mother Superior undertook to supply them. Assisted by the other nuns, she roamed the countryside in search of knives, daggers, bayonets, pistols, guns, and grenades ... The first four grenades received gratefully by the fighters were the gift of the Mother Superior, who instructed Abba Kovner in their proper use, as they were of a special type unfamiliar to him. She later supplied other weapons. Although she worked selflessly, tirelessly, she felt that not enough was being done.

> 'I wish to come to the ghetto,' she said to Abba Kovner, 'to fight by your side, to die if necessary. Your fight is a holy one. You are a noble people. Despite the fact that you are a Marxist and have no religion, you are closer to God than I.[15]

Kovner and the others dissuaded Mother Anna from such an attempt, partly to spare her from such a risky venture but also on the pragmatic grounds that she was far more useful to their movement as a civilian. Reluctantly, she agreed. Kovner and the other Jews returned to the ghetto, but they remained in contact with the convent, where Jewish refugees and occasional members of the resistance movement continued to find shelter when they needed it.

In an attempt to put aside their pre-war differences and unite against the common foe, members of the Jewish youth movements and older political activists created a new body in late January 1942 entitled *Fareinikte Partisaner Organizatzie* ('United Partisan Organisation', or *FPO*). The overall leader was Itzhak Witenberg, a Communist, and it had two battalions, one headed by Kovner and the other by Joseph Glatzman. In addition to representing different parts of the various Jewish groups, these men had other advantages – Glatzman was a member of the ghetto police and was thus able to obtain useful information. An intelligence unit of the *FPO* was also formed to help gather information, and a small *FPO* group was created within the accommodation of the *Kailis* leather factory. But the ambitions of the resistance fighters extended far beyond Vilnius. In early 1942, Haika Grossman travelled from Vilnius to Białystok and thence to Warsaw, where the Jews lived in the largest ghetto of all in terms of population – about 400,000 people squeezed into just three square kilometres of urban space. Her intention was to encourage the other ghettoes to adopt similar policies, for all the disparate factions to unite and oppose the Germans. She had a mixed reception; many of the Jews in the Warsaw ghetto believed that they were simply too numerous for the Germans to attempt mass killings, and that armed resistance would merely risk antagonising a dangerous enemy. Nevertheless, she was able to return to Vilnius with a modest sum of donations that could be used to purchase more weapons.

A second delegation was sent to Białystok and Warsaw in April, equipped with written testimony from people who had survived the killings in Ponary. Two sisters, Sara and Ruzhka Zilber, were accompanied by Shlomo Antin; they reached Białystok safely and spent three days in the ghetto, but when they attempted to travel on to Warsaw, they were arrested in a routine document check in the railway station of Malkinia, midway between the two cities. They were taken to Pawiak Prison in Warsaw, where they were executed a few weeks later.[16]

In addition to trying to establish a network of Jewish resistance groups in the ghettoes of major cities, the *FPO* also tried to contact other anti-German groups. The rival pre-war claims to the Vilnius region complicated matters a great deal. The most effective resistance group was the Polish *Armia Krajowa* ('Home Army' or *AK*), which was formally created in February 1942 from pre-existing resistance groups and was loyal to the Polish government-in-exile in London, but the *AK* units in the Vilnius region were markedly anti-Jewish in their outlook, persisting in the view that large numbers of Jews had cooperated with the Soviet authorities in 1940. At about the same time as the formation of the *AK*, a pro-Communist movement arose under the name of *Zwiazek Walki Czynnej* ('Union for Active Struggle', or *ZWC*), made up largely of Poles. At first, this group had no links with the Soviet Union and it became an active partner of the *FPO*. As the year progressed, pro-Soviet partisan groups began to appear, many of them equipped by the Soviet Union and possessing radios through which they maintained contact with Soviet authorities.

In an attempt to avoid lengthy discussions via intermediates, the *FPO* decided to send couriers directly to the Soviet Union. Two female members, Sonia Madeysker and Cesia Rosenberg, were given false documents and were to travel east where they would attempt to cross the front lines near the city of Velikiye Luki with the aid of pro-Soviet partisans and would then travel on to Moscow with the intention of publicising the slaughter of Jews in Vilnius and Kaunas. When they approached the front line, the two women were detained by a German patrol; fortunately, their Jewish identity remained concealed, and they were dispatched back to Vilnius, where they succeeded in slipping away from their guards.

For the Jews working in Plagge's *HKP 562*, conditions remained bearable – the additional food supplied on Plagge's orders allowed the workers to divert some of the rations given to them in the ghetto to their families. Early in 1942, the newly promoted Gefreiter (corporal) Alfons von Deschwanden joined the unit. He was aged 19 and had trained as a car mechanic in Germany before being conscripted into the Wehrmacht. Deschwanden came from a Catholic family and his father was openly opposed to the Nazis; through family and church contacts, the young Gefreiter was aware of some of the persecution of Jews being carried out by the Germans all across Europe, but he learned of the full horror of what was happening when he was posted to *HKP 562*. Here, he worked in a store for spare parts and had about 24 Jewish workers assigned to him, and they told him of the killings at Ponary and elsewhere. Although he didn't meet Plagge until later, Deschwanden was aware of the prevailing mood in *HKP 562* and he regularly accompanied his workers on their return to the ghetto, seeking to vouch for them at the gates – as a result, they were less likely to be searched. It was one of many small acts of kindness performed by personnel in *HKP 562* that helped alleviate the ordeal of the Jews working in the camp.

Another German who joined *HKP 562* in 1942 was Oberleutnant Alfred Stumpff, who had grown up close to Plagge's hometown of Darmstadt. He had known of Plagge before the war, but only distantly, as an older student in his school. He later described how Plagge ensured that all personnel in the unit treated the Jews with consideration:

> One day, by chance I saw how a Feldwebel in *HKP 562* from Wiesbaden, who was very proud of his civilian membership of the SS, threatened a Jewish worker and stamped on his leg. When I promptly spoke to the Feldwebel about this, he justified himself that the Jew had lied to him and made the usual National Socialist comments that the Jews were our enemies and didn't deserve protection. When I made a sharp reproach that it was unworthy of a soldier to assault a defenceless person and that he should perhaps request a front-line assignment, he reminded me again of his SS membership and made veiled threats that he would report me to them. I reported the incident to Plagge, who reprimanded the Feldwebel in the sharpest manner and immediately removed him from any activity in which he could come into contact with the Jewish workers and even gave him official papers to assign him to the front, which is what I believe happened.[17]

There were glimmers of hope for those living in the Vilnius ghetto. Towards the end of winter in early 1942, Mascha Rolnikaite experienced something quite new:

> Last night was something to celebrate: an air raid.
>
> We were already asleep when a large explosion suddenly set the plates rattling. We leaped up in alarm, thinking that the ghetto was being blown up. Then there was another crash. Someone shouted, 'Bombs!'
>
> Hurrah! They're going to liberate us! But Mama was a very sober person. She said that the Germans wouldn't be brought to their knees by a single air raid. Fine, they would get even more bombs thrown at them. That was what everyone thought.

> Gens and his policemen were beside themselves – if they saw anyone with a lit cigarette at a window, they promptly threw stones at them. Bombs exploded, plates were shattered, policemen blew whistles – a complete uproar.
>
> It was still once again. The planes flew into the distance and we were once more alone, locked in the ghetto, in the jaws of the enemy.[18]

One bomb landed within the ghetto. The following day, Hauptsturmführer Rudolf Neugebauer, head of the Gestapo in Vilnius, appeared in the ghetto offices raging that two flares had allegedly been fired into the sky from the ghetto to signal to the Soviet bombers. In a manner that became characteristic of his behaviour, he informed the *Judenrat* that he had no intention of trying to seek out those responsible. Instead, he regarded all of the Jews as being collectively responsible and threatened to set the entire ghetto ablaze if there were any recurrence.

The air raid was a clear demonstration that the Soviet Union was far from beaten, but little more than that. Despite their setback at the gates of Moscow, the Germans remained unchallenged in their control of most of Europe, but other signs of resistance were also appearing, and one such act of defiance proved to be a suitable nemesis for the man who was responsible for so much of the suffering of the Jews.

In addition to his numerous duties within the German security apparatus, Reinhard Heydrich was appointed Acting Reich Protector of Bohemia and Moravia at the end of September 1941. The Protectorate was largely what is now the Czech Republic, with a population of a little under eight million people. Of these, fewer than a quarter of a million were ethnic Germans. It was the intention of the Nazis ultimately to turn the Protectorate into a part of Germany, but before this could happen, the Slav population would have to be eliminated; they would either have to leave the region, or if they were deemed racially suitable they would be permitted to become Germans. However, this population engineering would have to wait until the end of the war. Until then, a government with strictly limited powers was in office in Prague, headed by President Emil Hácha, but effectively under the control of the Germans.

Heydrich's predecessor as Reich Protector was Konstantin von Neurath, a professional diplomat. Hitler dismissed him as foreign minister in 1938, replacing him with the more politically reliable Joachim von Ribbentrop. Although he was known as an urbane and experienced politician, Neurath applied strict controls to the Czech press; he also enacted the full panoply of Germany's anti-Jewish laws, but he was relatively lax in their implementation. In the last quarter of 1941, Prague, Brno and other major industrial areas – all of which were essential to the German war effort – were gripped by a wave of strikes and other industrial action, at a time when Hitler was increasingly minded to bring forward his plans for removing all Jews from Central Europe. He therefore summoned Neurath, Heydrich and Karl Frank, the Higher SS and Police Leader in the Protectorate, to his headquarters in East Prussia, and informed Neurath that he was being sent on indefinite sick leave. Heydrich would run affairs in Prague in his place.

This appointment coincided with Hitler telling his inner circle that the three major cities of the Reich – Berlin, Vienna and Prague – would be the first to be made *Judenfrei*. The appointment of Heydrich, who had organised the *Einsatzgruppen* that were destroying the Jewish population in the western parts of the Soviet Union, was therefore particularly appropriate. Immediately, Heydrich moved to deal with the pressing matter of industrial unrest and growing resistance. There were large-scale arrests and summary executions, and within a few weeks the reign of terror brought an uneasy peace to the region.

In Britain, there were increasingly elaborate plans to encourage and support resistance networks across Europe, with many of these activities taking place under the aegis of the newly created Special Operations Executive (SOE). Discussions about a possible assassination of Heydrich began almost immediately after his appointment, under the codename *Anthropoid*; he was widely seen as the iron hand behind Himmler, and his death would greatly reduce the power of Himmler in upper circles. There were concerns – completely justified, as events demonstrated – that such an assassination would lead to terrible reprisals, but the cold-blooded calculation was that any such German atrocities would merely encourage people to oppose the Germans. In late December 1941, A British bomber carrying nine parachutists set off to deliver the assassination team and two other teams that would work with the resistance to improve coordination and communication with the government in exile in London.

All the members of the team were Czech volunteers, and they rapidly made contact with sympathetic locals after the parachute drop. Two of the parachutists, Josef Gabčík and Jan Kubiš, then began careful planning for the assassination attempt, trying to identify a suitable location for an ambush. Alfréd Bartoš, the leader of one of the communications teams, was doubtful that the operation could proceed, given the widespread repression that Heydrich had unleashed. He was particularly concerned about the consequences of any attempt, and when he discovered that the assassination attempt was proceeding despite his requests that it be cancelled, he made his concerns clear to his controllers in London in a signal in May 1942:

> Judging by the preparations which Ota and Zdenek [the codenames for the two assassins] are making ... we assume in spite of the silence they are maintaining that they are planning to assassinate 'H'. This assassination would in no way benefit the Allies and might have incalculable consequences for our nation. It would not only endanger our hostages and political prisoners, but also cost thousands of other lives. It would expose the nation to unparalleled consequences ... We therefore ask that you issue instructions ... for the assassination to be cancelled.[19]

This signal was actually intercepted and decoded by the Gestapo, but – presumably on the basis that it looked as if an operation was being cancelled, and because of the success of the widespread repressive measures taken by Heydrich – no action was taken.

On 27 May, Heydrich was to travel to meet Hitler in Berlin. He planned to describe the successful measures that he had taken to restore order in the Protectorate and would use the opportunity to discuss how such measures – under the control of the SS, and thus furthering the influence of Himmler and Heydrich – might be applied against resistance movements elsewhere in occupied Europe. Accompanied only by his driver, Heydrich left his home in mid-morning. The assassins were aware of Heydrich's travel plans and had identified a hairpin bend where Heydrich's car would have to slow. They positioned themselves for an attack and waited.

Confident of the measures that he had taken to suppress dissent, Heydrich routinely travelled without an escort. As his car decelerated for the hairpin bend, Gabčík stepped out of cover and pointed a submachine-gun at the vehicle. But when he pulled the trigger, the weapon jammed without firing a single shot. Seeing the lone assassin, Heydrich ordered his driver to stop and stepped out of the open topped car, drawing his pistol to deal with Gabčík. At the same moment, Kubiš threw a bomb at the car from the opposite direction. The bomb exploded by the rear wheel of the car. Kubiš was injured by shrapnel and reeled away, grabbing a bicycle to make his escape.

Heydrich stepped forward towards Gabčík, but the bomb explosion had showered his back with shrapnel. One piece, which included bits of horsehair from the stuffing of the car's upholstery, penetrated into his abdominal cavity and angled upwards, rupturing his liver and diaphragm. As his lungs deflated, he suddenly collapsed. Gabčík fled, and people rushed to help the injured Heydrich. He was bundled into a baker's van and driven to a nearby hospital, where the extent of his injuries became clearer. Despite being in great pain, Heydrich refused to allow the Czech surgeons to operate and insisted that a specialist be flown from Berlin. Time was of the essence, and reluctantly he agreed to allow a senior surgeon from the German Surgical Clinic in Prague to carry out the vital surgery.

Although Heydrich had been badly wounded, his life did not appear to be in danger, but a furious Hitler demanded immediate reprisals. Frank, the local police commander, was ordered to commence executions of Czech civilians – Hitler wanted 10,000 to be killed, and Himmler ordered that 100 should be executed every day. Frank was certain that such measures would result in huge unrest in the Protectorate and immediately flew to Berlin to suggest less severe measures. At first, Hitler refused, insisting that the Czechs had to learn that such acts would result in terrible reprisals, but eventually Frank was able to persuade the Führer that concentrating on capturing the attackers should take priority.

When Himmler visited him in hospital on 31 May he was satisfied that Heydrich was recovering. But the surgeons who had treated Heydrich failed to remove all of the contaminating material from his abdominal cavity and an infection developed. It would have been a relatively simple matter to treat such a problem with antibiotics, but the Germans had no access to any such drugs (and nor did most). Early on 4 June, he died after several hours of great pain.

Eventually, the two attackers and other resistance fighters took refuge in an Eastern Orthodox church in Prague. In return for a substantial reward, a member of the resistance betrayed their location and the SS moved against the church. A gun battle continued for two hours; ultimately, the last surviving members of the resistance group shot themselves rather than allow the Germans to capture them.

The death of Heydrich was a huge blow to Himmler. Stahlecker's death had been marked by an elaborate funeral in Prague, but it was nothing in comparison to the ceremony that took place after Heydrich's death; in addition to a major service in Prague, there was a second ceremony in Berlin. Goebbels and the Propaganda Ministry portrayed Heydrich as an ideal Nazi, the epitome of both the Party and of Germany. Hitler gave a brief eulogy to Heydrich at his funeral:

> I have only a few words. He was one of the best National Socialists, one of the strongest defenders of the idea of the German Reich, one of the biggest enemies of all the foes of the Reich. He is a martyr. He died for the preservation and protection of the Reich. As leader of

> the party and as leader of the German Reich, I award you, my dear comrade Heydrich, the highest award that I give you: the Supreme grade of the German Order.[20]

Himmler spoke at greater length. He told those gathered that the National Socialist movement had made a tragic sacrifice and had lost a 'shining, great man' of 'unique abilities and pure character'. He described how 'sub-humans, such as Jews and assorted criminals' had feared and hated him, but that he had devoted himself to solving all the racial problems of the German people. Heydrich had been incorruptible and had put aside his personal sentiments in order to do his duty, placing great importance on teaching 'National Socialist morals' and showing great personal strength and determination. Heydrich's memory would continue to inspire his fellow Germans through the trials that lay ahead and he would be a model to the personnel of the security police and the SD. Himmler urged officers of the SS to regard Heydrich and other senior SS figures who had been killed during the war as role models, and to repay their deaths by devoting themselves to their duties. He listed the other senior figures who had died: Stahlecker, Fritz Weitzel (head of SS and police in Norway, killed in a British air raid on Düsseldorf in 1940); Paul Moder (head of SS and police in Warsaw with responsibility for the security of the Warsaw ghetto, transferred to the Eastern Front in 1941 after taking unauthorised leave, killed in action in February 1942); and Arthur Mülverstedt (commander of the infantry division *SS-Polizei*, made up of former police officers, killed in action in August 1941). He concluded with the words:

> But it is our holy duty to atone for his death, to take up his tasks, and pitilessly to destroy, without any sign of weakness, the enemies of our people. I have one last thing to say: You, Reinhard Heydrich, were truly a good SS man. On a more personal level I thank you for your unwavering loyalty and wonderful friendship, which united us in this life and cannot be obliterated by death![21]

Whilst Hitler may have agreed to concentrate on catching the perpetrators of the attack, the issue of reprisals was never far from German thoughts. There were widespread arrests of suspected resistance fighters and their supporters throughout the Protectorate; by 4 June, 157 people had already been executed.[22] Many of those detained, imprisoned or killed were innocent, but a large proportion of the resistance movement was eliminated. As a consequence, there was little active resistance against Nazi rule for most of what remained of the war.

Reprisals were not restricted to operations directly aimed at the resistance. Horst Böhme, head of the Security Police and SD in the Protectorate, contacted Himmler on the day of the funeral to inform him that the killers had been sheltered by people in the village of Lidice. Himmler passed this information to Hitler, who issued instructions via Frank: Lidice was to cease to exist. All male villagers were to be executed and the women sent to concentration camps; children who were deemed as potentially 'Germanisable' were to be given to German foster-parents.

The grounds for regarding Lidice as guilty of collusion with Heydrich's killers were weak at best. A Czech agent who was parachuted into the Protectorate in late 1941 was captured by the Gestapo shortly after, and during interrogation said that two families in the village had been his intended contacts. Members of both families had fled to Britain before the war, and the Gestapo was therefore already suspicious about their loyalties. Fifteen members of the two families were arrested almost immediately after Heydrich died, and on 10 June German police units surrounded the entire village. The men were separated from the women and taken in small groups to the farm where one of the two suspected families had lived and worked, where they were shot. By the early afternoon, 172 males aged 14 or more were dead. Even before the executions ended, the Germans had commenced the physical destruction of the village, setting fire to all the buildings and then dynamiting or bulldozing the ruins. Even the dead were not spared – the village cemetery was excavated and the remains of those who had been interred were destroyed. All of the animals in the village, livestock and pets, were also killed. Several men from the village, who were working night shifts in nearby factories, were rounded up in the days that followed and executed.

The 203 women in Lidice were held in the village school for three days. Four pregnant women were dispatched to the hospital where Heydrich had been treated before he died, where they were forced to undergo abortions. All of the women were then sent to concentration camps, primarily Ravensbrück, where they were used for hard physical labour; 53 died before the end of the war. A total of 105 children were first kept in the same school as the women and were then sent to an empty clothing factory in Łódź for screening. Only seven were selected for Germanisation. The rest were transferred to the custody of the local Gestapo office, which was under the control of Sturmbannführer Otto Bradfisch. Prior to taking up his role in Łódź, Bradfisch had led *Einsatzkommando 8*, part of *Einsatzgruppe B* in the central sector of the Eastern Front, where he and his men were responsible for the slaughter of thousands of Jews, suspected Communists and others. He ordered the children being held in the clothing factory to be sent to the concentration camp in Chełmno, where most of them were gassed in the modified vans that had been discussed at the Wannsee Conference the previous winter. Six of the eight who had been selected for Germanisation died in orphanages during the war, and only 17 children survived.

The reprisals resulted in over 1,300 people being killed. As a result of the discussions in Wannsee, the extermination of the Jewish population of the General Government – the region of Poland around Warsaw that lay to the east and south of the Polish territories that had been incorporated into the Reich – was gradually gathering pace by the summer of 1942, and this was now renamed 'Operation Reinhard', a final appalling tribute to the man who had assumed responsibility for implementing Germany's policies of racial purity. The three camps involved in 'Operation Reinhard' – Belzec, Sobibor and Treblinka – were the scenes of the deaths of over 1.5 million people by the end of 1943.

However horrific these figures might be, matters could have been worse. Hitler had vowed to deport millions of Slavs from the Czech lands as part of his reprisals, and many of them would have perished either in the concentration camps to the east or through starvation in the conquered territories of the Soviet Union. But the industrial demands of Germany made such a policy impossible – indeed, the seizure of the Sudetenland and the territory that became the Protectorate was driven by the German desire to take control of Czech armaments factories. With varying degrees of reluctance, Hitler and others postponed the ethnic cleansing of the Protectorate until the successful conclusion of the war.

There can be no doubt that Heydrich was ultimately responsible for the deaths of hundreds of thousands of innocent people. His men carried out his orders in Austria, the Sudetenland, Poland, the western parts of the Soviet Union, and the Protectorate of Bohemia and Moravia, competing to earn their chief's accolades for their murderous activities. Had he survived the war, he would unquestionably have been prosecuted alongside other Nazi leaders, and the weight of evidence against him was so great that conviction would have been a certainty, with the death penalty waiting for him at the end of the process. He died at a time when the Wehrmacht appeared to be triumphant once more in the east and before the impact of the United States had been felt to any major extent in Europe; for him, the defeat experienced by the Germans outside Moscow the previous winter were merely an inconvenient setback on the road to ultimate German victory. By the time that such a victory was achieved, he expected to have established the credentials of the SS as the undisputed means of delivering the population changes required for fulfilment of the Nazi nightmare.

Heydrich's wife Lina was pregnant at the time of Heydrich's death and gave birth to their fourth child – a daughter – on 23 July. She and the children, accompanied by Heydrich's mother Elizabeth, then moved into an estate that was donated to the family by Hitler, located in a village known to the Germans as Jungfern-Breschan and the Czechs as Panenské Břežany, immediately to the north of Prague. Himmler assigned a workforce of 30 Jewish labourers to the estate, and true to her longstanding anti-Semitic views and the career of her late husband, Lina treated them with contempt, abusing them physically and verbally.[23] Her personal losses continued in the years that followed. Her eldest son Klaus – he was 12 years old at the time – cycled out of the gates of the estate into the path of a small truck, which struck him. He died later that day. Lina Heydrich demanded that the driver and the other occupants of the truck be shot, but an investigation into the incident concluded that they were completely blameless. It is remarkable that – at a time when so many thousands of people who were equally innocent of any wrongdoing were being killed by the men who had served under Heydrich's authority – the occupants of the truck were freed without any action being taken against them.[24]

Near Kaunas, Jehoved Čartokaitė's carefree life in the country estate of her new friend Jonas Saunoris came to an end in the summer of 1942. In July, she was recognised by a woman from Kaunas. After a discussion with Saunoris, Čartokaitė decided that it was no longer safe for her to remain on the estate. Fortunately, she encountered Jurgis Inčiūria, a young man who had been interned by the Germans because he was a member of the Komsomol. He was perhaps fortunate not to be executed immediately, and in December 1941 he was released from captivity because of overcrowding but was required to report weekly to the local police. He returned home to find that his family's house had been destroyed by a bomb and his mother was in a nearby hospital – several members of his family were dead, and his sister had been taken away by the Germans and shot. He moved to the countryside, where he was joined by his mother after she recovered, and he worked as a hired farmworker. With him, Čartokaitė found sanctuary and ultimately married Inčiūria, and they had a daughter in 1943. They named her Halina, after Jurgis Inčiūria's sister, who had been killed by the Germans. That year, Inčiūria joined the growing anti-German partisan movement, and the family was finally liberated in 1944 by the arrival of the Red Army. Throughout her life, Jehoved Čartokaitė was haunted by guilt that she had abandoned her family in the ghetto.

7
Ghetto Life and Death

For the Jews living in the ghettos of Kaunas and Vilnius, life became quieter in 1942. The attempt by Jäger and others to proceed with the complete extermination of the Jews of Lithuania regardless of economic or other considerations was opposed by both the civil and military authorities, whose activities were – for the moment at least – regarded as more important than the pursuit of Nazi racial policies. Jäger had already expressed his frustration at what he saw as the obstructive attitudes of others in his report of 1 December 1941. Most of the original personnel of *Einsatzkommando 3* had been moved away from Lithuania, and the mass killings that were such a terrible feature of the second half of 1942 were no longer taking place. In his role as commander of the security police and SD, he found that he had little to fill his time – the meticulous reports that he had written in the preceding months were no longer needed, given the greatly reduced rate of killing, and for the moment at least the region was relatively quiet. He continued to languish in his post until the end of 1943.

As the large-scale 'actions' to reduce the population of the ghetto came to an end late in 1941, the *Judenrat* in Kaunas decided that the Jews stood a better chance of survival if they could make themselves useful to the German occupation forces. In addition to the workers who went out from the ghetto every day to labour at the airfield at Aleksotas, several dozen other groups also found work in different parts of Kaunas. The treatment of Jews in these groups varied, and workers in the 'better' groups were regarded with envy by many of their fellow inmates. But the efforts of the *Judenrat* concentrated on the creation of workshops within the ghetto itself. These were set up after negotiation with the German civil administration and expanded steadily, ultimately employing nearly 4,000 Jews. The work carried out by the workshops varied. Some activity involved carpentry, basket weaving, and other light industry, but a few of the workshops had a particularly harrowing task: they processed the clothing that had been gathered when Jews being taken for execution were forced to strip. Perhaps the greatest benefit for workers in these workshops was that there were no German or Lithuanian overseers present, but unlike workers who went out of the ghetto every day, there was no opportunity to engage in illicit trading with local people for food.

In Vilnius, the approach of spring brought with it renewed fears for the ghetto inmates. The 'yellow permits' that had been the source of so much anxiety and desperation the previous autumn were due to expire at the end of March, and there was widespread nervous discussion about what would happen. Would new passes be issued, perhaps in more restricted quantities? As unrest grew, Jacob Gens, head of the ghetto police, issued a warning notice: 'For circulating inaccurate reports and provoking a mood of panic among inhabitants, I punished two residents in the ghetto on 3 January 1942. I hereby announce that all who are convicted of the same offence will be punished with the utmost severity of the law.'[1]

When the fateful day came, the ghetto police insisted that all workers leave the ghetto for their workplaces as usual. Their dependants waited for their return that evening with a mixture of emotions. The optimists believed that the surviving Jews constituted a workforce that was too valuable to the Germans for further mass killings, but there had been too many such assurances before. In the evening, the workers returned without incident, but few slept that night, fearing that there might still be a major 'action'. Within days, new permits were issued with no expiry date. For once, the optimists were correct, but the respite for the Jews in Vilnius and Kaunas was at the expense of others.

In late January, Himmler had issued instructions to the *Reichskommissariat* heads in the Baltic region and Ukraine demanding the complete annihilation of the Jewish population, but Lohse decided that instead of pursuing this task in an indiscriminate manner, attention would focus for the moment on the ghettos in Belarus, which had not undergone the massive purges that had reduced the population of the Vilnius and Kaunas ghettos the preceding autumn. He could thus appear to be complying with Himmler's order, whilst at the same time not raising too many protests from other authorities that were demanding the retention of their workforce. For the moment, the surviving Jews in Lithuania were regarded as essential workers and the killing was focussed on the 'surplus' Jewish populations elsewhere.

A further development that indirectly gave the Jews a reprieve was an edict from Berlin that workers were to be sent from Poland and the occupied parts of the Soviet Union to Germany as compulsory labour in order to deal with the workforce shortages in German industry. The rather imprecise plans of the Nazi regime had been that this shortage of workers would only be temporary and would rapidly be alleviated by demobilisation of a victorious Wehrmacht once the Soviet Union had been defeated, but there was little sign of such demobilisation being possible by early 1942 – even if the Red Army was defeated, Germany was now at war with the United States, and it would have to reorganise its forces to deal with the threat.

Tens of thousands of civilians were forced to move to Germany where they worked in harsh conditions with severe punishments for minor infringements. Their pay was minimal, and although some were forced to write letters to their families portraying their lives in Germany in a positive manner, there was widespread resistance and resentment of this conscription, resulting in many people of working age fleeing into the forests to avoid being dispatched to Germany. Ultimately, many of these people then joined the growing partisan movement. But the forcible recruitment of labour and the increasing flight into the forests created severe worker shortages across the entire occupied region. The demands of Jäger, Himmler and others that the Wehrmacht and the civil occupation authorities should accelerate their training of non-Jewish workers so that the Jews could be killed became almost impossible to implement. In any case, the Jewish workers were paid such a small amount that replacing them with Poles, Lithuanians and others would be costly, even if the training expenses of the new workers were ignored.

The Vilnius ghetto had a smaller system of internal workshops than in Kaunas, but the number of workers grew steadily through 1942. By July, 1,393 people were employed in these workshops or for the *Judenrat* and ghetto police; by the end of the year, the total was 1,897.[2] Despite the repeated 'actions', Murer found himself facing a strange fact: the population of the Vilnius ghetto actually seemed to be growing. In February, there were a fraction under 14,500 ration cards circulating, but two months later this had risen to 18,500. Murer's initial reaction was that this was merely an attempt by the Jews to exaggerate the number of inmates so that they could secure more rations, but the reality was that the growing number reflected those who had remained hidden during the 'actions' of late 1941. In addition, some Jews who had been in hiding outside the ghetto now sought entry, joining work columns as they returned to the gates at the end of each day – it might have been safer to remain in hiding in the city during the repeated 'actions' in the ghetto, but now that those had ceased, the risk of being caught and promptly executed whilst living illegally outside the ghetto was greater than becoming an inmate.

In addition, several work camps near Vilnius were closed and their populations transferred to the ghetto. For the moment, Murer grudgingly accepted the increased number – the workshops in the ghetto and the workers who laboured at other locations were increasingly productive and financially lucrative. This was an important factor for the *Gebietskommissariat*. In addition to the small wages paid to Jewish labourers, those employing them had to pay an amount to Hingst's office. It was estimated that the result of this was an income of about half a million Reichsmarks per month.

In other ways the ghettos in Vilnius and Kaunas functioned similarly. The *Judenrat* in both ghettos took considerable precautions to ensure cleanliness and thus reduce the risk of disease. This was more than just a sensible precaution in an overcrowded environment; the Germans were almost paranoid about the outbreak of infectious disease within prison camps, concentration camps and ghettos. When such an outbreak occurred in Belarus in late 1941 with several prisoners developing typhus, the Germans imposed a strict lockdown and isolation of the camp, with the result that almost no food entered, exacerbating pre-existing near-starvation and increasing the death rate dramatically. Whenever an inmate contracted an infectious disease, they were treated covertly, either in their place of residence – which carried the considerable risk of onward transmission in such a crowded environment – or in the ghetto hospitals under a non-infectious diagnosis. If the Germans became aware of such a case, the person was immediately taken away and executed.

Bathhouses were organised in the ghettos, with a strictly enforced rota for attendance. Schools were set up for the numerous children, but these were relatively short-lived. There was a sweep through the Kaunas ghetto in February 1942 to seize books, which greatly hampered teaching. This was followed by orders in August 1942 stating that all the schools in the ghettos were to close. In many cases, teaching continued in a covert manner.

Other activities were also organised in the ghettos. Amongst the numerous possessions that the Jews had brought with them from their homes were musical instruments, and many of these were subsequently traded with local people in exchange for food. But within the Kaunas and Vilnius ghettos, there were sufficient instruments left to create small orchestras. In Kaunas, the orchestra consisted of 35 musicians and five singers; they first performed in the summer of 1942 and ultimately gave about 80 concerts. Many of the performances, particularly at first, featured songs and music of mourning for those who had been killed, but after a while a distinct pattern evolved. Each concert would commence with songs of pain and suffering, but the mood would gradually lighten with concluding pieces expressing hope for a better, brighter future.

The Vilnius ghetto's orchestra was organised somewhat earlier and gave its first performance in January 1942. Memories of the terrible slaughter of the closing months of 1941 were still raw, and most of the music and songs concentrated on mourning and loss. Despite being almost destitute, the audience paid small amounts for their tickets, and the *Judenrat* used this money for welfare activities in the ghetto. Some of the music that was performed was written in captivity – one song was composed by a resistance fighter named Hirsch Glick, with the title *Zog nit keynmol az du geyst dem letstn veg* ('Never say that you are walking the final road'). Glick was a poet from his teenage years onwards and was only 21 when the Germans invaded the Soviet Union. At first he fled into the forests and joined the partisans, only to be captured in one of the many German sweeps – he was fortunate not to be executed immediately. His song was written largely while he was working as a peat-cutter in the Rzeza work camp:

Never say that you are walking the final road
Though leaden skies obscure blue days;
The hour we have been longing for will still come,
Our steps will drum – we are here!
From green palm-land to distant land of snow
We arrive with our pain, with our sorrow,
And where a spurt of blood has fallen
There will sprout our strength, our courage.
The morning sun will tinge our today with gold
And yesterday will vanish with the enemy,
But if the sun and the dawn are delayed –
Like a watchword this song will go from generation to generation.
This song is written with blood and not with lead,
It's not a song about a bird that is free,
A people, between falling walls
Sang this song with pistols in their hands.
So never say that you are walking the final road
Though leaden skies obscure blue days,
The hour we have been longing for will still come –
Our steps will drum – we are here![3]

Resistance workers who moved from ghetto to ghetto spread the song to other cities, and it was widely known and sung by the end of the war.

But the performances were not met with universal acclaim. Some groups within the ghetto, such as the *Bund*, which had been a Jewish socialist political group in Poland before the war, demanded a boycott of all concerts on the grounds that 'theatrical performances should not be held in cemeteries,' but the uplifting effect of the performances on morale was undeniable and they became increasingly popular as time passed.

The authorities in the Kaunas ghetto – the *Judenrat* and the ghetto police – largely cooperated and worked in harmony, though the *Judenrat* was more popular in the eyes of the ghetto inhabitants than the police force. One ghetto resident later described the attitude towards the police, who were despised for their cooperation with the Germans and the extra rations they received as a consequence:

> We didn't want to have anything to do with members of the police ... To meet up with one of them could only mean trouble. We suffered from the blows and kicks of the police and being dragged out of our homes into one working brigade or another, not knowing if we would return. This is why we felt so bitter as we watched the Jewish police living well while we did the back-breaking labour ... we saw them working hand in hand with the Germans.[4]

But despite having to enforce the policies of the German authorities, the Jewish police in Kaunas attempted to remain distinctly Jewish in its identity and loyalty. In November 1942, the police personnel assembled to swear an oath of loyalty to the *Judenrat* and then marched through the ghetto, singing patriotic Jewish songs. Many of those who watched them pass joined in as they sang.

By contrast, the Jewish authorities in Vilnius often clashed. The head of the *Judenrat*, Anatol Fried, was not well known in the local Jewish community and had little respect from either the Jews or the Germans, despite his considerable and largely successful efforts to organise life within the ghetto. He had little by way of leadership experience, in contrast to Jacob Gens, the leader of the police. In early April 1942, Fried felt it necessary to write to Gens to complain about several areas of friction. Firewood was a commodity that was always in short supply and one of Gens's officers unilaterally issued instructions that effectively permitted the ghetto police to secure what others regarded as more than their fair share:

> I must express my astonishment at a directive which is liable to put askew all the order which has been introduced into the ghetto with such great effort, especially since it affects the heating problem. This

> directive is liable to destroy all existing discipline ... To prevent this in the future, I will ask you to issue appropriate instructions to the police personnel subordinate to you that, in all cases pertaining to the economy of the ghetto, they turn only to the *Judenrat*.[5]

The Germans were happy to exploit the friction between the two men, and Murer published a set of directives towards the end of April 1942 that effectively ensured the ascendancy of Gens and his police force. All orders of the *Gebietskommissar* would be implemented with the help of the Jewish police – there was no mention of any role for the *Judenrat*. Workers were to organise themselves into 'brigades' based on their place of work, and it would be the responsibility of each 'brigadier' or leader of the brigade to enforce the ban on smuggling food into the ghetto – many of the directives dealt specifically with the restriction of food supply and how it was to be enforced, showing that whilst the mass killings might have stopped, Murer and the German authorities intended to ensure that the Jews remained poorly fed. The new directives added that any food provided by employers of Jewish labour, including the Wehrmacht, was not permitted. These employers were warned that the provision of such food or other goods would be investigated, with possible severe repercussions: 'Jews, work column leaders and the Jewish police will in future face the death penalty if they disobey the instructions of the *Gebietskommissar* of Vilnius [Hingst].'[6]

The consequence of this was a stark choice: the Jews could either risk death by smuggling in food, or face slow starvation. Despite these strict injunctions, smuggling continued almost unchecked. Many workers had specially modified clothing with hidden compartments, and some of the ghetto police were willing to ignore orders for rigorous searches, often in return for a bribe. Ada Gens later described how her father had unofficial meetings with the 'brigadiers' in charge of each work brigade; he would tell them how many people were going to be searched and importantly, the sequence that was to be used on any one day – for example, he would tell them that every third or fourth person entering the gates would not be searched, so the brigadiers would then ensure that these individuals carried hidden food whilst the others didn't.

Although the ghetto police had orders to enforce the ban on smuggling food, Murer often played a personal role, if only to check that his orders were being followed. Mascha Rolnikaite was now old enough to join one of the work brigades, and in her diary, she recorded an occasion when she and her brigade returned to the ghetto:

> As we returned from work today, it was quiet at the gate. Suddenly there was a tumult – the ghetto police began to drive away the

people who were waiting for their relatives at the barrier and suppressed any disquiet. What was happening?

Murer showed up at the gate! He stood at the entrance and watched with disapproval how the police on gate duty carried out their task. If something displeased him, he took over personally. He found 20 pfennigs on one woman (we were meant to have only ten pfennigs with us). He ordered her to be brought to the guardhouse by the gate, and to be stripped and given 25 lashes with a stick. Five policemen beat her. Each of them gave her five lashes. But the sadistic Murer wasn't satisfied yet. He personally took hold of the stick. He beat the woman half to death before he finally left her alone and went back to the gate. The sadistic monster now had a taste for it and sought new victims.

He noticed that an old man had something under his jacket. It was a small pot full of soup. Murer ordered him immediately to drink all the soup on the spot. If that wasn't enough for him, said Murer, he was to eat until he burst. The man began to eat. But it wasn't easy for him: the kind fellow who had given him the soup had already fed him well. The soup was intended for his family. Murer threatened to send him to Ponary if he didn't lick the container clean. The man choked but swallowed it all.

Finally Murer was satisfied and simply said 'To the left' if he found something on anyone. His helpers took them to the prison. People had to risk death to bring a small piece of bread in for their children.[7]

Ada Gens lived outside the ghetto with her non-Jewish mother. Although many people within the ghetto knew their identity, they were able to evade detection by the Germans, even though they often visited the ghetto and spent considerable time there. In the months that followed the establishment of the ghetto, Ada and her mother often passed the ghetto gates and would check if Murer was present; Ada would then attempt to pass this information on to the returning work columns, which would detour into nearby alleys and discard items of food that they had intended to smuggle. In an attempt to counter this, Murer took to intercepting work columns some distance from the ghetto, which also gave him an opportunity to enforce another strict rule: Jews were not permitted to speak to non-Jews without express permission. Tova Rajzman and her sister Chaja were members of a work column during the summer of 1942:

We were about 40 or 50 people, on our way to work, when a car drove up to us and Murer climbed out. Murer shouted, 'Stand still!'

> and summoned the column leader. He struck him. The column leader's name was Abramowicz. Murer asked him what a Jewish woman had said to a Polish woman, as the Jewish woman who I didn't know had left the group and had spoken to a Polish woman. Abramowicz told Murer that the woman had asked for bread and firewood. Murer told Abramowicz to summon the woman. The woman asked Murer to let her keep the bread for her children. Murer went wild and said to her, 'Just come with me, I'll soon give you bread for your children!' Straight after this he shot the woman, who fell to the ground. Murer was very angry and went up to the group and said that if this happened again he would have all of us shot. Then he fired into the group and hit three women and a man. Their names were Chaja Pilowska – my sister Chaja, Eva Luna, Chaja Brujda. I didn't know the man or the woman that Murer had shot first.[8]

The outbursts of rage by Murer alternated with days when he seemed remarkably calm, almost another person. Ada Gens's father had a theory about this:

> Papa used to talk about Murer. He was of the impression that Murer was a drug addict. He said that there were days when you could talk to him like talking to a normal person, and there were days when he went berserk – you couldn't talk to him. He thought the withdrawal symptoms when he didn't have drugs were the main reason [for his behaviour] when he was so inhuman ... He said it's impossible to have the same person behave ... [so] erratically. Papa was suspicious that he was under the influence of drugs. He could compare Murer with the others, and nobody behaved like Murer. Nobody. He was the single person with that bestiality.[9]

Many of those who were arrested during the searches at the ghetto gates were later executed, but some were more fortunate. On several occasions, either Gens or other Jewish police officials were able to negotiate their release. The presence of soldiers from workplaces like *HKP 562*, who accompanied their workers back to the ghetto and prevented such events when they could, were thus particularly important. But some members of the ghetto police showed little sympathy for their fellow Jews. The head of the ghetto police section that guarded the gate was Meir Levas, and he was widely detested for the ruthless manner in which he attempted to enforce Murer's edicts. The last of several directives issued by Murer on 29 April specifically stated that any Jews, brigadiers or Jewish police who violated the orders regarding food smuggling faced the death penalty, but there were many occasions when instead of confiscating food and handing it over to Murer, Levas's gate police simply kept it for themselves.

Despite appearing to enforce the rules, Gens often acted to undermine them. Food that was confiscated at the gate was often returned quietly to the would-be smuggler later that evening, and Gens oversaw an extensive operation to smuggle food into the ghetto in large quantities, hidden in a variety of vehicles and other items, even in coffins. At some points of the ghetto perimeter, the boundary ran through a building, and hidden routes through the loft space were created for goods to be smuggled in. Sufficient food and drink – even alcohol – was brought into the ghetto to organise a number of restaurants for those who had the means to pay; in the summer of 1942, after Murer intercepted a shipment of alcohol, Gens ordered his police to close many of the restaurants.[10]

The situation in Kaunas was somewhat better, as Avraham Gollub recorded in his diary at the end of July 1942:

> Lately, the ghetto inmates have been somewhat relieved of concern over the food supply. The guards at the entrance gate have not been very strict. The Germans received an order to leave the control of the entrance gate to the Lithuanians, whereas the Germans are required to oversee them and refrain from taking anything for themselves. Seeing the indifference of the Germans, the Lithuanians also lost their willingness to confiscate goods passing through the gate. They could not enjoy their spoils, as every article confiscated at the gate must be brought to the German ghetto guard.
>
> As a consequence, a more relaxed atmosphere pervades the ghetto gate, and the inmates sense this. The price of various goods has gone down and – the main thing – the inmates have something to eat. There are no hungry people in the ghetto any more.[11]

In Vilnius, the constant friction between Gens and the increasingly impotent Fried came to a climax in mid-July 1942. *Gebietskommissar* Hingst and Murer, accompanied by Petras Buragas – the Lithuanian official with responsibility for Jewish affairs in the city's puppet Lithuanian administration – appeared in the offices of the *Judenrat*, where the assembled *Judenrat* and Gens awaited them. Murer told those present that the *Judenrat* had failed to act with the requisite alacrity and had instead spent too much time on debate. Consequently, it was being dissolved. Henceforth, Gens would be in charge of the ghetto. Fried would be his deputy for administrative affairs, and Salk Dessler, a senior officer in Gens's police, would he his deputy for police affairs.

Gens was a believer in the concept of 'Survival through work' – it was only by making themselves indispensible to the Germans that the Jews could expect to survive. He now issued a proclamation to that effect: 'The basis of existence of the ghetto is labour, discipline, and order. Every resident fit for work constitutes a pillar on which our existence is based. We must not have among us people who recoil from labour, behave improperly, or commit varied offences.'[12]

To mark his appointment as head of the ghetto, he announced that he was granting an amnesty to all the prisoners currently held in the small ghetto prison, but made clear that he wouldn't hesitate to fill the cells if there was any dissent.

The year of 1942 and the first part of 1943 might have been known in the ghettos as the 'quiet time', as there weren't any major clearances or mass killings, but it would be wrong to think that the Germans and their Lithuanian auxiliaries carried out no 'actions' at all. In July 1942, shortly after Gens was given the title of 'ghetto representative' and became its de facto leader, several Jews who were too old to work were gathered together and taken from the ghetto. Most of the elderly had been eliminated in earlier 'actions', and these new victims were largely those who had become too frail as a result of the harsh conditions in the ghetto. A home had been created there for these 'elderly' Jews and they were now loaded onto horse-drawn wagons. Gens and the ghetto police told them – and their relatives, who watched impotently – that they were being taken to a home in Pospieškis, but few believed the assurances, even when several of the ghetto police joined the elderly in the wagons.

Almost immediately, there were rumours in the camp that a new wave of killings was about to commence. As the elderly had been removed, there were fears that children would be targeted next, and Gens felt the need to tell the heads of each housing block that there were no plans for such an 'action'. Several more elderly people were detained the following day and although most were subsequently released, a small group was taken away.

To the surprise of the ghetto inmates, the elderly were indeed taken to a former resort building in Pospieškis, and photographs soon appeared to confirm this. Gens told the ghetto inmates that they would be returned to their families in a few short weeks once they had recovered sufficient strength to work. But on 26 July, Martin Weiss led a group of Lithuanian police to the resort building and the 84 frail Jews, together with the small group of ghetto police with them, were loaded into trucks. Their destination was not the ghetto, but Ponary. In the days that followed,

Gens apparently attempted to justify his actions to a number of Jews, telling them that he had no choice but to comply with the Germans; he maintained that they had demanded several hundred infirm people be handed over, but he had negotiated this down to just 100. It seems that few Jews blamed Gens, accepting that he had been forced to choose the lesser evil.

September 1942 saw the first anniversary of the establishment of the Vilnius ghetto. Almost as if he wished to mark this occasion with a special effort, Murer was at the ghetto gates to ensure the strict search of returning workers:

> Those who were guilty [of smuggling food] were brought to an empty room not far from the ghetto gate or to the Jewish police watch house, stripped, and beaten. The women emerged with tearful faces from these torture chambers and pulled their clothes into order; the men held up their trousers and remained silent, grinding their teeth in unconscious anger ... Next to [Levas] stood Murer, leading the beatings and punishment, and delighted at the sight of the injured, insulted and humiliated people.[13]

Whilst Gens in Vilnius and the *Judenrat* in Kaunas successfully managed to avoid any action against children in the ghettos, the Germans had already made clear their intention to move against future children. Early in 1942, the Germans informed the ghetto inmates that pregnancies would not be permitted beyond certain dates. The cut-off became the subject of intense negotiations – in Šiauliai, it was 15 August, in Kaunas it was mid-September – and any women who were still pregnant after these dates were required to have abortions. Any who attempted to evade this restriction faced execution, together with all members of their families. Inevitably, this meant that some women would have to undergo abortions at late stages of pregnancy. The distress of the women, and the medical staff who had to perform the abortions, is unimaginable. The *Judenrat* in the small ghetto in Šiauliai discussed the issue in March 1943, and one of the doctors of those present was not alone in wrestling with the appalling consequences of the restrictions, even several months after they came into force:

> There was a birth recently in Kaunas and all members of the family were shot and killed. Can the pregnant women be forced to have abortions performed? There are about 20 pregnant women in the ghetto, most of them in the first few months, but some who are already in the fourth or fifth month and one even in the

> eighth month. Only two of the pregnant women refuse to have an abortion ... They must be persuaded to have an abortion. They must be told what happened in Kaunas ... How can one perform an abortion on a woman who has already reached the eighth month of her pregnancy? And what will happen if despite everything the child is born alive? Shall we kill it? ... Perhaps we should let the child be born and give it to a Christian?[14]

In 1942, there were 257 recorded abortions in the Vilnius ghetto; this is almost certainly an underestimate, with many more taking place either under different diagnoses, or in private. Some of the children who were born illicitly remained hidden from the Germans, but many were later discovered and killed. A few were given to local people to bring up outside the ghettos, both in Lithuania and elsewhere. In once case near Warsaw, a baby was placed on the windowsill of a cottage when he was just four weeks old and was raised as a Catholic; he later became a Catholic priest, only discovering his Jewish origins as an adult.[15]

Parts of Belarus adjacent to Lithuania were transferred to the control of the German occupation authorities in Vilnius in the second half of 1942. This area included a number of small ghettos and in October Gens and a group of Jewish police were taken by Weiss to the town of Ashmyany, where there was one such small enclave. Gens spoke to a meeting of senior Jewish representatives in the Vilnius ghetto about what happened:

> A week ago Weiss came and ordered us on behalf of the SD to proceed to Ashmyany. He said that there were about 4,000 Jews in the ghetto there and that it was impossible that such a number remain there, that the ghetto must be reduced, that people for whom the Germans had no need should be selected out and shot ...
>
> We had been ordered to select at least 1,500 people [for execution]. We answered that we couldn't fill such a quota. We haggled, and ... the figure was reduced to 800. After I went with Weiss to Ashmyany, the quota was dropped once again, this time to 600 ... The truth is that 406 elderly were collected at Ashmyany and were handed over.
>
> When Weiss first came and demanded women and children, I told him instead that he should take old people. He replied, 'The old ones will die off anyway during the winter, and we are obliged to reduce the ghetto population now.' ... May these aged Jews forgive us, they were the sacrifice for our Jews and our future.[16]

It was revealed later that in order to persuade Weiss to accept barely a quarter of the number of Jews that he had originally demanded, Gens bribed him with a quantity of gold. Ada Gens commented in her post-war interview that when it came to bribery, the chances of success were always greater if the recipient of the bribe was from the Gestapo or SD; although Murer and Hingst seem to have been prepared to conduct seizures of Jewish money for personal gain, they were almost impossible to bribe.

Whilst many regarded Gens as a man in an impossible situation who was often forced to choose between collaborating in the deaths of a small number of Jews in order to protect the majority, others in the ghetto regarded him with contempt and loathing. After the war, Samuel Esterowicz looked back on his personal view of Gens:

> As far as I am concerned, and I had the possibility of observing personally the activities of Jacob Gens in the ghetto of Vilnius, there can be no doubt that he was performing a treacherous job according to the instructions and the plans of the Gestapo whose goal was our complete annihilation ...
>
> Eagerly carrying out the Gestapo's instructions, Gens was on one hand applying the rule of 'divide and conquer', suppressing any attempt at organised resistance ... on the other hand, by constantly assuring us that the ghetto would continue to exist, Gens was stretching out to us the straw for which we, the drowning, would eagerly reach and thus silently endure the sequential bloodlettings. The moral countenance of Gens can also be seen by the fact that he surrounded himself with a plethora of mistresses of great beauty, whom he would reward with the lives of their families ...
>
> The Gestapo realised that, in order for Gens to carry out successfully his mission of sending us to our deaths while keeping us submissive and non-resisting, it was indispensable to keep us in the dark as to his real function ... The news that Gens succeeded in grasping someone from the claws of death would spread through the ghetto with lightning speed – it naturally fell on fertile soil; after the almighty Jehovah continued to be deaf to our pleas and pitiless toward our sufferings, there was an immense need to find a saviour in Gens.[17]

Mendel Balberyszski, another Jew in the ghetto, had a very different view:

> I am convinced that at the start of his career [as head of the ghetto police and of the ghetto itself] he had the best intentions to help

> save whatever was possible to save. I believe even when he handed Jews over to the German murderers he believed that in this way he saved the remainder of the population of the ghetto. It is my opinion that Gens believed that in the end he would be the new Moses who would one day lead the Jews out of the ghetto. If there had to be sacrifices – that could not be helped. But the ghetto had to be saved. And to save the ghetto, according to his thinking, Jews had to work for the Germans, to drag out the process and win time. I say that this was his thinking, because Gens wasn't the only one who thought this way. Many people in the ghetto, driven by the inner wish to survive, clung to the illusion that survival was possible and if in the process some Jews had to be sacrificed by meeting German demands, then that was what was needed to be done. The Germans, of course, through their diabolical planning, did all they could to nurture and perpetuate such illusions.[18]

The truth is perhaps that both or even all opinions of Gens were in some way correct. He undoubtedly collaborated with the Germans and hid their intentions from the ghetto inmates, and it is noteworthy that none of his family members, nor the members of families of the other ghetto police, were caught up in any of the German 'actions'. But had he refused to cooperate – and had all other Jews refused to cooperate – it is likely that the rate at which Jews were killed would have been even faster. Much of the apparent cooperation of Jews in all the ghettos was based upon the belief that either the Germans would cease to carry out their plans of extermination, or would be prevented from doing so by being defeated; some also believed that Hitler would be overthrown sooner or later by the German Army. In that context, the willingness of some Jews to cooperate and permit – even collaborate in – the deaths of some Jews can be seen as an attempt to save a greater number in the hope and expectation that the ordeal would soon be over.

During this period, the Jews who worked for Plagge's *HKP 562* were relatively safe and continued to benefit from the steps that he took to alleviate their harsh conditions. Not all of the Jews held Plagge in high regard, with some later recalling that despite the extra rations, their lives remained very hard. Harry Sheres was a teenager who worked in the camp and later recalled that regardless of any orders that Plagge might have given, some of the Wehrmacht personnel treated Jews badly, beating them for trivial infractions. Carpenters working in *HKP 562* manufactured several items of furniture, which Sheres believed were then sent to Plagge's family in Germany. He also remembered an occasion when Plagge ordered a shoemaker to make him a pair of boots and then became angry with the shoemaker when the boots didn't fit properly.[19] It is perhaps worth remembering that Plagge was crippled by polio from his days in a British prison camp at the end of the First World War, and the boots would have had to take this into account – in any event, however angry he may have been with the shoemaker, he limited his response to a loss of temper. Other Germans in similar positions would have imposed a severe punishment.

In the Vilnius ghetto, Murer continued to terrorise the inhabitants. Late in 1942, he appeared unannounced in the ghetto and kicked open the door of a building where several families were crowded together. He searched for contraband food or clothing that didn't have the obligatory Star of David, and when he found a small fragment of lipstick he subjected the nearest woman to a severe beating. After several further searches, the Jews began to use their *malines* to hide food and clothing that might attract Murer's wrath. In the autumn of 1942, Jakob Kagan, a 19-year-old Jew, and his father Abraham were returning to the ghetto from their workplace at the railway station when they learned that Murer was at the door. The two men were carrying a considerable amount of meat, and when they reached the gates Abraham Kagan attempted to run past Murer and his ghetto police helpers. Jakob later described what happened:

> Murer ran straight after him and shouted 'Halt!' but at the same moment also fired at him. My father fell to the ground about 6m from me. I ran over and hoped that I could help my father. The Jewish police wanted to drag me away. But I said that it was my father. We then took him to the Jewish hospital, he was still alive and moving. Dr Sedlis took over from us and didn't let anyone see him. I waited for two hours, and then Dr Sedlis came up to me and said that my father was dead, as the bullet had struck his heart.[20]

As the weather grew colder in late 1942, the Jews in the ghetto braced themselves for the harsh weather that lay ahead. Herman Kruk, the Jewish librarian from Warsaw, established and then managed the ghetto library and was also heavily involved in welfare work. One of the tasks he was ordered to undertake by the German authorities was to cooperate with the *Einsatzstab Reichsleiter Rosenberg* ('Reichsleiter Rosenberg Task Staff'), a body set up by Alfred Rosenburg's *Ostministerium* to collect Jewish and other artefacts for a future museum; he succeeded in hiding most of the texts and other items that the Germans were seeking. At the end of October, he wrote about preparations for the cold months that lay ahead, and the mixed news from outside the ghetto. On the one hand, it was clear that the war in the Soviet Union wasn't going well for the Germans, but on the other hand, there were ominous reports from within Germany:

> Here in the ghetto, people are preparing for the second winter. Some say the last, really the last, because soon they will finish us off. But in the meantime, we live and prepare: the ghetto is excited about winter aid. Everyone is preparing for winter. Once again people put up the iron stoves, little ones with small panes instead of big and bright windows.
>
> Everywhere, people pull out old rags. The better clothes have already been sold. From the old things, they intend to alter clothing. They match, darn, re-knit. They make soles out of an old belt; from two pairs of torn underwear, they patch together one. Poverty now creeps into the street. The clothes, the rags – everything shows clearly the distance from a year ago to now. All statistics show this: the lines for social aid, the distribution of free lunches – everyone says that the ghetto is growing poorer. But Jews do not lose their courage. And everyone is satisfied: we are getting a winter, 'they' are getting a disaster. And a comrade helps me:
>
> 'A nastoyashtsher brokh!' [An honest-to-goodness disaster!] …
>
> The centre of the winter aid campaign is seething with work. Diligent women, girls, young men are numbering, assembling, and arranging the collected clothing …
>
> A day of art was held in Düsseldorf, and the main speech of the celebration was by none other than my boss Alfred Rosenberg. What he said there is not important. But what interests us here are his remarks on the Jewish Question:
>
> 'The Jewish Question is now being brought to its last stage. We must remove Jews from all European countries so that they will no longer interfere in our affairs.'
>
> Jews blink, ask, terrified, what that means – does it mean they will finish with the Jews forever?[21]

The Vilnius ghetto was increasingly divided into factions. In November 1942, Nosn Schlossberg, a Jewish policeman, was shot by partisans whilst supervising a work party in a village outside the city – he had a reputation for mistreating other Jews, and apparently word reached the partisans who took matters into their own hands. He died a few days later. This coincided with the death of a teacher named Gerstein, who had been popular with the ghetto community. When the two funerals were held, almost none of the ghetto authorities – the *Judenrat* and the ghetto police – attended Gerstein's funeral. By contrast, Gens declared a day of mourning for Schlossberg and organised a funeral with considerable pomp – but although the police turned out in force for the ceremony, few of the ordinary ghetto residents attended.

The deaths of Jews from Ashmyany continued to cast a shadow over Gens and the ghetto police, and many still suspected him of collaborating too easily with the Germans. In an attempt to restore confidence, Gens met Kruk in November 1942 in an attempt to explain his actions. He told Kruk that in addition to the Ashmyany incident, Weiss had ordered the ghetto police to carry out a similar operation in the town of Kiemieliszki, but Gens refused; he now regretted this, telling Kruk that all of the Jews in Kiemieliszki had been killed, and that if he had cooperated with the Germans, he might have been able to save at least some of them. Kruk was unconvinced, but could see the dilemma that Gens faced, particularly when he had to deal with Martin Weiss.

The Jews became aware that even in the ranks of the Gestapo, many disliked Weiss, and referred to him as '*Weiss, der Schwarz*' – 'White, the black', an expression that many Jews rapidly adopted. As soon as he took up his post, Weiss established a reputation for arbitrary cruelty. In late 1941, he shocked many who had already endured the horrors of the various 'actions' when he selected a young girl apparently at random, took her to the ghetto gate, and calmly shot her. A year later, he executed another young woman, allegedly because she had had sex with a non-Jew. Men like Gens would have been aware that Weiss was quite capable of deciding that their usefulness was at an end and a desire for self-preservation was probably one of the numerous motives that drove Gens to cooperate.

The behaviour of the Germans was often erratic. Whilst food supplies to the Kaunas ghetto improved for a while in the summer with the relaxation of gate searches, stricter rules were soon back in force. There were also repeated raids to search for money and valuables, and the threat of sudden and arbitrary death was never distant. In mid-November, a young Jew names Meck was caught attempting to leave the ghetto via a hole in the wire fence. He was armed and fired four warning shots into the air, but was nonetheless arrested. Three members of the *Judenrat* were arrested and threatened with execution unless they revealed the identity of another Jew who was believed to have been with Meck. A search of Meck's room in the ghetto revealed a substantial treasure – before the war, he had been a jeweller and over 2kg of gold, jewels and other items were taken away. Meck was hanged in the public square in the ghetto and his corpse was left hanging as a warning to other ghetto inmates. As a further punishment, Meck's mother and sister were taken away to Fort IX and executed.[22]

Although the possession of radios was strictly forbidden, the Jews had a small number of radio sets with which they listened to various news services. As 1942 drew to a close, they were therefore aware that the tide of war seemed to be turning against Germany. In North Africa, the Germans and Italians seemed to be in full retreat, and although the Germans announced that their offensive operations in Stalingrad had been successfully concluded, it was clear from British and Soviet broadcasts that parts of the city continued to resist. On 13 December, Kruk noted the growing signs of resistance to German occupation, though it was difficult to separate rumour from fact:

> In Bezdany [immediately outside Vilnius to the northeast] on Thursday 10th [December], at night, a train carrying soldiers, military ammunition, and equipment was blown up. In Wieluciany, a little town about 12 km [7 miles] from Vilnius, there are also partisans. There they are in complete control. They come in the middle of the day, and the Germans are terrified to show their faces. All the partisans there are Russians.
>
> Through the radio, we listen to orders for the partisans. Among other things, they are told: Group 82 fulfilled its orders. Group 32 is ready. Attention Group 76, you are warned. Such and similar codes are heard often.
>
> From one day to the next, the matter is apparently more organised and centralised.[23]

On 18 December, Kruk noted that it seemed as if the world was finally waking up to the terrible reality of what was happening to the Jews of Europe:

> Only now has the world grasped that the Germans are murdering Jews by the hundreds of thousands. Only now! ...
>
> Today I learned from the radio: the governments of London, the Soviet Union, and the United States issued a joint declaration today about the persecution of the Jews in all countries occupied by the Germans. The signatories of the declaration include the governments of Belgium, Poland, Holland, South American countries, and others.
>
> The declaration is 'in view of the persecution of the Jews, taking place through the German-occupied countries in a way unprecedented in history, aiming at the annihilation of the Jews of Europe.' The declaration was supposedly broadcast simultaneously on Moscow, London and Washington radio.

> [British Foreign Secretary Anthony] Eden described, among other things, materials he has outlining a total extermination plan in Eastern Europe which was carried out in an unfathomable manner ... He says that not long ago, half a million Jews were taken from Western Europe to the east and all of them, with few exceptions, were killed. He says that the nations will take steps to punish the guilty with all severity and save the future of the Jewish people.
>
> Hearing that, a local Jew smiled behind his moustache ... 'If they had only remembered us a year ago,' more than one says mockingly.[24]

On 28 December 1942, Murer was once more at the gate. Several Jewish men and women were forced to strip naked and were beaten; the much-hated Meir Levas was a particularly enthusiastic member of the police squad on this occasion. Those attempting to smuggle contraband were given 25 lashes and then forced to run naked to their homes, clutching their clothes while Murer and the police laughed loudly. Murer was noted to be particularly keen on making younger Jewish women strip naked, and often appeared at the communal bathhouse to watch the women washing.

The inmates of the ghetto in Vilnius ranged from the very poor to some who had been famous in the years before the war. One of the latter was the opera singer Ljuba Lewicka. After she and the other Jews were forced into the ghetto, she soon became known as the 'nightingale of the ghetto'; she took part in several concerts and joined the staff of the school in the ghetto, giving singing lessons. She was arrested by the Gestapo on suspicion of pro-Communist tendencies, but after a period of interrogation – which included torture – she was released back to the ghetto. During one of the 'actions' of late 1941, she hid under the floorboards of one of the houses and was stabbed in the back by Horst Schweinberger, who was probing between the floorboards with a dagger, but she recovered from her injuries. She was one of the Jews employed by Oskar Schönbrunner and as she left her workplace, she asked him if she could take a bag of peas with her. Schönbrunner had no objection, but she encountered Murer on her way back to the ghetto. He had her taken to Lukiškės Prison and rejected repeated requests from Schönbrunner for her release, telling Schönbrunner that he was too tolerant and should be much firmer and unyielding towards his Jewish workers.

On 27 January 1943, Lewicka and six other Jews were taken to Ponary. According to some accounts, Lewicka sang the entire way despite being ordered to stop. When the prisoners reached Ponary, they were taken to a pit, forced to kneel, and were then shot. There are different accounts of who actually killed the Jews; some described Martin Weiss as firing the fatal shots, while others believed that a German woman named Helen Degner, who was Weiss's lover, killed them.

As the days began to grow longer in 1943, the tide of the war was turning decisively against Nazi Germany. A Soviet counteroffensive swept across the frozen steppe in November 1942 to encircle the German Sixth Army in the ruins of Stalingrad, and after enduring a terrible few weeks the remnants of the German divisions surrendered to the Red Army in early February. In North Africa, the Germans were driven back to Tunis where they were ultimately forced to surrender in May. For the Jews of Eastern Europe, there were also changes: the relatively quiet time was coming to an end. A sign of this came in the form of a radio speech given by Joseph Goebbels. Avraham Gollub wrote in his diary on 19 February:

> 'Alarm! The West is in danger!' This is the headline of today's Kaunas newspaper, which printed the full text of Goebbels' most recent speech. Ghetto inmates who read it were overcome with anguish. In his speech Goebbels said, among other things: 'The Jews are the root of evil in the world; they are the devil which pushes the West toward its downfall; they are the carrier of ruin and destruction within the body of Western civilisation; they are the instigator of chaos in the world. The crocodile tears shed abroad over the persecution of Jews in German-occupied territory will not deter Germany from carrying out its plans and ideas. On the contrary, Germany will pursue its course with more vigour – by any available means, if necessary – in order to implement its plan for the total extermination of Jewry.'[25]

The intention of the Germans to exterminate the Jews of Eastern Europe had always been intended as a prelude to the killing of the rest of the European Jews. Once Eastern Europe's ghettos had been cleared, Jews would be dispatched there from the west. Implementation of this clearance of the ghettos of the Baltic region was now in the hands of Oberführer Friedrich Jeckeln. He was appointed as the higher SS and police commander for Ostland and the neighbouring parts of the Soviet Union shortly after the region was occupied; he had previously held a similar post in Ukraine, where he had devised a new method of mass killing in an attempt to make the process more efficient. This became known variously as the *Jeckeln-System* or *Sardinenpackung*: victims were taken to the killing ground in columns of between 500 and 1,000, where three prepared pits awaited them. After being stripped, the victims ran a gauntlet of guards who beat them and ensured that they had no remaining clothing or possessions; they were then forced to lie face down in the pits, often on the corpses of earlier victims, and were then shot with individual shots to the back of the head in order to conserve ammunition. Any who were not killed outright were simply buried with the rest.

Anticipating Himmler's orders to clear the ghetto prior to the arrival of more Jews from the west, Jeckeln had already implemented this process in Riga as early as November 1941, with the killings taking place in Rumbula, immediately to the southeast of Riga; over three days commencing on 30 November, about 27,500 people were killed, including about 21,000 women and children. In contrast to killings elsewhere in the Baltic States, all of those killed in Rumbula were executed by Germans, perhaps a dozen men that he had personally selected.[26] A Wehrmacht engineer, Hauptmann Otto Schulz-Du Bois, happened upon the scene. Hearing sounds of gunfire, he decided to investigate, and later described the scene to friends in Germany:

> The first thing he came upon was a huge pile of clothes, then men, women, children and elderly people standing in a line and dressed in their underclothing. The head of the line ended in a small wood by a mass grave site. Those first in line had to leap into the pit and then were murdered with a pistol bullet to the head. Six SS men were busy with this grisly chore. The victims maintained a perfect composure. There were no outcries, only quiet sobbing and crying, and soothing words said to the children.[27]

The first train carrying 1,000 Jews from the west left Berlin on 27 November 1941 and arrived in Riga two days later. This early transfer was marked by some confusion amongst German officials, with initial orders suggesting that they were simply to be liquidated. At the very last moment, it seems that Himmler decided that rather than being killed immediately, these Jews were to be housed in the Riga ghetto, but by the time that he issued an order to Heydrich, all of those on the train had been taken to Rumbula and killed. A week later, two more trains arrived in Riga, one from Vienna and one from Breslau (now the Polish city of Wrocław. Jeckeln had been ordered to house them in the ghetto, but despite the slaughter at Rumbula he decided that there was still insufficient space for them and diverted the train to Kaunas. When he was informed of their arrival, Jäger ordered that they should be taken immediately to Fort IX and executed.

The transfer of Jews to the east began in earnest after the Wannsee Conference, but the plans had changed. Instead of housing these Jews in the ghettos of Riga, Kaunas, Vilnius and elsewhere, they were taken directly to the death camps of Auschwitz, Treblinka, Majdanek, Sobibor, and Belzec. The summer of 1942 saw the beginning of the plan of the Germans to eliminate the largest ghetto of all – designated the *Grossaktion Warschau* ('Great Warsaw Action'), the operation saw more than 250,000 Jews moved from the Warsaw ghetto. They were told that they were being resettled elsewhere, but their destination was the Treblinka death camp. Partly in reaction to this, the Jews of Warsaw began to organise for armed resistance. The consequences would see the end of all the ghettos of Eastern Europe.

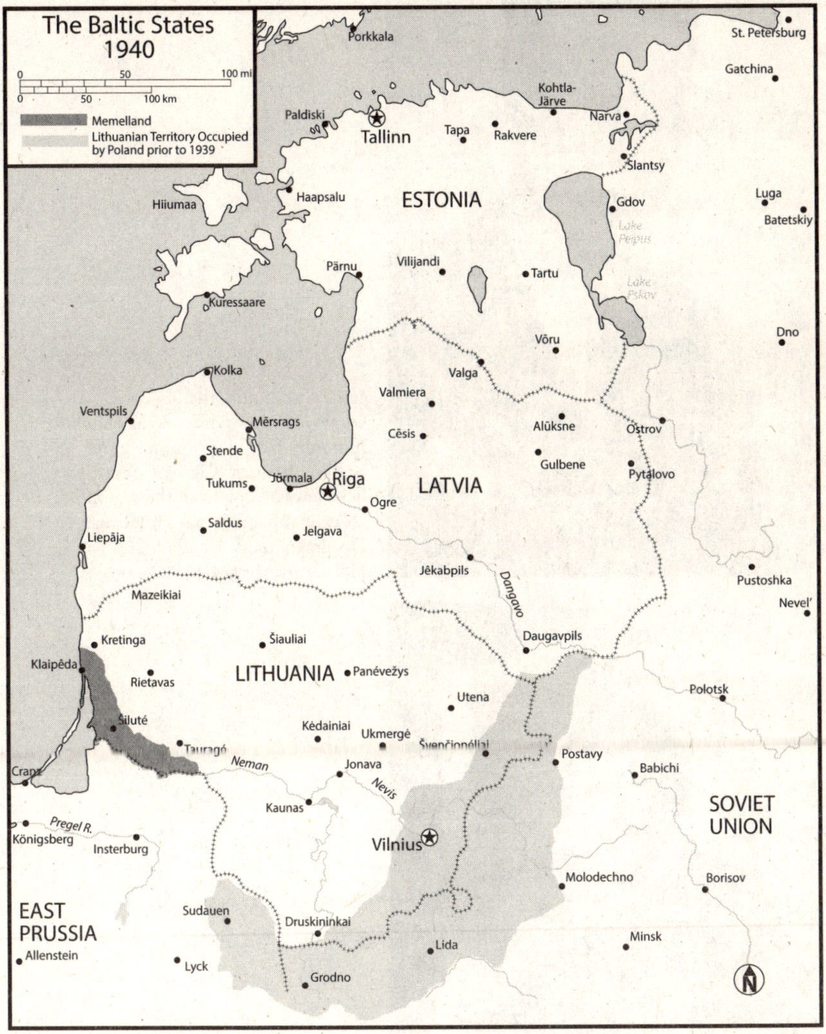

Map of the Baltic region.

Jan Zwartendijk, the Philips employee who in his role as Dutch honorary consul in Kaunas gave out hundreds of 'Curaçao Visas' to help Jews escape from the region. (National Institute for Holocaust Documentation, United States Holocaust Memorial Museum)

Chiune Sugihara, the Japanese vice-consul in Lithuania, defied orders from Japan and provided documentation for hundreds of Jews to leave Lithuania.

Above left: Reinhard Heydrich, often seen as the most powerful figure in the SS after Heinrich Himmler, was the architect of the *Einsatzgruppen* and their policy of mass murder after the invasion of the Soviet Union.

Above right: Like many senior officers in the *Einsatzgruppen*, Franz Walter Stahlecker, commander of *Einsatzgruppe A*, was a highly educated lawyer.

Right: Karl Jäger, commander of *Einsatzkommando 3*, was older than most of his peers. Despite being haunted by nightmares, he showed no inclination to stop the wholesale slaughter of Jews in Lithuania.

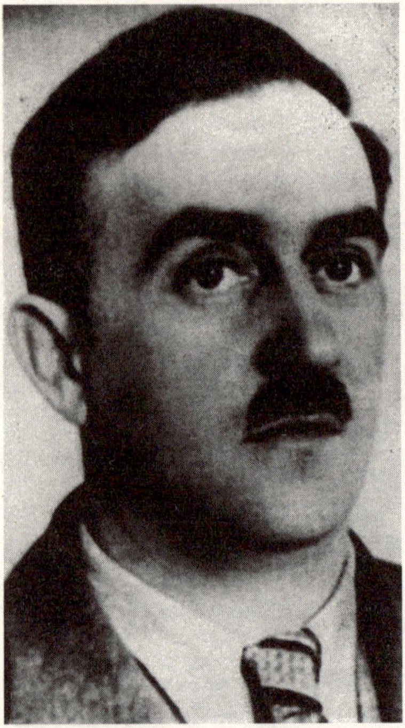

Left: Feldwebel Anton Schmid, the Viennese NCO who willingly risked his life to try to save Jews in Vilnius.

Below left: Solomon (Solly) Ganor was a Jewish teenager in Kaunas when the Wehrmacht invaded. He endured life in the Kaunas ghetto and several concentration camps before liberation. (National Institute for Holocaust Documentation, United States Holocaust Memorial Museum)

Below right: Karl Plagge was a veteran of the First World War and contracted polio as a prisoner. He was head of HKP 562, a German vehicle repair facility; he did all he could to protect the Jews who worked in his workshops. (Yad Vashem, 14486959)

Hans Christian Hingst was the *Gebietskommissar* of the Vilnius municipality, responsible for implementing instructions from *Reichskommissariat Ostland*, the regional authority.

Clarence Matsumura was a Japanese American whose family was interned after Pearl Harbor. He served with 522nd Field Artillery Battalion and was the man who liberated Solly Ganor. (Eric Saul, Visas for Life Project)

Above left: Bruno Kittel, the suave killer of the later part of the German occupation of Lithuania, was responsible for several massacres. (Yad Vashem, 4577/581)

Above right: The Baltic region came under the control of *Reichskommissariat Ostland*. Hinrich Lohse, its head, was simultaneously *Gauleiter* of Schleswig-Holstein. (Yad Vashem, 4613/808)

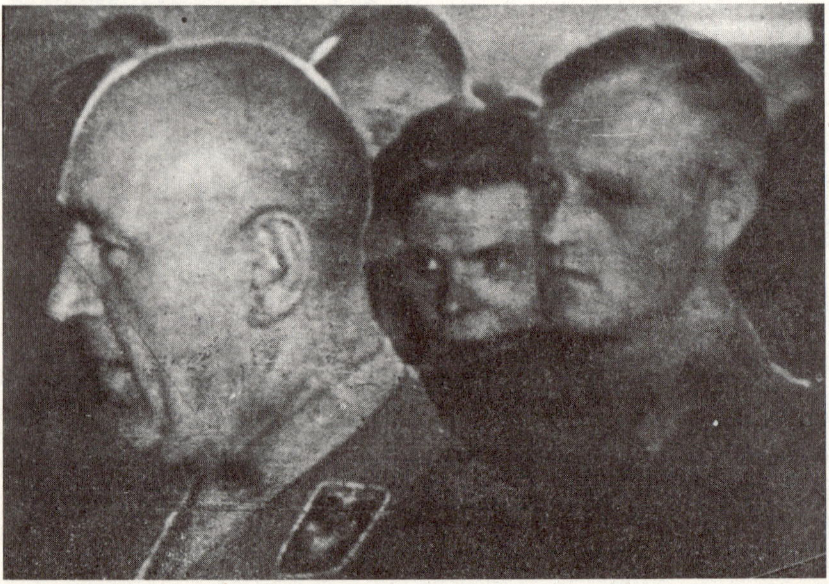

Murer (right), pictured here standing behind Hingst, was known to the Jews as the Butcher of Vilnius. (Yad Vashem, 4570/1)

Above left: Martin Weiss was a low-ranking SS soldier who conducted a reign of terror in the Vilnius ghetto. (Yad Vashem, 3380/146)

Above right: Jacob Gens, head of the Jewish Police in the Vilnius ghetto, tried to tread a fine line between collaborating with the Germans and saving the lives of the Jewish inmates. (Yad Vashem, Borowicz Collection 338)

Right: The *Totschläger von Kauen* ('Death Dealer of Kaunas'), who was seen by numerous witnesses beating to death several Jews shortly after the arrival of German troops in Kaunas.

The execution ground at Ponary.

Entrance to the Vilnius ghetto.

Jews being transferred from the Kaunas ghetto to Klooga in Estonia. (National Institute for Holocaust Documentation, United States Holocaust Memorial Museum)

8

Liquidation

The *Grossaktion Warschau* was the result of specific orders from Heinrich Himmler. In July 1942, he ordered that the 'resettlement' of the entire Jewish population of the General Government was to be completed by the end of the year.[1] Sturmbannführer Hermann Höfle was a deputy of the infamous Odilo Globocnik, who was instrumental in the creation of the death camps; at the end of July, Höfle met the *Judenrat* in the Warsaw ghetto and informed them that he required 7,000 Jews to be handed over every day for resettlement in the east. If the *Judenrat* refused to comply, the SS would execute 100 Jews every day until they acquiesced. Only those who worked in German-run enterprises or were essential for the running of the ghetto were to be left behind.

Although the death camps had been operating since the first months of 1942, their activity was still relatively unknown and the *Judenrat* cooperated. Trains left every day for Treblinka, with 100 people crammed into each cattle truck. As the programme continued, new gas chambers became operational in Treblinka, capable of killing 3,000 people every two hours. At this stage of the war, carbon monoxide was used; this would be replaced with *Zyklon B* at a later date. Until this operation, the Jews both in Warsaw and other ghettos had regarded Warsaw as relatively safe – with a population of over 400,000 Jews, many believed it was just too big for the Germans to liquidate; but from the outset, Adam Czerniaków, the head of the *Judenrat*, had little doubt that the intention was to kill the Jews. When the Germans refused to permit orphaned children to remain in the ghetto, he committed suicide by swallowing a cyanide capsule. In his last notes to his wife and colleagues in the *Judenrat*, he wrote:

> They demand that I kill children of my nation with my own hands. I have no choice left but to die … [Hermann] Worthoff [a Gestapo

> officer who worked for Höfle] and his colleagues visited me and demanded that a children's transport be prepared for tomorrow. With this my bitter goblet is filled to the brim because I cannot deliver defenceless children to their deaths. I have decided to resign. Do not consider this an act of cowardice or escape. I am powerless, my heart breaks with sadness and pity, I can't take it any longer. My deed will make everyone see the truth and perhaps put it on the right path of action. I am aware that I am leaving you a difficult legacy.[2]

On 18 January 1943, the Germans began what was intended to be a second wave of mass deportations to the death camps. By now, the Jewish resistance movement had decided that this was the moment to take a stand and had steadily built up its armament with help from the local Polish resistance groups. As soon as the Germans arrived, there was a fierce exchange of fire. Although the Jews suffered heavy losses, the Germans were forced to stop their operations after removing about 5,000 Jews from the ghetto over the next few days. For the moment, there seemed to be a reprieve, but few of the Jews expected it to last for long.

In the Vilnius region, the ultimate liquidation of the main ghetto was preceded by the elimination of smaller ghettos and camps in the area. Rumours reached the Jews in March about mass killings in Grodno in nearby Belarus, and in March 1943 the Germans informed the *Judenrat* that the small work camps were being closed; the workers from these camps would be moved to Vilnius and Kaunas. At the end of March, about 1,200 Jews arrived in the Vilnius ghetto. In early April, assisted by the Jewish police from Vilnius, the Germans put several hundred Jews who still remained in the small camps into trains, and notices were posted in the Vilnius ghetto advising the Jews that if they had families in Kaunas, they could apply to join the trains when they passed through the city. About 340 people decided to take advantage of this. The train was sent to Ponary. The Jewish police personnel on the train, including Gens, were offloaded and taken back to Vilnius.

When they realised that they were in Ponary, many of the Jews in the trains attempted to escape. Some were armed and opened fire on the Germans and Lithuanians, who fired back. Several thousands were killed, but perhaps 40 or 50 Jews escaped. Some reached the Vilnius ghetto with news of the terrible events. The journalist Kazimierz Sakowicz witnessed those events:

> One section of the column of people was halted by the first trench. From the other section, about half of the group, continued further. From this second half of the column a few daredevils fled when they reached a spot in dense woodland.

> The first half of the group, who were standing by the first trench, had to strip. Sobbing, groaning, pleading, many threw themselves at the feet of the Lithuanians and Germans. The latter stamped on them and shot some of those who were more persistent. Whilst being beaten, they were forced back about 10m from the trench.
>
> The Jews, who were clad in only rags, didn't have to strip. They were taken to the trench and the Lithuanians standing around the edge opened fire. Then a man who was already half-undressed carried a senseless or perhaps dead woman to the foot of the trench, as ordered by a German. After he had placed the woman in the trench and had undressed, a Lithuanian shot him at close range in the head. One could see clearly how his skull burst and he dropped like a felled tree. At the same time the rest of the Jews were being beaten and five, including a woman and three girls, had to kneel at the edge of the trench, facing over the edge. The Lithuanian with the revolver shot them from behind and they all disappeared into the trench.[3]

As the killings came to an end, Sakowicz saw a young Jew aged perhaps 11 creeping towards his house. He and his wife dressed his leg wounds and told him the best route away from the area.

Some witnesses said that they saw Murer at the railway station in Vilnius, and others described how Martin Weiss shot a woman and her child who refused to disembark at Ponary. Some of the survivors who fled into the woodland testified that both Weiss and Murer were present and had opened fire on the would-be escapees; Ariel Koslowski, one of those who fled, was shot in the right foot and was thrown into the trench but survived.[4]

On 6 April, Weiss went to the ghetto and demanded that a party of 25 Jewish police be organised. These men were sent to Ponary to bury the dead. Weiss accompanied them, as one of the policemen later described:

> Just before Ponary, the car stopped and we were ordered to continue on foot. We could see peasants hurrying to their homes, bent with loads on their backs: they had profited from the belongings of the murdered ... The whole area was strewn with bodies and human limbs ... Weiss took us to an enormous pit full of corpses and told us to cover them with earth ... After we completed this work, Weiss led us to a second grave ... At the end of it all, he took us on a tour of the whole area and gave us explanations as though he were a guide at an exhibition: 'Here are the graves of Jews kidnapped by abductors [i.e. snatched at random by Lithuanian partisans] in 1941; here is a second grave of the "Provocation Action".' He then went on to the graves of [other] 'actions'.[5]

The Jewish police and their families had feared that they would be executed at the end of the day, but they were returned to the ghetto that evening. A few days later, Gens summoned the 'brigadiers' of the working parties and told them that the deaths had been because the German authorities in charge of the Kaunas ghetto had refused to accept the transferees, but confidence in Gens's ability to protect the ghetto plummeted. Some of the younger Jews began to slip away into the surrounding forests to join partisan groups, and others attempted to procure weapons. In an attempt to head off German reprisals, Gens ordered the brigadiers to report any of their work parties who attempted to 'disappear' while outside the ghetto, but it proved to be an ineffective measure – many of those wishing to escape managed to persuade their brigadiers to exclude them from the count of Jews leaving the ghetto in the morning.

In the Vilnius ghetto, the news of German setbacks in the Soviet Union in the opening weeks of 1943 resulted in an upsurge of grim humour, as Herman Kruk recorded in his diary:

> A German asks a Jew to lend him 20 roubles. The Jew immediately takes the sum out of his pocket and gives it to him. The German wonders: 'How can this be? You don't know me at all, and you trust me with such a sum?'
>
> I have the fullest trust in the Germans,' answers the Jew. 'You took Stalingrad and gave it back; you took Kharkov and gave it back. I'm sure that you will give me back my 20 roubles.'
>
> What is the difference between General Rommel and a watch? A watch goes tick-tock and goes forward; Rommel goes tock-tick and goes backward …
>
> What city is the largest in the world? Stalingrad, because it took the Germans months to get from the outskirts to the centre.[6]

But any German defeats were too far from Vilnius for the Jews to have much hope of immediate rescue. Murer continued to terrorise the Jews, inflicting whippings on anyone who was guilty of the slightest transgression.

On 19 April, the SS moved against the Warsaw ghetto again. Once more they ran into armed resistance and sustained casualties with 59 killed or wounded and two armoured cars set ablaze by Molotov cocktails. Exasperated by the resistance, Himmler dismissed Oberführer Ferdinand von Sammern-Frankenegg, the SS and police commander for the Warsaw area, replacing him with Brigadeführer Jürgen Stroop. After regrouping, the Germans attacked again. The Jews rejected a demand that they lay down their weapons and were driven back by SS troops using flamethrowers and automatic weapons. At the same time, the Polish *Armia Krajova* attacked Germans at several points around Warsaw, but the balance of power was massively in favour of the Germans. By the end of April, the uprising was effectively over, with some of the surviving fighters breaking out and escaping through a tunnel. Sporadic clashes continued in the days that followed.

In the reports that he submitted to his superiors, Stroop claimed that his men lost 17 dead and 93 wounded, but other reports suggested that this was a deliberate underestimate.[7] About 13,000 Jews were killed in the fighting, and many more were taken away to the death camps. The final act of the German suppression was the demolition of the Great Synagogue of Warsaw, which lay within the ghetto, on 13 May. Stroop described the moment:

> What a marvellous sight it was. A fantastic piece of theatre. My staff and I stood at a distance. I held the electric device which would detonate all the charges simultaneously ... I glanced over at my brave officers and men, tired and dirty, silhouetted against the glow of the burning buildings. After prolonging the suspense for a moment, I shouted 'Heil Hitler!' and pressed the button. With a thunderous, deafening bang and a rainbow burst of colours, the fiery explosion soared towards the clouds, an unforgettable tribute to our triumph over the Jews. The Warsaw Ghetto is no more. The will of Adolf Hitler and Heinrich Himmler has been done.[8]

Many of the surviving buildings in the ghetto were set ablaze. The remaining Jews of the ghetto were taken away to work camps or to Treblinka. Many were simply executed on the spot. In place of the ghetto, a concentration camp was established to house Jews from Western Europe prior to their final disposal in the death camps.

Warsaw wasn't the only ghetto where there was fighting between the Germans and the Jews. The clearance of the Białystok ghetto began in February 1943 with a major 'action'. About 10,000 Jews were taken away and put on trains for Treblinka, but this triggered armed resistance by the Jews, who had succeeded in building up a substantial stockpile of weapons. The battle was inevitably very one-sided; for the loss of about 50 men, a mixture of Germans and Ukrainian paramilitaries, the Germans killed about 2,000 Jews in the fighting. A further group of nearly 8,000 Jews were taken to an interim camp before being sent on to the concentration camps at Auschwitz and Majdanek.

Mordechai Tenenbaum, who had encountered Anton Schmid in Vilnius, was in Białystok at the time. After the fighting was over, he and his fighters attempted without success to free Itskhok Malmed, who had blinded a soldier of the SS by throwing a bottle of acid in his face; the soldier had then fired wildly, killing another SS soldier. In response, Sturmbannführer Fritz Friedel, head of the Gestapo in Białystok, had the body of the dead SS soldier taken to the offices of the *Judenrat*, and told the head of the *Judenrat* that unless the 'culprit' surrendered, all the Jews in the ghetto would be killed. Malmed surrendered to the Germans, who tortured him in an unsuccessful attempt to extract information about the resistance group. He was then hanged in the main street of the ghetto.

The plans discussed in the Wannsee Conference in early 1942 had explicitly described the increasing pace of mass murder that would be required to exterminate Europe's Jewish population, and the 'actions' in Warsaw that precipitated the ghetto uprising were part of that programme. But partly in response to the rising and to prevent any further unrest, on 21 June 1943 Himmler issued an order to all areas where ghettos were still in existence. The order sent to the Baltic region stated:

> I order that all Jews still remaining in ghettos in the Ostland area are to be collected in concentration camps.
>
> I prohibit the withdrawal of Jews from concentration camps for work [outside the camps] from 1 August 1943.
>
> A concentration camp is to be built near Riga to which will be transferred the entire manufacture of clothing and equipment now operated by the Wehrmacht [in factories outside the ghettos]. All private firms will be eliminated. The workshops are to be solely concentration camp workshops ...
>
> Inmates of the Jewish ghettos who are not required are to be evacuated to the east.
>
> As many male Jews as possible are to be taken to the concentration camp in the oil shale area for the mining of oil shale.[9]

There could be no doubt about the fate of those who were 'evacuated to the east'. There was also an additional consequence of the change of designation from 'ghetto' to 'concentration camp'. Ghettos were under the control of the civilian occupation authorities; all concentration camps came under the control of the SS. This would give Himmler far more control over the rate at which the Jews could be killed.

On 1 July, the Jews in the Vilnius ghetto learned that Murer was being moved to a new post. Their relief was limited; most feared that he would be replaced by someone just as hostile to the ghetto inmates. Murer later suggested that he and Hingst were no longer on quite as friendly terms as before. At first, there were rumours that Murer had been sent to the Eastern Front, and many hoped he would meet a grisly death in the front line, but he was actually returned to the Luftwaffe and assigned to a light anti-aircraft unit in Vienna. Later in 1943, he was selected for training as an officer and in January 1944 became a Leutnant in an artillery regiment in an airborne division – like anti-aircraft units, German airborne forces were part of the Luftwaffe rather than the army. His unit was deployed in Italy near Anzio and Rome, and he remained with the division until the end of the war. He then surrendered to the British in May 1945. With documentation identifying him as a junior artillery officer in the Luftwaffe, he attracted little attention and was released in September.

Murer's replacement was the dapper, urbane Bruno Kittel, who held the comparatively low SS rank of Oberscharführer. Most accounts give his birth year as 1922, but this is likely to be an error; if it were correct, he would have been only 21 when he arrived in Vilnius, and by this time he had already served in the German departments of Jewish affairs in Paris and Riga. He had also enjoyed considerable success in his native Austria as an actor, singer and musician. He played both the saxophone and piano with considerable skill, and after his arrival in Vilnius he was given a regular radio show on Sunday evenings in which he played pieces on the saxophone. It is therefore likely that he was born earlier than 1922. Almost immediately after he reached Vilnius, Kittel put in an appearance at the ghetto gate:

> He has quickly made himself at home and came privately to the apartments of the ghetto leaders ... He and two assistants stood at the ghetto gate during the return from work. There was a series of searches, which generally went quietly. All units were immediately warned not to 'carry' [i.e. smuggle] anything, and his first outing didn't yield any results. But therefore, this morning, he went through the ghetto and hit a few Jews for passing by him without greeting him.[10]

Salk Dessler, the deputy commander of the ghetto police, contrasted Murer and Kittel:

> Kittel doesn't strike anyone on the face, nor does he stamp on anyone; instead, he kills his victims in a cynical manner – quietly, thoughtfully, with delicacy.
>
> When he shoots people himself, he asks them politely not to be afraid or anxious, and whilst he says that he aims his pistol at the heads of the unfortunate people and shoots them one after another, like sparrows, quite calmly and without any fuss.[11]

Throughout the 'quiet time' in the ghettos, the workers at Karl Plagge's *HKP 562* had continued to benefit from his benevolent regime, but on 10 July there was an incident that showed clearly that no Jews were completely safe. From time to time, workers from *HKP 562* were sent to a peat camp in the nearby forest to chop firewood. Mascha Rolnikaite learned about the events from one of the workers who escaped:

> Kittel is simply bestial, not human at all! The worst human being couldn't be so horrible!
>
> In a brilliant mood, he appeared at the peat work camp at Kena [to the east of Vilnius] with his followers and took gifts with him – cigarettes, tobacco and jam. He gave the cigarettes and tobacco to the best workers and the jam to the children. He looked around the camp and the work areas and asked if there was a barber in the camp and let himself be shaved.
>
> The camp elders and the workers couldn't decide what this meant. One quipped that things must be going very badly for the Germans if they were now visiting the Jews and even bringing them presents. But most remembered only too well that better rations were marked on people's ration cards before the 'actions'. This raised suspicions that the jam was poisoned.
>
> Kittel even condescended to conversation, unlike the usual behaviour when dealing with *Untermenschen*. He gave optimistic answers to anxious questions about the future of the camp. At the end of his tour of the camp and after his shave he ordered all workers to gather in the barn – he wished to speak to them.
>
> In his speech, he urged them to work hard, and above all not to have anything to do with the partisans. The German rulers weren't interested in killing the Jews – on the contrary, they needed the workforce. Whoever worked would remain alive! The Germans would try to improve working conditions and rations. Today only the best workers had received cigarettes and tobacco, but in future all would receive such gifts.
>
> However unbelievable his words were, a few people felt their spirits lift.
>
> After finishing his speech Kittel went to the door. He gave a short whistle – and as if from under the ground, soldiers suddenly appeared. They let him out and secured the door from the outside. The people were terrified and began to scream, striking the door and walls with their fists. But nobody replied.
>
> Everyone pressed against the door in the hope that they could force it open, they screamed and shouted and jostled each other.

A few tried to bring the panic under control and tried to hide their own anxiety. Calmly, they told everyone: the doors had probably only been secured while the camp was searched for weapons. Others made people more anxious – Kittel intended to deport their family members and leave only workers in the camp. Fear escalated. Shouts, cries, chaos. Panic broke out. Some tried to force the door from its heavy iron hinges with their shoulders or to break through the walls with their fists. But iron door hinges are stronger than the strongest shoulders, and walls are deaf to fists. Deaf and remorseless too were the soldiers who laughed loudly outside.

Suddenly smoke came through the slats of the door and gaps in the walls. Fire! The cries for help turned into wild screams. Many grabbed at the roof planks to try to escape through the roof.

The smoke grew ever thicker. A young man pulled a revolver from his pocket. In other circumstances he wouldn't have been permitted to use it, but now everyone urged him to do so. He fired into the air. Once. Twice. No response. He emptied the magazine and didn't leave a round for himself.

Flames broke out and rose higher, ever closer. The people fought against the choking smoke, screaming and pleading for help: perhaps the women in their barracks would hear and come to their aid.

The fire grew and came dangerously close. Those who were standing close to the walls retreated before the flames and pressed into the middle. But everyone was now pressed together in the tight space and could no longer move from the spot. The clothes and hair of some were already alight. Writhing in pain, they pushed into the centre of the barn with all their strength, where the flames hadn't yet spread. In doing so, they spread the fire to others. A few tried in vain to help by putting out the flames on their neighbours. A few people were already unconscious. Others then fell. The flames rose ever higher, as if wanting to embrace and devour them and wrap them all in the murderous heat.

Suddenly, screams and cries were heard from the women's block. The women called for help. They too were being set alight. And the children, the small children! The fading consciousness [of the men in the barn] was cut through by terrible horror.

The roof collapsed followed by the walls, a great pyre of people and wood blazed.

And Kittel stood with his followers on a nearby hillock and gazed upon the scene. A real Nero!

One of his companions quipped that it was a shame about the cigarettes and jam. Another replied that it would sweeten their journey to join their forefathers. Kittel offered a thousand

Reichsmarks to whoever could find the hands of the barber who had shaved him. And the stupid Jew had taken such care! ...

When Kittel had had enough of this theatre, he climbed into his car and drove away ... Only two people escaped from this dreadful hell – they had slipped out of the barn. When they saw what the Germans were preparing, they ran away, crept into the ghetto and told everyone what had happened.[12]

Herman Kruk described what is almost certainly the same incident but assigned it to the nearby Bezdany work camp; in any event, both camps were liquidated and the workers in them killed. Over the following days, Kittel and his team went from one remote work camp to another, killing all the workers and their families.

As the summer progressed and news of the fighting in Warsaw and Białystok reached the Vilnius ghetto, the mood of the resistance movement began to harden. Until now, many had believed that the large ghettos elsewhere would be safe from liquidation purely because they were so populous, but it was clear that the Germans now had the means to kill as many people as they wished. Throughout 1942 and the first half of 1943, Gens and the ghetto police had studiously avoided taking any steps against the resistance fighters, but Gens was now under pressure from the Germans to take such measures. There were regular searches for weapons caches, and Gens and some of the senior ghetto police were permitted by the Germans to carry guns; on at least one occasion, they used them against Jews who refused to hand over their weapons.

Matters came to a head on 8 July when Kittel ordered Gens to arrest Itzhak Witenberg, the Communist co-leader of the *FPO*. Gens invited the leadership of the *FPO* to meet him in his home. Accompanied by Witenberg, the group went to his house, where Witenberg was seized by two Lithuanian police officers led by Salk Dessler, Gens's deputy. But when they attempted to take Witenberg back to the guardhouse, they were ambushed by a group of *FPO* fighters led by Shmuel Kaplinsky. Witenberg was rescued, and the resistance fighters mobilised.

This triggered a serious breakdown in relations between the two sides. Gens demanded that the *FPO* surrender Witenberg, as Kittel had promised to liquidate the entire ghetto if he wasn't handed over, and he persuaded the brigadiers to support him. In addition, he was able to call upon the ghetto's criminal groups, known colloquially as the *Shtarke* ('strong ones). But Witenberg was no longer in the *FPO* houses, having slipped away disguised as a woman. Even when the *FPO* reluctantly decided that it was in the greater interests of everyone for Witenberg to surrender, he refused and remained in hiding. Terrified that the Germans would send in their troops, ordinary inmates joined the search for Witenberg and found his refuge, but Witenberg managed to flee to the *FPO*. After further argument – the *FPO* wanted him to surrender to the Germans, whereas he maintained that the Germans intended to liquidate the ghetto in any case – he handed himself in and was transferred to the German Security Police. However, Witenberg managed to avoid interrogation. The Germans had stipulated that he must be handed over alive, but he managed to hide a cyanide capsule and took it whilst in the German cells.

One of the consequences of what became known as the Witenberg Affair was that the *FPO* was acutely aware that their support was limited, and a large group of fighters – about 21 in all – left the ghetto on 24 July to join the forest partisans. Perhaps by chance, or possibly because they were betrayed, they ran into a German group about 20 miles (32km) from Vilnius, and nine of the *FPO* fighters were killed. Some of the nine were wounded and taken prisoner, dying during or after interrogation, and the following day the Security Police went to the ghetto and demanded that the families of all those who had escaped be taken into custody. A total of 32 people were taken to Ponary and executed.[13]

Throughout Lithuania, the mood of the civilian population began to change as a consequence of the growing realisation that German victory in the war was by no means guaranteed, particularly after the entry of the USA into the conflict. In late May 1943, Jews in the Kaunas ghetto became aware of a new anonymous leaflet that was circulating in the city. The pamphlet read:

> There are clear and reliable indications that preparations are afoot for new massacres of the Jews. The previous acts of murder of the Jews brought neither honour nor benefit to Lithuania. Lithuanians will be called upon to explain to the world the fact of the participation of many of their compatriots in those criminal acts. From now on, in order not to be implicated in the crime of mass murder, Lithuanians are also called upon to refrain from carrying out the instructions of the Gestapo; when risk of their life is involved, they should flee to the forest.[14]

Whilst the changing attitude of Lithuanians was welcome to the Jews in the ghetto, the first sentence of the leaflet was ominous. In addition, a Wehrmacht soldier who had known one of the members of the *Judenrat* before the war warned him that when the Red Army attacked Velikiye Luki the previous autumn – over 250 miles to the east – a substantial quantity of firearms and ammunition was moved from Riga to Kaunas, possibly in preparation for the extermination of the ghetto's inhabitants before the Red Army could arrive.

The pamphlet may have called upon Lithuanians not to cooperate with the Germans, but thousands of Lithuanians actively collaborated with the occupying authorities with varying degrees of enthusiasm. The Germans raised SS divisions in both Estonia and Latvia but were unable to secure the cooperation of the Lithuanians for similar formations to be raised; however, several air defence units were created to defend Lithuanian cities and German airfields in Lithuania from increasingly frequent Soviet attacks. In addition, several police battalions were raised under the authority of the *Ypatingasis Būrys* ('Special Office'). These battalions provided much of the manpower for the early shootings in Ponary and the forts around Kaunas, and although some justified their brutal acts on the grounds that they were taking revenge for real or alleged crimes by the Soviet authorities and their Jewish collaborators, many in the police battalions were deeply troubled by what they witnessed. The head of the Vilnius police force told Gens that he couldn't sleep and was haunted by visions of bodies without heads, or eyes, or faces, streaming with blood.[15] Many of his subordinates may have felt the same way, but sufficient remained willing to help the Germans for the killings to continue.

The change of mood in 1943 affected Germans, too. The official in charge of the ghetto workshops in Kaunas was a man named Gilow, who was widely disliked by the Jews. He frequently ordered them to make items for his personal use – boots, clothing, even gold rings – and was often violent towards the workers that he regarded as slaves. In June 1943, Gilow drove to Šiauliai to collect some leather. He was accompanied by his driver and several Jews. On the return journey, the truck developed engine trouble and while the driver fixed it, the Jews were permitted to climb out and rest for a moment. A nearby German soldier wandered over and tried to strike up a conversation with them:

> The Jews signalled to the German soldier … that they were Jews. They pointed to another German who was standing not far away, meaning that it was forbidden for them as Jews to speak with them. The German soldier, however, failed to take the hint. Instead, he began spewing out fire and brimstone against the war and against Nazi rule. Then the Jews showed him the yellow badges on their clothes, as if to say, 'We are Jews, we have no rights.' But the soldier was unconvinced. 'What, you have no rights? Before long you'll have all the rights.'
>
> When the soldier saw Gilow's brown trousers and Nazi uniform, his anger reached boiling point. He ran up to him: 'Just what exactly do you think, you idiots from the brown gang? You are to

> blame for this war.' Gilow's flushed red face made the soldier even angrier: 'The brown pigs stuff their faces and drink themselves silly for days on end, while we, the soldiers, must fight on every front and spill our blood for the Party parasites.' He picked up a heavy stone and set upon Gilow, who fled to the driver's cabin and slammed the door shut behind him. The driver had just finished repairing the engine and was ready to start the truck. The soldier threw a stone through the window but missed Gilow.
>
> Gilow tried to pacify the soldier: 'Comrade, you're mistaken. I served at the front for two years.' The soldier refused to be appeased: 'Your end will not be long in coming. The war is lost anyway.' ...
>
> Since then, Gilow has lost some of his self-confidence. The soldier implanted doubt in his heart, and this doubt has been gnawing at him recently. He no longer wears his Nazi uniform on all occasions; he feels better wearing civilian clothes.[16]

The behaviour of this Wehrmacht soldier is unusual. Despite the growing awareness of the setbacks suffered by German forces on every front, ordinary soldiers largely remained loyal to Hitler – even during the summer of 1944, when the Red Army was pouring west through Belarus and the Western Allies were firmly established in Normandy, most soldiers were genuinely shocked and angered by the attempt to kill Hitler in July. The contempt for the 'golden pheasants' of the civil administration was a different matter, but to express such anger in this manner ran the risk of serious consequences; the soldier must have been confident that Gilow wouldn't be able to identify him and report him to his superiors.

In light of the sense of growing threat from the anonymous leaflet and other sources, the family of Fruma Kučinskienė decided even before the liquidation of the Kaunas ghetto could begin that she would be safer outside the ghetto, as there were persistent fears that the Germans would decide all the children there who were too young to work should be eliminated. Decades later, Kučinskienė recalled what happened:

> I didn't want to be separated from my parents and my brother. At that time my mother worked in a laundry in the ghetto and I could see her from time to time. The long sleepless night before parting! The unknown future seemed threatening to me.
>
> A Jewish policeman led my friend Debora and me out of the ghetto on a cold wintry evening. We passed between the men returning from work as if through a stream of water. They hid us ...

> and soon we were far from the ghetto gate. I knew that two women were waiting for us. I had to ask for a codeword. They were the two Natashas, two Russian women with the pseudonym Engel. That evening was the last time I saw my father and my brother.
>
> Natasha later recalled that I was silent on our long walk and couldn't be persuaded to say anything. I was full of fear. When we reached Natasha's house in Žaliakalnis [northeast of the city centre] and I saw my Aunt Rivka, I began to cry. Rivka had disappeared from the ghetto at the beginning of 1942 with the family of her friend Gerda Bogriansky. She had been hiding with the Natashas for nearly two years. As soon as the threat of an 'action' against children appeared, she wanted to save me. That evening, I was to forget my name of Fruma for a long time ... [I became] Danutė Vitkauskaitė.[17]

Although Himmler had ordered the ghettos to be converted into concentration camps by 1 August, the difficulties faced by the German administrators meant that the process dragged on into the autumn, not least because Lohse's administration in Ostland was determined to retain as many workers as it could. Large numbers of Jews from the Kaunas ghetto were transferred to the concentration camp created outside Riga, including the family of Fruma Kučinskienė; she never saw any of them again. Others were dispatched further north to the Baltic coast of Estonia, where the Germans had established a network of camps.

The first concentration camp in Estonia was established in Tartu as early as August 1941. The town had been liberated from the Red Army by anti-Communist Estonian partisans known as the Forest Brothers. When they arrived the Germans invited the partisans to organise themselves as part of the *Omakaitse* ('Home Guard'). One of the first tasks assigned to the *Omakaitse* was the establishment of a prison camp in the town's Exhibition Square, where Jews and suspected Communists were interned. As the number of detainees grew, the camp was moved to the nearby Kuperjanov Barracks. Executions took place regularly and in the three years of the camp's existence, it is estimated that about 12,000 people were killed.[18] Most were taken in groups twice a week to a nearby anti-tank ditch that had been excavated by the Red Army. Lilli Lõoke, who lived close by, remembered seeing Jews being executed: 'The bus drove close to the trench. Those who walked were taken to the edge of the trench, but a small child, almost a baby, was held up by the legs, head hanging. A man shot him in the head and dropped him in the trench as if he were a puppy.'[19]

Most of the killings of Jews were carried out by Estonians, as a guard later described:

> The commandant of the camp [Karl] Linnas brought the list of people sentenced to execution to the chief of the guards and announced the time of the transportation to execution; also, other guard officers at the camp were allowed to join. The Special Department ordered a vehicle for that occasion ... Nobody except the execution unit and the leadership of the camp was to see the departure of the inmates to be executed ... A guard officer selected an execution squad from among the guards, and two special guards to be on watch duty at the time of the shooting. In Kuperjanov Barracks, all executioners were selected from among the guards at the camp; earlier there had also been members of the *Omakaitse* among the executioners ... There were always enough volunteers ...
>
> The inmates, about 10-12 people, were brought to the site in a truck ... The inmates were lined up facing the trench and thereafter shot on the orders of [Aleksander] Koolmeister.[20]

In August 1942, a concentration camp was established on the orders of Heinz Jost at Jägala, near Tallinn. The following month, the first inmates – Jews from the Theresienstadt concentration camp in Czechoslovakia – arrived, followed by Jews from Germany. Originally, these Jews had been intended for Riga, but as had been the case in late 1941 Jeckeln refused to accept them on the grounds that he lacked the space. Those deemed capable of work were sent to labour camps; the rest were executed.

The German plans for the war against the Soviet Union in the second half of 1942 had centred on the capture of the Caucasus oilfields, without which Germany would struggle to supply its armed forces with fuel. Although the campaign became concentrated around the city of Stalingrad, this had originally been purely an objective to secure the flank of the main thrust into the Caucasus region. After the defeat at Stalingrad, the Germans had to abandon their positions in the Caucasus. Although they had overrun some Soviet oil facilities, the extensive demolitions carried out by the retreating Red Army had made it almost impossible for the Germans to extract any oil. With no further prospect of capturing any territory where oil could be obtained, Germany was largely dependent on the Romanian oil wells and on the production of synthetic fuel. There was a pressing need to secure other sources of oil.

Recognising this, Goering wrote in March 1943 that the exploitation of Estonian oil shale was of critical importance. Extraction facilities had existed on the northern coast of Estonia before the German occupation but had been largely destroyed during the Soviet retreat, and work progressed only slowly. In order to accelerate the programme, Sturmbannführer Martin Sandberger, the chief of security police and the SD in Estonia and formerly commander of *Sonderkommando 1b*, part of *Einsatzgruppe A*, began to take steps so that Jewish workers could be used in a variety of activities. Part of this was the creation of a new concentration camp in Vaivara in August 1943, close to the oil shale mines.

The regime in the new camp was harsh. Unlike in the ghettos, men and women were kept in separate blocks. At first, there were several hundred children who lived with the women. Originally, Vaivara had three satellite camps but after October 1943 this grew steadily in order to increase oil shale processing. Of these subsidiary camps, Klooga became the most important. In addition to the physically demanding and unpleasant job of mining oil shale, the workers in the camps were also used for building field fortifications and other construction work, and for logging in Estonia's vast forests. In an attempt to secure better medical resources, Sturmbannführer Franz Freiherr von Bodman, the senior camp doctor, submitted a report describing the productivity of the workers and therefore the loss of production if they were too ill to work, also stressing the potential for oil production if the workers were kept healthy: 'Each inmate extracts two cubic metres of oil shale daily and, in two hours, this will give us 100 litres of oil.[21]

As the year progressed, a series of German delegations visited the Kaunas ghetto and inspected the workshops. There was considerable concern within the ghetto: did this mean that the ghetto would be liquidated and the workshops closed down? Or was it a good sign, showing that the Germans were assessing the work output of the ghetto and would thus be inclined to permit it to continue functioning? The Jews were aware of the transfer of inmates from the Vilnius ghetto to Estonia and the deaths of many, particularly when the smaller ghettos were closed down earlier in the year.

In addition to the Jews sent to Riga and Vaivara from Kaunas, there was another significant departure from the city in August 1943. After having been in the city for two years, first as head of *Einsatzkommando 3* and then as commander of the SD, Karl Jäger was replaced and given a new assignment. He took command of a small unit involved in anti-partisan operations – the details of this unit's activities have not survived – before returning to Berlin. He had been told informally that he was to be appointed as 'house commandant' at the headquarters of the RSHA, but this was not to his liking and he complained to Ernst

Kaltenbrunner, who had replaced Heydrich at the head of the RSHA. He told Kaltenbrunner that Heydrich had promised him a post as head of police in a German city; this was clearly the role that he had hoped would be his last before a long and prosperous retirement. For the moment, he was sent home on leave, but in June 1944 he finally got the post that he desired and became head of police in Reichenberg in the Sudetenland (now the Czech city of Liberec).

At about the same time, the Gestapo became suspicious of the activities of Sister Anna Borkowska in her convent near Vilnius. After the arrests of several clergy who had been helping Jews the previous year, the Germans had kept a close watch on the convent and in the summer of 1943 they arrested all of the nuns and shut down the convent. The women were interrogated and sent to concentration camps.

When the Germans attempted a further clearance of the Białystok ghetto in August 1943, the Jews were once more prepared to resist. Until now, the resistance had been largely composed of two groups, one made up of Communists and one of Zionists, but a unified command was now created. The SS units involved were under the command of Gruppenführer Odilo Globocnik, one of the most notorious figures involved in the Holocaust. At this stage, the Germans had learned from their experiences in Warsaw and fully anticipated armed resistance, particularly as the Białystok Jews had already fought them earlier in the year. A force consisting of German SS personnel reinforced by Wehrmacht soldiers, former Soviet prisoners of war who had volunteered to serve in German units (known as *Hilfswillige* or *Hiwis*) and Ukrainian paramilitaries encircled the ghetto. They were opposed by about 300 resistance fighters. The battle continued for five days from 16 August and Globocnik's troops were repeatedly driven back, even after they deployed armoured vehicles and air strikes.

A counterattack by the Jews briefly recaptured the central area of the ghetto, but the final result was never in doubt. After most attempts to break out of the ghetto failed, Tenenbaum and the other fighters fought to the last bullet. Tenenbaum committed suicide to avoid capture. About 150 fighters managed to escape into the surrounding forests, where they joined pro-Soviet partisan groups. The ghetto was then systematically liquidated, with its surviving residents taken to a variety of camps, where most of them were eventually killed. About 1,000 children from the ghetto were taken first to Theresienstadt, and thence to Auschwitz where they were all killed.[22]

The first steps to move Jews from the Vilnius ghetto to Estonia were carried out at the beginning of August. About 3,000 workers were told that they were no longer needed by their workplaces, but the numbers of labourers working on the railways and at a nearby airfield were increased. Rumours spread through the ghetto that people were about to be shipped off to Riga and elsewhere and many tried to avoid leaving the ghetto to go to their workplaces, fearing that they would instead be marched off to an uncertain fate. Gens reacted by placing many of these workers under arrest; he was forced to release them when their families gathered en masse outside the prison and threatened to break in.[23]

The following day – 6 August – most of the workers assigned to the airfield labour team reported for work, only to find themselves surrounded by Estonian troops when they reached their workplace. Fearing the worst, many tried to flee. Some were caught on the barbed wire around the camp and dragged back, while others were gunned down by the guards. Only a few escaped. Other workers were also rounded up at their workplaces and taken to the railway station, where about 1,000 Jews were herded into cattle trucks. After the incident in which Jews who had been told that they were being taken to Kaunas were actually shipped to Ponary and executed, there was understandable fear amongst those on the trains, but on this occasion they were spared immediate execution and were sent instead to Estonia to try to increase oil production.

Some of those who managed to slip away attempted to return to the ghetto; most were captured by German and Estonian troops who had been deployed in anticipation of such an attempt, but some succeeded in re-entering. Once word spread, there was widespread unrest and many refused to believe Gens's assurances that their family members were safe and had been sent to Estonia. On 9 August, Obersturmführer Rudolf Neugebauer, the head of Security Police and SS in Vilnius, visited the ghetto and addressed the brigadiers, reiterating Gens's statements. He urged the Jews to continue attending their workplaces, and two days later one of the brigadiers who had been dispatched to Estonia returned to the ghetto to confirm that the Jews had reached Vaivara. He brought several letters with him, and for the moment the mood in the ghetto calmed, though the contents of the letters painted a grim picture: 'We are still alive and working. Our employer is Todt [the Todt Organisation, responsible for major construction projects]. Food is scarce, 400g bread a day, [the] work is hard, but the main thing for me is clothes … I don't have a coat or any underwear. It rains hard here and it's very cold.'[24]

Despite the assurances of Neugebauer, the demands for labour in Estonia in order to improve oil shale extraction required further influxes of Jews. The front line was now the old frontier between Estonia and the Soviet Union, and the Germans wished to accelerate their operation in Vaivara to secure as much oil as they could before the area became a war zone. Consequently, Gens was told that he had to provide an additional 5,000 workers. In an attempt to avoid forcible deportations, Gens asked for volunteers. Many, particularly those whose family members had already been sent to Estonia on 6 August, agreed to go, but when the new group departed on 24 August it numbered fewer than 1,500 and included many children, far short of the workforce that the Germans had demanded. As a result, the German and Estonian forces returned to the ghetto on 1 September and sealed it off. Gens was told that he had to dispatch 3,000 men and 2,000 women without delay to Estonia.

Immediately, the *FPO* ordered its personnel to mobilise. It was organised into two battalions; one battalion managed to reach its concentration area safely and armed itself, but the other was betrayed and ambushed. Most of its personnel were captured but some managed to slip away and join the first battalion. At noon, the *FPO* issued a proclamation to the entire population of the ghetto:

> Jews! Defend yourselves with arms! The German and Lithuanian hangmen have arrived at the gates of the ghetto. They have come to murder us! Within a short while, they will lead us group after group through the gate. Thus they led out hundreds on Yom Kippur [in 1941]! Thus they led us out on the night of the White, the Yellow and the Pink Passes. Thus they led our brothers and sisters, our mothers and fathers, our children. Thus were tens of thousands taken out to their death. But we shall not go! We shall not stretch our necks like sheep for the slaughter ... Do not believe the reassuring prevarications of the murderers. Do not believe the statements of the traitors. Anyone who goes out of the ghetto gate has only one route – to Ponary. And Ponary means death! Jews! We have nothing to lose, death will snatch us up in any event ...
>
> Jewish masses! Go out into the street! Whoever has no weapons, take up a hatchet; whoever has no hatchet, take steel and cudgel and stick! For our fathers, for our murdered children! To revenge Ponary, strike the murderers! In every street, in every courtyard, in every room, inside the ghetto and outside it. Hit at the dogs! Jews! We have nothing to lose! We shall save our lives only if we wipe out the murderers. Long live freedom! Long live armed defence, death to the murderers![25]

In the most desperate situations, it is natural for people to cling to whatever hope there might be. Faced with the choice between almost certain death in fighting against the Germans and the possibility of surviving a little longer – after all, the letters from Vaivara confirmed that the first trainload of Jews had reached its destination safely and was actually so near to the front line that liberation might be close at hand – few of the ghetto inhabitants joined the resistance fighters. Even the *FPO* had mixed feelings about a call to arms, as Kovner later described:

> We cogitated more than anything else over the moral aspect. Were we entitled to do this, and when? Were we entitled to offer people up in flames? Most of them were unarmed – what would happen to all of them? And if in the meantime it turned out that this was not liquidation. We were terribly perplexed as to what right we had to determine their fate.[26]

Aware of the concentration of *FPO* combatants from the first battalion, Gens managed to persuade the Germans to withdraw from the ghetto and promised to deal with matters personally – he wished to avoid an armed clash between Germans and the *FPO*, which might easily overflow into general violence against the entire ghetto. Despite ordering the ghetto police to round up as many men as possible to satisfy the German demands for labour, Gens was able to hand over only 600 by the end of the day, and the Germans and Estonians re-entered the ghetto and rapidly closed in on the *FPO* stronghold. Mascha Rolnikaite recorded the events in her diary:

> A few officers accompanied Gens into the courtyard and announced over a loudspeaker that all those who were hiding in the cellars were to come out into the courtyard immediately. If they didn't, they would be blown up. If the women wished to save their husbands and brothers, they should urge them to leave their hideouts. Gens made the same announcement, but in vain. Nobody appeared. The most senior officer ordered the women to leave the courtyard within five minutes. The soldiers prepared explosives. They placed them on the left side of the house, directly over the cellar.
>
> Dreadful panic broke out amongst the women. A few hurried to leave the courtyard as quickly as they could, others tried to stop the soldiers from preparing the explosives, still others ran desperately back to the cellar, some screaming for their men to come out and some urging them to stay there. The women who kept their composure stood by the entrance to the cellar and pushed the panicking women away. They tried to explain that the cellar was deep and made of concrete and wouldn't be harmed by the explosives.

> When they saw that the soldiers had left the courtyard, they too ran, their eyes wide with terror, arms outstretched, as if they were trying to protect someone.
>
> A huge explosion was heard. I was standing some distance away but was still deafened by it. The brick walls collapsed and fell in. A huge cloud of smoke rose up. When it cleared, we gazed on the ruins. Where there had been houses there was now just rubble.[27]

Desperate to avoid further armed clashes, Gens once again persuaded the Germans to allow him time to round up sufficient workers. Over the next two days, the ghetto police – assisted by volunteers – succeeded in gathering sufficient women for the required quota, but the total of Jewish males still remained short. Meanwhile, Abba Kovner, who was in command of the surviving *FPO* fighters, discussed with his fellow fighters how best to proceed. For the moment, they decided to remain in the ghetto – their chances of escaping to join the partisans outside Vilnius would be greater if they waited until the German 'action' was over. After clandestine discussions with Gens, an agreement was reached: the *FPO* would refrain from combat provided that Gens managed to keep the Germans from initiating any similar actions.[28]

Amongst those who were rounded up to be sent to Estonia after the demolition of the *FPO* house were several hundred workers from *HKP 562*. As soon as he heard, Plagge gathered together a group of soldiers from his workshop and went with them to the railway station. He succeeded in locating the prisoners and ordered his men to remove them from the train and to ensure that they remained safe. He then left the railway station, but shortly after Neugebauer appeared. He immediately ordered the Jews to be put back onto the train. Although Plagge had left armed soldiers to protect the Jews, any attempt to do so would have resulted in a direct clash with the SD and police personnel present, and Plagge's subordinates could only watch helplessly as the Jews were pushed back into the cattle trucks. This led to a furious exchange between Plagge and Neugebauer, but it was in vain: the trains had already left.

It was clear to Plagge that while the Jews working for him remained in the ghetto, they were at the mercy of Neugebauer, Kittel and others. He decided that the best way to proceed was not via further confrontation with Neugebauer, but instead wrote to higher authorities and suggested the establishment of a work camp outside the ghetto, close to the workshops of *HKP 562*. He had identified two large buildings in the east of Vilnius, originally built by a Jewish industrialist as housing for his workers. Discussions took several days, and Plagge travelled first to

Kaunas and then to Riga. The SS were resistant to the plan, especially when Plagge made it clear that he wished to re-house not only his workers, but also their families – he eventually overcame objections by his repeated insistence that if families were separated, this would have a negative impact upon the morale and hence the productivity of his workers. After patient and dogged negotiations, Plagge succeeded. In addition to re-housing his remaining workforce and their families, he also inherited many of the workers from the Kailis clothing factory. Mira Rolnikaite, sister of diarist Mascha, was able to join those moving to Plagge's new work camp; she took advantage of the moment and disappeared into the city streets.

The surviving members of the *FPO* left the ghetto in the first two weeks of September with the tacit approval of Gens. On 14 September, Gens was summoned to the headquarters of the Security Police. He received a tip-off – either from a German or a Lithuanian – that he was about to be arrested and that he should attempt to flee, but fearing that this would trigger fresh reprisals against the ghetto he decided that he had no choice but to comply with the German demands. He was accompanied by his assistant Dessler, who was ordered back to the ghetto by the Germans. Gens was arrested by Neugebauer and Weiss and taken to a small prison near the SD headquarters. The two Germans took him into the back yard of the building where a grave had already been dug, and Neugebauer executed Gens with a single shot to the head.

When he returned to the ghetto, Dessler told the Jews that Neugebauer had confronted Gens with the words: 'There is a nest of Jewish partisans in the ghetto who fought us. You, as chief of the ghetto, did not turn them over to us. I arrest you for that.'[29] The day after the killing, Kittel went to the ghetto and addressed the ghetto police, telling them that Gens had been executed because he had failed to follow the directives given to him by the Germans. Dessler was appointed as the new head of police.

Gens remains a controversial figure even today, with opinion divided on whether he was a cynical collaborator or someone who genuinely believed that he could save his fellow Jews by limited cooperation with the Germans, as touched upon earlier. Samuel Esterowicz had few doubts about Gens – although he refers to the Gestapo, this is effectively a shorthand for the various overlapping German administrations responsible for the persecution of the Jews:

> In my opinion, the different evaluations of Gens' role in our tragedy are due to a fact that his defenders do not take into account: the reality [is] that in the Gestapo we had a merciless and treacherous

enemy whose aim was not only to exterminate us, [but that] we should also disappear quietly and without resistance. Even though resistance on our part was senseless given the huge inequality of forces, the Germans could still be offered resistance from people who knew that they had nothing to lose ...

Gens was needed by the Gestapo for the accomplishment of a second aim. [The] Gestapo needed a Jew who on the one hand would convince us that we could save ourselves through work and on the other hand would, working from the inside, smother any attempt at organised resistance.

[The] Gestapo wanted us to trust Gens and give him authority – on this depended his efficacy in carrying out his mission. Thus they tried to lead us astray about his real role. Thus we see Gens in the role of the deliverer of Jews arrested by the Gestapo, the patron of the arts and one who helped the *Judenrat* in the organisation of life in the ghetto.

One has to admit that it is possible that Gens got induced into his treacherous work only gradually, and that he had been made the obedient tool of our deadly enemies through coercion.

The judgement of history in this case should be tempered by this circumstance. After all, Gens' refusal to obey would have brought his immediate death and thus demanded heroism of him – a trait we have no right to demand. But even though Gens' guilt might have been tempered (but not excused) by a circumstance which we have no right to exclude, the judgement of history has to apply all its severity in its condemnation of Gens for the extraordinary zeal displayed by him in his treacherous work, his heartless brutality and his shameless brazen favouritism.[30]

Others took a more charitable view. One ghetto inmate wrote in his diary:

The report of the killing of Gens spread like lightning throughout the ghetto and hit the inhabitants like a thunderbolt. If there had ever been two opinions about Gens, if Gens had supporters and opponents – there were no longer two opinions nor any who hated him. All, virtually all, understood that the ghetto had lost in the person of Commander Jacob Gens one who was important to them all, a man of wide vision and great understanding of historical moments.[31]

Even members of the *FPO* showed some sympathy:

The hearts of the Jews mourn the tragedy of Gens. It may be charged that his course was harmful, but everyone knows he was

> never a traitor. All that he did during his tenure as chief of the ghetto was for his people ... Everyone knows that Gens had many opportunities to save himself ... but he renounced his personal safety to devote himself to the ghetto. He believed in his ability and was convinced to the last moment that he would be able to save [the last inhabitants of the ghetto].[32]

Kittel continued his operation to eliminate the ghetto. On 18 September, German and Lithuanian police sealed it off and Kittel demanded from Dessler that several hundred labourers be handed over. Realising that Plagge's work camp was likely to be a haven for Jews when the long-delayed liquidation of the ghetto took place, Dessler moved his parents and two friends into the camp and went into hiding – he had already prepared somewhere to hide outside the ghetto. The workers that he had forced to gather promptly disappeared into their *malines* in the ghetto and Kittel took personal charge of the ghetto police, ordering them to search for those in hiding. Only a few were found, and they were soon released. Furious at Dessler's disappearance, Kittel had his parents removed from the *HKP 562* work camp and executed.

On 23 September, the Germans informed the remaining Jews that the ghetto was to be liquidated. Mascha Rolnikaite recalled the moment when the announcement was made:

> The Germans stood on the steps to Dessler's accommodation and had a megaphone brought to them. One read out an order from the Gestapo chief: the Jews of the Vilnius ghetto who had first come here two years ago were to be evacuated to two work camps. One was in Estonia, the other here in Lithuania near Šiauliai. The evacuation would take place today. Everyone should take with them only what they could personally carry.
>
> On his own initiative, the speaker added that he meant a bucket, saucepan, and other kitchen equipment, as these items wouldn't be available at the new work camps. We were to be ready for the journey in four hours. Departure from the ghetto would be at 1100 precisely ...
>
> Mother packed our things. The little ones sat on the bunk bed and watched her. When they saw that she was crying, their eyes also filled with tears ...[33]

Several hundred Jews attempted to hide in their *malines*, but most obeyed through a mixture of resignation and hope that there would indeed be work camps for them. They were marched out of the ghetto gates – where Neugebauer, Kittel, Weiss and other Germans watched and kept a tally of those leaving – walking down streets lined with soldiers, many with dogs. The column trudged through cold drizzle to a large square near the railway station. Here, they watched as Kittel paraded three captured *FPO* fighters before them; one of them had shot and killed a Gestapo officer when they were arrested. Kittel oversaw the erection of a gallows, and all three men were hanged in front of the gathered Jews.[34]

The following day, the Germans began the process of selecting relatively fit workers:

> There were two rows of Gestapo [again, this is shorthand for the mixture of German and allied police and paramilitaries] facing each other for about 200 feet ... they took my father immediately ... My brother put rouge on my mother to make her look younger. But when we went through the Gestapo with my mother, they pulled her from his arms to the left and he went to the right. I was left stunned ... The Gestapo hit her to make her keep going ... My sister and I went to the right. Right was the path to work, left to death. The older men went to wagons with the older women.[35]

Some of the women and children were forced to pass through a narrow door, one at a time, as Mascha Rolnikaite described:

> Mother was worried that we would be separated and let me go first. Ruwele was to follow behind me, then Rajele and finally Mother herself. In this manner we would all remain in sight of each other.
>
> I went through. A soldier grabbed me by my coat and pulled me to one side. There were no trucks to be seen. I turned and wanted to speak to Mother but she was not there. The soldiers had formed a chain across the entire road. Behind this chain – and another beyond it – was a great crowd of people. Mother was there. I ran to the soldier and asked him to let me through. I explained that I had been separated by mistake from my mother. She was standing over there. They were my family and I had to reach them.
>
> I spoke to him and argued, but the soldier didn't even notice me. He looked at the women coming through the door. And he continued to pull one or other to our side. The rest were pushed into the crowd of people where Mother was standing.
>
> Suddenly I heard Mother's voice. She cried out that I just shouldn't go to her side. And she asked the soldier not to let me through, as I was still young and could work hard.

> 'Mama!' I cried as loud as I could, 'come with me!'
>
> She shook her head and called in the same clear voice, 'Live, my child! At least you can live! Take revenge for the little ones!' She bent down to them, said something and arduously lifted them up one by one so that I could see them. Ruwele looked so odd, he waved at me with his hands. Then they were pushed to one side. I couldn't see them any more.[36]

Mascha was one of about 1,600 fit women who were selected for work. Of her three siblings, only Mira, her sister, survived the war; she was hidden with 11 other Jews by a Lithuanian priest. Her mother and her two youngest siblings, Rajele and Ruwele, were amongst about 5,000 taken from the Vilnius ghetto who were dispatched to the Majdanek death camp as unfit for further work. Several people had attempted to flee while being marched from the ghetto and were shot on the spot, and those unfit for travel were taken to Ponary where they were shot.

About 2,000 Jews had hidden in the *malines* in the ghetto and the police searched diligently for their hiding places. Most were located, often when the inmates were forced into the open when they ran out of food and water. A few managed to escape via the sewers into the city; some were able to contact Lithuanians they had known before the war and were given shelter. Plagge was able to persuade the SS to release 100 men who were found in hiding in order to replace the personnel from his workforce who had been sent to Estonia, but the rest of those who were captured were marched to Ponary in small groups and executed. Together with the last of his *FPO* comrades, Abba Kovner escaped from the ghetto through the sewers.

The formal abolition of the Kaunas ghetto and its conversion into a concentration camp resulted in many of the enterprises that had relied on work brigades from the ghetto moving to Riga; others closed down entirely. Within the camp, conditions remained hard for the inmates, who were now further traumatised by so many of their family members being shipped off to Riga or the Vaivara camps. Obersturmbannführer Wilhelm Göcke, who was the camp commandant, rapidly implemented changes, as Avraham Gollub described:

> Göcke's initial plan was to break up the ghetto, dispersing those ghetto residents who could still be exploited for their work among seven or eight labour camps. Children were to be left in the ghetto, their fate undetermined. This plan was opposed by various economic and military bodies, including the city governor and governor-general, as well as by factories and other enterprises

> which used Jewish labour to manufacture most of their products. As a result of this opposition, Göcke's plan was modified.
>
> According to the new plan, the smaller labour brigades will gradually be broken up and joined to larger units. People will leave for work escorted by policemen from the ghetto [technically now a concentration camp]. They will return to the ghetto at the end of the working day, marching in close formation. As a result, the Jews will disappear from the city streets, since they will no longer go to work ... as part of small labour brigades. Thus they will not fill up the city streets; the feelings of the Aryan city residents will no longer be offended.[37]

On 25 October, Göcke informed the *Judenrat* that he required 3,000 workers for transfer elsewhere. Only a small number of those designated by the *Judenrat* appeared the following morning, and Göcke ordered the ghetto police backed by Ukrainian paramilitaries to round up Jews indiscriminately. About 2,000 were dispatched to the Vaivara camps to work on oil shale processing; 758 were deemed to be unfit for work and were sent to Auschwitz where they were killed.[38] The remaining 8,000 Jews were still about four times the number that the SS had intended to leave in the camp, but for the moment no further 'actions' took place.

Not long after, Göcke caused considerable anxiety when he informed the *Judenrat* that he wished to centralise care for all children in the ghetto so that their mothers could be released for work, and many feared that this would be a prelude to widespread killings. If the Jews had any doubts about Göcke and his intentions, opinions hardened a few days later when a Jew from the Palemonas work camp returned to Kaunas and told the inmates about the fate of a young Jewish woman:

> She tried to bribe a Ukrainian policeman to allow her to go to a nearby Lithuanian house to purchase food. Someone heard about her request to the Ukrainian and informed the head of the camp. At about the same time, Göcke arrived at Palemonas in his car. When he learned what had occurred, he ordered the two of them – the Jewish woman and the Ukrainian policeman – to be shot. The Ukrainian begged for his life. Göcke pardoned him, on condition that he kill the Jewess with his own hands ... Having unsuccessfully tried to evade this devilish assignment, the Ukrainian finally accepted.[39]

After the liquidation of the Vilnius ghetto, the Germans turned their attention to the killing ground at Ponary. A workforce of about 70 Jews and perhaps a dozen Soviet prisoners of war was taken to Ponary where they were kept in an underground bunker. Every day, they were brought out with fetters and chains on their legs and forced to dig up the corpses of those murdered in preceding months and years; the remains were then piled into heaps, which were set ablaze.

Yitzhak Arad, who was one of the *FPO* fighters who escaped from the ghetto with Kovner, later looked back on the fate of the Jews of Vilnius:

> Jewish Vilna had its origins in the late 15th century. Over many generations, the Jewish community of Vilna grew and prospered, and by dint of its writers, scholars, rabbis and institutions devoted to the Torah and the intellectual content of its existence, that community won a central and enduring place in the spiritual life of the Jewish people the world over. Such was Jewish Vilna until its annihilation by the German Nazis and their Lithuanian collaborators. The period of the Holocaust was, for the Jewish citizen of Vilna, one of struggle without prospect; the forces of extermination that were arrayed against him were simply too overwhelming. Out of a total of approximately 57,000 Vilna Jews subjected to the Nazi regime, only some 2-3,000 survived, one third of them in the forests – a pitiful remnant of the terrible destruction of the 'Jerusalem of Lithuania'.[40]

In Kaunas too, the Germans tried to destroy evidence of the mass killings. Avraham Gollub described how 75 prisoners – one Polish woman and the rest Jews, a mixture of ghetto inmates and Soviet prisoners of war – were assembled; 11 were found to be unfit for labour and were executed. The rest were divided into several groups:

> One group, the 'diggers', had to dig out the dead corpses – to scrape off the upper layer of the earth from the pits, and then, with spades, remove the first layer of corpses. This group then had to go down into the pit by ladder and, using pitchforks, toss the remaining bodies up to the surface. The German supervisors used to make cynical remarks such as 'Stick the pitchfork in the belly of that disgusting Jew' or 'Toss up that Jewish woman – that Sarah – by digging your pitchfork into her hair' …
>
> When the corpses were brought up, the gold teeth had to be extracted, all rings and bracelets removed, and searches made for gold and jewels in the rotting garments of the dead. Then all valuables had to be cleaned and polished and handed over to the German supervisors. Most of the corpses were half or totally

> decayed, but some were well preserved. More than once, the diggers recognised their own acquaintances ...
>
> Once the belly of a woman in her last months of pregnancy cracked in the terrible heat of the pyre, and from inside her burst a small baby's body. The Jewish prisoners were stunned. Even the Nazi guards were astonished ...
>
> After the corpses had been brought out of the pits by the diggers, the members of the second group, 'porters', piled the bodies on special wooden pallets, counted them in the presence of a Nazi supervisor, and took them to the pyres. There, a third group, the 'firemen', were at work, headed by an expert on burning – the *Brandmeister*. This group had to prepare the pyre once every 24 hours as follows: in the courtyard of the Fort, not far from the pits, they would lay out a long row of logs, put a row of bodies on it, then lay another row of logs on top of the bodies, and another row of bodies on the second pile of logs. The daily quota was fixed at 300 bodies. To make it easier to light the fire, kerosene was poured into holes dug in the ground as well as over the corpses themselves. On either side were narrow trenches, into which ran the fat of the burning corpses ... After each fire there remained heaps of ashes and bones, which were pounded in huge mortars. This 'flour' was flung into the air or dug into the soil.[41]

Similar scenes occurred wherever mass killings of Jews and others had taken place in Eastern Europe. Faced with the growing likelihood of being driven out of these territories, the Germans were determined to hide as much physical evidence of their crimes as they could. But while former residents of the ghettos survived, their testimony would remain.

9

The Approaching End

By late 1943, there could be little doubt about the final outcome of the war. German cities were being bombed to rubble by British and American bombers, and it seemed that the creation of the long-awaited 'second front', an invasion of Western Europe would surely take place soon. Within the Soviet Union, the Wehrmacht was in retreat almost everywhere. The German armies had been driven back across central Ukraine, Kiev was once more in Soviet hands, and the hopes of the Germans that they would be able to bring the Red Army to a halt along the Dnepr River were dashed when Soviet forces raced to reach and cross the river even as German units were withdrawing to the west bank. In the north, the Siege of Leningrad – the terrible, prolonged agony that cost the Soviet Union more lives than British Empire war dead from both World Wars combined – had been lifted, and the Red Army was planning its advance towards Estonia. Liberation of the Baltic States from German occupation seemed to be only a matter of time. The key for the Jews was to survive long enough to see it.

For the Lithuanian Jews who were sent to work camps elsewhere in the region, conditions varied. In Vaivara, the insistence of the authorities on strict Nazi rules resulted in considerable inefficiencies – Jews were not permitted to mix with non-Jewish civilians or prisoners of war, often resulting in almost daily rearrangements of the makeup of each shift. In an attempt to ensure that the labourers could cope with the heavy work, rations were comparatively good, but inmates were often subjected to arbitrary acts of violence. Abram Krein, one of the Jews who was sent to the camp, described how a German medical orderly forced an inmate to undress and stand in the Baltic cold air for two hours, and then shot him. Other Jews – especially those regarded as no longer being fit for work – were simply pushed off the nearby cliffs into the sea.[1]

Mascha Rolnikaite and other women selected for work from the Vilnius ghetto endured an uncomfortable journey in cattle trucks. Their first fear had been that they would find themselves in Ponary, but instead were taken to a camp:

> A camp! Barracks! A long, single floor, made of wood. Through the windows leaked a weak light. People were busy all around. All wore odd striped pyjamas. We saw something strange at one barracks building: people in striped clothes jumping out of the windows. They leaped out and rushed back into the barracks, jumped out of the windows again and then went back once more. Soldiers beat them and urged them to make haste. The people fell but scrambled up under the blows, ran on and jumped again. What did it mean? Were they lunatics that the soldiers were using for their entertainment?
>
> We were ordered to leave our bundles [of belongings] in a square next to the barracks. They wouldn't let us take anything with us.
>
> Two soldiers guarded the square. A couple of men in striped pyjamas came up to us shamefully. Quietly, they began to talk to us, asking where we came from. We also wanted to know where we had been sent. It turned out that we were in the Kaiserwald concentration camp not far from Riga. But apparently we would not remain here and would be sent on. The men in striped pyjamas were concentration camp prisoners. If we had cigarettes or bread, we would be better off sharing with them as the overseers would take them away from us. The people jumping out of the windows weren't insane, just normal people who were being punished for some insignificant offence. The smallest misdemeanour was punished here ... Fleeing was impossible as the barbed wire fence was electrified. There was very little to eat – 250g bread and a quarter litre of so-called soup. Often, people were punished by not getting any food all day. Everyone was hungry. As we had nothing to give them, they ran off quickly, as speaking to women would result in 25 lashes.[2]

After having their hair shorn, the women were given an ill-fitting assortment of clothes. Rolnikaite was one of several who were taken to a work camp a short distance away. Here, the workers – both men and women – were roused before dawn and then marched to a construction site, where Rolnikaite was ordered to load rocks into carts:

> The stones were dreadfully heavy. Carrying a stone between two people or rolling it was forbidden. Speaking during work was not

> permitted. Stopping work [for a toilet break] was permitted just once a day, but we had to wait until others had returned.
>
> My fingers were soon bloody. They were swollen and looked awful.
>
> To make matters worse, it rained heavily.
>
> I was completely exhausted when the signal for the midday meal sounded. We had to leave quickly and were taken back into the work camp. Those who were at the front received a bowl of soup. Those at the end of the line had to wait until a bowl was free. We pressed forward a little out of fear of not getting any.
>
> And thus it was. No sooner had I started to slurp my soup than a soldier chased us out again. One of the guards struck my soup spoon from my hand and the soup spilled on the floor. For better or worse, I had to form up in my rank. The couple of spoonfuls of soup had given me an appetite.
>
> Once again, I carried stones. Now it was even harder. And the rain was even worse. A stone slipped from my hands and landed on my foot.
>
> I could hardly wait for evening. When we were back in the camp we were each given a piece of bread and some murky water – they called it coffee.[3]

Herman Kruk was one of the many Jews who were sent to the northern coast of Estonia. Conditions were grim but much depended on the personalities of the guards. Generally, the Estonian and Ukrainian guards behaved well, but there were isolated incidents of violence. The Germans varied in their attitudes. Some were content merely to ensure that work was carried out as ordered; others imposed arbitrary punishments.

The Jews in *HKP 562* were the most fortunate of those in work camps across the Baltic States. Food remained in limited supply, but nobody starved and there was little or no mistreatment of individuals – Plagge and his officers continued to ensure that the workers were treated well. Worried that the SS might attempt to remove Jews who had no obvious work, Plagge managed to negotiate for those who had worked in the *Kailis* factory before being transferred to his work camp to set up sewing machines in the lofts of his two apartment buildings. Here, they worked to repair clothing for the Wehrmacht, fulfilling a contract with the Rietz and Meier clothing companies. The amount of work that was carried out was relatively modest, but it was sufficient to give the impression that the Jews – including many of the children – were safely employed. As the end of 1943 approached, Plagge ordered his men to give small gifts to their Jewish workers. It was a unique and kind gesture in the monstrous system of forced labour camps across the occupied territories.

Amongst the Jews working in the camp was Joseph Panzer, who had been a teacher before the war. He was one of the many workers who had no skills or qualifications for such work, but Alfons von Deschwanden and a few other soldiers in the camp began a series of impromptu classes to teach the workers the basics of engine mechanics. Panzer proved to be an able pupil and impressed Deschwanden with his understanding of the complexities of gearboxes. He was soon made responsible for overseeing the repair and replacement of such parts, and often astonished the Germans by being able to recall from memory the details of engines that had been sent back to Germany for replacement, or when specific parts could be expected to be delivered. He and Deschwanden became close friends, and from Panzer, the young German learned more about the horrors that the Jews had endured.

However, like all work camps employing Jews, the camp remained technically under the control of the SS, and the SS NCO who oversaw the camp, Oberscharführer Richter, was known to the Jews as *Golosheyka* ('little bare neck') on account of his scrawny appearance. The SS also provided the guards who kept watch on the camp at night, and there was a small group of Jewish police who were responsible for keeping order in the camp. One day towards the end of 1943, there was a graphic demonstration of the limits of Plagge's ability to protect his workers. Samuel Esterowicz described what happened when the Germans captured two workers who had tried to escape from the camp compound:

> After all the workers had been mustered out on the yard where the Jewish police had previously (on the orders of the Germans) built a gallows, the gate suddenly opened and three Gestapo men, led by Bruno Kittel, the liquidator of the ghetto, drove in, in an open car.
>
> They brought with them two fugitives from our camp that they had caught – a woman ... nicknamed *Pozhar* ['Fire'] and her fictitious husband [i.e. like others, they had declared themselves married in order to avoid an 'action'] whom I had known as an employee of the stationery store of Zhabinski on Niemecka Street.
>
> The deathly silence that reigned as the Gestapo men moved towards the gallows with the condemned couple was broken by a piercing cry of 'Mama!' which suddenly sounded from a window on the upper floor of one of the buildings, where we saw a child's head.
>
> Within a minute a little girl, perhaps eight or ten years old, ran out of the building and with a joyous cry of 'Mama!' rushed to embrace her mother, Pozhar.

> Here, we witnessed a horrible, heartrending scene – the joy of the child who thought that she had found the mother she was longing for, and face of the mother, distorted by suffering, who was passionately embracing her child, knowing that she was walking to her death. When the whole group arrived at the place of execution, Kittel motioned with his hands for Grisha Shneider, the camp's blacksmith ... to step forward from our lines and ordered him to be the executioner. However, when the man, whom they were hanging first, fell twice when the noose broke, Kittel ordered him to kneel down and killed him by a shot to the back of the head. Afterwards, while he was killing the woman, one of the other Gestapo men killed the child.[4]

Other accounts of this episode differ in detail – one witness recalled that the child was hanged first, and that after the noose around the neck of the man – David Zalkind – broke, Kittel laughed and said that if it broke a hundred times, he would hang him a hundred times. But even after the three people were dead, the incident wasn't over. Perela Esterowiccz recalled what happened the following day:

> The next morning, after the men had gone to work, the Gestapo ordered the Jewish police to chase all the women and children out of the rooms into the huge yard adjacent to the buildings.
>
> When the policeman Miganz, a man my parents knew, chased us down into the yard, we were immediately surrounded by rifle-wielding Lithuanian police. Kittel mustered us out into rows and stood before us with his arms crossed. My mother and I were in the first row, Kittel was standing just in front of us. He was very handsome, like a film actor. I will never forget him standing before us, regarding us for a very long time – I had nightmares long afterward imagining huge, flashing fluorescent green eyes staring at me. Then Kittel smiled and, I guess at a sign from him, the Lithuanian police started to club us, herding us around the side of the building, toward where they were grabbing and dragging women into the black van standing between the two buildings. My mother said, 'Let's go, why be beaten up before we die?' But I wanted to live so passionately, I was looking at the tiny barred basement windows and wishing I could squeeze through them. I pulled my mother away from the side from which they were dragging women to the black van, at the risk of being clubbed. My mother was anxiously repeating, 'I have the golden cigarette case on me, Dad will have nothing to live on after they take us!' Then suddenly, my father broke through the clubbing Lithuanians, the

> only man who came to stand with his family. When it was over – they had filled their quota of victims – and we could leave the yard, we ran like arrows to the upper floor of the building. The ecstasy of being able to this simple thing was indescribable. Through the high window we looked down on the yard – the black van was still there, we saw a frenzied man in a paroxysm next to it, vainly begging the Germans to let his wife out.[5]

A total of 36 women were taken away and executed at Ponary as a collective punishment for the escape attempt of David Zalkind and Pozhar. Once more, Kittel's actions concentrated the minds of the Jews – whilst they were fortunate to be in Plagge's work camp, they weren't immune from the capricious wrath of the Germans. When he was informed of the incident, Plagge's reaction was characteristically muted. He was aware that there was nothing that he could do to prevent Kittel and the SS from such activities. When he met some of the workers shortly afterwards, he told them, 'Regrettably, the war has destroyed moral values as well as the material ones.'[6] Quietly, many of the Jews began to prepare *malines* in the two accommodation blocks.

A few days later, Kittel returned to the work camp. Since the liquidation of the Vilnius ghetto, Salk Dessler – Gens' replacement as chief of the Jewish police – had been hiding with his wife Rega, and Kittel remained determined to find him. One of the Jews in the camp, Petya Sakin, was a friend of Dessler, and Kittel put a noose around his neck, threatening to hang him on the spot unless he revealed Dessler's location. Sakin had no idea where Dessler was and fortunately managed to persuade Kittel of this. But another inmate named Altaszewski had been an editor of a Polish newspaper in Łodź, Rega Dessler's hometown. Under pressure from Kittel, he told the Germans that Alpern, a member of the ghetto's Jewish police and now a police officer in the work camp, had helped Dessler construct a *maline* outside the ghetto in the basement of a baker's shop that had once belonged to Alpern. Here, the Germans found the Desslers, still in hiding since the liquidation of the ghetto. They were both arrested and later executed, even though Rega Dessler was not a Jew.

Many had suspected Dessler of being too close to the Germans, even acting as their spy and informer, and there were few tears shed when his fate was announced. Many of the Jews who had survived over two years of persecution and often random killings had become hardened to their plight, as an incident recounted by Samuel Esterowicz shows:

> The Germans brought to our camp a man named Fikhler, after they had been informed that he was a converted Jew. When Fikhler ...

> was able to see his Gentile wife in the reception building, they both could not stop sobbing. I remember that the Jewish girl who worked in the reception building and I, as I witnessed this scene accidentally, were deeply astonished. People didn't cry in the camp, not so much because we knew that tears didn't help – we just had no more tears, and we took what was happening to us for granted. We had been hurled into a bottomless pit, and the 'normal' people – the Gentiles on the surface – and their concerns were beyond our horizon.[7]

Everywhere across the vast stretches of Eastern Europe, the Germans were in retreat, with their armies under huge pressure from the pursuing Soviet forces. Despite the destruction of mass graves, the scale of the atrocities committed by the Germans in the Soviet Union were becoming increasingly well known and most Soviet divisions and regiments kept diaries in which soldiers could record incidents that had occurred to their families; these entries were then read out to soldiers by the political commissars of the divisions and regiments in order to strengthen the resolve of the men to continue fighting.

The war between Germany and the Soviet Union had, from the outset, been brutal with little regard for the usual rules of conflict. Throughout the long months of bitter fighting, both sides often executed prisoners without compunction, but by late 1943 the Red Army was undoubtedly in the ascendancy and was taking its revenge on those it regarded as responsible for terrible crimes against the Soviet people. Members of the SS in particular were lucky to survive capture. The black uniforms worn by many of the SS and the *Totenkopf* ('death's head') insignia worn on their shoulder tabs owed their origins to the black uniforms worn by Prussian 'death's head' hussars in previous centuries and had been adopted by both the SS and the crews of German panzer units. The latter were often killed by Soviet soldiers who assumed that their black uniforms meant that they, too, were members of the SS. At first, there were attempts to differentiate – the SS personnel wore the German eagle-and-swastika badge on the sleeve of their uniforms, while the Wehrmacht personnel wore it on their chests – but as the war progressed and it became increasingly clear that many if not most Wehrmacht units had been involved in atrocities, less attention was paid to this distinction and men in black uniforms were often executed out of hand, regardless of whether they were SS or panzer crewmen.

There was growing awareness in senior German circles that the atrocities committed during the war could have serious repercussions. After the war, many of those accused of war crimes would attempt to justify their actions on the grounds that they were following legitimate orders given by the legitimate government of their nation, but from the outset, most senior figures in the German hierarchy had been careful to issue instructions regarding mass killings verbally rather than in writing, suggesting that there was an awareness that these actions were illegal.

On 4 October 1943, Himmler organised a conference for senior figures in the SS and gave a speech that lasted for three hours. It should be remembered that all of his audience would have been aware of the devastation inflicted on German cities and the widespread defeats on the Eastern Front, but Himmler remained resolutely confident and the speech is important for the glimpses it gives into the mindset of the highest German leadership. He blamed the setbacks at Stalingrad on the inability of Romanian and Hungarian units to defend the flanks of the German forces and highlighted the German counteroffensive that followed, not least because armoured formations of the *Waffen-SS* played such a major role. When it came to the current state of affairs, he took the same stance as many others – given its huge losses, the Soviet Union had to be close to the end of its resources: 'Without doubt, the Russians have already thrust large numbers of men into their ranks from younger year groups, even those born in 1928. The division *SS-Das Reich* reported that some of the divisions it faced had entire companies made up of 14- and 15-year-olds.'[8]

This estimate was far from the truth – despite its huge losses, the Soviet Union remained capable of fielding large armies without recourse to child soldiers, though the years that followed the war would see great shortages of manpower. Moreover, Himmler ignored the fact that Germany was also running out of men. In particular, the loss of experienced soldiers and officers resulted in a steady reduction in the fighting power of German units. Nonetheless, Himmler told his audience that he remained optimistic. If the current wave of Soviet offensives could be weathered, the tide would turn in favour of Germany.

He then turned his attention to his SS, stressing the importance of their loyalty purely to the German people:

> One principle must apply absolutely to the men of the SS: we have to be honest, decent, loyal, and comradely to members of our own blood, and to no one else. How things are for the Russians, how things are for the Czechs, is entirely irrelevant to me. If there is any good blood of our people amongst them, we will get this if necessary by taking their children and raising them with us. Whether other people live in prosperity or whether they perish from hunger is of interest to me only insofar as we need them

> as slaves for our civilisation, and doesn't interest me otherwise. Whether or not 10,000 Russian women die from exhaustion while digging an anti-tank ditch, interests me only insofar as whether that ditch was completed for Germany. We will never be cruel and heartless when we don't need to be: that is clear. We Germans, who are the only people in the world who have a decent attitude towards animals, will of course also adopt a decent attitude towards these human animals, but it is a crime against our own blood to be concerned with them and to be idealistic if as a result our sons and grandchildren will suffer. If someone comes to me and says: 'I can't dig an anti-tank ditch with children, or women. It's inhumane, because it'll kill them,' then I have to say, 'You are a murderer of your own blood, because if the anti-tank ditch isn't dug, German soldiers will die, the sons of German mothers. That is our blood.' That is what I want to instil into the SS and – I believe – have instilled, as one of the most sacred laws of the future: our care, our duty, is to our people and our blood: that is what we should concern ourselves and think about, what we should work and fight for, and for nothing else. All else is irrelevant. I hope that the SS will face the problem of all foreign, non-German people in this manner. Everything else is froth and a betrayal of our own people and an obstacle to winning the war.[9]

Later in his speech, he turned his attention to the Jews:

> I would also like to talk about a difficult chapter here in all frankness. Let it be discussed openly amongst us, yet we will never talk about it in public. Just as we showed no hesitation on 30 June 1933 [when the SS moved to purge the SA] to do our duty as ordered and to stand up against the wall and shoot those comrades who had erred, we have not spoken of it and we will never speak of it. Thank God that it was a matter of course that we never spoke to each other about it or talked about it. Everyone shuddered, yet everyone knew that they would do it again if it was necessary and war ordered.
>
> I refer now to the evacuation of the Jews, the extermination of the Jewish people. It is one of those things that is easy to say – 'The Jewish people will be exterminated,' says every Party member, 'it is clearly stated in our manifesto that we will eliminate the Jews, exterminate them.' And then they all come to us, the good 80 million Germans, and each has his decent Jew. 'It's obvious that the others are all swine, but this is one is a great Jew.' None of those

> who speak thus have watched, none has experienced [the reality]. Most of you know what it means when 100 corpses lie together, when 500 lie there, or when 1,000 lie there. To have endured this and – apart from exceptions due to human weakness – to have remained decent, that has made us tough. This is a glorious page of our history that is not written and never will be written, because we know how difficult it would be for us if there were still Jews today as saboteurs in every city – with the bombing, the burden and privation of war. We would probably now have reached the stage of 1916-1917 if the Jews were still part of the German nation.[10]

Bruno Kittel had wide-ranging duties that took him to Kaunas and Riga as well as to Vilnius. It seems that he was convinced – with some justification – that wherever there were Jews, there would be resistance fighters. In Kaunas, he persuaded a Jewish black marketeer named Fain to try to seek out members of the resistance and find caches of armaments. The Jews became aware of Fain's activities and a special tribunal of resistance fighters heard evidence against him, concluded that he was guilty, and sentenced him to death. They then killed him and disposed of his body.

Near Riga, Mascha Rolnikaite worked at a number of locations, and wherever she worked the need to find more food was a dominant feature of the lives of the prisoners. Despite the obvious impact of hunger and malnutrition on productivity, the Germans continued to search workers for hidden food and punished severely anyone they caught, often in a sadistic manner. She recorded the events of the previous evening in her diary:

> When the building workers returned in the evening from their work, they were thoroughly searched at the gate. One of the guards had reported that he had seen how a passing civilian had given a piece of bread to each of them. Bread was found on two men – a mouthful each. During the evening roll call, a further report was made to the Unterscharführer.
>
> After the roll call, the Unterscharführer didn't give the usual order to dismiss the work party, but instead ordered the two 'offenders' to be brought forward, to turn around in front of us and to strip to their underwear. The two were terrified: it was bitterly cold and snowing hard. But the whips forced them to comply. We had to stand at attention and witness everything – as a lesson for the future.
>
> Then, two buckets of warm water were brought from the kitchen and tipped over the heads of the two men. The poor souls

> shivered and their teeth chattered, and they wanted to tear their damp clothing from their bodies, but the soldiers had brought another two buckets of water. They poured these once more over the unfortunate men. Desperately they began to jump and dance. The soldiers and the Unterscharführer derived great entertainment from this show.
>
> They let this go on for 20 minutes. The poor souls soon no longer looked like men – The older of the two had a thin layer of ice on his chilled body, while the younger pulled at the frozen roots of his hair in pain. Their underwear was frozen stiff, and their legs were as white as the dead.
>
> The guards were gasping with laughter. They were delighted with this great Christmas show. They all offered suggestions on how the water should be poured on the prisoners. 'In their underwear!' shouted one. 'On the head! Pour it on the head!' shrieked another.
>
> When the buckets were tipped over them again, the two poor guys tried to jump to one side, but they were caught and brought back to their places like escaped animals. If even a little water missed them, they brought a further full bucket. There was no option for the unfortunate men than to lift their deathly white feet in turn so they didn't get frozen to the snow …
>
> Today, the old man died while at work. He collapsed next to his wagon and didn't get up again. The other was able to work but could barely stand upright and was feverish and confused. When the guards weren't watching, his friends helped where they could and he was able to survive until the end of work.[11]

Over the first three months of 1944, the military situation continued to worsen for Germany. In the south, the Red Army continued a series of rolling offensives that took its troops across the great rivers of Western Ukraine, unmasking many of the sites of massacres carried out by *Einsatzgruppe C* and *Einsatzgruppe D* in the first year of the conflict. With the Siege of Leningrad lifted, Soviet forces advanced steadily towards the Narva River, and soon the inmates in the camps around Vaivara could hear the unmistakable rumble of artillery to the east. And in the west, the British and Americans continued their preparations for a second front. It seemed to the Jews that liberation was almost within reach – but how many of them would survive to see it?

In the north, the approach of the Red Army triggered the evacuation of the most eastern of the work camps in Estonia, in and around Narva; the workers were taken to the main camp at Vaivara. Fearing that the Red Army was about to break through to Vaivara, the SS ordered the evacuation of the least fit prisoners – about 600 who were ill and 185 children. Shortly after, a further group of nearly 2,500 was ordered to head west on foot. They marched for three days through deep snow until they reached Kiviõli; 44 died on the journey, either through exhaustion and exposure, or because they were shot by their guards because they couldn't keep up with the column.[12]

The constant flow of bad news from the front line began to have an effect on German personnel in the camps. In early 1944, one of Plagge's junior officers came to him and made him aware of a conversation the previous evening, in which another officer in the unit – Hauptmann Plisch – had said that Adolf Hitler should be shot, the sooner the better. Had this comment been made in a small group of like-minded individuals, it might have been easy to overlook, but the officer who reported the incident to Plagge told him that the unit paymaster, Oberzahlmeister Mueller, was also present at the time. Cautiously, Plagge summoned the paymaster to his office and discussed the matter with him. To his relief he soon realised that Mueller had no intention of reporting Plisch's words to higher authorities and was just as hostile towards the Nazi Party. Plagge was minded to drop the matter, but the officer who had made the complaint insisted that it should be taken further. In response, Plagge drew up a report that glossed over the matter. He showed it to the reporting officer and asked him why he had felt it necessary to denounce a fellow officer. At first, the reporting officer remonstrated with Plagge, but then let the matter drop. He was a heavy drinker and had made controversial comments himself in the past and was perhaps concerned that he might come under scrutiny personally if he persisted with his complaint.[13]

In the First World War, the ability of armies to function effectively was hugely dependent on railway lines – the quantities of food and ammunition needed was so great that it was almost impossible to operate far from a railhead. In the Second World War, the widespread use of motor vehicles alleviated this problem, but of course was dependent upon three factors. Firstly, trucks had to be available in sufficient numbers. Secondly, the trucks needed fuel. Thirdly, the trucks were useless without adequate roads. Throughout the conflict on the Eastern Front, the poor state of the roads was a limiting factor for both sides, and civilians were routinely conscripted as labourers to improve them – Soviet memoirs describe the way that the local population willingly helped the Red Army, but the reality is that they had little choice. For the Germans, the main limitations on using trucks as a replacement for rail transport were shortages of trucks and particularly shortages of fuel, and the Wehrmacht remained hugely dependent upon railways, both for supply and mobility – when the vital panzer divisions were shuffled from one sector of the front line to another to try to shore up the defences, their heavy equipment was almost always moved by rail.

Locomotives and rolling stock were always in short supply, yet throughout this period the Germans continued to allocate considerable quantities of both to the ongoing extermination programme. Trains rolled without interruption into the death camps, delivering tens of thousands of Jews to the gas chambers and the crematoria. For the remaining Jews in the Baltic region, monitoring foreign radio stations with clandestine radio sets – in the *HKP 562* camp, the workers had made a radio set from components they pilfered from the workshops – there was a very real possibility that the Germans would kill them all before the Red Army could reach them. The work of preparing *malines* continued.

At the beginning of 1944, Plagge tried to take steps to assume complete control of his work camp. He held meetings with senior SS figures, suggesting that if the work camp came under his jurisdiction, he would ensure that the workers were made available for any tasks required by the Wehrmacht. Aware of some of the motives behind the desire of the SS to retain control of all camps, he suggested that the money paid by the Wehrmacht and private firms for Jewish labour would continue to be given to the SS. Plagge's work camp was classified by the SS as a satellite camp of the Kaunas concentration camp, and consequently all negotiations were via Göcke, the camp commandant. He wrote to Plagge on 8 February rejecting Plagge's suggestion and instead suggested a somewhat bureaucratic arrangement by which the workers of *HKP 562* and those of the Reitz and Meier companies should effectively be regarded as three separate workforces, all of which would remain under the control of the SS. It seems that Plagge was particularly concerned that those working for the two clothing companies might be transferred, together with their work, to Kaunas, and he responded forcefully to Göcke's letter:

> The motivation and effectiveness of the Jewish labourers [in *HKP 562*] is essentially dependent on the fact that not only the men but also their wives and children can remain in Vilnius … *HKP 562* sees a risk that the SS is now in a position to control the female workers at will and transfer them, even to the Kaunas concentration camp … This would not only break the principle that the male specialists of *HKP 562* stay with their wives in the interests of their motivation, but also that the Vilnius camp will be deprived of highly valuable workers.[14]

Plagge's proposal required the consent of both the SS and the local Wehrmacht command; the latter effectively torpedoed the scheme by stating that it lacked the administrative capacity for the Wehrmacht to take control of the work camp. The workers would remain at the mercy of the SS, even though they were under the day-to-day supervision of Plagge and his men. At about the time of this exchange of letters, fearing that a further 'action' was imminent, a Jewish worker named Samuel Taboryski spoke to the soldier Alfons von Deschwanden and asked if he would permit his wife and small daughter to hide in the workshop. Deschwanden agreed and created a hiding place in the storeroom where he worked. Two other German soldiers worked in the storeroom, but Deschwanden told them bluntly that the hiding place and its occupants were not their concern. When no 'action' took place, Taboryski took his family back to the main camp. It proved to be a premature move.

As described above, most of the Jews assumed that their struggle to survive had left them with no more tears to shed. It is a measure of the tragedy that occurred the following March that this belief proved to be incorrect. As part of the ongoing programme to eliminate all Jews incapable of work, Himmler issued orders in 1943 that children in the ghettos and camps who were aged under 14 were to be killed, but the order was widely ignored. This was rarely due to any sense of compassion, but more out of recognition that killing children would hugely undermine morale in the camps and might have an impact on the productivity of the workforce. With the ghettos either liquidated or converted into concentration camps, Himmler no longer needed to rely on the cooperation of civil occupation authorities and issued fresh instructions early in 1944.

Sunday 26 March saw the Jews of *HKP 562* celebrate the festival of Purim; as was traditional, the children of the community put on a show, including a modified version of Hansel and Gretel, in which two children were threatened by a monster dressed in German uniform who threatened to eat them. Some of the German personnel of the camp were invited as guests, including Berger, the senior NCO who had been consistently kind and helpful to the Jews. He and his fellow Germans had little difficulty understanding the Yiddish jokes and roared with laughter and applauded as the German monster was humbled by the children, and the day ended with mirth and optimism. For many, it was the last time that they would feel so happy.

On 27 March, the Jewish police in the Kaunas concentration camp were ordered to assemble. One of the policemen later told Solly Genkind what happened:

A day before the action started, our chief Moshe Levin was ordered by Göcke of the Gestapo to assemble the whole police force … we were going to be instructed on air raid procedures. We were surprised, but we suspected nothing. Even after four years of lies, deceit and murder, we still believed them!

It was a beautiful spring morning and that added to our good feeling. At 8am sharp, 130 of us, dressed in our best uniforms, stood at attention in the courtyard of the ghetto administration building.

Göcke, resplendent in his grey leather coat and matching gloves, inspected our ranks carefully. He then smiled and ordered the policemen who were playing in the ghetto orchestra to step forward and enter the administration building.

Suddenly I had doubts. Something was wrong here. But before anyone could say a word, a large group of SS men came running out from behind the building. They were armed and surrounded us on all sides.

We were ordered to sit on the ground. Some of the policemen who were not fast enough were clubbed. Within seconds several large army trucks drove into the yard and we were ordered to crawl to them on all fours, the guards kicking and clubbing us all the way. The surprise was complete. There was no chance for us to resist, which we would have done had we any inkling. Many of us were trained by the underground in hand-to-hand combat.

We knew that our turn to die had come. One policeman, by the name of Levner, was absolutely paralysed by fear and couldn't move. He was shot on the spot.

As we neared the fort [IX] two of our officers, seeing that they had nothing to lose, decided to make a break for it. One was a lawyer named Zilberkweit and the other was someone called Levin. They didn't get very far. The Gestapo accompanying the convoy shot them down.

At the fort they took everything away from us. They beat us systematically until we could barely stand … Moshe Levin and his two lieutenants … had been very active in the underground and helped many young men to escape to the partisans' groups. The Gestapo and the SS had their informants and probably knew to some extent what was going on.

Our chief and his two lieutenants were beaten so mercilessly that we barely recognised them. But we recognised Moshe's voice.

'Listen, they are trying to extract information from us about the hiding places and the resistance movement in the ghetto. Comrades, let us die with dignity! Not a word to the murderers!'

> Moshe was a very strict boss, even a bastard sometimes, but when he spoke to us that day I knew that I was standing before a hero.
>
> Some time later the Germans and their Ukrainian helpers dragged us from our cells … Kittel was already waiting for us. Kittel was notorious for his sadism. He was an expert at extracting information from his victims by employing the most sophisticated methods of torture.
>
> Moshe Levin was the first to be interrogated while the remainder of us were forced to watch. No amount of torture brought a single word from him.
>
> Kittel kept repeating the same questions: 'Where are the ghetto hideouts? Who are the leaders of the partisans in the ghetto?'
>
> Then Kittel leaned too near and Moshe spat a mouthful of blood and saliva into his face. The infuriated Kittel couldn't control himself. Drawing his revolver he shot Moshe dead.[15]

After interrogation, 40 of the police were executed. When they returned to the concentration camp, the Germans began a systematic sweep to round up children and the elderly – the latter had been spared because they had been given responsibility for caring for the children of the camp, but now that the decision had been taken to kill the children, the elderly too were regarded as surplus. Kittel oversaw the operation, during which loud music was played from loudspeaker vans to drown out the desperate screams of distraught mothers and children. Some of the Jews recalled how the Germans called to each other and their helpers, asking if there were any more *Kätzchen* ('kittens') to be found. Many of those who tried to hide in *malines* were located and dragged out. A few suffocated to death. Anyone who attempted to stop children being taken away was beaten, and in some cases the police set their dogs on those who resisted. By the end of the day, about 900 children and elderly had been taken away.

On the same day, the Germans carried out a similar action against the *HKP 562* camp in Vilnius. Perela Esterowicz described the manner in which events unfolded:

> In the early morning, after the men had left for their workplaces, the gates of the camp were opened suddenly and into the yard of our camp drove in trucks carrying a large contingent of the Gestapo and of the Lithuanian police, led by Martin Weiss, an executioner whose hands were already crimson with the blood of many tens of thousands of the inmates of the Vilnius ghetto.

> The new arrivals scattered swiftly through the accommodation from which they began dragging out children and teenagers up to the age of 15, as well as those few elderly who had managed to get to our camp. They took those they captured to the trucks and pushed their prey aboard. Heartrending scenes took place in our camp when the sobbing children looked in vain to their parents for protection. Mrs Zhukovski, the mother of the boy whom Kittel, amazed by his beauty, had sent with his mother to our camp from Ponary, was killed by Weiss with a shot from his pistol after Mrs Zhukovsky called him a murderer. I saw with my own eyes as the Lithuanians wrenched Boris Beniakonski's talented daughter from his arms with brutal force. She had enchanted us just the evening before. In some cases the mothers, not wanting to abandon their children in this terrible moment, shared their children's fate voluntarily ... I avoided this horrible fate by hiding in a *maline* that our neighbour, the attorney Zmigrod, had built in the cellar, which I had found a few days before. I was sitting on the seat of our carry-out toilet in the cubbyhole under the stairs when I noticed an opening in the floor. A few hours later there was no trace of the opening – that was suspicious, and I remembered it. When we heard that the camp was surrounded I went to check the 'hole' and found Zmigrod going down through it into the cellar. I ran to get my mother and we went into the cellar with Zmigrod – one could never refuse entrance into a hiding place [because] anyone left outside could reveal it to the executioners. Gershon, the eight-year-old son of my Uncle Mula, ran away from the Lithuanians who had grabbed him and were taking him down the staircase from their third-floor room; he saved himself by sliding down the banisters to his father's workplace where Mula managed to hide him.[16]

In the years that followed, many of the Jews of *HKP 562* were haunted by memories of that terrible day. One described how children were seized by their legs and unceremoniously tossed into the trucks. Steven Rotschild-Galerkin was ten years old at the time and when the Germans and Lithuanians entered the accommodation block, he tried to reach a *maline* in the loft:

> We could hear the commotion downstairs, the Germans were searching everywhere. What to do? Where to hide? The women were at a loss as to how to save us, so I told them about the hiding place in the loft. We ran to the stairwell and up the stairs ...

At the landing in a corner stood a little boy, I knew him. I don't remember his name, he was about my age, but smaller. He was an artist. He made magic with a pencil and a piece of paper. In a minute there appeared on paper amazing drawings of people, objects or landscapes. He mostly kept to himself and didn't run with our gang, and didn't know of our hiding place. I asked him to come with us, but he didn't respond, just stood there in the corner of the landing, frozen. I had to run. Once more I called to him from the top of the stairs, but he remained where he was, his large dark eyes staring from his upturned pale face ... The boy on the landing who could have been a great painter, maybe? I never saw him again.[17]

In the midst of this devastating tragedy, this story at least has a happy ending. Many years later, after Michael Good published Rotschild-Galerkin's recollections in his book *The Search for Major Plagge*, he received a communication from the owner of an art gallery in Boston. The child artist remembered by Rotschild-Galerkin and his mother both survived their time in the camp, and the child – Samuel Bak – fulfilled his early promise and became a successful artist. Nearly 60 years after the terrible events of 27 March 1944, the two survivors were put in contact with each other again.

There were children and older women in the work camp where Mascha Rolnikaite was confined, and these too were the target of the Germans:

During the evening roll call a bunch of soldiers burst through the gate. At first we took no notice. But when we saw that some were encircling us while the others went into the [accommodation] blocks we became anxious.

What were they going to do? ...

What were the soldiers doing in the blocks? A search? And my diary was in my straw mattress ... And why had they encircled us? To stop us rushing into the blocks in case we had hidden anything in our mattresses? In any case it wasn't a normal search – there were just too many guards ...

Two old women who were from Riga were led out from the second block. They were ill and hadn't been able to come to the roll call. They were taken to two vehicles with black folding canopies. We hadn't noticed when these vehicles came into the courtyard. Other soldiers took away the children from the women at the end of the row. At first, everyone was stunned, but suddenly terrible

> screams and cries broke out. The mothers rushed to the vehicles, they didn't want to hand over their children, they cried and cursed. One begged the soldiers to be allowed to accompany her children. Another threw herself to the ground and clung to the legs of a soldier to stop him carrying away her child. He kicked her in the face with his boot and dragged the screaming child away. One tried forcefully to pull her child from a soldier. She bit his hand but two other soldiers grabbed her, pulled her arms behind her back and dragged her aside ...
>
> One mother personally carried her small daughter to the vehicle. A soldier took the child and wanted to throw it aboard but the child wrapped her arms around his neck and clung to him. The mother touched her child's head and then collapsed. The SS man climbed over her and pushed the little girl into the vehicle.[18]

Could anything be worse than the terrible scenes that unfolded in Kaunas, Vilnius and elsewhere? When the trains carrying the victims arrived at Auschwitz, the numbers exceeded the capacity of the gas chambers to cope. As there was nowhere for the children and smaller number of adults to be kept while awaiting execution, many were simply sent directly to the crematoria.

Samuel Esterowicz described the sense of shock and horror after the children had been driven away from the *HKP 562* camp: 'The air was filled with the cries of disconsolate mothers; people moved about the camp like shadows. I ran into Boris Beniakonski who had lost his daughter. In a state of anguish he declared, "We are worms, you hear? We are nothing but crushed worms!"'[19]

Every society in the world places a special value on children. All wars are terrible and the Second World War featured many horrific crimes; amongst those crimes, the *Kinderaktion* must rank as one of the cruellest acts. Plagge was on leave at the time, but even if he had been present, it seems highly unlikely that he would have been able to prevent Weiss and his men from carrying out the 'action'. As had been the case in Kaunas, many children – between 20 and 30 – escaped the searchers by hiding in *malines*, but they now faced a deeply uncertain future. They had to remain out of sight at all times, and not only to avoid being seen by the Germans or their Lithuanian allies: many of the Jews who had lost their children became hostile to the survivors and refused to shelter them. For the children, there was the added trauma of no longer being able to see their friends. Many spent the following weeks in hiding believing that they were the only children to have survived.

Almost immediately after his return to Vilnius, Plagge received a small delegation of senior Jews. He apologised to them for the *Kinderaktion*, but they came with a request on a different matter. They explained that the Jewish holiday of Passover was imminent, on 8 April. They explained the importance of the holiday to the Jews and asked if Plagge would be willing to grant the workers reduced working hours. The holiday would be a Saturday, and Plagge agreed that *HKP 562* would not work normally on that day; instead, the Wehrmacht personnel would carry out equipment inspection and stocktaking. The Jewish workers would be able to take the entire day as a holiday, and would work instead on the day after, a Sunday, which would normally have been a rest day. The Jewish delegation then made a second request. They explained that it was traditional for Jews to have a dinner known as *Seder* on Passover, which would feature *Matzoh*, a special type of unleavened bread. Therefore, they requested permission to use the ovens of *HKP 562* to prepare *Seder* for what might be their last Passover – they knew the end of the war was approaching, and feared that the SS would kill them all before the arrival of the Red Army. It is likely that even if the *Kinderaktion* hadn't taken place, Plagge would have agreed to both requests; in the circumstances, he had no hesitation in giving permission. He also authorised the use of 'army' wheat flour by the Jews for the preparation of their *Matzoh*. It was a small gesture of atonement for the massacre of the children of the work camp.

10
Liberation

Twice a year – in the autumn and in the spring – the war on the Eastern Front almost came to a halt. In the autumn, heavy rains turned the roads into bottomless rivers of mud, and the best option was to wait for the winter to freeze the ground solid before resuming operations; in the spring, the accumulated snow and ice melted and again turned the landscape into a muddy morass that was almost impossible for wheeled – and often even tracked – vehicles to cross. One of the most remarkable achievements of the second half of 1943 was the manner in which the Red Army was able to overcome these difficulties, maintaining a high tempo of operations through the autumn rains, but by the spring of 1944, the fighting had to stop. The Soviet forces had advanced a considerable distance across terrain in which the Germans deliberately destroyed roads, railways and bridges, and that infrastructure had to be repaired before sufficient supplies and men could be brought forward to resume operations.

Throughout the first four months of 1944, the Soviet forces that had rolled back the Wehrmacht from Leningrad tried in vain to break into Estonia. The frontier between Estonia and Russia runs along the line of the Narva River from the Baltic coast to Lake Peipus; at the southern edge of the lake, the frontier turns towards the southwest for 32 miles (52km) to the Latvian border. With Lake Peipus covering 77 miles (124km) of frontier, the invasion routes for the Red Army were effectively limited to the two narrow land corridors to the north and south of the lake. The configuration of roads and railways further limited matters, making an attack north of Lake Peipus, over the Narva River, the most effective route. But repeated assaults against the city of Narva and the defences to either side achieved little, at the expense of a growing number of dead and wounded. The Red Army was able to establish a substantial bridgehead over the river to the south of Narva but building up sufficient forces in this forested and swampy area for a decisive breakthrough proved almost impossible. After weeks of listening with anxiety and hope to the sounds of battle not far away, the inmates of the Vaivara camps and the oil shale works faced the disheartening truth: liberation was still weeks, if not months, away.

For the surviving Jews in Lithuania, the prospects of rescue from their plight were rather more remote. The Red Army had concentrated its energies in the north and south in 1943 and early 1944, lifting the Siege of Leningrad and sweeping west across Ukraine. The German Army Group Centre, to the east of Belarus and Lithuania, was driven back from Smolensk in September 1943, but at a huge cost – the Red Army lost over 450,000 men killed, wounded or missing, compared with German losses of a little over 70,000.[1] But these casualty figures disguised important truths.

Until this battle, there had remained the possibility, however remote, that the Germans might mount a new offensive towards Moscow – this threat could now be completely discounted. More importantly, in combination with the offensives to the north and south, the fighting around Smolensk left the Germans in an exposed position. Army Group Centre occupied a huge bulge in the front line projecting towards the east, almost inviting the Red Army to launch converging attacks. If this were to happen, the German units in the area – worn down by the heavy fighting of 1943 – could not be expected to hold back the tide for long. Nonetheless, the front line was currently over 200 miles from Vilnius, and even if the Red Army advanced faster than expected, there was still the question of surviving any last attempts by the Germans to exterminate their prisoners, as Solly Genkind recalled: 'The big question in everyone's mind was how we would get through the dangerous moment when the Russians finally arrived. The saying around the ghetto was that liberation was under our noses, but the knife was at our throats.'[2]

After the horror of the *Kinderaktion*, the Jews were increasingly fearful that the approach of the Red Army would result in further 'actions', not excluding the complete slaughter of the workforce. Perela Esterowicz described the measures taken to construct *malines*:

> Working diligently, the men blocked off the farthest room in the basement by a brick wall and excavated an underground passage to gain access to this isolated space. For this we had to chisel a large hole through the stone foundation of the house. The shaft leading to the crawlspace we camouflaged by covering it with an

> earth-filled flat wooden box. We fastened wires to two sides of the box. By pulling on the wires we could raise the earth-filled box. The needed materials – cement, boards and so on, we stole from the Germans. The car battery we needed for illumination we acquired by the same means.[3]

For the moment, much of the activity in *HKP 562* continued as it had in the days after the *Kinderaktion*. Whilst the 12-hour working days were long, the work itself wasn't onerous, and growing shortages of replacement parts for the workshops reduced activity still further. The strain of the war on Germany was beginning to show in several ways. Men returning to the front line from leave brought back stories of cities reduced to rubble by American and British bombing raids, and the huge task of trying to fulfil military duties whilst at the same time offering what protection he could to the Jews left Plagge increasingly exhausted. On 21 June, he wrote to his wife:

> As a result of all my experiences here – perhaps also due to my health – my whole mood is very pessimistic. You know that I can't and am not permitted to write to you about what I see, hear and experience here and I don't want to write how I feel about my health. There is nobody amongst my superiors or my subordinates with whom I can discuss things. I can't join in with the defeatism of my colleagues and I don't understand the devil-may-care attitude of my superiors. So I am quite alone and isolated. I do my duty and much more with calm, quiet determination ... I stand here in another world. In the unearthly, dimensionless world of the east ... My view of the world, my perception of things, are shaped by events, experiences and knowledge that I am not permitted to write and also do not wish to relate. And yet they shape my overall mood ...
>
> I find life a very, very heavy burden. Sometimes I almost feel as if I can hardly deal with it. But I fight my way through time after time. Logic, emotions and my physical state are often at odds with each other. Again and again, strong humanitarian urges break through, completely contrary to the inhumanity around me. This is the biggest conflict for me. As a National Socialist I have to say 'yes' to the mass slaughter, the policies in Poland that see these people as an inferior class of human beings, and other people too. As a human being I see that it is insanity and that everything must be reduced to rubble, as it will all lead repeatedly to the most violent upheavals ... I can't tell you how depressed I am by the manner in which the

> reputation of Germany has suffered so indescribably here because of the wrong policies, unsuitable personnel, dubious politics and mismanagement. How humiliating are many of the things that have occurred here. How they make every German grind his teeth. How deeply ashamed one is about the messy situation in which we Germans find ourselves here.[4]

By the time that Plagge wrote this letter, the long-awaited second front in the west had become a reality. The Western Allies were ashore in Normandy and slowly expanding their beachhead. Hitler had followed a policy of stubborn defence in the east whilst holding sufficient forces in the west for a counterattack that would inflict a major defeat on the British and Americans, which would then allow him to dispatch more units to the Eastern Front, but every attempt to strike the bridgehead failed as the Western Allies repeatedly tied down the German units and prevented their concentration. As the balance of power in Normandy shifted steadily against Germany, the reality of ultimate defeat grew ever more apparent in the minds of soldiers of all ranks.

In the east, the Wehrmacht waited anxiously for a resumption of Soviet offensive operations. Although the build-up of Red Army units opposite Army Group Centre was at least partially detected and officers at both a local and higher level were certain that a major attack was coming, it seems that Soviet attempts to mislead the Germans into believing that their main effort would come further south had considerable success. As a result, when the hammer blow fell on 22 June, a day after Plagge's letter to his wife Anke and exactly three years after the German invasion of the Soviet Union commenced, the Germans were taken by surprise by the weight of the assault. Within days, Army Group Centre was crushed in a series of local encirclements at Vitebsk, Orsha, Mogilev and Bobruisk. Although the Wehrmacht's panzer divisions were motorised and highly mobile, most of the infantry units of the German Army were heavily dependent upon horses to move their equipment – a typical infantry division had over 2,000 horses in its establishment, and the losses of previous years had not been replaced. As a consequence, when the Red Army broke through, much of the heavy equipment of the army had to be abandoned and the retreat across Belarus rapidly became a rout. Briefly, the line stabilised around Minsk, but this was followed by another encirclement. The front line was now rapidly approaching the frontier with Lithuania, and the battered Wehrmacht had no resources with which to stop the Red Army.

The Jews in the various camps became aware of the rapid advance of the Soviets through a number of sources. In some camps, there were clandestine radios and people listened to the reports from Moscow, London and elsewhere, frustrated by the lack of detail about precisely where the fighting was taking place. In her work camp, Mascha Rolnikaite and her fellow inmates had to rely on sporadic information gained from German guards or from German newspapers, but the small trickle of Jews escaping increased steadily. Those who were left in the work camp lived in fear of mass punishment, and after one incident in which nine inmates fled, the Germans selected others at random and took them away for execution. Even the guards were warned: if there were any further escapes, they would be sent to the front.[5]

Many of the Jews who escaped were subsequently captured and executed, but others simply disappeared, often hidden by local people. Whilst the prevailing mood in Lithuania in 1941 might have been strongly pro-German, if only because the Germans were driving the Soviet 'occupiers' from the region, the attitude of local people was now very different. Few were entirely supportive of a return of Soviet authority, but most were now aware that this was inevitable. The violent hostility to Jews in 1941 by a radical minority of the population was now replaced by awareness that the Germans had committed huge crimes against the Jews, and the general mood of the population towards the Jews was far less unfriendly.

Jonas Paulavičius, born in 1898, was in many respects typical of many Lithuanians who lived in the countryside. He managed a small farm with his wife, daughter and son. Although he had been inclined to support the Communists before the war, he carefully kept his distance from politics. During the pogroms of the summer of 1941, he saw a Jew escape from a group of people being taken away for execution; the Lithuanian militia chased him and gunned him down in the street, and Paulavičius decided that if the opportunity ever arose, he would do what he could to help Jews.

After the *Kinderaktion*, a friend who lived in Kaunas contacted him. The friend knew a Jew in the Kaunas concentration camp, Yitzhak Shames, whose four-year-old son had been successfully hidden during Kittel's operation against the children of the camp. The friend was too scared to provide shelter for the child, but asked if Paulavičius was willing to help, as it might be safer to hide the boy in the countryside. Paulavičius spoke to his wife and they agreed to take him under their care.

At first, the arrangements seemed to work well, but the small child was understandably upset at being separated from his parents and cried frequently. Fearing that neighbours or someone visiting the farm might notice, Paulavičius and his wife decided that separating the boy from his parents was causing too much distress but returning him to the camp was out of the question, so they offered to give shelter to the parents, too. Yitzhak Shames' wife Lena worked outside the concentration camp and Paulavičius had visited her regularly to keep her up-to-date on her son. He now suggested to her that both she and her husband should join their son in hiding at the farm. Lena replied that they cared for her mother in the camp – one of the very few elderly Jews to survive the multiple 'actions' directed against those unable to work. She felt that she couldn't leave her behind, so Paulavičius agreed to shelter her as well; in order to house his small group of four Jews, he and his son excavated a shelter under the cellar of his farmhouse.

Over the days that followed the arrival of the new residents, Paulavičius learned more about the appalling treatment of the Jews in the concentration camp. The shelter that he and his son had built provided fairly roomy accommodation by the standards of the ghetto and subsequently the concentration camp, so he asked the Shames family if they knew of any other Jews who might want to escape from the camp. In particular, he suggested that it might be helpful to shelter Jews with professional training, as their skills would be vital to help rebuild Lithuania after the war. The Shames knew a couple in the camp, Chaim and Tania Ipp, who were doctors, and managed to get a message to them suggesting that they try to escape from the camp. At first, Chaim Ipp was sceptical and feared a trap, but concluding that staying in the camp meant that they would be killed sooner or later, he agreed to take a chance. The couple slipped out of the camp and joined the small community in the farm cellar.

In the weeks that followed, several more Jews were added to the group. Yochanan Fein was a 14-year-old boy who had attended the same school as Paulavičius' son. He had survived the *Kinderaktion* by jumping from the window of the bus taking some of the children away for execution. Learning that he was still alive, Paulavičius's son suggested that he slip out of the concentration camp and go to the farm. Not long after, Mania Niemark and then her husband Aaron also escaped and joined the group. By now, the shelter was nearly nine square metres in size, with double bunks, a table, basic toilet facilities, and even a radio set.[6]

Others also escaped from the Kaunas concentration camp. Avraham Gollub was encouraged by Dr Elkes, the head of the *Judenrat*, to take advantage of an opportunity to flee in March. He had buried several boxes of documents and diaries in the ghetto, and after telling Elkes and another *Judenrat* colleague the location of the boxes he managed to escape into the city. Father Bronius Paukštys, who had forged documents for Jewish children earlier in the occupation and had helped many escapees, sheltered him overnight and put him in touch with a Lithuanian woman who owned a farm and was already sheltering two Jews, Pnina Sheinzon and her daughter Shumalit; Sheinzon's husband had been killed during one of the massacres of 1941. She and Gollub had become close during their time in the ghetto, and they remained in the farm until they learned of the Soviet army's arrival in Kaunas.

The war was now getting closer to Lithuania, though the front line was still too distant for the surviving Jews in Plagge's camp to be able to hear the sounds of battle. The Wehrmacht was scrambling to move units into position to rebuild the shattered front line; the Soviet offensive against Army Group Centre, codenamed *Bagration*, had accounted for over 400,000 German soldiers killed, wounded or taken prisoner. Red Army losses were higher at nearly 800,000, but the Soviet Union was in a better position than Germany to endure such casualties, especially as they were part of a battle that was such a decisive victory. When the Western Allies broke out of the Normandy beachhead shortly after, they inflicted further heavy losses on the Germans, effectively guaranteeing the final outcome of the war. Units like the security divisions and police battalions that had played a leading role in the killing of Jews and others in 1941 and 1942 were now inserted into the front line. Lacking heavy weapons, training and experience of such combat, they were rapidly consumed in the fighting. The Soviet advance slowed more owing to lengthening supply lines than German resistance.

Fearing that the SS would kill all of the workers before the Red Army arrived, the Jews began to make final preparations for taking shelter in their *malines*. The biggest problem was one of timing. It was impossible to stockpile sufficient food and water for a long occupation of the hideaways and taking shelter too soon would result in rigorous searches by the SS – the Jews had to wait until the last moment, when the Germans were in the process of leaving, if they were to maximise their chances of survival. They would therefore be very dependent either on spotting signs of German preparations for departure, or receiving some kind of warning. Fortunately for them, Plagge rose to the occasion.

The military situation was very confused. When the Wehrmacht advanced into the Soviet Union in 1941, there was a more-or-less orderly system of responsibility for each area to be passed from the control of the front line units first to rear area military commands, and then ultimately to civilian German occupation authorities, but as the war turned against Germany and the Red Army drove back the Wehrmacht, there was no equivalent return of areas to military control. Instead, the retreating combat units found themselves in territory where there were overlapping agencies, each with their specific requirements. Matters were worsened by huge reluctance on the part of civilian authorities to hand back control to the military, thus losing their lucrative control of work camps and other resources and effectively making themselves redundant.

In Lithuania, in addition to the civilian administration of *Reichskommissariat Ostland*, there was the rear area military authority and the SS and security police. Plagge's *HKP 562* was subordinated to the rear area military authority, and it ordered him to prepare his men for immediate withdrawal to the west. At the same time, the combat units that were attempting to organise defences capable of at least delaying the Red Army were anxious to use any military personnel they could find to increase their strength. Furthermore, Hitler had adopted a policy of declaring locations on the Eastern Front to be fortresses. These had to be held to the last man, an order that was rarely rescinded until it was too late to withdraw the mixture of exhausted front-line and hastily organised rear area units; the result was that almost every such 'fortress' became a death trap for its garrison. Plagge would have been aware that if he delayed, his men were likely to find themselves trapped in Vilnius with no prospect of escape, and as soon as he received a warning order that he was to move his unit west, he acted promptly in order to extract his men in good time. But he knew that the Jews would not be moving with his military personnel, and even in this situation he found time to give them a warning of what lay ahead. Perela Esterowicz later described what happened:

> On Saturday 1 July 1944, Major Plagge … came to talk to us. We clustered around him, eager to hear what he would tell us about what lay before us. Major Plagge warned us that the German Army was leaving Vilnius and our camp would be evacuated westward in connection with the nearing of the Russians. To emphasise his warning Major Plagge informed us in his speech that we would stop being a *HKP* work camp and would be entirely in the hands of the SS – he then carefully commented: 'And you all know how well the SS takes care of their Jewish prisoners.' This speech of Major Plagge aroused terrible fear in us. According to the British radio station BBC, before retreating the Germans had shot without mercy all the Jewish inmates of the camps [to the east]. The vast majority of us understood, especially after Major Plagge's veiled warning, that for our camp the moment had come which we all feared and for which the dwellers of our landing had made feverish preparations.[7]

Plagge chose his words carefully, as 'Golosheyka', the SS NCO in charge of the camp, was present. When one of the Jews asked if they should prepare luggage to take with them when the SS evacuated the camp, Plagge replied that they would not need any luggage, not even soap or towels – a further hint that the evacuation would lead to their deaths. The Jews were informed that their evacuation would begin on 3 July, in two days' time. That evening, they saw that the SS guards around the camp had been reinforced and decided that the moment for them to go into hiding was imminent. They would wait until the following day, and then take to the *malines*.

Plagge took one last step to help the Jews that he had tried to protect for so many years. He suspected that some of the Jews would attempt to escape from the camp that night and knew that the SS were increasing security around the perimeter. By this stage, it seems that he had a fairly good grasp of which of his men were of a similar opinion to him with regard to the Jews, and on the afternoon of 1 July, the *HKP 562* master sergeant – presumably on Plagge's orders – informed Alfons von Deschwanden, who had consistently been friendly and protective towards the Jews under his authority, and two of his friends, that they were to man a guard post on the camp perimeter near the blacksmith's workshop. This was highly unusual – Deschwanden and his comrades had never been told to mount guard on the camp before, and it was explicitly a task reserved for the SS. Still puzzled by this turn of events, Deschwanden and his friend Collet – the third soldier originally nominated for duty was ill and was replaced by a man who Deschwanden didn't know – duly took up their post at 9pm. They manned a machine-gun, and had orders to fire on anyone attempting to escape.

About 30 of the Jewish workers planned to attempt an escape via the blacksmith's workshop; one of its windows overlooked an adjacent street, and the workers had weakened the wire mesh that was intended to seal off the window. The July night was bright, with the waxing moon approaching its brightest, and Deschwanden could see small groups of Jews slipping out of the accommodation block and heading for the workshop. When they were briefly alone, Deschwanden asked Collet if he knew what was going on. Collet replied that he had noticed the weakened mesh around the window in the workshop a couple of days before, and that he suspected the Jews were escaping into the city. Neither man felt prompted to take action, as they suspected that any Jews left in the camp when the SS arrived on the following Monday would be shot.

Not long after, the third guard returned to the post. Deschwanden and Collet had no idea of his views about the Jews, and they kept silent about the shadows they could see slipping away towards the blacksmith's shop. Finally, the third guard asked them acerbically if they shouldn't start firing. Deschwanden shook his head and replied that it was too dark to identify the shadows, and he was fearful that he would end up opening fire on German or Lithuanian police. At first, the third guard seemed inclined to argue with them, but in the face of the united position adopted by Deschwanden and Collet, he retreated into silence.

Towards morning, there were muffled gunshots from beyond the blacksmith's shop and the soldiers assumed that someone had spotted the escapees and had opened fire on them. As it grew lighter, a truck appeared with a mixture of SS personnel and soldiers from another unit. The SS officer in charge of the detachment ordered Deschwanden and his two colleagues to help in an urgent roll call – aware of the escape attempt, the SS wanted to check how many had got away. The Jews in the camp were paraded and carefully counted, and the total was 23 short.

Deschwanden and Collet were increasingly alarmed that the SS would interrogate all the guards about the escape to see if anyone had seen anything; they feared that the third guard would give them away. Fortunately, just as the roll call was finally concluded after repeated counts, a senior NCO from the main *HKP 562* workshops arrived and ordered them to return to their unit. The unit was preparing for its imminent departure with trucks being loaded with equipment. Deschwanden and Collet were hugely relieved when they were ordered to board one of the first vehicles that were departing for the west. Just as it is likely that their appointment as guards had been deliberate, so it is equally likely that their swift departure before any escapes could be investigated was organised by Plagge or one of his subordinates.

Towards the end of Sunday 2 July, the Jews began to slip away to their hiding places. There were sufficient *malines* for fewer than a third of the approximately 1,100 Jews that remained in the work camp, but many of those who had not been able or willing to prepare hiding places in advance now demanded admission. Knowing that refusing entry would leave people to the mercy of the SS – and moreover might endanger the *malines* if those left outside gave away their locations – the occupants of the *malines* allowed more people to squeeze in. The *maline* constructed by the neighbour of Perela Esterowicz was intended for about 25 people, but a group of desperate young Jewish men demanded access and badly beat Zmigrod, the man who had constructed the *maline*, forcing him to tell them where the entrance was. As a result, the *maline* now had nearly 100 crowded into it. This of course placed an even greater demand on the limited resources of food and water that had been stockpiled. All would depend on how long the Jews had to remain in hiding. Perela Esterowicz described the conditions she and the others had to endure:

> A small electric bulb connected to a stolen car battery barely illuminated the space where about 100 of us were lying down on the bare ground. With the coming of morning [on 3 July] and the moment when the Germans would discover that a few hundred people did not appear at the inspection, our tension increased ...
>
> Added to the fears of discovery by the Germans, or that we would perish under the ruins of the building, came excruciating physical suffering from the lack of fresh air. We had not appreciated the importance of this and thus did not arrange for sufficient ventilation. Because of the unforeseen crowding, our hiding place was rapidly becoming more and more stifling. Being faced with death by suffocation, our leaders, Zmigrod and Mintz [the latter was one of those who had demanded entry at the last moment] broke through the outside walls with pickaxes to make some tiny openings, risking that this would bring us to the attention of our enemies.
>
> The scanty trickle of air thus generated saved us from suffocation but was insufficient to protect us from the effects of oxygen deficiency ... oxygen deprivation together with the terrifying psychological burden we were subjected to evoked ... many cases of insanity. As a result, truly infernal scenes were enacted among those of us suffering in the *maline* ... the strained silence in our shelter was interrupted by a piercing scream of a male voice repeating, 'But why, why do you want to slaughter me?', seconded by a woman crying 'Such a brilliant future would await our children, after all.'[8]

In order to conserve battery power, Zmigrod decided to extinguish the single light bulb for a few hours:

> Unexpectedly, soon after our shelter was plunged into darkness there came sudden desperate calls for help. When the light was put on the following picture stood before our eyes: Gutman [the man who had been screaming earlier] was standing up, wild-eyed with a bloody pocketknife in his hand, on the ground before him lay Malkes [a Jew who had sat down next to him to try to quieten him], saved from death by his winter coat but bleeding from the numerous wounds inflicted on him by Gutman ... This was followed by events that shook us to our depths. After a short conversation, the bunch of youths who had attacked Zmigrod killed the Gutmans, braining them with some bricks that lay on the ground nearby.

> This did not end the horror: with every passing moment I realised that my mother was hallucinating. Her speech was becoming ever more irrational and pointless. I remember that my despair ... was deepened by the realisation that if she should start to scream she would be killed ... Two young girls, the Arluk sisters, were hiding in our *maline*. When one of the girls began to show signs of violent insanity, our leaders strangled her before our eyes.[9]

By the end of 2 July, Plagge's men had left the city where they had lived and worked since 1941. The front line was drawing ever closer, and late that day the BBC transmitted a codeword for the Polish *AK*. Under an overall plan with named *Burza* ('Storm'), the *AK* was to try to seize control of cities across what had been eastern Poland before the arrival of the Red Army. The specific operation for Vilnius was codenamed *Ostra Brama* ('Gates of Dawn', the name of a famous landmark in the city), but almost immediately a further message was transmitted, postponing the operation until 7 July. Estimates of the number of *AK* fighters in the Vilnius region vary between 4,500 and 9,000; they were generally equipped only with rifles and pistols with just a few automatic weapons and no heavy weapons.[10] Their seizure of the city could be little more than a political gesture, but given the disputed status of the Vilnius region, the Polish government in exile felt that it was imperative for Poles to state their ownership of the city.

Early on 3 July, the SS arrived in the *HKP 562* camp. About 500 Jews had either failed to persuade the occupants of the *malines* to give them shelter or had decided to await their fate. Many had lost all their family members and were emotionally exhausted by their ordeal and could no longer think of resistance. Amongst their number was Joseph Panzer, who had worked with Deschwanden. They were all taken to Ponary where they were executed. At the same time, a second SS detachment rounded up the last workers at the *Kailis* factory and put them on a train to Kaunas. Shortly after their arrival, they were taken to Fort IX where they were murdered.

The SS then began a careful search of the two accommodation blocks of Plagge's camp to locate the *malines* of the Jews, and about 200 of those who were hiding were discovered. They were shot in the compound of the camp and buried there. Driven by thirst and the increasingly stagnant air in their *malines*, a few of the hidden Jews emerged from hiding too soon; they, too, were killed on the spot. The rest waited in fear, wondering how long they would have to endure. When water ran out, some resorted to trying to filter water from a sewer through a piece of cloth.

On 4 July, the Vilnius region was formally assigned to the control of the retreating Third Panzer Army. One of the soldiers in 170th Infantry Division was part of a battalion that was sent by train to Vilnius, as he recorded in his diary: 'What a night. We spent the entire day in the railway station. In the evening we detrained. The Russians have already taken Minsk. The first units of our division are already engaged in heavy fighting. We're not going forward, but are to hold Vilnius. We drove to the fortifications through another air raid.'[11]

This was the only substantial element of 170th Infantry Division that would reach Vilnius; the rest of the division was driven away to the south by the pace of the Soviet advance. There were repeated air attacks on the city as Soviet bombers began to prepare the way for the ground troops that were closing in. For those awaiting liberation, the growing intensity of these attacks was a welcome sign that the German occupation was in its last days. This was also the day that Hitler declared that Vilnius was a fortress. The troops that were designated as the 'fortress garrison' would be expected to hold out to the bitter end, in the hope that the Red Army would have to divert significant forces to encircle and reduce it. It was a policy that had failed repeatedly but remained Hitler's preferred way of trying to hold back the tides that were closing in on Germany from all sides.

Meanwhile, late on 4 July, the first scouts were sent out of the *maline* where Perela Esterowicz and her family were hiding. They returned quickly: the Germans had abandoned the camp but were clearly still in control of the city. A small group was sent out with wire cutters to create a gap in the perimeter fence and the Jews then began to emerge. At the same time, groups of local people were entering the camp to see if they could find anything worth looting. All that remained in the accommodation blocks were the few pots and pans and items of clothing that had belonged to the Jews, but the legends of the fabulous wealth of the Jews persisted and many of the local people began to tear up floorboards to search for hidden treasures. Hearing the commotion, many Jews feared that the SS had made a surprise return to the camp and went back into hiding. On the morning of 5 July, the searching Poles found the entrance to Zmigrod's *maline* and ordered the occupants to leave. They were forced to pay the Poles before they were permitted to go. Like many others, the Esterowicz family was able to find shelter with non-Jewish residents they had known in the years before the war.[12]

Desperately scrambling to organise a defence of the city, Generaloberst Hans-Georg Reinhardt, commander of Third Panzer Army, issued orders on 6 July that the rear area units such as *HKP 562* were to continue their work as long as possible; thereafter they were to make their personnel available for front-line service. Plagge had acted just in time to get his men out safely. The following day the delayed uprising by the *AK* codenamed *Ostra Brama* began, creating a complex three-way fight between the Germans, the Poles and the leading elements of the Red Army. The commander of the Polish *AK* forces was General Aleksander Krzyżanowski, who had been an artillery commander before the war. He had spent the months prior to the uprising trying to establish a coalition that included his Poles and Lithuanian, Belarusian, Jewish and pro-Soviet groups, but following increasingly hostile actions by the pro-Soviet groups, he held secret negotiations with local German officials in early 1944. The Germans offered him weapons, including light artillery, if he would agree to fight against the Red Army; Krzyżanowski refused, but the two sides were able to reach a verbal accommodation to avoid unnecessary clashes.

The Germans also ensured that weakly guarded weapons and ammunition would be left in places where the *AK* could capture them, if a German withdrawal became necessary. The Poles now moved to take control of these supply dumps, but when they attempted to capture the eastern parts of Vilnius – they already controlled much of the local countryside – they were held off by a German armoured train. But other Polish units threatened to isolate the city from the west, and Soviet tanks now reached the airfield to the south of Vilnius where a German paratrooper unit had just arrived by air. Eventually, under heavy pressure from all sides, the German garrison was forced to fight its way out in an attempt to link up with German forces to the west. About 5,000 men managed to reach safety; roughly twice that number were killed, wounded or taken prisoner.[13]

Perela Esterowicz described the last moments of the German occupation of Vilnius:

> The Russian army came close to the city during the night from Friday to Saturday [7-8 July)] and the artillery shelling began ... Directed by the janitor, we ran to the bomb shelter in the basement of a many-storied building ... [It] was overfilled by people seeking refuge from the bombing, which was getting worse every minute ...
>
> The ceaseless roar of the shelling shook the walls of our shelter. To make matters worse, on Monday morning [10 July] it dawned on the Poles that we were Jewish; one of the Poles suddenly said that he remembered having encountered my father before the war and knew he was a Jew ... The news about our being Jewish spread like wildfire through the shelter and evoked different reactions, from reserved coolness to expressions of outright hostility.[14]

Finally, on the morning of 12 July, a Red Army patrol reached the shelter. All of those in the basement emerged into the daylight of a city battered by the short but intense battle for control. For the Esterowicz family and others who survived, it was a moment that they had hardly dared to believe would ever come: safety from the Germans. Of the approximately 1,200 Jews who were in the *HKP 562* work camp when Plagge warned them that his unit was being withdrawn, between 250 and 300 were now safely outside German control. It was the single largest group of Jews from Vilnius to survive the war and the German occupation.

The Red Army suffered considerable losses in the battle for Vilnius; in particular, General Pavel Rotmistrov's Fifth Guards Tank Army was drawn into close-quarters urban fighting, a situation that Rotmistrov had been explicitly ordered to avoid. The consequence was his dismissal, and the Red Army was forced to regroup before it could continue its surge towards the west. This gave just enough time for the Germans to complete the evacuation of the Kaunas concentration camp. On 6 July, Elkahan Elkes, the head of the *Judenrat*, was summoned by Göcke who told him that the camp would be cleared in the coming days, and most of the inmates would be shipped south by barge. Many of the younger Jews, who formed the majority of the resistance groups, decided to try to escape. Solly Genkind and some of his family were invited to join a friend, Jakov Schuster, and his family in a *maline,* but Solly's father Chaim was reluctant – he felt that the *maline* was a death trap and would be easily located. Under pressure from his family, he gave in:

> The entrance to the cellar was below a small wood stove. Jakov was very handy and had cleverly fastened the stove to a trapdoor, fashioning it in such a way that the opening couldn't be detected. A few wooden steps led down to a small room. The low ceiling was supported by wooden beams and wooden bunks were built along the walls. A tin pipe ran up to another stove above and then to the roof, to supply air. In one corner stood several large water bottles and two straw baskets full of food. Besides Jakov, cousin Frieda and Esterke, Jakov's uncle and aunt and two teenage daughters were there. They greeted us with unsmiling faces, barely nodding their heads. They were half undressed and wet with perspiration.
>
> Small wonder that they received us with sour faces. The heat was suffocating and our bodies only increased it.
>
> Without saying anything Aunt Anushka, always practical, stripped to her underwear and the rest of us followed suit.[15]

The heat meant that they drank their water supply faster than they had anticipated and Jakov and Solly ventured out of the *maline* later that day to fetch more water from the nearby well. They remained in the *maline* until 10 July when they heard vehicles entering the camp and the barking of dogs. At first, they were terrified that the dogs would sniff them out, but Jakov had taken precautions, sprinkling a mixture of spices and turpentine around the house in the hope of confusing them. Even more alarming than the barking of dogs was the sound of explosions and after a while the *maline* began to fill with smoke. Deciding that they would not be able to survive, the group decided to surrender and hope that they could still be evacuated. Chaim Genkind volunteered to see what was happening. He returned to the *maline* with the news that the Germans had moved on.

The group survived another two days, and then the Genkind family decided to move to the cellar of a house that had already been searched, reasoning that the Germans wouldn't return to the same building. The following morning, when the Germans began systematically to burn the remaining buildings in the camp, the Genkind family had no choice but to emerge from hiding and surrender. They watched helplessly as the Schuster family were shot by the Germans and the survivors were then marched out of the gates. After two hours of walking, they reached a railway station outside the city. The Genkind family and many others were crammed into cattle trucks that took them to the concentration camp at Stutthoff, close to the estuary of the Vistula River. From there, Solly and his father and several others, mainly men capable of work, were taken to Dachau in Bavaria. Some, including the few children who had remained undetected and were discovered at this time, were put on trains to Auschwitz where they were killed. The complete evacuation took several days and about 5,000 Jews were marched out.

Perhaps half of the Jews who attempted to hide in the camp were found and killed. Nonetheless, some 900 survived, either hiding in the ruins or escaping into the city. With its advance slowed by those lengthening supply lines, the Red Army reached Kaunas on 1 August and took the city almost without a fight. The city had been under German control since late June 1941, and in the 37 months that had passed, the Germans and their Lithuanian helpers killed about 30,000 of the 35,000 Jews who had been living in the city when the Wehrmacht arrived.

Elkes, the leader of the *Judenrat*, was dispatched to a series of concentration camps, ultimately reaching one of the satellite camps of Dachau near the town of Landsberg am Lech. He worked there as a doctor, but he joined a hunger strike of inmates in protest at the conditions in the camp. He died on 17 October 1944.

One column of Jews was forced to leave Kaunas on foot as there was insufficient railway capacity. The column included Miriam Šumacher, a woman aged 20. As they were crossing a narrow pedestrian bridge, one of the Jewish men jumped over the railing into the river in an attempt to escape. The Germans rushed to the railing and opened fire, and Šumacher took advantage of the confusion to remove the yellow Star of David from her dress. As the column reformed, she stood slightly to one side and assuming she was a passing civilian, one of the guards pushed her away. She went down to the riverbank as the column trudged on:

> I kept walking along the river when I saw a man in a boat with a sack of flour. He called to me in Lithuanian and I answered his greeting. He asked me if I saw what happened on the bridge, and I told him that I didn't know. I kept walking. A few minutes later, I heard the man's voice again behind me. I turned around and asked him why he was following me in his boat. He said that he felt I needed help. I firmly answered that I was in no need of any help and to please stop following me. The man told me … that the Germans were checking everyone's personal documents and I would be caught by them. I told him that I didn't have any money or jewellery to give him and asked him why he wanted to save me. The man asked me to trust him. I didn't really trust him, but I had no place to go.[16]

She was fortunate: the man was Jonas Paulavičius, the farmer who was already sheltering a growing colony. In the next few days, two more Jews and two escaped prisoners of war – former members of the Red Army – also joined the group, as well as two Lithuanians who had been imprisoned by the Germans under suspicion of helping the partisans. When the Red Army took control of the area around Paulavičius's farm, the Jews, Lithuanians and Russians emerged into daylight; most of the time, they had lived in their underwear, as the underground cellar was stiflingly warm with so many occupants. But unlike so many of their family members, they were alive and healthy.

On the same day that the Soviet forces took Kaunas, there was a further significant development. Pursuing the broken remnants of the Wehrmacht into the Baltic region, the Red Army was determined to reach the Baltic coast in order to isolate the two German armies fighting further north. With almost the last of its remaining reserves, the Soviet force advancing across Latvia and northern Lithuania sent a group on a thrust towards the north. Almost unopposed, this column reached the Gulf of Riga. The Red Army had smashed the German Army Group

Centre and advanced a remarkable 280 miles (450km) in a little over a month.

It proved to be a disastrous day for the Third Reich. American forces breaking out of the Normandy beachhead overran much of Brittany and reached the Loire valley. Shortly after, the American forces turned first east and then north, creating an encirclement around the town of Falaise on 21 August. About 50,000 Germans were trapped; although some escaped, all of their heavy equipment was lost.

Amongst those isolated by the Soviet thrust to the Gulf of Riga were the inmates of the concentration camp outside Riga, and its satellite work camps. Mascha Rolnikaite, now aged 17, was marched down to Riga harbour with several hundred other prisoners. After several days at sea confined to the hold of the ship, they were put ashore and marched to the Stutthoff camp. Here, they found themselves subject to a brutal regime. Their overseer was a fellow prisoner named Max, who had apparently been imprisoned 11 years previously for murdering his wife and children but escaped execution for his crimes as his brutality made him useful to the Germans. The rations were even poorer than in Riga, and prisoners were taken away from time to time for execution in the camp's gas chamber.

Further to the north, the Red Army renewed its attempts to drive the Germans out of Estonia. The Wehrmacht pulled back from the line of the Narva River in the last week of July and took up defensive positions about ten miles (17km) further west, in the area around Vaivara. Most of northern Estonia is relatively flat, with large areas of swamp and forest to the south – this leaves a small corridor about 12 miles (20km) from north to south, which has historically been the main route for armies marching either towards Russia or out of Russia. Around Vaivara are the three relatively small Sinnemäed Hills, and here the Germans had prepared extensive fortifications known as the Tannenberg Line. In the first days of August this area became the scene of bitter fighting. Although the Soviet forces succeeded in capturing the eastern hill, they were unable to break the German lines and the thrust towards Tallinn came to a halt, but other Soviet forces marched into Estonia to the south of Lake Peipus forcing the defensive line through the Sinnemäed Hills to be abandoned. The Germans pulled back in stages to Tallinn. Eventually, the remaining troops were evacuated by sea.

The proximity of the fighting forced a further evacuation of work camps. Despite Hitler insisting as late as July 1944 that the shale oil extraction work had to continue and even be expanded, various small camps were evacuated through the month and the last of the Jews were marched out in the first week of August. Some were put on trains to the south, while others were herded west into the remaining camps in western Estonia. From here, many were taken to Tallinn, from where they were transported by sea, eventually reaching Stutthoff. A camp to the west of the German defences at the Sinnemäed Hills in Ereda was formally closed at the end of July but many of the Jews were marched back to the camp a few days later – in the growing chaos, it had not been possible to organise their evacuation. Shortly after, they were taken out of the barracks in groups of about a dozen and were shot, their bodies burned.

When Soviet troops moved into the area, a Major Aavik from the NKVD wrote a report on the findings at Ereda, documenting five separate sites where bodies had been burned; in some, the partially destroyed remains of skulls and other bones were clearly visible. From the records of the camp, he reported that the number of victims was about 2,000. But this is likely to be inaccurate due to the manner in which Jews and others were first marched away from the camp and then some – but not all – returned. To complicate matters further, the final total would also include workers who were brought to Ereda immediately before the killings took place.[17]

The last camp in Estonia was at Klooga, to the southwest of Tallinn; Herman Kruk, the diarist of the Vilnius ghetto, was incarcerated here. He and his fellow inmates knew that time was running out for the camp, but they were unsure about their fate. Would they be transferred to Germany, or would they be executed? On 17 September, he carefully buried his diary manuscripts in the camp, witnessed by six other prisoners, hoping that at least one would survive to reveal the location.

That day, the final evacuation of all German forces from Estonia began, and on the next the Germans began the removal of prisoners from Klooga. About 300 Jews were selected as being fit for arduous work, but instead of being evacuated they were tasked with carrying logs to a clearing in woodland a short distance from the camp. The remaining prisoners were then taken from the camp to the clearing in groups of between 50 and 100. Here, they were ordered to lie down on a pyre that had been assembled from the logs taken there earlier and were shot in the back of the head. Once a layer of dead had accumulated, a new layer of logs was placed on them. About 18 Jews attempted to flee, and were gunned down by the soldiers, who seem mainly to have been members of an Estonian *Waffen-SS* training battalion; surviving members of the battalion – almost inevitably – denied that they had taken part, with some claiming that all of the killings were carried out by German personnel. Other Jews were killed in the accommodation blocks in Klooga before the Germans and their Estonian helpers departed on 20 September.

The Red Army arrived two days later. The Soviet soldiers found four pyres that had been constructed, three of which had been set alight. It is estimated that about 1,800 men and women were killed. Amongst the victims was Herman Kruk. One of those who witnessed the interment of his diary survived and dug it up later.

For the prisoners taken from Lithuania to Stutthoff, liberation was still several months away. After its huge advance of 1944, the Red Army needed to gather its strength and bring forward supplies and reinforcements. In the west, the British and Americans overran France and Belgium, but they too needed to pause to regroup. In the meantime, Nazi Germany sent out its last drafts to shore up its divisions, but when the Red Army attacked again on 12 January 1945, the German lines were once more shattered. Soviet tanks and soldiers raced across Poland, reaching the Baltic coast at several points and fragmenting the German forces left defending the eastern approaches to Germany. On 27 January, the men of the Soviet 1st Ukrainian Front, advancing towards Silesia, came across the huge concentration camp of Auschwitz-Birkenau. The previous year, the Red Army had already liberated Majdanek and had found the remains of the camps at Treblinka and Bełzec, but the horror the men of the Soviet Sixtieth Army found at Auschwitz dwarfed all that had gone before. Vasily Gromadsky was an infantry officer with one of the leading Soviet units:

> I realised that [the people in the camp] were prisoners and not workers so I called out, 'You are free, come out!' ... They began rushing towards us, in a big crowd. They were weeping, embracing us, and kissing us. I felt a grievance on behalf of mankind that these Fascists had made such a mockery of us. It roused me and all the soldiers to go and quickly destroy them and send them to hell.[18]

Another officer, Grigori Elisavetsky, was haunted for the rest of his life by what he saw as he and his fellow soldiers burst into a barrack block and surveyed the skeletal victims on the bunks:

> As in fog, I hear my soldiers saying, 'You are free, comrades!' I sense they don't understand, and begin speaking to them in Russian, Polish, German, Ukrainian dialects; unbuttoning my leather jacket, I show them my medals ... Then I use Yiddish. Their reaction is unpredictable. They think I am provoking them. They begin to hide. And only when I said to them: 'Do not be afraid, I am a colonel of the Soviet Army and a Jew. We have come to liberate you.' ... Finally as if the barrier collapsed ... they rushed towards us

> shouting, fell on their knees, kissed the flaps of our overcoats, and threw their arms around our legs. And we could not move, stood motionless while unexpected tears ran down our cheeks.[19]

In Bavaria, Solly Genkind and his father were sent to a satellite camp of Dachau. Solly and his friend Zelig and two others were fortunate enough to be assigned to fetching food from a nearby inn for the kitchens that prepared food for the guards:

> I thought I would faint looking at the things they finally began bringing out of the inn. There were slabs of butter and big round cheeses, eggs, whole smoked hams, and even fresh rolls. There were tomatoes, cucumbers, onions, carrots, and more. I wanted to jump into the cart and eat myself to death, but two Germans stood at the door watching us.
>
> After we finished loading the cart, with the smell of the food driving us crazy, the owner of the inn brought us a loaf of bread. She was a slim woman with dark hair and kind eyes, and she looked at us with pity. 'Tomorrow I will have some soup for you boys,' she said. We thanked her profusely, and Zelig even grabbed her hand and kissed it.
>
> I was disgusted with his performance and told him so, but he explained to me that she reminded him of his mother. 'Besides,' he said sadly, 'this is the first time a Christian woman has been kind to me since before the war.' I had to admit that I, too, was touched by that simple act of kindness. We were as starved for affection as we were starved for food.[20]

Solly's father Chaim was growing increasingly weak and if he was unable to continue working, he would be killed. Solly wanted to get him assigned to less arduous work, but the Jew in charge of work assignments demanded cigarettes in return. When he returned to the inn the following day, Solly decided to ask the innkeeper for help.

> The lady innkeeper was true to her promise and gave us each a bowl of soup that day. Thick with meat and potatoes, it was the most delicious and nourishing meal I'd had since the invasion. I wished I could bring some to Father.
>
> After we finished eating I took the four bowls back to her. I was terribly frightened of what I was about to do, but I had to do it.
>
> 'Dear lady, you are so nice to us. God will repay you for your kindness. But you could do something else that might save my

father's life.' I quickly told her what was happening and begged for some cigarettes in order to save him. She looked at me as if I had proposed something indecent.

'A likely story,' she said, but when she saw the tears in my eyes she realised that I was telling the truth. Suddenly she exclaimed, 'My God, what are they doing to you in that camp? I understood it was a working camp, and everyone was treated decently.'

This time it was my turn to be astonished. With all that was going on around them, how could the German people still believe government propaganda?

'It is a working camp, and they work us to death. We do hard labour 12 hours a day, on practically empty stomachs. They are starving us. Even the youngest and strongest will perish within a few months,' I said, looking her straight in the eye.

She recoiled as if I had personally insulted her. I suddenly realised I had exposed myself to terrible danger. If she was a Nazi, which was likely, I was doomed. I broke out in a cold sweat. She must have noticed my alarm, because she told me not to worry, but added that I shouldn't go around saying things like that if I wanted to continue living. Then she disappeared inside.

When we finished loading the cart, she came out and gave us another loaf of bread and slipped a small parcel into my hand.

On the way back to the camp I was almost jubilant. Wrapped up in newspaper was a pack of 20 German cigarettes, a veritable treasure.[21]

From the perspective of the 21st century, it is difficult to know just how much ordinary Germans knew about what was being done in Germany and the occupied territories. It is quite conceivable that people living in a small village in the Bavarian countryside would be largely in the dark – listening to foreign radio stations was forbidden, and it is unlikely that such an area would have had a significant Jewish population before the war, so local Germans wouldn't really have noticed the disappearance of their Jewish neighbours. Nonetheless, her warning to Solly Genkind suggests that the innkeeper wasn't entirely ignorant of the crimes being committed.

Hitler's 'Thousand Year Reich' was rapidly coming to an end. He made what would be his last public radio broadcast on 30 January, assuring the German people that the current setbacks would soon come to an end and Germany would emerge triumphant. On 11 February, the Red Army captured Budapest after a bloody siege, and at the beginning of March the Western Allies crossed the Rhine. Having reached the line of the Oder River, the Red Army was once more gathering its strength for a final assault that would take it to and beyond Berlin. And wherever the enemies of Germany approached a concentration camp, the SS drove the inmates out on what became known as the Death Marches. The intention was to move the prisoners to other camps, but this was often impossible due to blocked roads or the advance of opposing forces. Any who were too weak to continue were simply executed; thousands perished from hunger or exposure as they staggered along the frozen roads of Europe in the first weeks of 1945. Whilst the end of their ordeal was close, it was by no means certain that those who were still alive would survive the end of the conflict.

Stutthoff was left in one of the enclaves still held by the Wehrmacht along the Baltic coast, and it would be the very last concentration camp to be liberated. Throughout the remaining months of the war in Europe, German ships – both civilian and naval – attempted to evacuate German civilians and soldiers from the enclaves and take them to the west, where it was hoped that they would be able to come under British or American occupation. Those same ships also brought in ammunition and supplies to permit the troops defending the enclaves to continue fighting, and slave labour from Stutthoff and its satellite camps was used to unload the supplies. Any prisoners who became too weak to continue their labour were executed. Large groups of Jews and other prisoners were marched out of Stutthoff in late January and forced into the freezing waters of the Baltic, where they were machine-gunned to death.

Mascha Rolnikaite spent most of the winter working on a farm near the Stutthoff camp but returned to the camp in mid-November 1944. She and her fellow farmworkers had at least enjoyed adequate rations during the preceding weeks, but they were now forced to live in the same crowded barracks as the other prisoners, surviving on completely inadequate rations. Over 40,000 inmates, including Rolnikaite, were marched out of Stutthoff in January. They were meant to proceed to Lauenburg in Pomerania, but it was impossible for them to reach their destination. Many were taken back to Stutthoff, where another contingent was marched into the sea and executed.

Suffering both from starvation and illness, Rolnikaite knew that to remain in the camp meant certain death. She dragged herself along the road with her fellow prisoners:

> We went on and on, and there was no end in sight. Every day, a few women fell by the wayside. They collapsed and even with the help of others could no longer stand. The guards then shot them in the head, dragged them a pace or two, and another

corpse rolled into the ditch. When we passed a village, the guards reported that a body lay a few kilometres back and would have to be buried.

A column of Soviet prisoners of war passed us. They looked dreadful – yellow, starving and emaciated. And yet – with what compassion they gazed at us!

I didn't want a single face to pass me without my looking: perhaps Papa was amongst them?

Now the others had to help me. I couldn't go on unaided. With my last strength I tried to put one foot in front of the other and not to lean too hard on the other women. But it was endless and hard. And besides, the snow clung to my wooden clogs and made the going even harder.

I was terribly hungry. They no longer gave us anything to eat. Sometimes the farmers, in whose barns we were locked at night, let us have a bucket of potatoes. Everyone got one or two potatoes.[22]

When the column reached a farm in the middle of the Pomeranian countryside, the prisoners were left in a barn. Rolnikaite was at the end of her strength and knew that any further marching would result in her death. During the night they heard several loud explosions and they feared that they were about to be killed, but as it grew light there was silence. A Polish voice outside the barn told them that the German guards had fled:

There were loud men's voices behind the barn. Russians? The Red Army? Was it really them? I wanted to go out. How could I get on my feet?

The barn filled with soldiers. They came up to us, seeking out those still alive, helping them up. When they found those for whom help came too late, they took off their caps.

'Do you need help, little sister?'

I was pulled to my feet but couldn't move as my legs were trembling. Two Red Army men took my hands, lifted me up and carried me into the open.

Ambulances were approaching the village and more soldiers arrived. One wanted to help carry me, another gave me a piece of bread, a third offered me his gloves. Their willingness to help affected me so much that I wept. They comforted and soothed me. One even pulled out a grubby handkerchief and, as if speaking to a small child, urged me to dry my tears.

'Don't cry, little sister, we won't let anyone harm you.'[23]

Several thousand of the prisoners who were still in Stutthoff were loaded onto open barges on 29 April. The Jews must have feared that they would be taken out to sea and drowned, but after enduring three days of being towed across the Baltic through bitterly cold rain they reached Neustadt Bay, near the city of Lübeck. Here they found several ships that were no longer able to take part in the evacuation of the eastern enclaves as a result of breakdowns or fuel shortages. Some of the ships had been commandeered by the SS and were now full of concentration camp prisoners, mainly from the Neuengamme concentration camp. The barges were taken to the ocean liner *Cap Arkona*, but the ship was already overloaded with several thousand prisoners and instead the barges were beached near Neustadt. Many of the prisoners were taken to a nearby sports hall, but others were simply gunned down on the shore. By this time, Hitler had been dead for two days.

British troops were now less than a day from Neustadt. For the prisoners from Stutthoff and Neuengamme, cowering in the sports hall and aboard the *Cap Arkona*, the liner *Deutschland*, and two small freighters, *Thielbek* and *Athen*, it must have felt as if their long ordeal was about to come to an end. On 3 May, several squadrons of British Typhoon fighter-bombers dived from the morning sky and attacked the ships in the bay with rockets. It seems that there were fears that the SS had commandeered the ships in order to transfer large numbers of SS troops to Scandinavia, with the intention of continuing resistance in the mountains of Norway, and although the Swedish Red Cross had made the British aware of the likely presence of concentration camp prisoners, there remains controversy about whether these warnings were passed to the relevant RAF commanders. Within minutes, *Cap Arkona* and *Thielbek* were both ablaze and sinking. About 2,800 prisoners were aboard *Thielbek*, and only 50 survived. Several hundred prisoners aboard the liner *Deutschland* had been transferred to *Athen* before the air attack and were taken ashore, but over 4,500 prisoners perished aboard the *Cap Arkona*. Some managed to swim ashore, where SS personnel, aided by sailors from a U-boat training school, shot them. That evening, British troops reached Neustadt and rescued the few survivors.

Many of the women from Stutthoff who had been taken to the sports centre had also been executed. Amongst the survivors was Fanny Genkind, the sister of Solly; she leapt from a barge as it approached the shore and managed to swim to dry land, and hid until the arrival of British troops later that day. Her mother had died of malnutrition and illness in Stutthoff.

The senior commander of German forces in the area was Field Marshal Erhard Milch, a Luftwaffe officer in charge of the armaments programme for the Luftwaffe. An aide to General Evelyn Barker, commander of the British VIII Corps that took control of Neustadt and Lübeck, later described his experiences:

> The brigadier [Derek Mills-Roberts, commander of I Commando Brigade] took me through Travemünde, a pretty little holiday resort. We walked along the river towards the beach, where we started to find dead bodies, not many at first but more and more as we came to the beach … The beaches for a good few hundred yards were covered with bodies. I would imagine the figure to be in thousands. The two Dutch barges, which were very deep, had had their ladders removed and it was impossible for the victims to escape. These people had been mown down by machine-guns …
>
> The children had been clubbed to death and judging by the shape of the wounds, rifle butts had been used. We assume these had been used because the troops concerned were running out of ammunition, but the tragic sight of those small heads bashed in is one I shall never forget.
>
> The brigadier had found out from locals that German marines were responsible for the slaughter. I reported to the general who came immediately. While waiting for him, Milch, the German field marshal, surrendered to the brigadier with a 'Heil Hitler' and his field marshal's baton in his outstretched hand. The brigadier snatched it out of his hand and broke it over his head …
>
> The general ordered me to take the field marshal to see the beaches. I took an interpreter and followed the same route as the brigadier had taken. After Milch had seen a few bodies at the river mouth, he asked to be taken back but I insisted that he should go and see the beaches. When we reached them and all the horror of the incident could be seen, I noticed the field marshal was staggered. He could see how all the people had been killed, and also climbed up onto the decks of the two Dutch cargo barges and saw for himself the awful carnage that had taken place. He came down from the second barge, and with tears streaming from his eyes, told the interpreter to tell me that he felt ashamed of being a Reich field marshal and a German.[24]

Just how shocked and ashamed Milch was is open to question. After the war, he was tried at Nuremburg on charges of knowingly using slave labour in armaments programmes and of being complicit in the use of prisoners for medical experiments. He was found guilty of the first charge and sentenced to life imprisonment, though he repeatedly insisted that he was innocent. It is inconceivable that a man of his rank in such a position was unaware of the use of slave labour, and of the numbers of slave workers who died due to mistreatment, if only because he would have known about the constant demand for replacement labourers. His sentence was later commuted to 15 years' imprisonment. He was released in 1954 on parole.

Solly Genkind and his father spent the first months of 1945 hoping desperately that they would be rescued before they were killed or died of starvation. There was a crisis when Chaim Genkind's old boots disintegrated – without proper footwear, his feet would freeze and he would die. Solly managed to trade food that he had pilfered from the kitchen that prepared meals for the guards for a new pair of boots. They were returned to Dachau from their satellite camp to find that the site was now hugely overcrowded, as all of the satellite camps had been abandoned. As American forces closed in, the able-bodied inmates, including several Soviet prisoners of war, were marched out into the countryside. They trudged through drizzle and rain, and as they passed through the town of Wolfratshausen to the south of Munich, they were attacked from the air by American fighter planes, which mistook them for a column of German soldiers:

> We remained in the woods that day, trying to recover our strength. From a distance we could hear faint explosions, and as they continued and the volume increased we realised they weren't bombs. Then one of the Russians came crashing past, laughing and singing like a madman.
>
> 'What is it, comrade? What's happening?' my father shouted at him.
>
> 'That's field artillery! The front is upon us! It's the Americans!' he shouted back, throwing his hat in the air.[25]

It proved to be a false hope, at least for the moment; the sounds of gunfire died away. The march continued into the foothills of the Bavarian Alps, and men began to fall by the wayside through exhaustion and hunger. At some point, Chaim Genkind disappeared, and Solly laboured on. The road was littered with the bodies of those either killed trying to escape or who had died on the march. The following day, Solly awoke with a start to silence. He walked over to a wrecked cart and tore strips of meat from the belly of the dead carthorse. He started a small fire to make some soup:

> Below me, on the road, a tank appeared. Then what looked like a jeep. I closed my eyes, waiting for a bullet to put me out of my

> misery. Then I heard someone speaking English. When I opened my eyes, four men in khaki uniforms were approaching. They looked unshaven and tired. Their oriental features astonished me. They looked like Sugihara and his family. I stared at them, unable to grasp the situation. Japanese? I continued to sit and stir my soup. My throat constricted. I dared not think and could not speak.
>
> One of the men came up and knelt in front of me. He gently touched me on the shoulder and said, 'You are free, boy. You're free now,' he said, and then smiled.[26]

They were from the US 522nd Field Artillery Battalion. The first person Solly saw was Clarence Matsumura, a Japanese American, whose family had been interned in the United States after Pearl Harbor; it was a bitter irony that Solly's rescuer was someone whose family had also been confined to a camp purely because of their ethnicity.

After being ordered out of Vilnius, Plagge and the rest of his unit were moved back to Germany. *HKP 562* was disbanded and the remaining personnel designated as merely a workshop. In some respects, it was a significant step down from its previous role, and Plagge regarded it as a personal slight; he attributed it to a belief amongst his superiors that he had been too lenient towards his Jewish workers. He no longer had any prisoners in his care and devoted all his energy to ensuring that his men reached the end of the war alive. His unit provided mechanical support for German units facing the US Army and when the front line broke up after the Western Allies crossed the Rhine, he took advantage of the chaos of collapse and surrendered together with his men to the Americans. He didn't lose a single man in the fighting.

11

Different Fates: The Imperfections of Justice

By the end of the war, many of those responsible for the mass murder of the Jews of Lithuania were already dead. Franz Walter Stahlecker and Reinhard Heydrich died in 1942, as did Fritz Jordan, who had terrorised the Kaunas ghetto in 1941; he was sent to a front-line unit and was killed on the Eastern Front in the same year as Stahlecker and Heydrich. Lina Heydrich, the widow of the man who was so instrumental in the planning and implementation of the Holocaust, fled from the estate near Prague as the Red Army approached. Heydrich's mother who had been living with the family also left and went to stay with other relatives in Dresden. She was there when British bombers smashed the city on 13 and 14 February 1945 but survived the attack. However, most of her family were killed and she was left homeless and without any means of support. She died from a mixture of starvation and exposure in the last weeks of the war, a fate shared by so many of her son's victims.

Lina Heydrich moved back to her family's estate on an island in the Baltic Sea. The pro-Soviet Czechoslovak government that was created after the war sought in vain to secure her extradition on charges of abuse and cruelty to the Jewish workers on her estate, but neither the British nor the German authorities were prepared to cooperate. She managed a small hotel and restaurant on the island, which became a favourite retreat for former SS officers, and in 1956 and 1959 she was able to overturn the refusal of West Germany to award her a lucrative pension to which she claimed entitlement as the widow of a senior officer. In 1976, she published a book entitled *Leben mit einem Kriegsverbrecher* ('Life with a War Criminal') and remained resolutely unrepentant. She wrote repeatedly to authors and newspapers to object to published material, seeking retractions or corrections, and died in 1985 aged 74, openly contemptuous of the manner in which Germany had failed to recognise the great achievements and contributions of her dead husband.

Other perpetrators of the Holocaust in Lithuania died in the closing weeks of the war or immediately after the cessation of hostilities. Wilhelm Göcke, the commandant of the Kaunas concentration camp that was created after the liquidation of the ghetto, was transferred to the Adriatic region where he took command of a battlegroup deployed against partisans. He was killed in fighting on 20 October 1944. Joachim Hamann, the merciless hater of Jews whose eponymous *Rollkommando* was responsible for the deaths of tens of thousands of Jews in the late summer and autumn of 1941, was sent to Berlin after his involvement in the failed *Zeppelin* operation and took up a post in the *RSHA*. He was actively involved in the hunt for the conspirators behind the July 1944 plot to kill Adolf Hitler and was one of the men sent to arrest Field Marshal Erwin Rommel. Not long after, the head of the *RSHA*, Ernst Kaltenbrunner, appointed him as his personal representative. He avoided capture after the war but committed suicide on 13 July 1945. Rudolf Neugebauer, who was head of the German Security Police and SS in Vilnius in 1942 and 1943 and oversaw the liquidation of the ghetto, was sent to Budapest in late 1944. He is recorded as being buried in Salzburg with a date of death of December 1944, but the circumstances of this death are unknown. It is conceivable that this record was faked to permit him to disappear.

Gerhard Kortkampf and Gustav Grauer, who along with Hamann were the subunit commanders of Karl Jäger's *Einsatzkommando 3*, both survived the war. Like Hamann, Kortkampf was assigned to a post at the *RSHA* in Berlin but was then sent to join the new 38th SS-Grenadier-Division *Nibelungen*. He surrendered to the Americans near the town of Traunstein in the Bavarian Alps. He remained in American custody until mid-1948; by this time, the initial determination to seek out and prosecute war criminals was waning, not least because of the sheer numbers involved, and he was released – his most recent identity documents all related to his time with *SS-Nibelungen* and any link to his time in Lithuania was overlooked. He never faced any charges relating to his involvement in *Einsatzkommando 3* and resumed his pre-war career as a bookseller.

Grauer's fate demonstrates the complexity of relationships that developed after the war. He became part of 16th SS-Panzergrenadier-Division *Reichsführer-SS*, a unit that was raised in 1943. This division was involved in numerous atrocities in Italy and was responsible for the murder of up to 2,000 Italian civilians – it is likely to have been involved in more war crimes in Italy than any other German division.[1]

Although the division surrendered to British troops in Austria at the end of the war, Grauer was handed over to the Soviet occupation forces by American troops, probably having been detained in West Berlin – he had returned to a desk job in the city before the final collapse of the Third Reich. What happened to him next is unclear. Like many thousands of other German prisoners, he was detained in the Soviet Union for several years. Some of those held were charged with a variety of crimes, but whilst some faced serious charges, the 'crimes' of others were often spurious – one Luftwaffe officer was sentenced to a long term of hard labour for destroying Soviet state property, the items in question being the Soviet aircraft he had shot down during the war. Many of those detained, including hundreds of German civilians, never faced any charges. In September 1955, the West German chancellor Konrad Adenauer visited Moscow in an attempt to normalise relations between West Germany and the Soviet Union. High on his agenda was a desire to achieve the repatriation of the surviving prisoners. At first, the Soviet authorities refused to consider a release but eventually agreed, and about 9,200 prisoners were permitted to return to Germany.

At least twice this number of prisoners had died during the decade of captivity since the end of the war. It was now time for the Soviet Union to provide the Germans with dates and places of death. It soon became clear that in many cases the Soviet authorities had not kept accurate records of when and where the prisoners had died. As a consequence, a suspiciously large number of prisoners were recorded as having died in the months immediately before the survivors were released. Amongst these was Gustav Grauer, who was recorded as dying in a prison camp in the Ural Mountains not far from Sverdlovsk in 1955.

The case of Grauer should have ended there, but in February 1962 a CIA officer in Germany wrote a report on an incident that had taken place a year previously involving an agent of the *Bundesnachrichtendienst* ('Federal Intelligence Service' or BND, the intelligence agency of West Germany) with the name of Gustav Grauert. Although the name was spelled differently, the date and place of birth was the same as the Gustav Grauer who had served in *Einsatzkommando 3*. The CIA report described how Grauert had been a passenger in a car driving through West Berlin at night; the car was stopped by a police officer who warned them that they were about to cross into the Soviet sector of the city. Grauert apparently assumed that it had been an honest mistake until the other two occupants of the car, codenamed UJDROWSY and UJDRUM in the CIA document, were later arrested and charged with spying for the Soviet Union, whereupon he claimed that it had been an attempt by Soviet agents to abduct him.

A second report a year later spelled Grauer's name correctly, and recounted information about the incident obtained by an agent codenamed FLEMING:

> FLEMING also mentioned some more details concerning the possible attempt UJDROWSY and UJDRUM had made to kidnap GRAUER in Berlin in early 1961 – saying that further review of the episode indicated that there was a probability that there was something fishy about GRAUER's story. He had reported the matter to the chief of his Bremen District after returning from the trip to Berlin when the incident occurred. The chief thought it was too weird to report to Headquarters and did not forward the report until after hearing of the arrest of UJDROWSY and UJDRUM. FLEMING said it made no sense that UJDROWSY and UJDRUM would try to kidnap GRAUER and said that when UJDRUM had been asked about the incident ... apparently in a rather foolish manner UJDRUM had replied by asking if they were pulling his leg. FLEMING also mentioned –
>
> A. GRAUER was a member of the Waffen-SS and SD. At the end of the war he had some sort of job with the Berlin [administration]. The Americans turned him over to the Soviets after the end of the war. He was a POW until circa 1955 and has alleged that the Soviets never realised he was an SD man.
>
> B. UJDROWSY knew GRAUER from the war and became very interested in his activities and background upon learning GRAUER had joined [the BND]. UJDROWSY tried to get GRAUER's address from [BND] files and also tried to get information from Ludwigsburg concerning GRAUER's wartime activities, claiming he was sure GRAUER had been involved in some sort of dirty business.
>
> C. It seems likely that on the basis of UJDROWSY's knowledge of GRAUER's background that he discussed GRAUER with the KGB and possibly recommended that sufficient handles existed to make a recruitment possible.[2]

Given the correlation of date and place of birth in these documents, there can be little doubt that the person referred to is the same Gustav Grauer who served under Jäger's command. It is quite possible that he managed to hide his identity while in Soviet custody, and on his return to West Germany his wartime experience working for the SD would have made him a prime candidate for recruitment by the newly formed BND; he wouldn't have been the first suspected war criminal to be employed, and perhaps he knew sufficient details about the wartime past of other members that he was able to persuade people in positions of authority to employ him in return for keeping silent about their previous histories.

The incident in Berlin raises a further possibility. Was this really an attempt to kidnap him with a view to recruiting him, as the CIA agent FLEMING implied? An alternative possibility is that the Soviet authorities learned about Grauer's past during his period of captivity and the KGB had already recruited him prior to his release in 1955. He was then encouraged by the KGB to join the BND as an infiltrator. The Berlin incident may have been an attempt to debrief him; when the other two agents were arrested, fearing that his role as an agent of the KGB was about to be revealed, Grauer then invented the story about abduction. The CIA report added that FLEMING intended to interrogate UJDRUM in the near future, but no record of that interrogation is available. Nor has it been possible to obtain more information about what ultimately became of Grauer.

Karl Jäger, the former commander of *Einsatzkommando 3*, ended the war as chief of police in Reichenberg. He had been living there for a year with his second wife Lotte, during which time she gave birth to a child. As the Red Army approached the region, he considered shooting his family and himself but instead opted to flee to the west. He and his small family set off on a hazardous road journey through the chaos of refugees, shattered Wehrmacht units and advancing enemy forces; after travelling for five weeks, they ended up in the city of Tecklenburg in Westphalia. This does not seem to have been their intended destination, merely the place where they were washed up by the tides of German defeat and collapse, and neither of the Jägers had any contacts in the area. Fearing arrest by the British occupation forces, Jäger decided that he would be safer in an area that he knew, and where he had friends. The day after the family arrived in Tecklenburg, he left his wife and child there and headed south, first to the city of Freiburg and thence to his old hometown of Waldkirch. He told Lotte that he hoped to be able to find work close to the town in a sewing machine factory where he had worked briefly in the 1930s. He gave her a contact address via which they would be able to keep in touch until it was safe for her to join him. She never heard from him again.

As the case of Gerhard Kortkampf demonstrated, the initial intention of the Western Allies to conduct a policy of comprehensive prosecution for war crimes rapidly ran into difficulties, not least because of the huge number of potential cases. Another problem was that, at first, the Western Allies had limited knowledge and understanding of the details of what had happened in Eastern Europe. The ignorance was ultimately corrected by an unlikely source: one of the main perpetrators of the killings obligingly provided them with all the details.

When the unconditional surrender of Germany came into force on 8 May 1945, Gruppenführer Otto Ohlendorf was in his office in Flensburg, which had effectively become the capital of the shrinking Third Reich after Admiral Karl Dönitz, nominated by Hitler as his successor, moved his headquarters to the town. Ohlendorf was an economist and lawyer by training and education and was working on projects intended to help Germany establish a stable currency after the war. He helped Heinrich Himmler slip away from Flensburg before Dönitz and the rest of his staff surrendered to the British; Himmler had failed to persuade Dönitz to appoint him as deputy leader of Germany and had been dismissed from all of his posts on 6 May. Using false documents in the name of Feldwebel Heinrich Hitzinger, Himmler left Flensburg with Ohlendorf and a small number of others, but on 21 May the former head of the SS was arrested together with Ohlendorf in the small town of Bremervörde, where released Soviet prisoners of war had set up an impromptu checkpoint.[3] Himmler's true identity was discovered shortly thereafter and he committed suicide by using a hidden cyanide capsule, but Ohlendorf was handed over to the British.

What began as a routine interrogation of a Nazi bureaucrat rapidly assumed new dimensions. Like so many others in the SS, Ohlendorff was born too late to participate in the fighting of the First World War and was aged only 11 when the conflict came to an end. He joined the Nazi Party in 1925, aged 18, and went on to study at a variety of universities. Heydrich recruited him to the SD in 1936 and he was given the task of running the domestic intelligence office of the SD. At first during his interrogation, Ohlendorf had restricted himself to giving details to his interrogators about the structure and functioning of the SD; the British knew about his role in domestic intelligence, and his interrogators seem to have been more interested in his knowledge of other high-ranking SS and Nazi officials and the structure of SS and SD organisations than in Ohlendorf per se. But on 11 August 1945 he told the British that he had been commander of *Einsatzgruppe D* in Crimea in the opening months of the war against the Soviet Union. Until this date, British and American knowledge about the activities of the *Einsatzgruppen* had been very limited, though at about this date the Americans had informed the British that Ohlendorf was suspected of being involved in mass killings in the Soviet Union, but – apparently with little pressure from his interrogators – Ohlendorf proceeded to enlighten them, as an interrogation report from late September shows:

> Between June 1941 and June 1942 [Ohlendorf] went as an RHSA delegate attached to the staff of Eleventh Army at Simferopol [in

> Crimea] to deal with security tasks in Eleventh Army area. He was commander of Sipo [security police] and SS *Einsatzgruppe D*. He was also responsible for the voluntary recruiting of Tartars. His *Einsatzkommandos* were directly responsible, under his command, on orders received from Heydrich and Himmler, for liquidating a total of approximately 7,000 Jews at Nikolayev (June 1941 to November 1941) and Simferopol (December 1941).[4]

These figures were a significant underestimate. It seems that Ohlendorf believed that he could make himself useful to the British after the war, convinced that his economic experience would be invaluable in helping re-establish Germany. Furthermore, he offered information expecting that whilst it might be used against other senior German figures, he would not face prosecution himself. On 18 October, the Americans took custody of Ohlendorf, intending to use him in the planned prosecution of Ernst Kaltenbrunner, the successor of Reinhard Heydrich.

As had been the case with the British, Ohlendorf behaved as if he expected the Americans to use his expertise in future and freely offered detailed information about the SD, German economic matters, and the activities of the *Einsatzgruppen*. He showed no remorse for what he and his men had done, repeatedly telling his interrogators that the execution of non-combatants had been a legal act because it was done under the orders of superiors and was a military necessity during wartime. He stressed that he had taken steps to ensure that the killings were as humane as possible and had preferred mass execution by firing squads rather than individual shots to the back of the head, as the former method would alleviate personal responsibility for any one death and would therefore be less stressful for his men; he personally oversaw several of the mass killings to ensure that military discipline was maintained throughout.

The sheer frankness of Ohlendorf's account of the mass killings, and the chilling details that he provided, stunned some of his interrogators. Some even questioned his sanity. An army psychologist struggled to reconcile his conduct and lack of remorse with his obvious intelligence and high level of education, concluding that he must have been a sadist, a pervert or a lunatic, as it seemed to the psychiatrist that only someone in one of these three categories could have been involved in such atrocities and could show so little remorse afterwards.[5] Nonetheless, the information that he provided – and his testimony at the International Military Tribunal in Nuremburg – helped convict several senior figures. Kaltenbrunner was hanged on 16 October 1946 at least partly on the basis of evidence from Ohlendorf.

After the conclusion of the International Military Tribunal, the full horror of what had taken place across Europe was clear, but further prosecutions faced thorny problems. The Americans had found it very difficult to work with the Soviet Union during the tribunal for many reasons, both procedural (due to very different legal systems) and ideological. Subsequent prosecutions at Nuremburg were carried out exclusively by the Americans and continued until late 1948. There were 12 separate trials, including one of Erhard Milch, the Luftwaffe field marshal who surrendered to the British at the time of the *Cap Arkona* sinking. The growing weight of evidence against Germans who had been part of the *Einsatzgruppen* led to demands for major prosecutions, but there were potentially so many defendants that the eventual trial, which commenced late in September 1947, limited itself to just 24 officers, including Ohlendorf.

By this stage, vital evidence in the form of the almost daily reports written in 1941 by Heinrich Müller, head of the Gestapo, were available to the prosecutors, and these effectively confirmed what Ohlendorf had revealed in late 1945. Amongst the defendants, only two had been active in the Baltic region: Heinz Jost, who replaced Stahlecker as head of *Einsatzgruppe A*, and Martin Sandberger, who commanded *Sonderkommando 1a* and was subsequently head of the German security police and SS in Estonia.

Jost's attempts to defend himself during the trial were disastrous because they were so often mutually contradictory. He insisted that he had been sent to the east as a replacement for Stahlecker as a punishment for being too soft, and that he was assured that his role would be purely administrative. He told the court that he had suffered health problems – thyroid disorders and rheumatic pains – as a consequence of the mental conflict brought on by his duties, but he had no choice but to follow orders or face punishment himself. The killing of Jews was, he testified, unnecessary, and he had taken every possible measure to have this order revoked, though he provided no evidence to support this.[6]

Sandberger said that he had tried to secure a transfer out of *Einsatzgruppe A* to the Wehrmacht before deployment and on several occasions thereafter, but this was contradicted by the simple fact that he remained in the Baltic region for a little over two years, far longer than the assignments of most men in the *Einsatzgruppen*. He attempted to draw a distinction between legal executions – carried out in accordance with higher orders – and illegal killings, which he blamed exclusively on local paramilitaries. He claimed that the 'few' killings of Jews by his men were the result of fair trials and exhaustive investigation, and that a system of appeal had been available to those convicted and sentenced, even though he could produce no evidence either of any due process prior to execution or even the existence of an appeal system, let alone any evidence of it ever functioning. The court had documents from SS personnel records that showed Sandberger in a different light:

> He is distinguished by his great industry and better than average intensity in his work. From a professional point of view, Sandberger has proved himself in the Reich as well as in his assignment in the east. Sandberger is a versatile SS leader, suitable for promotion ... Because of his political service and his efforts, which far exceed the average, the Chief of the Security Police and SD already supports his preferential promotion.[7]

This was in stark contrast to the picture he attempted to portray of a man trying his best to be assigned to a different role. His attempts to exonerate himself on the grounds that he was personally responsible for only a few of the killings were also unconvincing. When challenged about the execution of 1,000 suspected Communists, he claimed that he was personally responsible for only 350 of the killings. He admitted being responsible for ordering prisoners to be held in camps where they faced almost certain death but claimed that he hoped Hitler would withdraw or change the order.[8]

Ohlendorf, the man whose interrogation had started the series of steps that led to the trial, faced a particularly difficult problem defending himself, as his interrogation records showed him freely confessing to the killings. Denial of involvement was clearly impossible, and instead he argued that he had carried out the killings because of superior orders and military necessity, without any hatred of his victims. He claimed that when he received an order from Hitler – via Bruno Streckenbach, who was head of the SS Personnel and Administration Office at the time and organised the key conferences in Pretzch and elsewhere – that Jews were to be killed in the Soviet Union, he protested and tried to have the order rescinded. When he made this statement, he and his interrogators believed that Streckenbach was dead, but he was one of those being held in captivity by the Soviet Union. After his return to Germany in 1955, he denied that he had passed on any such order. However, at the time of what had become known as the *Einsatzgruppen* Trial, the account given by Ohlendorf and others of the transmission of the order was widely accepted. This made little difference to the views of the court, but Ohlendorf offered it as evidence that he was nothing more than a small cog in a greater machine.

On the subject specifically of killing Jews, Ohlendorf and others defended themselves on the grounds that this was not due to anti-Semitism;

rather, it was because everyone knew that Jews and Bolsheviks were essentially the same people, and as the war in the east was explicitly intended to destroy Bolshevism, this necessitated the killing of all Jews. When challenged about the killing of children, Ohlendorf replied that this, too, was a military necessity. If they were permitted to live, they would be likely to seek revenge when they grew up.[9]

At the end of the trial, both Jost and Sandberger were found guilty of crimes against humanity, war crimes, and membership of an illegal organisation. Jost was sentenced to life imprisonment, and Sandberger was sentenced to death by hanging. Ohlendorf was also found guilty of all three charges and sentenced to death. But a number of factors intervened between sentencing and execution. There was growing opposition in Germany to the prosecution of suspected war criminals, boosted by evidence that showed irregularities in some of the legal processes. For example, at no stage had Ohlendorf and many others been warned that anything they said during interrogation might be used in evidence against them, nor had they been offered legal representation until the court proceedings were announced. There were signs that some American proceedings against Germans involved in the massacre of US soldiers at Malmédy during the Battle of the Bulge were flawed – some of those accused had been coerced or intimidated into incriminating themselves and others. Supported by prominent members of the German clergy, German lawyers repeatedly lobbied American military authorities for clemency and even the complete vindication of some of those convicted.

There was also a growing need for Germany to be reintegrated into the international community, and the increasing tension with the Soviet Union undoubtedly influenced American thinking. In August 1950, an Advisory Board on Clemency recommended reducing Jost's sentence to ten years' imprisonment; Sandberger remained on death row. When the military authorities looked at these recommendations, Sandberger's sentence was reduced to life imprisonment. Jost was paroled in 1952 and subsequently worked as an estate agent in Düsseldorf; he died in 1964, aged 60. Sandberger remained in captivity until February 1958 when he was paroled. He worked as a lawyer and successfully fought attempts at further prosecution in 1970 on the grounds that he had already been tried and had served his sentence. He died in 2010, aged 98. He never expressed a word of remorse and when asked by a journalist whether he felt any sense of shame, he replied that he preferred not to talk about it.

Ultimately, only four of those sentenced to death in the trial – Ohlendorf, Paul Blobel (commander of *Sonderkommando 4a* in Ukraine), Werner Braune (commander of *Einsatzkommando 11b* in Crimea), and

Erich Naumann (commander of *Sonderkommando 7a* in Belarus) – were executed. Nine others had their sentences reduced, and all were free men by February 1958.

The justice faced by others involved in war crimes was also limited. Otto Bradfisch, who commanded *Einsatzkommando 8* and subsequently was head of the Gestapo in Łódź, in which role he played a part in the brutal massacre of the people of Lidice after the death of Heydrich, was head of the Security Police and SD in Potsdam at the end of the war and succeeded in escaping to the west with false documents identifying him as Karl Evers, a junior officer in the Wehrmacht. He was briefly held by the Americans and British but was released in August 1945 and remained free for several years. He resumed using his real name and was identified as a potential war criminal in 1958, when he was imprisoned for his role in the liquidation of the Łódź ghetto; originally sentenced to ten years, this was increased to 13 years in 1963, but he was released in October 1965. It is estimated that his total time served amounted to one hour for each of the 37,000 victims attributed to him.[10]

Amongst the senior figures involved in the German occupation of the Baltic region, Hinrich Lohse, the Reichskommissar, was captured by the British in Schleswig-Holstein at the end of the war. He was found guilty of involvement in the deportation of Jews to the death camps and sentenced to ten years' imprisonment in 1948. He was released just three years later on the grounds of ill health but remained alive until 1964, when he died aged 68. Friedrich Jeckeln, who had been the higher police and SS commander for all of Ostland and earlier in the war had overseen the massacres of Jews in Ukraine and was praised in SS circles for his policy of *Sardinenpackung* to make mass killings more efficient, became a prisoner of war in 1945 when commanding V SS Mountain Corps against the Red Army. He was then sent to Riga where he was tried for multiple war crimes including murder in January 1946 alongside Wolfgang Ditfurth, commander of 403rd Security Division, and several others. Jeckeln and Ditfurth were both found guilty and hanged in February 1946.

Franz Murer, who personally executed several Jews and terrorised the ghetto with his repeated obsessive searches for smuggled food, returned to his native Austria at the end of the war and resumed rural life, living on the large farm that had belonged to his father-in-law. Some of his acquaintances, knowing something of his past, suggested that he and his family might be safer moving to the American zone rather than staying in a British-controlled area, but Murer chose to remain in familiar surroundings. He made no attempt to hide his name and was arrested as a result of a chance event.

Many of the territories controlled by Nazi Germany were teeming with refugees – people who had fled the heavy fighting of the closing months, and hundreds of thousands of those who had been forcibly taken to Germany as labour to keep German industry and agriculture functioning during the conflict. In order to care for these people and to help them return to their homes or to travel on to other destinations, a new agency – the United Nations Relief and Rehabilitation Administration or UNRRA – set up a series of displaced persons' camps across Europe. Many of these housed mixed populations, but one of the largest in the British occupation zone of Austria, in the town of Admont in Styria, was home to about 2,000 people, almost all of them Jews.

As Yom Kippur – the holiest day in the Jewish calendar – approached in the autumn of 1946, two Jews in the camp, Mair Blitz and Moses Kussowitzki, ventured out with a large bag of chocolate and other goods given to them as part of their rations in the camp. They wished to exchange them with local people for live chickens, which they intended to use in the ceremony of *Kapparot*. To their disappointment, a local farmer told them that they would be unlikely to find any chickens that could be exchanged – there was a widespread shortage of eggs, and the farms were operating a registration system for chickens. He told them that there was a large farm not far from Admont, near Gaisdorf am See, where there were at least 2,000 chickens. But whilst the owner of so many chickens might be expected to exchange one or two old birds for other foods, the farmer warned them that the farmer hated Jews, and was believed to have been a 'senior Nazi'.

At the time, there were rumours that Adolf Eichmann and other senior figures were hiding in the neighbourhood and Blitz and Kussowitzki immediately set off for Linz, in the American sector. The town – where Adolf Hitler spent most of his youth – was home to an institution set up by Simon Wiesenthal that was dedicated to tracking down those responsible for the Holocaust, and Blitz and Kussowitzki confidently informed Wiesenthal that they thought they had located Eichmann's hiding place.

Wiesenthal had doubts that the 'senior Nazi' in the chicken farm was Eichmann, but he and Mischa Lewin, who had been a Jewish partisan in Eastern Europe, travelled to Gaishorn with Blitz and Kussowitski. The group visited the gendarmerie office in the town where they learned the name of the owner of the farm – any disappointment on the part of Blitz and Kussowitzki that it wasn't Eichmann was offset by Wiesenthal's recognition of Murer's name. From the gendarmerie, the four men went to the camp at Admont to seek witnesses to the crimes that Murer had committed, and rapidly found seven witnesses from the Vilnius ghetto. Four of them made sufficiently clear statements to form the basis of legal action and Wiesenthal returned to the Gaishorn gendarmerie office: 'Without a word I handed over the statements to the old [gendarmerie] commander. He read them with great concentration. At one point he stared helplessly at the Madonna on the wall. Then he ordered two gendarmes to go up the hill and to arrest Murer, and notified the officers of the British military police.'

When the two gendarmes reached Murer's farm, they found him about to leave – someone from the gendarmerie had warned him that his arrest was imminent. Nonetheless, they took him back to the gendarmerie office, where he was handed over to the British authorities. The following day, Wiesenthal was surprised to find that the British military police officers were more interested in asking him about illegal Jewish migration to Palestine; they threatened to detain him when he refused to answer any questions. When Jews from the displaced persons' camp protested outside, British soldiers set up two machine-guns to cover them. The situation was in danger of deteriorating rapidly, but after discussions with his superiors, the British officer in charge released Wiesenthal.

It seems that the British authorities were actually aware of Murer's presence and had already detained him twice during the summer of 1946 and had carried out a search of his house but had insufficient evidence to detain him – at no point had they visited the displaced persons' camp to ask if any of the Jews in the camp might be able to assist them. In the weeks that followed, Wiesenthal worked to gather further testimony against Murer, who insisted to the British that he had been employed purely in an administrative role in Vilnius, but evidence of his crimes accumulated as witnesses from all over Europe responded to Wiesenthal's enquiries. Many of the accounts lacked the precision required for legal proceedings, but nonetheless a substantial file was placed before the court in Graz in 1947. The court seemed reluctant to prosecute, as Murer's name had not featured on any of the lists of wanted war criminals that were circulating, but the British then suggested that the solution might be to hand him over to the Soviet authorities.

At first, the Soviets seemed to have little interest in Murer, but after further discussions they changed their minds; supporters of Murer muttered about the British liaison officer who worked with the Soviet authorities being a 'Viennese Jew'. Murer and his wife later claimed that the British were inclined to be sympathetic to his cause, even encouraging him to flee and assuring him that they would do nothing to intervene. Murer also said that the reason that he didn't take advantage of this suggestion was because he fully expected to be acquitted by the Soviet courts.[11] The suggestion regarding possible British complicity in an escape attempt seems highly unlikely given the nature of the crimes with which Murer was charged, and there is nothing to suggest that he was of any use to western intelligence services, a factor that might otherwise have counted in his favour. And even if he genuinely believed that he was innocent, he would have known that the chances of the Soviet legal system agreeing with that assessment were almost non-existent.

In February 1948, Murer was handed over to the Soviet occupation authorities in the town of Semmering. A month later, in a cattle truck of the sort used by the Nazis to transport Jews by train, he was transferred to Vilnius where he underwent lengthy interrogation before being brought before a military court in September. Witnesses testified to Murer's violent searches of prisoners returning to the ghetto and to several killings, including his involvement in the arrest and murder of Ljuba Lewicka, the opera singer. The court's judgement was damning:

> When the German Nazis ruled Vilnius, the capital of Lithuania, they severely persecuted the people. The main initiator of these acts in Vilnius was the Nazi Franz Murer ... In September 1941 Murer established the Vilnius ghetto and under his leadership about 40,000 Soviet Jews were housed here. He himself persecuted, punished and degraded there, whenever anyone broke Nazi laws or the rules of the ghetto. Murer had 5,000 Jews taken to the special camp at Ponary and shot ...
>
> As head of the ghetto Murer personally wrote and developed the rules and documents – which bear his signature – that discriminated against Jewish Soviet citizens. He made the Jews work in impossible conditions.[12]

Despite being found guilty of murder as well as the less severe but still serious charges of mistreatment of ghetto inmates, Murer escaped the death penalty by chance. Just a few weeks before his conviction, the Soviet authorities had abolished the death penalty. It was reinstated not long after, but Murer was sentenced to twenty-five years' hard labour. At the beginning of 1949, he was transferred to a labour camp near Vorkuta, close to the Arctic Circle, where he worked in a coalmine; the temperature was far below zero for much of the year and rations in the camp were limited, though still a little better than the limits that Murer had imposed on the inmates of the Vilnius ghetto. He was again fortunate in that at the end of 1950, he was transferred out of the camp, where he would almost certainly have died within a few years, and eventually sent to work in an asbestos factory in the Ural Mountains.

Helmut Rauca, who worked with Jordan in Kaunas, was detained by the Americans at the end of the war for a time before being released with no charges brought against him. After working as a coal miner he travelled to Canada in 1950, taking a number of manual jobs before running a restaurant. He became a Canadian citizen in 1956 and retired as a moderately wealthy businessman in 1973. Günther Wieland, who was a prosecutor in East Germany, tracked Rauca to Canada but the Canadians refused to extradite a Canadian citizen to a country on the eastern side of the Iron Curtain. Wieland passed his files to the West German authorities, who then sought his extradition. An arrest warrant relating to the slaughter of Jews in the *Grosse Aktion* in Kaunas in 1941 was issued in September 1961 but no action was taken by the Canadian authorities. Another attempt in 1972 foundered because of a dispute about the spelling of his name, and an arrest warrant was only issued in June 1982 after the personal intervention of Robert Kaplan, the Canadian attorney general. Rauca was finally placed under arrest shortly after; one of the most important witnesses against him was Avraham Gollub, who was able to disprove Rauca's assertions that he had not been in Kaunas during the war. Rauca remained in captivity pending extradition and after a lengthy legal battle he was finally flown to Frankfurt am Main in May 1983. He died in custody of cancer in October 1983, aged 72.

There are several aspects to the case of Rauca that are noteworthy. His initial custody in American hands was very short, and there are different accounts of how long it lasted. His name was mentioned on several occasions during the International Military Tribunal proceedings in Nuremburg, and his involvement in the crimes committed in Lithuania was therefore documented within a few months of the end of the war; this should have been sufficient to render impossible his emigration to Canada, and his assumption of Canadian citizenship. The manner in which the 1961 arrest warrant and extradition request was ignored is extraordinary, and the obstruction of the second attempt in 1972 is also curious. The only single explanation that can account for all of these factors is that Rauca had provided useful service to western intelligence agencies in exchange for being protected from prosecution.[13]

Martin Weiss was one of so many Germans who earned a reputation for brutality in Lithuania, even before his involvement in the *Kinderaktion*. He left Vilnius at almost the last moment before the arrival of the Red Army and returned to Germany, where he was arrested in 1949. The following year he was charged in Würzburg with multiple murders. The court heard that he had been present at the shooting of at least 30,000 victims during his time in Lithuania, had overseen all aspects of the murder operation, had ordered the killers to open fire, and had personally killed several victims. He had never shown any remorse; a Jewish witness testified that she had worked in an administrative role in his office and that he had often returned from Ponary with his uniform bearing bloodstains; on one occasion he told her: 'Now I have killed your fathers, your mothers, or your sisters. I still need you for work. But later you too will be killed.'[14]

Weiss was found guilty and sentenced to life imprisonment.

Horst Schweinberger, who oversaw many of the mass killings at Ponary, was one of many who escaped any punishment. An attempt to prosecute him in 1973 for the killings after the 'Great Provocation' incident was rejected on the grounds that he was on leave at the time of the killings; documents available both at the time and later showed that this was untrue. He died in obscurity several years later. Another who escaped entirely was Bruno Kittel, the dapper, cold-blooded killer who terrified the Jews of Vilnius and Kaunas in 1943 and 1944. At the end of the war, he simply disappeared. It is possible that he was one of the numberless corpses that littered the devastated towns and cities of Europe in 1945, but it is perhaps more likely that the former actor merely took on another role and lived out his remaining years in safety.

Throughout the 1950s, Karl Jäger remained at liberty. He lived under his real name and made no secret of his past as a senior SS officer, at least as far as casual acquaintances were concerned. He left Waldkirch in the summer of 1945, moving to Wiesenbach, near Heidelberg, where he secured work as a labourer in a grain mill. In 1951, he moved to Kümmelbach. Like all Germans, he was required to complete registration papers for the occupation authorities, and although he registered under his real name and date of birth, he failed to report his membership of the Nazi Party and SS. By 1948, he was being sought by the Americans in connection with his wartime activities, but Karl Jäger is a very common name and there was no obvious link between the manual labourer and the senior SS officer who had led *Einsatzkommando 3*.

It wasn't until late in 1956 that the German authorities began to search for him; despite circulating requests for information including photographs of Jäger in SS uniform, they were unable to locate him. The woman who owned the hotel where he rented a small room in Heidelberg later confirmed that she knew that her tenant had been a senior SS officer and had commanded Security Police units in the east, but like so many Germans she remained silent and made no attempt to inform the authorities. In the 1950s, especially the first half of the decade, the prevailing mood in West Germany was to try to forget about the past. In many cases, German civilians actively helped fugitives to hide or to leave the country in order to avoid facing prosecution for their crimes. Some Germans who attempted to inform the police about the whereabouts of former Nazis faced intimidation and threats of violence from their neighbours.

But time was running out for Jäger. In April 1958, the German authorities in the city of Ulm prosecuted ten former members of *Einsatzkommando Tilsit*, a unit that had operated in the area of Lithuania immediately adjacent to the northern border of East Prussia. The trial was marked by the defence strategy – already seen repeatedly at Nuremburg – of portraying the defendants as men who had merely acted under orders, and as a result the sentences passed were relatively light compared to the severity of the crimes. The men were charged with the murder of over 3,900 individuals, but although all ten men were found guilty, the sentences ranged from just three years to 15 years. Nonetheless, the trial and the widespread press coverage tore away the veil that so many Germans had attempted to draw over the past and forced them to confront the reality of what had been done in the name of Germany.[15]

One of the consequences of the trial was the establishment of the *Zentrale Stelle der Landesjustizverwaltungen zur Aufklärung Nationalsozialistischer Verbrechen* ('Central Office of the State Justice Administration for the Investigation of National Socialist Crimes') in Ludwigsburg, with the aim of identifying previously unprosecuted war criminals. It commenced work at the end of 1958 and one of its earliest objectives was to renew the search for Jäger, whose name had featured in the recent Ulm trial. Investigators who visited Waldkirch interviewed Otto Weber, whose sister Emma had been Jäger's first wife; Weber gave them Jäger's address in Kümmelbach, and the former commander of *Einsatzkommando 3* was finally arrested in April 1959. He had lived at liberty, taking no real steps to hide his identity, for 14 years.

In his early interrogations, Jäger admitted freely to having held senior rank in the SS and even to having commanded *Einsatzkommando 3*, but denied any involvement in the mass murder of Jews and others in Lithuania. He adopted the same position as others, namely that he had merely passed on orders from above. He stated that he had to obey orders as it was wartime, but at the same time denied being the originator of any orders himself – he had merely passed them on.[16] A few weeks after his arrest, he was handed over to the Ludwigsburg team and over four days underwent about 23 hours of interrogation. He repeatedly denied any personal involvement in war crimes, often claiming to have no memory of important events, but he seemed to have little difficulty recalling relatively trivial incidents, such as the damage to one of his vehicles from a landmine after *Einsatzkommando 3* first entered Lithuania. He insisted that he had acted diligently in carrying out his instructions, and even made a virtue of the fact that he had refused sick leave when suffering from stress during his time in Kaunas: 'I have always been a person with a higher sense of duty ... I was of the opinion that as a soldier in wartime, as I thought myself, I always had to do my duty, regardless of where I was sent.'[17]

It was impossible for Jäger to deny that Jews, suspected Communists, Roma, and the mentally ill had been executed, but he tried to pass all responsibility for this to others. He told his interrogators that men like Hamann had operated on their own initiative. At this time, the document that later became known as the Jäger Report – the detailed compilation of statistics and other information that Jäger sent to Stahlecker on 1 December 1941 – had not yet been unearthed. Nonetheless, he admitted writing such reports, stressing that he had merely collated information for higher authorities.

If found guilty, Jäger faced what would probably have been a relatively short time in prison; he was 74 years old and the death penalty was no longer in force, and he would likely have been released after a few years on medical grounds. But Jäger wrote a letter to his son-in-law, Sepp Fackler, in which he repeated that he was not responsible for any crimes and felt no sense of guilt, and on 22 June 1959, he hanged himself in his cell.

In 1955, as part of the treaty recognising the new Austrian state, Murer and other war criminals were repatriated. Murer was met at the railway station in Wiener Neustadt by his wife and sons. The court in Graz considered his case once more but decided at the end of the year to take no further action. At the time, Austria was seeking assiduously to portray itself as the first victim of Nazi Germany rather than as a willing collaborator. Like many in West Germany, most Austrians simply wished to forget about the past and the involvement of so many Austrians in the terrible crimes that had been committed.

Whilst Lina Heydrich lived for the last years of the war on the lavish estate awarded to her and later successfully sued the West German government to secure the pension accorded to the widow of a dead general, Steffi Schmid, whose husband Anton was executed in Lithuania in 1942 for trying to save Jews, endured several years of insults and persecution in Vienna. Max Salinger, who had been transformed by Schmid into Gefreiter Max Huppert, survived the war and visited Steffi and her daughter Gertha after the war. It was the first time that the family heard the full details of what had happened in Vilnius in 1941 and 1942. Salinger was also able to provide Steffi with a small amount of financial support. After the war, Steffi continued to run Schmid's radio shop. Nazi Germany had refused to grant her a widow's pension, and after the war the Austrian authorities similarly refused to recognise the rights of family members of men who had been killed for desertion or other crimes. But the mood changed during the 1950s and in 1956 Steffi received a certificate confirming that she was the widow of someone who had been victim of political persecution during the Nazi era. She was finally awarded a pension in 1957. She died in 1984.

Like Salinger, Luisa Emaitisaite also survived the war, as did Schmid's friend Hermann Adler and many of the Jews who had been part of the resistance movement, including Abba Kovner. Adler published a prose poem in 1945 entitled *Gesänge aus der Stadt des Todes* ('Songs from the City of Death') in 1945, in which he described some of Schmid's actions; it was the first time that Schmid's name entered the public realm.

Karl Plagge surrendered with his men to the Americans on 2 May 1945. As a former member of the Nazi Party, in order to secure appropriate documents that would enable him to get work after the war he had to go through a denazification process, which involved him appearing in court. At first, many of these courts were run by the Western Allies, but the sheer number of people who had to go through the process meant that the task was rapidly handed over to the German legal system, which many British and American authorities regarded as having survived the Nazi era untainted, even though so many senior Nazis had been lawyers. Many of the judges who then sat in these denazification courts had without hesitation passed judgement on their fellow citizens during the Nazi era; these men, who were often responsible for the implementation of Nazi laws relating to race, now convened to consider the guilt of others. In the case of Plagge, there was more at stake than merely his former membership of the Nazi Party: he had also been involved in the use of forced labour.

The proceedings took place in February 1948 in Darmstadt. Many of the soldiers who had served in *HKP 562* either gave evidence in person or submitted affidavits, confirming that Plagge had always acted with decency towards the Jews who worked for him. Heinz Zeune told the court that Plagge had been very concerned about the poor food supply for the Jews and tasked Zeune with securing additional supplies; he added that Plagge insisted on weekly weighings until he was satisfied that the prisoners weren't losing weight and repeatedly asked Zeune to ensure that the prisoners received the same rations as German officers. Alfred Stumpff, who had the rank of Oberleutnant (lieutenant in the British Army) in *HKP 562*, testified that Plagge had rejected the extermination policies towards the Jews and employed far more Jewish workers than he actually needed. In addition to the incident when Plagge arranged for the 'Jew-hating' Feldwebel to be transferred to a front-line unit, Stumpff gave an account of Plagge's efforts to get Jews who had been locked up by the SD released from prison; Christian Bartholomae corroborated this, telling the court that he had been tasked with securing the release of four prisoners from SD custody, and that Plagge had also protected two Jewish doctors so that they could help other members of the Jewish community. Georg Raab and Friedrich Asmus also spoke out in defence of Plagge.

The denazification court could assign people to one of five categories. At either end of the scale, it could find a defendant not guilty of any wrongdoing, or guilty of potential war crimes, which would then necessitate further prosecution. In between these two extremes the court had three further options. The lesser was to find a defendant guilty of being a 'fellow traveller' of the Nazi Party, i.e. someone who had been a party member but had not done anything to further its interests or aims. The middle grade was 'lesser offender', someone who had aided the Nazis in numerous minor ways, and the higher intermediate grade was an offender who had been an activist or had made personal profit from involvement in the Nazi Party. Plagge faced one of the more serious classifications, because of the use of forced labour in *HKP 562*. It was so commonplace for former comrades to make exonerating statements that it was relatively simple for the court to assume that the testimonies submitted by men he had commanded were little more than attempts to whitewash his past. Unless some of the people that Plagge had protected came forward, it looked likely that he would be found guilty of one of the higher grades of involvement with the Nazis.

Fortunately, fate took a kind turn for Plagge. Maria Eichamueller was a civilian resident of Darmstadt, and she presented herself to the court and insisted on giving evidence. Her statement proved to be crucial:

> Today was the first time that I have seen Mr Plagge. I do not know him. I wish to say the following. At Christmas I was in Ludwigsburg near Stuttgart on a visit. My friend, with whom I was staying during my visit, knows the Jewish lawyer Dr Paula Zanka, who cares for the Jews in the camp [a displaced persons' camp near Stuttgart]. Via my friend, she asked me to seek out someone named Plagge here in Darmstadt for the reason that in the camp there were several Jews who wished to offer their thanks to Plagge. They said that Plagge had been kind to them and had done whatever he could for them. They are prepared to support him with food and money if he is in need. There is also a Jewish father in Stuttgart who explained that his son was saved by Plagge. On my return, I immediately went to the police to try to locate Plagge and found several Plagges, but none of them were the person being sought. On Saturday I happened to read in the newspaper that a court case about Plagge was about to begin. I immediately came here but couldn't find the chairman in question on Saturday. I therefore came today to find out whether this was the right Plagge from Vilnius.[18]

It proved to be a decisive moment. Although it seems from the court transcript that Plagge's lawyer was confident that his client would be acquitted, Plagge chose to plead guilty to the charge of being a 'fellow traveller' of the Nazis. It seems that he was haunted by a sense of guilt, that he could and should have done more, and wished this to be recognised by the court. The presiding judges accepted his plea and fined him 100 Marks, together with court costs of 9,000 Marks. Their judgement suggests that if Plagge's treatment of the Jews had been motivated by opposition to the Nazi regime, they would have found him not guilty, but remarkably, they decided that saving the Jews on humanitarian grounds was insufficient for such a verdict. After the trial, Plagge lived quietly with his wife Anke until he died of a heart attack in June 1957; he was 60 years old.

Alfons von Deschwanden, who was a junior NCO in *HKP 562*, did not testify at Plagge's denazification trial. He returned to his home town and worked as a vehicle mechanic. For many years after the war, he received a crate of oranges every Christmas, sent to him from Israel by one of the Jews that he had befriended and protected. He was overjoyed in 1971 to be contacted by two of the Jews who had slipped out of the blacksmith's shop after Plagge's warning about the camp's imminent transfer to the SS, and he and the two Jews – now married – made reciprocal visits to each other's homes in Germany and Israel.

Rauca and Kortkampf were of course not the only war criminals to benefit from the attention of the intelligence agencies of both sides. In many cases, these individuals worked directly for the agencies concerned, but in other cases they were sheltered lest they reveal information about the pasts of other, perhaps more prominent people. This is probably true in the case of Adolf Eichmann. He rose to the rank of Standartenführer during the war and was widely seen in the SS as something of an expert on Jewish matters, though his qualification for this was minimal. He oversaw the deportation of Jews to death camps once the industrialised killing of the Jews began after the Wannsee Conference and evaded capture in the years that followed the German surrender, moving to Argentina in 1950.

It is highly likely that both the CIA and the BND were aware of his location by 1958 at the latest, but they decided to take no action in order to protect a man named Hans Globke who had been a colleague of Eichmann during the war. Globke was a lawyer who helped draft some of the details of the anti-Semitic Nuremburg Race Laws of 1936 and then went on to draw up legislation that progressively reduced the rights of Jews. After the war, he claimed at his denazification trial that he had been an opponent of the Nazis, stating that he had close contacts with the plotters who tried to kill Hitler in 1944. Whilst this is probably correct, he was also undoubtedly responsible for many acts against the

Jews of Europe, including playing a major role in the deportation of Jews from Slovakia and Greece to death camps in Poland, but the presiding judges in his denazification trial were much more willing to exonerate him than the judges in Plagge's trial. Cleared of any responsibility for Nazi war crimes, Globke rose to become a senior figure in the post-war German government, remaining an adviser into the 1960s, and due to concerns that Eichmann might make incriminating statements against Globke, both the BND and the CIA left Eichmann alone.

The Israelis had no such concerns and agents of Mossad, the Israeli secret service, abducted him in May 1960, and took him back to Israel to face trial. Eichmann was extensively interrogated and appeared in court in 1961, and the prosecutors took the opportunity of the trial to publicise many aspects of the Holocaust that had little relevance to Eichmann's duties. Like so many other Nazi war criminals, Eichmann refused to acknowledge any sense of personal guilt – he openly admitted to disliking Jews but attempted to claim that he had never been in favour of their extermination. The prosecutor then challenged him about a statement he had made in 1945: 'I will leap into my grave laughing because the feeling that I have five million human beings on my conscience is for me a source of extraordinary satisfaction.'[19]

In response, Eichmann claimed at first that he had been speaking of Soviet citizens as a whole, but later admitted that he had been referring to the Jews. He said that this reflected his opinion in 1945 but couldn't account for how this was consistent with his previous statement that he hadn't approved of the extermination policy.[20]

Despite attempts to portray Eichmann as some sort of master figure in the story of the Holocaust – Robert Musmanno, who had been the presiding judge at the *Einsatzgruppen* trial in Nuremburg, stated without any justification that Eichmann had been responsible for the organisation and deployment of the *Einsatzgruppen* – the truth was that Eichmann was merely one part of the killing machine that slaughtered so many innocent people. He was found guilty of 15 counts of crimes against humanity, war crimes, crimes against the Jewish people, and membership of a criminal organisation, but acquitted of personally killing anyone and of organising the *Einsatzgruppen*. He was hanged shortly after midnight on 1 June 1961.

Eichmann wasn't the only target of Mossad. A Latvian by the name of Herberts Cukurs was a member of a paramilitary unit known as the *Arājs Kommando*; this formation was responsible for mass killings in Latvia and Belarus, and after the war Cukurs moved to South America where he became involved in the aviation industry, resuming a pre-war career. He consistently claimed that he had no personal involvement in the killings carried out by the *Arājs Kommando*, but in 1965 he was invited to a meeting in Montevideo with a group of businessmen who were interested in setting up a new airline. A few days later, an announcement appeared in the press offices of German and South American newspapers:

> Taking into consideration the gravity of the charge levelled against the accused, namely that he personally supervised the killing of more than 30,000 men, women and children, and considering the extreme display of cruelty which the subject showed when carrying out his tasks, the accused Herbert Cukurs is hereby sentenced to death. [The] accused was executed by those who can never forget on 23 February 1965. His body can be found at Casa Cubertino Calle Columbia, Séptima Sección del Departamento de Canelones, Montevideo, Uruguay.[21]

The Eichmann abduction and trial triggered a further investigation of Franz Murer. Wiesenthal reviewed the case in 1960 and, believing that Murer was either dead or still in Soviet captivity, telephoned the Gaishorn gendarmerie office to clarify a few points concerning the earlier arrest in 1946. To his surprise, the officer he spoke to replied that he would phone him back shortly after checking with Murer. The astonished Wiesenthal contacted the justice ministry in Vienna and enquired why Murer's name had not been recorded on a list of war criminals who had been returned by the Soviet Union. The reply was that it was a simple error; the Soviet authorities had not provided the Austrians with a comprehensive list of those released, and processing of the men on their return to Austria had not been completely thorough.

Murer's father-in-law had died in the years that Murer was in Soviet captivity, and he was now running the family farm. He had also become a representative of local farmers in the farmers' union and was a widely respected figure in his rural Styrian community – a post he now resigned, at least until the new investigation was resolved – and at first the justice ministry seemed reluctant to proceed against him. Just as the temporary suspension of the death penalty in the Soviet Union had saved him from hanging, a change in Austrian law in 1957 now came to Murer's aid: he could not be prosecuted for being part of the machinery of the Holocaust but would have to face specific new charges. Had he been prosecuted immediately on his return from the Soviet Union in 1955, he would have had no such protection.

Wiesenthal was undeterred by the requirement to produce fresh charges, as he had accumulated a wealth of witness statements showing Murer's involvement in several acts of murder, and in May 1961 the justice ministry finally issued an arrest warrant. Despite intensive lobbying by Murer's friends and relatives, he was finally brought to trial in June 1963 in Graz before a jury of eight individuals. The presiding judge was Dr Egon Peyer; the prosecuting lawyer was Dr Schumann; and the defence was led by Dr Karl Böck. Murer was charged with 15 counts of murder, and a guilty verdict in any of these could result in life imprisonment.[22]

From the outset, Murer's defence strategy was clear: he declared that he had never fired a shot at anyone, had never been involved in any violent acts against Jews, and had served purely in an administrative capacity. When he was presented with documents bearing his signature imposing harsh conditions on Jews and threatening them with death if they broke these conditions, he replied that he had no memory of signing them, and he claimed that his imprisonment by the Soviet authorities was purely because he had diverted food resources from the civilian population to the Wehrmacht.

The proceedings soon took on an extraordinary character. Murer's two sons sat in the front row of the court, laughing mockingly and grimacing at witnesses, with no intervention from Judge Peyer. Dr Mosche Feigenberg, who had worked as a urological surgeon in the ghetto hospital, described Murer's orders that pregnant women had to undergo abortions and how he had been widely feared in the ghetto for his arbitrary violence. When Feigenberg described how Murer repeatedly visited the bath house where Jewish women stripped to wash and how he had forced women returning to the ghetto to remove all of their clothes, Judge Peyer cut him short, insisting that the court did not need a 'moral history lesson', rather it needed to hear specific evidence against Murer.

The witnesses might have believed that their shocking stories would receive a considerate audience, but their reception was anything but sympathetic. On the third day of the trial, Tova Rajzman described how Murer had shot her sister Chaja; as she began her evidence, she broke down and wept at the memory of the killing. Judge Peyer reprimanded her with the words 'Don't cry in the court room!' She replied, 'Forgive me, Sir, but it was terrible. My sister's blood was splattered over my feet.' Some witnesses considered taking matters into their own hands. On a 'rest day' in the trial, Wiesenthal spoke to a witness in a nearby hotel. The witness showed him a long knife that he had concealed under his jacket. He had lost faith in justice, both human and divine, he told Wiesenthal. The place where Murer sat in court was close to the witness stand, and he intended to spring across the short distance and stab the man who had killed his son. It was only with difficulty that Wiesenthal was able to persuade him to hand over the knife.

The quality of the witnesses varied considerably. Some reported that Murer had killed people, but they hadn't personally seen him carrying out the murder. In other cases, Böck – the defence lawyer – exploited the difficulty that witnesses had in giving an accurate date for events, suggesting to the jury that if they were unable to provide a date, the rest of their evidence was also of questionable accuracy. Franz Engelmann, who had been a Wehrmacht Hauptmann in Vilnius, told the court that he had visited Murer's office to protest about the poor nutrition of the Jews sent to work for his unit. Murer, he said, had replied that if the Jews became too weak to work, he should simply shoot them. In many cases, Murer claimed to have no recollection of the specific events described by the witness, but on this occasion he replied that he had told Engelmann to go upstairs, where he would find plenty of potatoes to give to his workers. When entries from the diary of Herman Kruk were submitted as evidence, Judge Peyer responded that the entries did not describe specific murders, and the court had no means of knowing how accurate the entries were, as Kruk was long dead. For the defence, Martin Weiss – released on parole from his life sentence – told the court that Murer had only been responsible for general civil matters; he knew of no occasions when Murer had shot anyone, and that the incidents described in the charges against Murer were broadly similar to several other episodes for which he – Weiss – had already been convicted.

If matters weren't already moving from the extraordinary towards the scandalous, there was a further development on the day of the closing speeches. Julius Kloiber, one of the jurors, informed the court that he felt himself to be compromised. During the last weeks of the war, he had been mobilised as part of the *Volkssturm* – the German equivalent of the British Home Guard – and had been ordered to fire on Jewish prisoners. Kloiber was removed from the jury and replaced by one of two 'reserve' jurors who had been in court throughout proceedings. This was contrary to strict observance of the rules that applied at the time.

In his closing speech, Schuhmann admitted that the prosecution had failed to produce sufficient evidence in six cases. He left the jury to decide in four further cases, but he argued that Murer was undeniably guilty in the remaining cases, including those in which witnesses described seeing their family members shot and killed. His concluding words were: 'Put yourselves in the terrible situation of seeing with your own eyes, your child being killed. I believe that the testimony of these witnesses is without doubt sufficient to find Murer guilty.'[23]

In response, Böck didn't deny that the killings had taken place; he simply rejected the suggestion that his client was responsible. He suggested that numerous Jewish organisations had encouraged witnesses to come forward, and that the many Jewish witnesses were only alive because men like Hingst and Murer had held a 'protective hand' over them, acting in the best interests of the German Reich. The allusions to some great Jewish conspiracy against Murer were reminiscent of the pre-war talk of a 'worldwide Jewish conspiracy', but there was no reprimand from Judge Peyer.

The verdict of the jury was shocking. They appeared to have been more inclined to believe the testimony of the convicted mass murderer Martin Weiss than the statements made by several Jews. On almost every count of murder, the jury returned a unanimous verdict of not guilty. In two cases – the shootings of the father of Jakob Kagan and of Abraham Schmigel – the jurors were evenly split, and Judge Peyer was required to cast a deciding vote in favour of the defendant. With loud cheers, Murer's family and friends carried him from the court. Journalists described how many celebrated the verdict in a café opposite the courthouse, accompanied by most of the jurors, who were clearly on good terms with Murer's supporters and seemed to know them well. The right-wing newspapers of Austria and Germany reported the outcome with approval, but others were less pleased; the *Volksstimme*, a left-wing Austrian newspaper, concluded that those celebrating the outcome in the café outside the court were marking the burial of justice: 'With the Graz verdict, not only Murer was set free. Mass murder, committed in the uniforms of the Hitler area, has been declared free of punishment.'[24]

There were widespread protests, both in Austria and elsewhere. Many who marched in Vienna sewed yellow Stars of David to their clothes. Large crowds gathered in cities in Israel, and the Austrian ambassador warned his government that relations between the two countries would be damaged for many years. But even worse was to come: an anonymous letter to Simon Wiesenthal's institute stated that Judge Egon Peyer had been an enthusiastic supporter of the Nazis during the war. Both in the days after the trial and the months and years that followed, Peyer refused to answer any questions about this.

There were some attempts to have Murer prosecuted again – there were plenty of other murders with which he could be accused, and the publicity around the trial and its disgraceful outcome resulted in more witnesses coming forward – but no further trial took place. After the scandal of the trial had faded from attention, Murer resumed his life as a prosperous and respected Styrian farmer. In 1989, Gerulf Murer, one of the two sons who had mocked several witnesses without any rebukes from Judge Peyer, announced that a forthcoming book would prove his father's innocence. No such book has ever been published. Franz Murer died in 1994, and like many other perpetrators of the Holocaust, he showed no remorse whatsoever for his deeds.

The various Poles and Lithuanians who helped the Jews had differing fates. Father Andrzej Gdowski, the priest in the Church of St Teresa of Avila in Vilnius, survived captivity and resumed his duties as a priest after the war. Mother Anna Borkowska, who sheltered several resistance fighters and other fugitives in her convent, also survived, but she turned her back on religion, feeling that a just God would never have allowed such terrible events to take place. Bronius Paukštys, who had helped several hundred Jews in Kaunas and had been fearless in his opposition to the Germans, showed similar determination in the face of the Soviet authorities. Avraham Gollub, who had married Pnina Sheinzon in August 1944, returned to the ruins of the ghetto to try to recover his diaries. He was arrested by the NKVD, who demanded that he reveal to them the location of the documents, but after he was released he recovered three of the five buried crates and took them to Vilnius. Here, he made contact with a Zionist group that offered him an escape route from the area. Deciding to take advantage of this, he first returned to Kaunas:

> I went to see [Father Bronius] Paukštys and suggested that he join me in my escape from Lithuania, warning him that, as a priest, he would not be able to carry on his humanitarian work or national traditions under Soviet rule, and that sooner or later he would be exiled to Siberia ... But that noble man refused to leave, saying that he could not leave his community and that he would continue on his chosen path regardless of the peril or the threat of exile. He had not given in to the Nazis. He would not give in to the Bolsheviks either.[25]

Gollub travelled first to Lublin in Poland, where he was joined by his wife Pnina and her daughter Shumalit, on an odyssey that took them to Czechoslovakia, Hungary, and Romania before finally reaching Italy, carrying the documents he had recovered from the Kaunas ghetto site. They remained in Italy until 1947, when they were able to travel to Palestine; Gollub changed his surname two years later, from Gollub (the Russian word for 'dove') to Tory (the Hebrew equivalent). As Gollub had feared, Father Paukštys was arrested by the KGB in August 1946 and sentenced to ten years in a Siberian camp for helping anti-Soviet partisans. He was forced to work breaking stones for roads and the ordeal proved to be a tough one for a man in his fifties. He returned to Lithuania in 1956 and worked in a church in Alytus, but was forced to go into hiding briefly after giving a sermon that was critical of the Soviet authorities. He died in 1966.

Life was not kind to Jonas Paulavičius, the farmer who steadily accumulated over a dozen fugitives. His home – which he had personally built – was washed away by a flood and his daughter died shortly after the war of tuberculosis. He endured insults from some of his neighbours after the war for having helped the Jews; some of this seems to have been straightforward anti-Semitism, but many resented his actions on the grounds that he had endangered others in his community, because the Germans might have resorted to collective punishment if he was discovered. In 1952, a man shot and killed him through an open window in what was at first thought to be a burglary attempt, but the perpetrator was a strongly anti-Semitic Lithuanian nationalist. He was arrested, charged with murder and executed.

After the war, Jan Zwartendijk, who had been the acting consul in Kaunas before the war, continued to work for Philips and made no mention of his activities in Kaunas. In 1976, when he was aged 80 and was dying of cancer, he was briefly in contact with David Kranzler, an American historian who had emigrated to the USA as a child with his family in 1937 from Germany to escape the growing persecution of the Jews. Kranzler became aware of Zwartendijk's efforts to help Jews escape from Kaunas and campaigned steadily over the following 18 years to secure recognition for the man who had, purely by chance, become an honorary consul. In 1998, the Yad Vashem organisation in Israel awarded Zwartendijk the title of Righteous Among the Nations.

After he closed the Japanese consulate in Kaunas, Chiune Sugihara was assigned to other diplomatic duties in Europe and was in Romania when the Red Army drove out the Germans in late 1944. At first, he was interned with other diplomats, but in August 1945 the Soviet Union declared war on Japan. Together with his wife and three small children, Sugihara was transferred to an old Romanian Army barracks in Bucharest, which was being used as a prison camp – it isn't known whether his suspected involvement with the White Russian community of Harbin contributed to his imprisonment. At the end of 1946, the Sugiharas were informed that they were to be permitted to return to Japan and they journeyed for several months on slow, unheated trains to the Pacific coast. Finally, in April 1947, they returned to Japan.

Sugihara contacted the Japanese Foreign Ministry to report his return, and not long after he was summoned to a meeting where he was dismissed from the diplomatic service, at least partly due to his activities in Lithuania. He took what work he could find in a Japan laid waste by the war, at one time as a door-to-door salesman trying to sell light bulbs to people who often had no electrical supply. Slowly, his fortunes improved and he finally worked in Moscow as a representative of a Japanese company until he retired in 1976. Eight years later, his activity in Kaunas was recognised by Yad Vashem and he was awarded the title of Righteous Among the Nations.

In 1985, a year before he died, he explained his actions in an interview:

> It is the kind of sentiments anyone would have when he actually sees refugees face to face, begging with tears in their eyes. He just

> cannot help but sympathise with them. Among the refugees were the elderly and women. They were so desperate that they went so far as to kiss my shoes ... Also I felt at that time that the Japanese government did not have any uniform opinion in Tokyo. Some Japanese military leaders were just scared because of the pressure from the Nazis, while other officials in the Home Ministry were simply ambivalent ... So I made up my mind not to wait for their reply. I knew that somebody would surely complain about me in the future. But I myself thought this would be the right thing to do. There is nothing wrong in saving many people's lives.[26]

The few Jews who survived the Lithuanian Holocaust had to deal with the loss of most of their families and friends, but some had moments of unexpected joy. Chaim Genkind, the father of Solly, had disappeared during the last death march and Solly believed that he had died by the roadside. But shortly after he was liberated by American troops, he found his father in an American field hospital. The two were later reunited with Solly's sister Fanny, who survived the massacre in Neustadt Bay. His brother Herman, who was last seen by the family when they were returning to Kaunas from their abortive attempt to flee the German invasion, was reportedly seen being held with a group of Soviet prisoners of war in 1942, but Solly could find no other trace of him. Fluent in Lithuanian, German, Russian and Yiddish and able to speak some English, Solly was a useful interpreter for the US occupation forces. He moved to Israel when the new Jewish state was created. At the time, he was intending to travel to Canada, but he fought in the war that saw the birth of Israel. He later recalled that many of those who fought and died for Israel were survivors of the Holocaust:

> I remember a fierce battle in the Galilee [area], when I came across a wounded soldier and dragged him to safety. He had an Auschwitz tattoo on his arm. I dressed his wounds and tried to reassure him, but he only smiled. 'I witnessed the two things I wanted to see – the downfall of Hitler and his Third Reich, and the establishment of the State of Israel. Now I can die in peace.'
>
> Later that evening, after the fighting was over, I spoke to the young doctor who had treated him and discovered the soldier was already dead.
>
> 'I'll be damned if I know what he died of. His wounds weren't that serious,' the doctor said.
>
> 'There was nothing you could have done for him, Doctor. He died with his family in Auschwitz a long time ago,' I replied.[27]

After the war, Solly became a merchant seaman before settling in Canada. In a conscious attempt to put the nightmares of the past behind him, he changed his surname from Genkind to Ganor. He suffered from occasional nightmares about the past for the rest of his life.

Mascha Rolnikaite was one of the very few Vilnius Jews to return to the city where she had lived before the war. Like Solly, she was overjoyed to find that her father had survived the war; unable to return to his family on the night before the beginning of the German occupation, he had been forced to leave with the last units of the Red Army and had spent the war fighting in its ranks. Mascha's sister Mira, who had escaped from the ghetto and remained hidden with non-Jewish friends in Vilnius, also survived. The rest of the family disappeared after Mascha was separated from them on the day of the liquidation of the Vilnius ghetto, and it is likely that they were taken to Auschwitz and killed there. Mascha studied at the Literary Institute in the Russian city of Gorki before returning to Vilnius, where she worked until 1964 in a government literary department, translating Russian works into Lithuanian. She then moved to the city that was still known as Leningrad and remained there after it resumed its old name of St Petersburg in 1991. She died in 2016, aged 88.

Two of the Jews who sheltered in Plagge's work camp, Samuel and Perela Esterowicz, moved to the United States after the war. Perela met and married Vova Gdud, who survived the German occupation by hiding from the Germans outside the Vilnius ghetto. They anglicised their names to Pearl and William Good. They were part of the tiny minority that escaped the attempt by Nazi Germany to exterminate the Jews of Lithuania. It is estimated that the Jewish population in the country was about 210,000 immediately before the German occupation, though this figure may be a significant underestimate, not taking into account many unregistered Jewish refugees from Poland and elsewhere. About 8,500 Jews were able to flee east into Soviet Russia before the arrival of the Germans, and between 3,500 and 5,000 either escaped from the ghettos and concentration camps or survived to the end of the war. The rest – at least 196,500, and according to some estimates as many as 254,000 – were killed. The great majority were slaughtered by the *Einsatzgruppen* and their local paramilitary helpers in the first months that followed the German invasion.

12

Remembrance and Motivation

In 1953, the Yad Vashem institute was created by an act of the Israeli Knesset with the mission of commemorating, documenting, researching into and educating about the Holocaust. The institute grew steadily over the years that followed, and one of its many functions was to identify non-Jewish people who had taken risks with their personal safety to help Jews during the war. These people were then awarded the title of 'Righteous Among the Nations'. The largest number to receive this award are from the Polish community, reflecting the large numbers of Jews who lived in Poland before the war and who perished there in the Holocaust. A total of 916 Lithuanians and 638 Germans have also been honoured.

Although Herman Adler's prose poem of 1945 spoke about Anton Schmid, his story remained relatively unknown to most of the world; Yad Vashem described his attempts to save Jews in a Hebrew publication, which resulted in some Yiddish newspapers in America repeating the story, but in the non-Jewish West Schmid remained unrecognised, and for many his story remained completely unknown until the trial of Adolf Eichmann. Amongst those who gave evidence at the trial were Hermann Adler and Abba Kovner. The latter claimed in court that Schmid had told him about Eichmann, but it seems unlikely that a Feldwebel would have known the identity of such a bureaucratic figure; however, both Schmid and Eichmann were from Vienna, and perhaps Schmid had heard something about Eichmann's activities. When Kovner told the court about Anton Schmid and what he had done to save Jews, the effect was profound:

> During the few minutes it took Kovner to tell of the help that had come from a German sergeant, a hush settled over the courtroom;

> it was as though the crowd had spontaneously decided to observe the usual two minutes of silence in honour of the man named Anton Schmid. And in those two minutes, which were like a sudden burst of light in the midst of impenetrable, unfathomable darkness, a single thought stood out clearly, irrefutably, beyond question – how utterly different everything would be today in this courtroom, in Israel, in Germany, in all of Europe, and perhaps in all countries of the world, if only more such stories could have been told.[1]

The Eichmann trial received widespread coverage in news media across the world, and by the 1960s there was growing interest in Germany and elsewhere of the activities of men and women like Schmid. Hermann Adler commenced a campaign to have Schmid recognised by Yad Vashem as Righteous Among the Nations. In order to achieve this, he had to demonstrate that his friend had satisfied four criteria: that he had instigated or assisted in demonstrable acts to save the lives of Jews; that by doing so he had placed himself at considerable risk; that he had done so without any personal gain; and that he was not a Jew himself. Despite initial setbacks, Adler remained determined and in 1967, Feldwebel Anton Schmid became the first soldier of the Wehrmacht to be recognised as Righteous Among the Nations. It was a fitting tribute to the humble Feldwebel from a working-class neighbourhood of Vienna whose 'big heart' led him to treat everyone as a fellow human being. Steffi Schmid was presented with a medal to commemorate the occasion by Dr Michael Simon, the Israeli ambassador in Vienna. He told her:

> This badge, which is exclusively given to the Righteous Among the Nations, has on its front a picture of the Yad Vashem Memorial Institution in Jerusalem and the name of the person honoured with the dedication 'With Thanks from the Jewish People' and the inscription in Hebrew: 'Whoever saves a single human life, saves the entire world.'[2]

Austria was slow to face up to the responsibility of so many of its citizens for the crimes of the Nazi era. Karl Renner, who had been the first Chancellor of Austria after the First World War, supported Hitler's *Anschluss* and offered to serve in the Nazi administration during the war. As the Red Army entered Austria, he made contact with the Soviet forces and Stalin invited him to form a provisional government in late April 1945, and despite all that had happened during the war, he was at best equivocal with regard to the Jews of Austria who had fled before the arrival of the Nazis or who had suffered and died in the concentration camps. At a very early stage of his new premiership, he stated:

> Restitution of property stolen from Jews ... [should be] not to individual victims, but to a collective restitution fund. The establishment of such ... is necessary in order to prevent a massive, sudden flood of returning exiles ... A circumstance that for many reasons must be paid very close attention to ... Basically the entire nation should be made not liable for damages to Jews.[3]

This was a widespread view in Austria – despite the evidence that Austrians had formed a disproportionately large percentage of the guards and officials in the concentration camp system, Austria was determined not to admit any liability and the great majority of Austrians who had been members of the Nazi Party, the SS and other organisations deemed to be illegal by the International Military Tribunal in Nuremburg escaped any punishment. Whilst Yad Vashem was prepared to honour Anton Schmid and the city of Haifa renamed an area near the port as Anton Schmidt Square – unfortunately adding an extra T to his name – his home city of Vienna didn't commemorate him until several more years had passed. In 1990, when the area of Brigittenau where he had lived was being redeveloped, a memorial plaque was erected in the entrance to one of the blocks of apartments that were built, including a quote from one of his letters to Steffi: *Ich habe ja nur Menschen gerettet* ('All I did was save people').

In the last decade of the 20th century, there was a growing awareness in Germany of the need to remember those who had opposed the Nazis. Rudolf Scharping, the German Defence Minister from 1998-2002, proposed in 2000 that the Rüdel Barracks of the Bundeswehr should be renamed in honour of Anton Schmid. A poll of the soldiers and civilian workers in the barracks suggested that almost 60% wished to retain the old name but Scharping decided to proceed with the plan anyway. On 8 May 2000, precisely 55 years after Germany's unconditional surrender, the barracks were renamed but many military personnel and locals refused to adopt the name, preferring to refer to the barracks by the old title. The barracks were later closed as part of defence cuts and the plaque commemorating Schmid was transferred to a firing range; when that closed, the plaque moved to a museum.

Ten years after Schmid became the first member of the Wehrmacht to be recognised by Yad Vashem, the same honour was accorded to Oskar Schönbrunner, the paymaster who used his duties in Vilnius as an opportunity to save Jews. He gave evidence at several trials of men charged with war crimes and died in 2004.

The efforts of Jonas Paulavičius and his family were also recognised by Yad Vashem. Jonas, his wife Antonina and their children Danute and Kestutis were awarded the title of Righteous Among the Nations in 1984. A year later, Yad Vashem awarded the title to Anna Borkowska, the former sister superior; she and seven of her Dominican sisters were all honoured. Some of the Jews she had sheltered believed that she had died in German captivity and were overjoyed to learn that she was still alive, though living in poverty in Warsaw. They made contact with her in 1984, and Abba Kovner travelled to Warsaw to present her with her medal. In the ceremony that was held in her honour, Kovner said: 'In the days when angels hid their faces from us, this woman was to us Anna of the Angels – not the angels that we invent for ourselves, but angels that help us build our lives for an eternity.'[4]

After lobbying by Avraham Tory, who as Avraham Gollub had been a member of the Kaunas *Judenrat*, Father Bronius Paukštys of Lithuania was also recognised by Yad Vashem in 1977, 11 years after his death. Pnina Tory's submission of evidence to Yad Vashem stated:

> The very appearance of a man like Bronius Paukštys instilled in our hearts the hope that not all was lost, that not all men had turned into predator animals or cowards. That there are still people with morals and conscience, goodhearted and compassionate, and on top of that, gifted with a unique courage and urge to combat evil.[5]

Father Paukštys' brother was also awarded the title of Righteous among the Nations on the same day.

Karl Plagge's role in saving the Jews of Vilnius was largely forgotten until a family visit to Vilnius. Pearl Good – who as Perela Esterowicz had lived in the *HKP 562* camp – and her husband William had three children. One, Michael Good, travelled with his wife, children and parents to Lithuania in 1999. For William and Pearl, it was their first return to the scene of so many painful memories, and Pearl told her son about the kind German officer Plagge, without whose help she and so many others wouldn't have survived. On his return to the United States, Michael Good started on a long process of research to uncover the story of this remarkable man. In 2002, he petitioned Yad Vashem to recognise Plagge as Righteous Amongst the Nations, but the authorities rejected his application; they declined to give any reasons, on the grounds that this was their normal practice.

Good and those working with him appealed against the rejection, adding further testimony from survivors, but this application was also rejected. However, the second rejection was at least accompanied by a note of explanation:

> We fail to understand what possible risks he had to fear from his superiors. He was not involved in hiding Jews, or arranging their illegal flight and escape. He simply put them to work in a workshop that was serving the German military. The fact that he treated his Jewish, as well as non-Jewish, workers in a decent manner can only with great difficulty be construed as acting contrary to the interest of the Wehrmacht. On the contrary, he could probably claim, and perhaps he indeed did so, that his good treatment of his workers was for the interest of the war effort, that is, that they were producing more efficiently.[6]

In some respects, this explanation accorded with the rejection of the defence put forward by accused war criminals, who had tried to justify their crimes on the grounds that if they refused, they would have faced severe punishment. The truth of the matter was that whilst refusing involvement in atrocities against Jews and others might well have had serious consequences for the career of the person involved and might have attracted hostile comment from contemporaries and peers, there were no cases in which such refusal resulted in the person being punished severely.

The group working with Michael Good was dismayed by this second rejection but remained determined to honour the memory of Plagge. Their third application to Yad Vashem included further testimony from survivors. One, David Swirski, described how he had been caught smuggling food as he was leaving the *HKP 562* workshops and the SS guards had intended to beat him severely, perhaps to death; seeing what was happening, Plagge persuaded the SS guards to allow him to give Swirski and his companion an exemplary beating instead. He took the two Jews into a room where he gave them a razor blade and asked them to cut their faces. Taking up a piece of wood, he beat it repeatedly against a table, asking Swirski and his companion to cry out each time, and then returned them to the guards. Satisfied that they had been adequately punished, the guards took them away. In addition, Good and his colleagues submitted copies of the letters that Plagge had written to Göcke, unsuccessfully seeking to take over responsibility for the camp from the SS. This third application resulted in a favourable decision and in the summer of 2004, Plagge was bestowed with the title of Righteous

Among the Nations. Pearl Good wrote to the team that had worked tirelessly to achieve this: 'I am so grateful to you all – you all had crucial roles in this accomplishment ... My debt of gratitude, unpaid for almost 60 years, is at last paid in full – or can one ever pay for one's life?'[7]

In February 2006, the Bundeswher renamed its base in Pfungstadt, just outside Plagge's home city of Darmstadt, the Karl-Plagge-Kaserne.

Whilst the memory of people like Schmid, Plagge, the Paulavičius family, and Anna Borkowka has been celebrated, writing about some of the perpetrators of the Holocaust has stirred up memories that some Germans – and also many Lithuanians – would prefer remained forgotten. Many in West Germany preferred to look at the war on the Eastern Front purely in military and political terms, and the memoirs of many of the senior officers who commanded Germany's armies gave a deliberately distorted version of history. According to their accounts, the military, even the *Waffen-SS*, had fought a 'clean' war, and atrocities – when they were rarely acknowledged in these memoirs – were entirely due to rear area units like the *Einsatzgruppen*, or due to local paramilitary groups who were seeking revenge against their Soviet oppressors.

In the Baltic States as in other parts of the Soviet Union, there was a deliberate policy by Soviet authorities to portray the deaths that occurred during German occupation as being directed against Soviet citizens rather than specifically against Jews, and any role played by Lithuanian, Latvian, Estonian, Ukrainian and Belarusian paramilitary units in support of the Germans was both downplayed and distorted. The small numbers of such perpetrators had all fled to the west, according to Soviet historiography, where they were largely left undisturbed and faced few or no sanctions. There was no denial of the killing of Jews, but it was seen in the context of a deliberate policy of mass murder directed at the people of the Soviet Union as a whole. It wasn't until the end of the Cold War and the breakup of the Soviet Union – and access to many of the records that had been behind the Iron Curtain – that things began to change significantly.

The Soviet era in the Baltic states was marked also by little or no recognition of Vilnius, Kaunas, Riga and other cities as being major centres of Jewish culture – indeed, the long history of Jews in Lithuania was deliberately downplayed. One of the consequences of this was that the generations that grew up after the war had little concept of the cultural damage that was done to their countries during the German occupation, and immediately after the Baltic States gained their independence, the three countries focussed primarily on the years of Soviet occupation rather than the brief years of German rule. Things began to change in the mid-1990s. Algirdas Brazauskas, the Lithuanian president, visited Israel in 1995 and apologised on behalf of Lithuania for the crimes that Lithuanians had committed in the Holocaust. Whilst this was welcomed in Israel, it resulted in widespread criticism and protests across Lithuania, but at least started the process of questioning the past more thoroughly. Valdas Adamkus, who was Brazauskas's successor in 1998, established an official commission to investigate crimes committed during both the German and Soviet occupations of Lithuania. Liudas Truska, one of the members of the commission, summed up many of the problems that he and his colleagues faced:

> Up to the present, the Holocaust in Lithuania remains an incomplete matter. This was the conclusion of the largest newspaper in the country, *Lietuvos Rytas*. For Lithuanians, the Holocaust is not merely a historical problem, but also a political and moral one. The key question is whether Lithuanians today are prepared to recognise what happened in their country more than half a century ago, to condemn their guilty compatriots without reservation, and to accept moral responsibility for their deeds, or whether – as before – they will further seek to talk their way out of it, justifying the deeds of the murderers and even blaming the victims.[8]

Similar problems arose across all of the western regions of the former Soviet Union when they achieved independence. Many of those regarded as heroes for fighting against Soviet occupation and the imposition of the Communist system after the Second World War were individuals with extensive involvement in war crimes; this was a consequence of the manner in which the Germans had encouraged nationalist, anti-Bolshevik movements and had then used them to provide military and paramilitary formations in support of Germany. Memorials to many of these 'heroes of resistance' have proved to be controversial as aspects of their past have been uncovered.

A number of memorials have appeared across Lithuania, Latvia and Estonia marking the sites of former ghettos and concentration camps, and of mass killings like Ponary. The two housing blocks that were used by Plagge as accommodation for his Jewish workers are still used as social housing, and a large plaque in Lithuanian, English and Russian describes the history of the site. There is also a smaller memorial to the children who were killed in the *Kinderaktion* and those who were killed when the SS searched the buildings for *malines* after Plagge and his men had departed in 1944.

German towns like Waldkirch preferred to forget the role played in the crimes of the Second World War by their former residents. In 1989, Waldkirch residents took part in a cultural event that compared their town with how it had been in 1939, and for many of the younger residents this was the first time that they learned of the existence of Karl Jäger. The official publication of the festival used quotes from contemporaries of Jäger, describing him as 'subtle and cultivated' and 'a brilliant leader', and two of the authors felt the need to clarify this at a later date, writing that these characterisations were from contemporary witnesses and reflected the attitudes during years immediately before the war; they added that it was only after the festival book was published had they become aware of his involvement in the activities of 'the so-called *Sondereinsatzkommando* of the SS' in Eastern Europe.[9]

In Waldkirch and other German and Austrian towns and cities, there was a growing tension between the obvious need to face reality and accept the crimes committed by former residents, but at the same time a desire by the current generation to avoid accepting responsibility for those crimes. In addition, many feared that recognising these crimes would have a negative effect on the image of their towns and cities. Liesl Frick, a member of the Christian Democrats political party in Germany, spoke for many in 1990 during a radio broadcast when she said that she was tired of hearing endlessly about the Third Reich and having to cope with the suffering of that time; surely, she suggested, it was a time to draw a line somewhere and to stop constantly asking 'what we might have done wrong in the past'.[10]

The desire of so many people in Waldkirch to draw a veil over the past became a subject in itself. Some criticised the desire for silence on the grounds that it was only by a frank look at the past that future generations would be able to learn best how to avoid such problems in future. An article in the *Badischen Zeitung*, the largest circulation newspaper in the region, looked at the dissonance between the portrayal of Waldkirch as an idyllic small town and the deeds of Karl Jäger and contrasted those who asked 'How many Jägers are there amongst us?' with others who wished to stop looking at the past.[11] Ultimately, this debate led to a further discussion: how could someone like Jäger, who was widely regarded by his contemporaries as an intelligent, highly cultured individual, become a mass murderer?

This question of motivation is perhaps one of the most difficult to answer. The sheer number of Germans and Austrians who took part in war crimes creates its own problems: it is easy to define broad characteristics that seem to account for so many of the perpetrators, but equally there are either so many perpetrators who don't fit those characteristics, or there are people who, whilst they had similar characteristics to the perpetrators, didn't become war criminals.

An analysis of the officers of the *Einsatzgruppen* shows some of the problems. Most of the officers who commanded the *Einsatzgruppen* and *Einsatzkommandos* in Eastern Europe were of a generation that was too young to take part in the First World War. They were typically in their last years of school and experienced the collapse of Germany with a sense of impotence; they were also at an age where they were very susceptible to notions such as the view that circulated in Germany after the war that the army had been undefeated – Germany's defeat was due to the collapse of the home front, and the army had been 'stabbed in the back' due to left-wing agitation and unrest. Most of these young men were from fairly affluent middle-class backgrounds and had an instinctive aversion to socialism and Bolshevism, and anti-Semitism was very widespread across much of Europe at the time. As they went on to higher education in the early 1920s and saw violent political unrest on the streets of German cities, they were attracted to increasingly right-wing political groups, seeing these as an answer to Germany's problems. The disorder that gripped the country could only be controlled by strong, authoritarian government. This would require the suppression of those who wished to undermine the traditional order of German society.

An overview of these personalities also shows that most were highly educated. Two-thirds of the defendants in the *Einsatzgruppen* Trial in Nuremburg had at least one university degree and several had doctorates. But despite this, these men were able to embrace the full horror of Nazi racial policies and to carry out mass murder.

For most of the German perpetrators of the Holocaust in Lithuania and other parts of Eastern Europe, the link between Bolshevism and the Jews was self-evident. Once Hitler declared that the war against the Soviet Union was ideological and a clash of irreconcilable cultures, these men had little hesitation in seeing all Bolsheviks – the people they blamed for the unrest in Germany that brought about the end of the First World War – as enemies of Germany who had to be destroyed. Therefore, the destruction of Jews was also justified on the grounds that they were all, or nearly all, Bolsheviks. This matter was probed at length during the Nuremburg trial. None of the defendants was able to articulate a clear logical defence of the view that Jews were automatically Bolsheviks, and some accepted only with great reluctance that even if the great majority of Jews were Bolsheviks, the wholesale murder of Jews would still result in the deaths of some innocent people. Even the killing of children was justifiable to many of the defendants; Ohlendorf told the court that if Jewish children were allowed to survive, they would one day grow into adults who would seek revenge upon Germany, and therefore their killing was a military necessity.[12]

But there were exceptions to these general traits. Jäger and two of the Nuremburg defendants – Otto Rasch and Paul Blobel – were a generation older. Compared to many of his contemporaries and subordinates, Jäger had a comparatively modest education without any time in university. In his case, his determination to demonstrate how effectively he could carry out his instructions may have been motivated partly by his awareness that he was older, less educated, and also less experienced in police and security matters than most of his contemporaries and subordinates, and in the competitive world of Nazi Germany, he had to demonstrate his value.

The background of some of the lower-ranking individuals, such as Murer, Kittel, Weiss etc, were varied. The processes by which these individuals travelled the roads that led them to mass murder were complex. Even past political allegiances were no guide – an analysis of many of the men in *Orpo* battalions in the east shows that a large proportion were from working-class backgrounds in cities like Hamburg where membership of the Communist Party had been strong in the years before Hitler's accession to power. The Lithuanians who showed such enthusiasm for killing Jews included many who had suffered at the hands of the Soviet authorities in the months prior to the arrival of the Germans, and had come to regard the Jews as supporters of the Soviet regime; but despite the lurid tales of Jewish commissars committing acts of rape and cannibalism, many – probably most – of the Lithuanians who provided the manpower for the killing squads of Ponary, and the mobile execution teams of *Rommkommando Hamann*, had experienced no such acts themselves. Yet the speed with which some Lithuanians turned on their Jewish neighbours, and the savagery of the attacks – as demonstrated by the white-shirted blond man in Kaunas – is as remarkable as it is horrifying.

Much has been written about the use of dehumanisation of the enemy as a means of preparing combatants, and the manner in which such dehumanisation makes brutality and atrocity far easier to implement in all conflicts.[13] In the case of the Holocaust, the detailed bureaucratic administration of the Holocaust, as displayed in the reports of Jäger and Stahlecker and the daily reports published in Berlin by Müller, added a further veneer of distance between the officers who oversaw the killings and the murders themselves. As all of the senior figures involved are now dead and few were interviewed in a manner designed to encourage openness and honesty, it is difficult to be certain of motivation.

Many of the men who were charged in the Nuremburg *Einsatzgruppen* Trial were seen as ideologically motivated – nearly all were early members of the Nazi Party and even after the war, some still expressed complete devotion to Adolf Hitler and a compulsion to obey any orders that originated from him. The years of political turmoil and violence in Germany prior to the Nazi seizure of power; the decade or more of economic instability; the burning resentment at the manner in which Germany was treated at the end of the First World War; the longstanding sense of anti-Semitism – all of these factors contributed to creating the environment in which many individuals found it relatively straightforward to commit mass murder against an enemy regarded as less than completely human.

Almost all of those involved in wartime atrocities showed no regret or repentance when confronted with the evidence of their crimes. Some like Ohlendorf defended their deeds as military necessity: the war was intended to destroy Bolshevism; the Jews were synonymous with Bolshevism; therefore, all Jews had to be killed as a war aim, and children had to be killed to avoid problems in future. Others, including Karl Jäger, denied personal involvement, but saw nothing wrong with passing on orders that resulted in the mass killing of Jews and others. Many of the military figures who in their post-war memoirs denied any involvement in atrocities were actually culpable – Field Marshal Erich von Manstein, for example, widely regarded as one of the best commanders in the Wehrmacht, wrote in his memoirs, first published in 1955:

> A few days before the offensive started [i.e. the invasion of the Soviet Union in 1941] we received an order from the Supreme Command of the Armed Forces which has since become known as the 'Commissar Order'. The gist of it was that all political commissars of the Red Army whom we captured were to be shot out of hand as exponents of Bolshevik ideology ...
>
> Whatever one might feel about the status of commissars in international law, however, it inevitably went against the grain of any soldier to shoot them down when they had been captured in battle. An order like the 'Commissar Order' was utterly unsoldierly. To have carried it out would have threatened not only the honour of our fighting troops but also their morale. Consequently I had no alternative but to inform my superiors that the Commissar Order would not be implemented by anyone under my command.[14]

To call this passage of Manstein's memoirs misleading is a huge understatement: it is an outright distortion. Manstein was tried in Hamburg in 1949 for war crimes, where orders bearing Manstein's signature were presented as evidence showing that even if he didn't pass on the commissar order – which is disputable – he certainly passed on the related 'Severity Order' to his subordinates. The original version of this order was written by Field Marshal Walter von Reichenau, Commander of Sixth Army in Ukraine, and was then circulated to other senior officers, who were required to pass it on in their own words. Accordingly, in November 1941, Manstein issued the following order to his units in November 1941:

> The Jewish Bolshevik system must be wiped out once and for all and should never again be allowed to invade our European living space ... It is the same Jewish class of beings who have done so much damage to our own Fatherland by virtue of their activities against the nation and civilisation, and who promote anti-German tendencies throughout the world, and who will be the harbingers of revenge. Their extermination is a dictate of our own survival.[15]

During the first winter of the war against the Soviet Union, Manstein came to an agreement with Otto Ohlendorf, whose *Einsatzgruppe D* was operating in the same area as Manstein's Eleventh Army, whereby Manstein provided Ohlendorf with truckloads of small-arms ammunition in exchange for civilian fur coats. It is inconceivable that Manstein was unaware of why Ohlendorf required such large quantities of ammunition, or the fact that Ohlendorf acquired such large quantities of winter clothing from civilians that his men had killed, yet in his memoirs he sought to portray his war record purely in terms of front-line military operations. Clearly, by the time he wrote his memoirs, it was abundantly clear to almost everyone that the behaviour of the Germans in the occupied territories had been criminal on a huge scale, but it should also be noted that most of the perpetrators of war crimes were aware during the war years that their deeds were, at the very least, highly questionable. Himmler's speech to senior SS figures made this very clear: however important it might be for the future wellbeing of Germany to kill all European Jews, this was a deed that the perpetrators would never be able to discuss openly.

But even in the brutalising environment of Nazi Germany and the countries that its armies captured, some individuals – Anton Schmid, Karl Plagge, Andrzej Gdowski and others – remained true to their humanitarian principles. Just as it is difficult to identify universal traits amongst the perpetrators, it is difficult to see why these people were able to retain their moral compass when most of their contemporaries failed to do so. From Schmid's letters to his wife and the recollections of his friend Hermann Adler, it is clear that his strong Catholic beliefs were the cornerstone of his morality; he interpreted Christian teaching as a requirement to show kindness and compassion to all people, regardless of their ethnicity or nationality. But other Christians, both Catholics and Protestants, were able to reconcile their religious views with the persecution of Jews.

In the year before his death, Karl Plagge wrote a letter to a Jewish lawyer he had encountered in Stuttgart; the two men had met on a train journey and the lawyer had encouraged Plagge to write about his wartime experiences. In the letter, Plagge described some of the reasons why he had acted as he did, and his reflections offer an insight into both his behaviour and that of the men who were responsible for the atrocities:

> The fate of the unfortunate Jews and the suffering that these people had to endure seemed to me nothing other than what it really was, namely an appalling outrage.
>
> But this outrage is not directed in the same manner by a political person as it is by the people who became its instruments and murderers. I could not distinguish the boundary where the limits of guilt for these people began or ended, and in the wider sense, as a German I bear it too. There is no isolation from this plague. One had to witness this outrage and as a result the only choice remaining was whether to hate or love a God who permitted such things. This was the reason for me changing my spiritual view of the world and I turned my face from embracing a reality in which people are tortured and even children are gassed and people are deemed guilty, as happened here. In a world order that was determined by death, it was perhaps better for God not to believe in him and oppose death with all one's might, without raising one's eyes to the heavens where God remained silent. If all there was to be on Earth were 'scourges and sacrifice', then it was a duty not to stand on the side of the punishers but to take the side of the victims. I spoke to many of these 'scourges' who were responsible for the horror and have reflected long on their words. I felt as if these people were unseeing instruments of delusion and I have to say that I felt pity towards them too, as I saw how a terrible dichotomy existed in their souls. They were unable to defend themselves against the outbreak of stupidity, inertia and bestiality that is imparted to people as the unfortunate inheritance of their origins.
>
> Once, in my canteen, in which long distance drivers from all over the east came together to refuel or repair their vehicles, I

> encountered a drunken SD man who collapsed in tears because of the weight of his conscience. He belonged to an execution squad that had carried out its terrible acts for several months. He tried to drown his despair in alcohol. I sat next to him and tried to see into his soul. What I discovered was the wreckage of a man with fatal spiritual wounds, who was only held together through the strength of military discipline. At best he was only dimly aware of what he had done and his attempts to justify it sprang from a frightening ignorance.
>
> I realised that evil in the world is almost always born of unawareness, ignorance, and weakness. People are generally more good than evil, but they are more or less ignorant and this is termed virtue and vice. The worst vice is an ignorance that thinks it knows everything and thus has the right to kill.[16]

Plagge continued in his letter to explain that he had tried to act within certain constraints – he deemed it counterproductive to be too confrontational, as this might result in him being assigned to a different post, and instead had tried to present information to superiors and SD personnel in a manner that resulted in them agreeing to his proposals. He added:

> Perhaps in other cases, all that was needed to act similarly to prevent and mitigate atrocities was merely a little determination. I have never felt that it took any special courage. All that was needed was a conviction that anyone can draw from the depths of moral feelings that exist in everyone. In addition, a little goodwill, occasionally a kind thought and dedication to the task at hand may be necessary. I didn't feel that I was exposing myself to a particularly great danger because my arguments were always sensible, honest and incontestable, both on the human and factual level.[17]

This last statement is excessively self-effacing. By taking on Jewish workers in excess of what was needed, employing workers with no skills that were useful to *HKP 562*, rescuing arrested Jews who had little or no value to the Wehrmacht, and in several other respects, Plagge regularly overstepped the limits of what might be termed 'sensible, honest and incontestable' arguments. At the very least, he was under the constant threat of severe reprimand and dismissal from his post. Transfer to the front line was always a possibility.

He finished the letter with a stark warning, drawing on imagery from Albert Camus' book *The Plague*. In Camus' novel, the main character

Dr Rieux watches people celebrating the end of the plague outbreak in his city but considers how the plague bacteria never disappear completely – they lurk dormant and can resurface decades later. Plagge added that in his view, the murderers of the past were often not grim monsters but pitiful, psychologically damaged individuals with greatly reduced awareness; those who resisted weren't heroes, but merely possessed a fraction more insight and conscience than those around them.

The contrasts are striking. On the one hand, none of the perpetrators of these crimes expressed remorse for their acts and sought to justify them through a variety of excuses: the need to obey orders in wartime; military necessity; the fear of being punished if they failed to carry out these acts. On the other hand, soldiers like Feldwebel Berger in *HKP 562* recognised at the time that the crimes that were being committed would be a stain on Germany for generations, and many years after the war Plagge still felt a strong sense of collective guilt for what had been done.

In his account of the men of a battalion of *Orpo* personnel deployed in the east, Christopher Browning concluded with the words:

> Everywhere society conditions people to respect and defer to authority, and indeed could scarcely function otherwise. Everywhere people seek career advancement. In every modern society, the complexity of life and the resulting bureaucratisation and specialisation attenuate the sense of personal responsibility of those implementing official policy. Within virtually every social collective, the peer group exerts tremendous pressures on behaviour and sets moral norms. If the men of Reserve Police Battalion 101 could become killers under such circumstances, what group of men could not?[18]

In a similar manner, Wette's biography of Karl Jäger describes how the thin veneer of civilisation collapsed under the assault of the warlike and genocidal policies of Hitler's Germany:

> Despite two thousand years of Christian tradition, these developments brought to the fore a multitude of completely normal mass murderers like Karl Jäger. Amongst the approximately 200,000 German perpetrators and their helpers in the conquered territories there were dentists and opera singers, teachers and truants, lawyers, university professors, architects, even priests, Catholic and Protestant, young and old. Generally, these people came from the midst of German society and had at least some higher education ...

> Against the background of the nightmare of war and Holocaust, Germany today and all political and social thinkers elsewhere with an awareness of history swear that something similar must 'never again' take place. But at the same time people should remember that the fundamental lessons of recent German history give no guarantees for the future: everything remains possible.[19]

The history of the Holocaust demonstrates how easy it is for factors in the past of an individual to combine with the pressures of the present to create a toxic mix. In these circumstances, it is all the more important for everyone to remember the high moral standard and personal sacrifice of people like Anton Schmid, Karl Plagge, Andrzej Gdowski, Anna Borkovska, and Jonas Paulavičius. Whilst many may, in the words of Karl Plagge, lack complete awareness of what they are being asked to do, it seems that others can find sufficient awareness and an adequate sense of conscience not to succumb. These individuals and those like them give hope: if they could rise above the madness that engulfed Europe, others can do so in future.

Endnotes

1 The Birth of the *Einsatzgruppen*

1. Hitler, A, Mannheim, R (trans.) *Mein Kampf* (Houghton Mifflin Harcourt, Boston MA 1998) Vol.I p91
2. Quoted in Sebag Montefiore, S, *Stalin: The Court of the Red Tsar* (Vintage, London 2004) p318
3. Halder, F, Burdick, C, Jacobsen, H-A (eds), *The Halder War Diary 1939-1942* (Greenhill, Novato CA 1988) p31
4. For a full account of this largely forgotten act of genocide, see Olusoga, D, Erichsen, C, *The Kaiser's Holocaust: Germany's Forgotten Genocide and the Colonial Roots of Nazism* (Faber, London 2010)
5. For an excellent biography of Heydrich, see Gerwarth, R, *Hitler's Hangman: The Life of Heydrich* (Yale University Press, Newhaven CT 2011)
6. Bundesarchiv Berlin, R 581/256, f.90
7. Arnberger, H, Ardelt, R, *'Anschluss' 1938: Eine Dokumentation* (Österreichischer Bundesverlag, Vienna 1988) p440
8. Bundesarchiv Berlin, R 58/241, f.169, *Richtlinien für den Auswärtigen Einsatz der Sicherheitspolizei und des SD*
9. Mallmann, K-M, Böhler, J, Matthäus, J, *Einsatzgruppen in Polen. Darstellung und Dokumentation* (WBG, Darmstadt 2008) p121
10. Halder, F, Burdick, C, Jacobsen, H-A (eds), p346
11. Roth, A, *Aus der Kampfzeit des Deutschvölkischen Schutz- und Trutzbundes: Eine Erinnerungsschrift* (Schwitzke, Hamburg 1939) p18
12. Quoted in Longerich, P, *Politik der Vernichtung: Eine Gesamtdarstellung der Nationalsozialistischen Judenverfolgung* (Piper, Munich 1991) p298-299
13. Longerich, P, *Heinrich Himmler* (Oxford University Press, 2013) p540
14. Wildt, M, *Generation des Unbedingten. Das Führungskorps des Reichssicherheitshauptamtes* (Hamburger Verlag, Hamburg 2002) p557
15. Bundesarchiv Berlin, R 70 SU/32
16. Bundesarchiv Berlin, R 70 SU/31

17. Quoted in Wette, W, *Karl Jäger: Mörder der Litauischen Juden* (Fischer, Frankfurt am Main 2012) p35
18. Bundesarchiv Berlin, BDC S 60
19. Quoted in Paul, G, Mallmann, K-M, *Die Gestapo im Zweiten Weltkrieg. 'Heimatfront' und Besetztes Europa* (Primus, Darmstadt 2000) p111
20. Paul, G, *Die Täter der Shoah: Fanatische Natrionalsozialisten oder Ganz Normale Deutsche?* (Wallstein, Göttingen 2002) p52

2 Lithuania, the Jews and the Poles

1. Quoted in Bartusevičius, V, Tauber, J, Wette, W (eds), *Holocaust in Litauen: Krieg, Judenmorde und Kollaboration im Jahre 1941* (Böhlau, Cologne 2003) p40
2. For a history of the Teutonic Order, see Urban, W, *The Teutonic Knights: A Military History* (Greenhill, London 2003)
3. Morgenstern, M, *Martin Luther: Von der Juden und ihren Lügen* (Berlin University Press, 2016) p42
4. Brumberg, A, 'Poles and Jews' in *Foreign Affairs* (Congers, NY 2002) Vol.81 No.5 p175
5. Quoted in Brumberg, A, p176
6. For a full description of events, see Buttar, P, *Between Giants: The Battle for the Baltics in World War II* (Osprey, Oxford 2013) p31-49
7. Michlic, J, 'The Soviet Occupation of Poland, 1939-41, and the Stereotype of the Anti-Polish and Pro-Soviet Jew' in *Jewish Social Studies* (Indiana University Press, Bloomington IN 2007) Vpl.13 No.3 p140
8. Quoted in Paldiel, M, *Saving the Jews: Men and Women who Defied the Final Solution* (Schreiber, Rockville MD 2000) p78-79
9. Paldiel, M, *Diplomat Heroes of the Holocaust* (Rabbi Arthur Schneier Center for International Affairs of Yeshiva University, New York 2007) p41-42
10. Gold, A, *A Special Fate: Chiune Sugihara, Hero of the Holocaust* (TMI, Providence RI, 2014) p66
11. Palasz-Rutkowska, E 'Polish-Japanese Secret Cooperation During World War II: Sugihara Chiune and Polish Intelligence', lecture given to the Asiatic Society of Japan, Tokyo 13 March 1995

3 The First Days of German Occupation

1. Valentinas, B, *1941 m. Birželio Sukilimas: Dokumentų Rinkinys* (Lietuvos Gyventojų ir Rezistencijos Tyrimo Centras, Vilnius 2000) p183
2. Klein, D (ed.) *Hidden History of the Kovno Ghetto* (Bullfinch, Boston 1997) p222
3. Quoted in Bartusevičius et al, p41
4. Ganor, S, *Light One Candle: A Survivor's Tale from Lithuania to Jerusalem* (Kodansha USA, New York 2003) p54
5. Rolnikaite, M, *Ich muss Erzählen* (Rowohlt, Reinbek bei Hamburg 2004) p38
6. Quoted in Grossmann, V, Ehrenburg, I, Lustiger, A (trans.), *Der Schwarzbuch: Der Genozid den Sowjetischen Juden* (Rowohlt, Reinbeck bei Hamburg 1994) p626

7. Klee, E, Riess, V, Dressen, W, *Schöne Zeiten: Judenmord aus der Sicht der Täter und Gaffer* (Fischer, Frankfurt am Main 1998) p35-36
8. Klee, E et al, p38
9. Klee, E et al, p38
10. Klee, E et al, p39-40
11. Klee, E et al, p40-41
12. Klee, E et al, p32-35
13. Ganor, S, p85
14. Arad, Y, *Ghetto in Flames: The Struggle and Destruction of the Jews in Vilna in the Holocaust* (Holocaust Library, New York 1982) p46
15. Klee, E et al, p47-49
16. Klee, E et al, p49-50
17. Barusevičius, V et al, p31
18. Arad, Y, p47
19. Memoir of Samuel Esterowicz, available at www.searchformajorplagge.com
20. Memoir of Perella Esterowicz, available at www.searchformajorplagge.com
21. Quoted in the memoirs of Samuel Esterowicz, p303-304, available at www.searchformajorplagge.com
22. Wette, W, *Feldwebel Anton Schmid: Ein Held der Humanität* (Fischer, Frankfurt am Main 2013) p25
23. Quoted in Wette, W (2013) p25-26
24. Yad Vashem Archive, Jerusalem TR-10/823
25. Longerich, P, p346
26. Browning, C, *Ordinary Men: Reserve Police Battalion 101 and the Final Solution in Poland* (Harper Collins, London 2017) p12
27. Yad Vashem Archive, Jerusalem TR-10/823
28. Yad Vashem Archive, Jerusalem TR-10/823
29. BundesarchivMilitärarchiv Freiburg, Befehl SicherungsDivision 221 17/07/1941, RH 26-221/12
30. Yad Vashem Archive, Jerusalem 0-53/128/219
31. Browning, C, p14-15
32. Yad Vashem Archive, Jerusalem, TR-10/388 p41

4 The Gathering Darkness

1. Quoted in Klee, W et al, p32
2. Mallmann, K, Angrick, A, Matthäus, J, Cüppers, M (eds.) *Ereignismeldung UdSSR 1941: Dokumente der Einsatzgruppen in der Sowjetunion* (WBG Academic, Darmstadt 2011), p75-76
3. Bartusevičius, V et al, p28
4. Quoted in Burleigh, M, *Ethics and Extermination: Reflections on Nazi Genocide* (Cambridge University Press, 1997) p69
5. Mallmann, K et al (2011) p85
6. Hebert, V, *Hitler's Generals on Trial: The Last War Crimes Tribunal at Nuremberg* (Universtiy Press of Kansas, Lawrence KS 2010) p121-122
7. Mallmann, K et al (2011) p103

8. Mallmann, K et al (2011) p103
9. Quoted in Wette, W (2011) p90
10. Wette, W (2011) p92
11. Wette, W (2011) p92
12. Mallmann, K et al (2011) p273
13. Bartusevičius, V et al, p203-204
14. Quoted in Arad, Y, p471-477
15. Bartusevičius, V et al, p29
16. Bartusevičius, V et al, p33
17. Arad, Y, p77-78
18. Margolis, R, Tobias, J, *Die Geheimen Notizen des K Sakowicz: Dokumente zur Judenvernichtung in Ponary* (Antogo, Nuremburg 2004) p44
19. Transcript of Denazification File, Karl Plagge, Hessisches Hauptstaatsarcchiv Wiesbaden, p6, available at www.searchformajorplagge.com
20. Ibid
21. Rolnikaite, M, p57-58
22. Sachslehner, J, *Rosen für den Mörder: Die Zwei Leben des NS-Täters Franz Murer* (Molden, Vienna 2017) p22
23. YIVO Institute for Jewish Research, New York: Report from *Gebietskommissar* Gewecke to Lohse 11/09/1941, Occ.E 3/22
24. YIVO Institute for Jewish Research, New York: Occ. E 3/22
25. Wette, W (2013) p37
26. Rudashevski, Y, Matenko, P, *The Diary of the Vilna Ghetto June 1941-April* 1943 (Ghetto Fighters' House, Tel Aviv 1973) p32
27. Wette, W (2013) p39
28. Kruk, H, Harshav, B, Harshav, B (eds.) *The Last Days of the Jerusalem of Lithuania: Chronicles from the Vilna Ghetto and the Camps* (Yale University Press, New Haven CT 2002) p90-91
29. Kruk, H, p92-93
30. Interview with Ada Gens Ustjanauskas on 17/11/2008, available from US Holocaust Memorial Museum website at collections.ushmm.org/search/catalong/irn36962
31. Rolnikaite, M, p61-65
32. Memoirs of Perella Esterowicz, p20, available at www.searchformajorplagge.com
33. Jäger Report 1 December 1941, p8-9, reproduced in Wette, W (2011) Appendix 1
34. Stang, K, *Kollaboration und Massenmord: die Litauische Hilfspolizei, das Rollkommando Hamann und die Ermordung der Litausichen Juden* (Lang, Frankfurt am Main 1996) p102
35. Stang, K, p163
36. Stang, K, p170-171
37. Wette, W (2011) p107
38. Schur, G, Porudominskij, W *Die Juden von Vilna: die Aufzeichnungen* (DT Taschenbuch, Munich 1999) p94
39. Zuroff, E, Beruf: Nazijäger. *Die Suche nach dem Langen Atem: Die Jagd nach den Tätern des Völkermordes* (Ahriman, Freiburg 1996) p89

40. Quoted in Wette W (2011) p111
41. Memoirs of Vova Gdud, available at www.searchformajorplagge.com
42. Rolnikaite, M, p70
43. Quoted in Sachslehner, J, p106-107
44. Quoted in Sachslehner, J, p98
45. Tory, A, Gilbert, M, Porat, D, *Surviving the Holocaust: The Kovno Ghetto Diary* (Pimlico, London 1990) p26-28
46. Adler, H, *Meine Begegnung mit Feldwebel Anton Schmid* – radio broadcast on 9 March 1967, manuscript at Deutsche Nationalbibliothek Frankfurt, EB 2004/38 (NL 193) A.02.01
47. Transcript of Denazification File, Karl Plagge, Hessisches Hauptstaatsarcchiv Wiesbaden, Statement of Alfred Stumpff, available at www.searchformajorplagge.com
48. Transcript of Denazification File, Karl Plagge, Hessisches Hauptstaatsarcchiv Wiesbaden, Statement of Friedrich Asmus, available at www.searchformajorplagge.com
49. Memoirs of Samuel Esterowicz, p293, available at www.searchformajorplagge.com
50. Transcript of Denazification File, Karl Plagge, Hessisches Hauptstaatsarcchiv Wiesbaden, Statement of Georg Raab, available at www.searchformajorplagge.com

5 The First Winter

1. Bartusevičius, V et al, p204-205
2. Benz, W Neiss, M (eds.) *Judenmord in Litauen. Studien und Dokumente* (Metropol, Berlin 1999) p137
3. Ganor, S, p144
4. Bartusevičius, V et al, p208-209
5. Bartusevičius, V et al, p209
6. Tory, A, p54-55
7. Ganor, S, p163-164
8. Ganor, S, p175-177
9. Bartusevičius, V et al, p222
10. Bartusevičius, V et al, p213
11. Sutzkewer, A, *Vilner Geto 1941-1944* (IKUF, Buenos Aires 1947) p50
12. Memoir of Samuel Esterowicz, p299, available at www.searchformajorplagge.com
13. Balberyszski, M, *Shtarker fun Ayzn* (Hamenorah, Tel Aviv 1967) p259-260
14. Schur, G, Porudominskij, W, P63
15. Rolnikaite, M, p73-74
16. Memoir of Samuel Esterowicz, p296-297, available at www.searchformajorplagge.com
17. Testimony of Abram Suzkever at Nuremberg, 27 February 1946, available at http://law2.umkc.edu/faculty/projects/ftrials/nuremberg/suzkevertest.html
18. Quoted in Sachslehner, J, p116-227

19. Dworzecki, M, *Jerušolaim de Lite in Kamf un Umkum: Zichroines fun Wilner Geto* (Union Populaire Juive, Paris 1948) p89-90
20. Rolnikaite, M, p79-80
21. Memoir of Samuel Esterowicz, p300, available at www.searchformajorplagge.com
22. Memoir of Samuel Esterowicz, p299-300, available at www.searchformajorplagge.com
23. Priemel, K, *Rettung durch Arbeit: Handlungsspielräume von Wehrmachtsangehörigen im Kontext des Holocausts am Beispiel von Vilnius, Litauen* (Masters thesis, Freiburg 2002) p96
24. Tauber, J, *Argeit als Hoffnung: Jüdische Ghettos in Litauen 1941-1944* (De Gruyter, Berlin 2015) p340-341
25. Wette, W (2013) p134-135
26. Yad Vashem Archive, 0-4/53-1, p180
27. Yad Vashem Archive, 0-18/203
28. Wette, W (2013) p74
29. Grossman, H, *The Underground Army: Fighters of the Bialystok Ghetto* (Holocaust Library, New York 1988) p68
30. Quoted in Wette, W (2013) p116
31. Mallman, K et al, p764
32. Mallman, K et al, p555
33. Jäger Report p7-8, reproduced in Wette, W (2011) p243-244
34. Bundesarchiv Berlin, B 162/2537, 10046-48
35. Quoted in Wette, W (2011) p149
36. Gerwarth, R, p199
37. Goebbels, J, Fröhlich, E (ed.) *Die Tagebücher von Joseph Goebbels* (Institut für Zeitgeschichte, Munich 1996) Part 2 Vol.II p487-488

6 The Prices to Be Paid

1. Wette, W (2013) p234-235
2. Wette, W (2013) p236
3. Wette, W (2013) p122
4. Mallmann, K et al, p139
5. National Archives, Kew, HW 16/31
6. Mallmann, K et al, p272
7. Budesarchiv-Militärarchiv Berlin, N 510/48
8. Mallmann, K et al, p345
9. Mallmann, K et al, p690
10. Mallmann, K et al, p822-823
11. Dorries, R, *Hitler's Last Chief of Foreign Intelligence: Allied Interrogations of Walter Schellenberg* (Routledge, London, 2007) p80
12. Quoted in Wette, W (2011) p153
13. Quoted in Wette, W (2011) p153
14. Available at https://he.wikipedia.org/wiki/ חבטל_ןאצכ_ךלנ_לא!
15. Quoted in Friedman, P, *Their Brothers' Keepers* (Holocaust Library, New York 1979) p16-17

16. Korchak, R, *Flames in Ash* (Merhavya Sifriat Poalim, Tel Aviv 1946) p76-77
17. Testimony of Alfred Stumpff, p2, available at www.searchformajorplagge.com
18. Rolnikaite, M, p103
19. Public Records Office, Kew, HS 4/39
20. Text of speech available at www.futurefund.org/Reports/Heyrich/heydrichfuneral.htm
21. Text of speech available at www.futurefund.org/Reports/Heyrich/heydrichfuneral.htm
22. Kaplan, J, *Prague: The Turbulent Century* (Kinemann, Cologne 1997) p239
23. Schwarz, G, *Eine Frau an seiner Seite. Ehefrauen in der 'SS-Sippengemeinschaft'* (Aufbau Taschenbuch, Berlin 2001) p211
24. Williams, M, *Reinhard Heydrich: The Biography* (Ulric, Church Stretton 2002) Vol.II 'The Enigma' p248

7 Ghetto Life and Death

1. Kruk, H, p126
2. Arad, Y, p334
3. Gilbert, S, *Music in the Holocaust: Confronting Life in the Nazi Ghettos and Camps* (Oxford University Press, 2005) p71
4. Gordon, *The Shadow of Death: The Holocaust in Lithuania* (University Press of Kentucky, Lexington KY 2001) p74
5. Kruk, H, Harshav, B, Harshav, B, p143
6. Quoted in Sachslehner, J, p145
7. Rolnikaite, M, p110-111
8. Quoted in Sachsenlehner, J, p153-155
9. Interview with Ada Gens Ustjanauskas
10. Arad, Y, p308
11. Tory, A, p115
12. Kruk, H, Harshav, B, Harshav, B, p309
13. Schur, G, Porudominskij, W, p142
14. Chalmers, B, *Birth, Sex and Abuse: Women's Voices Under Nazi Rule* (Grosvenor House, Surbiton 2015) p73
15. Paldiel, M, p104-107
16. Moreshet Archives, Menashe, D.1.357
17. Memoir of Samuel Esterowicz, p294, available at www.searchformajorplagge.com
18. Balberyszski, M, *Stronger than Iron: The Destruction of Vilna Jewry 1941-1945: an Eyewitness Account* (Gefen, Jerusalem 2010) p217
19. Interview with Harry Sherez, available at www.searchformajorplagge.com
20. Quoted in Sachslehner, J, p164
21. Kruk, H, Harshav, B, Harshav, B p391-393
22. Tory, A, p153-155
23. Kruk, H, Harshav, B, Harshav, B p425
24. Kruk, H, Harshav, B, Harshav, B p432-433
25. Tory, A, p230

26. Ezergailis, A, *The Holocaust in Latvia, 1941-1944: The Missing Center* (US Holocaust Memorial Museum, Washington DC 1996) p241-242
27. Fleming, G, *Hitler and the Final Solution* (University of California Press, Berkeley CA 1987) p88

8 Liquidation

1. Longerich, P (2013) p573
2. Czerniaków, A, *In Warschauer Getto: das Tagebuch des Adam Czerniakow 1939-1942* (Beck, Munich 2013) p285
3. Margolis, R, Tobias, J, p225
4. Sachslehner, J, p188-189
5. Quoted in Arad, Y, p363
6. Kruk, H, Harshav, B, Harshav, B, p466-467
7. McDonough, F, *The Hitler Years. Volume II: Disaster 1940-1945* (Apollo, London 2020) p396
8. Moczarski, K, Fitzpatrick, M, Stroop, J, *Conversations with an Executioner* (Prentice-Hall, Hoboken NJ 1981) p164
9. Yad Vashem Archive, NO-2403
10. Kruk, H, Harshav, B, Harshav, B, p580
11. Quoted in Oevermann, J, *Vilnius 1944: Spurensuche* (Self-published, 1995) p95
12. Rolnikaite M, p148-151
13. Arad, Y, p387-399
14. Tory, A, p355
15. Bubnys, A, *Vokiečių Saugumo Policijos ir SD Vilnaiaus Ypatingasis Būrys 1941-1944 m* (Lietuvos Gyventojų Genocido ir Rezistensijos Tyrimo Centras, Vilnius 2019) p23
16. Tory, A, p386-387
17. Bartusevičius, V et al, p223-224
18. Laosson, M, Päll, E, Saat, J, *Saksa Fašistlik Okupatsioon Eestis Aastail 1941-1944* (Poliitiline Kirjandus, Tallinn 1947) p411
19. Quoted in *Estonia 1940-1945: Reports of the Estonian International Commission for the Investigation of Crimes Against Humanity* (Estonian Foundation for the Investigation of Crimes Against Humanity, Tallinn 2005) p697
20. Interrogation minutes of Juhan Jüriste by KGB 1 December 1960 in *Eesti Riigiarhiivi Osakond* SM 130-28195
21. Eesti Ajaloomuuseum, Tallinn, *Monatsbericht des SS Lagerartzt KL Waiwara 25/10/1943*, D152-2-40, p3-12
22. Bender, S, *The Jews of Białystok During World War II and he Holocaust* (University Press of New England, Lebanon NH 2008) p262-263
23. Dworzecki, M, p361-362
24. Kruk, H, Harshav, B, Harshav, B, p660
25. Korchak, R, p208-209
26. Quoted in Arad, Y, p417
27. Rolnikaite, M, p157-158

28. Lazar, C, *Hurban va-Mered* (Muze'on ha-lohamim Veha-Partizanim, Bet Z'abotinski, Tel Aviv 1988) p166-167
29. Arad, Y, p426
30. Memoir of Samuel Esterowicz, p145, available at www.searchformajorplagge.com
31. Quoted in Arad, Y, p426-427
32. Lazar, H, p181
33. Rolnikaite, M, p164-165
34. Kowalski, I, *A Secret Press in Nazi Europe* (Central Guide, New York 1972) p263
35. Beker, S, *Symphony on Fire: A Story of Music and Spiritual Resistance During the Holocaust* (Wordsmithy, New Milford NJ 2007) p58-59
36. Rolnikaite, M, p171-172
37. Tory, A, p481
38. Megargee, G (ed.) *The United States Holocaust Memorial Museum Encyclopaedia of Camps and Ghettos* (Indiana University Press, Bloomington IND 2009, 3 vols.) Vol.I p849
39. Tory, A, p490
40. Arad, Y, p470
41. Tory, A, p509-510

9 The Approaching End

1. KGB interrogation of Krein, A, Eesti Riigiarhiivi Filiaal Tallinn, SM 133-1-10 p134
2. Rolnikaite, M, p177-178
3. Rolnikaite, M, p190
4. Memoir of Samuel Esterowicz, p345-346, available at www.searchformajorplagge.com
5. Memoir of Perela Esterowicz, p44-45, available at www.searchformajorplagge.com
6. Memoir of Samuel Esterowicz, p346, available at www.searchformajorplagge.com
7. Memoir of Perela Esterowicz, p46, available at www.searchformajorplagge.com
8. Peterson, A, Smith, B, *Heinrich Himmler: Geheimreden 1933 bis 1945* (Propylaeen, Frankfurt am Main 1974) p269
9. Peterson, A, Smith, B, p272-273
10. Peterson, A, Smith, B, p275
11. Rolnikaite, M, p204-206
12. *Estonia 1940-1945*, p729
13. Plagge Denazification Process file, p15-16
14. Letter from Plagge to Göcke 18 February 1944, available at www.searchformajorplagge.com
15. Ganor, S, p245-246
16. Memoir of Perela Esterowicz, p49, available at www.searchformajorplagge.com
17. Rotschild-Galerkin, S, *Walking, Running, Hiding: Memories of a Child in Vilna During the Second World War* (self-published, Toronto 2003) p77
18. Rolnikaite, M, p211-212
19. Memoir of Samuel Esterowicz, p351, available at www.searchformajorplagge.com

10 Liberation

1. Glantz, D, *When Titans Clashed: How the Red Army Stopped Hitler* (University Press of Kansas, Lawrence KS 1995) p297
2. Ganor, S, p249
3. Memoir of Perela Esterowicz, available at www.searchformajorplagge.com
4. Letter from Karl Plagge to Anke Plagge, 21 June 1944, available at www.searchformajorplagge.com
5. Rolnikaite, M, p220-221
6. Paldiel, M (2000) p88-90
7. Memoir of Perela Esterowicz, available at www.searchformajorplagge.com
8. Memoir of Perela Esterowicz, available at www.searchformajorplagge.com
9. Memoir of Perela Esterowicz, available at www.searchformajorplagge.com
10. Tomaszewski, L, *Kronika Wileńska 1941-1945 z Dziejów Polskiego Państwa Podziemnego* (Oficyna Wydawnicza, Warsaw 1992) p221
11. Quoted in Oevermann, J, p102
12. Good, M, p80-82
13. Buttar, P, p188-192
14. Memoir of Perela Esterowicz, available at www.searchformajorplagge.com
15. Ganor, S, p254
16. Paldiel, M, p87
17. Eesti Riigiarhiivi Filiaal, Tallinn, SM 133-1-10, p134
18. Quoted in Stone, D, *The Liberation of the Camps: The End of the Holocaust and its Aftermath* (Yale University Press, New Haven CT 2015) p45
19. ibid
20. Ganor, S, p281
21. Ganor, S, p283-284
22. Rolnikaite, M, p267-268
23. Rolnikaite, M, p277-278
24. Quoted in Jacobs, B, Pool, E, *The 100-Year Secret: Britain's Hidden* WWII *Massacre* (Lyons, Guilford CT 2004) p155-157
25. Ganor, S, p342
26. Ganor, S, p346

11 Different Fates: The Imperfections of Justice

1. Gentile, C, *Wehrmacht und Waffen-SS im Partisanenkrieg: Italien 1943-1945* (Ferdinand Schöningh, Paderborn 2012) p20
2. National Security Archive Washington DC, Central Intelligence Agency EGMA-61049 available at archive.org/details/GrauerGustav/GRAUER%2C%20GUSTAV_008
3. Rhodes, R, *Masters of Death: The SS-Einsatzgruppen and the Invention of the Holocaust* (Vintage, New York 2003) p272
4. Public Records Archive, Kew, London, Combined Services Detailed Interrogation Centre Report 30/09/1945, RG 319, 165A
5. Quoted in Earl, H, *The Nuremburg SS-Einsatzgruppen Trial 1945-1958* (Cambridge University Press, 2009) p56-57

6. Earl, H, p156-158
7. Library of Congress, Washington DC, *Trial of War Criminals Before the Nuremburg Military Tribunals Under Control Council Law 10, Nuremburg October 1946-April 1949* D804. G42 A42 OCLC 315875936 Vol. IV p534 16 vols
8. Ibid, p533-536
9. Earl, H, p144-147
10. Sagel-Grande, I, Fuchs, H, Rüter, C, *Justiz und NS-Verbrechen. Sammlung Deutscher Strafurteile Wegen Natzionalsozialistischer Tötungsverbrechen 1945-1966* (University Press, Amsterdam 1977) Vol. XIX p657-708 49 vols
11. Sachslehner, J, p213-214
12. Sachslehner, J, p219
13. Margolian, H, *Unauthorised Entry: The Truth About Nazi War Ciminals in Canada 1946-1956* (University of Toronto Press, Toronto 2000) p114
14. Quoted in Sachslehner, J, p179
15. Müller, S, 'Zum Drehbuch einer Ausstellung. Der Ulmer Einsatgruppenprozess von 1958' in Finger, J, Keller, S, Wirsching, A (eds) *Von Recht zur Geschichte. Akten aus NS-Prozessen als Quellen der Zeitgeschichte* (Vandenhoeck & Ruprecht, Göttingen 2009) p205-221
16. Wette, W (2011) p163-165
17. Wette, W, p165-166
18. Testimony of Maria Eichenmueller, Record of Plagge Denazification Trial, available at www.searchformajorplagge.com
19. Knappman, E, *The Adolf Eichmann Trial 1961* (Gale Research, Detroit MI 1997) p335
20. Cesarani, D *Eichmann: His Life and Crimes* (Vintage, London 2005) p300
21. Time Magazine, 19 March 19656
22. For an excellent account of the trial, see Sachslehner, J, p230-256
23. Sachslehner, J, p252
24. Quoted in Sachslehner, J, p256
25. Tory, A, p526
26. Levine, H, *In Search of Sugihara: The Elusive Japanese Diplomat Who Risked His Life To Rescue 10,000 Jews From The Holocaust* (Free Press, New York 1996) p258
27. Ganor, S, p.xii

12 Remembrance and Motivation

1. Arendt, H, *Eichmann in Jerusalem: A Report on the Banality of Evil* (Penguin, Harmondsworth 2007) p231
2. Wette, W (2013) p190-191
3. Quoted in De Waal, E, *The Hare with Amber Eyes* (Vintage, London 2011) p286
4. Quoted in Paldiel, M, p217
5. From 'Father Bronius Paukštys and his Brother Juozas' available at yadvashem.org/righteous/stories/paukstys.html
6. Good, M, p169-170
7. Quoted in Good, M, p179

8. Bartusevičius et al, p262
9. *Die Zeit* (Hamburg) 18/02/1999, p11
10. Quoted in Wette, W (2011) p181
11. Wette, W (2011) p184
12. For a full discussion of this, see Müller-Hill, B, 'The Idea of the Final Solution and the Role of Experts' in Cesarani, D (ed.) *The Final Solution: Origins and Implementation* (Routledge, New York 1994) p62-70
13. See for example Dower, J, *War Without Mercy: Race and Power in the Pacific War* (Pantheon, New York 1993)
14. Manstein, E von, Powell, G (trans.) *Lost Victories: The War Memoirs of Hitler's Most Brilliant General* (Presidio, Novato CA 1994) p179-180
15. Melvin, M, *Manstein: Hitler's Greatest General* (Weidenfeld & Nicolson, London 2010) p243
16. Full text available at www.searchformajorplagge.com
17. ibid.
18. Browning, C, p189
19. Wette, W, p202-203

Bibliography

Bundesarchiv Berlin
BundesarchivMilitärarchiv Freiburg
Deutsche Nationalbibliothek Frankfurt am Main
Eesti Ajaloomuuseum, Tallinn
Eesti Riigiarhiivi Filiaal, Tallinn
Eesti Riigiarhiivi Osakond, Tallinn
Library of Congress, Washington DC
Moreshet Archives, Menashe
National Security Archive, Washington DC
Public Records Archive, Kew, London
Steiermärkisches Landesarchiv, Graz
United States Holocaust Memorial Museum Archive, Washington DC
Yad Vashem Archive, Jerusalem
YIVO Institute for Jewish Research, New York

Die Zeit (Hamburg)
Foreign Affairs (Council on Foreign Relations, Congers, NY 2002)
Jewish Social Studies (Indiana University Press, Bloomington IN 2007)
Naval Research Reviews (US Navy, Washington DC 1973)
Time (New York)

Arendt, H, *Eichmann in Jerusalem: A Report on the Banality of Evil* (Penguin, Harmondsworth 2007)

Arad, Y, *Ghetto in Flames: The Struggle and Destruction of the Jews in Vilna in the Holocaust* (Holocaust Library, New York 1982)

Arnberger, H, Ardelt, R, *'Anschluss' 1938: Eine Dokumentation* (Österreichischer Bundesverlag, Vienna 1988)

Balberyszski, M, *Stronger than Iron: The Destruction of Vilna Jewry 1941-1945: an Eyewitness Account* (Gefen, Jerusalem 2010)

Bartusevičius, V, Tauber, J, Wette, W (eds), *Holocaust in Litauen: Krieg, Judenmorde und Kollaboration im Jahre 1941* (Böhlau, Cologne 2003)

Beker, S, *Symphony on Fire: A Story of Music and Spiritual Resistance During the Holocaust* (Wordsmithy, New Milford NJ 2007)

Bender, S, *The Jews of Białystok During World War II and the Holocaust* (University Press of New England, Lebanon NH 2008)

Benz, W Neiss, M (eds.) *Judenmord in Litauen. Studien und Dokumente* (Metropol, Berlin 1999)

Browning, C, *Ordinary Men: Reserve Police Battalion 101 and the Final Solution in Poland* (Harper Collins, London 2017)

Bubnys, A, *Vokiečių Saugumo Policijos ir SD Vilnaiaus Ypatingasis Būrys 1941-1944 m* (Lietuvos Gyventojų Genocido ir Rezistensijos Tyrimo Centras, Vilnius 2019)

Burleigh, M, *Ethics and Extermination: Reflections on Nazi Genocide* (Cambridge University Press, 1997)

Buttar, P, *Between Giants: The Battle for the Baltics in World War II* (Osprey, Oxford 2013)

Cesarani, D (ed.) *The Final Solution: Origins and Implementation* (Routledge, New York 1994)

Cesarani, D, *Eichmann: His Life and Crimes* (Vintage, London 2005)

Chalmers, B, *Birth, Sex and Abuse: Women's Voices Under Nazi Rule* (Grosvenor House, Surbiton 2015)

Czerniaków, A, *In Warschauer Getto: das Tagebuch des Adam Czerniakow 1939-1942* (Beck, Munich 2013)

De Waal, E, *The Hare with Amber Eyes* (Vintage, London 2011)

Dorries, R, *Hitler's Last Chief of Foreign Intelligence: Allied Interrogations of Walter Schellenberg* (Routledge, London, 2007)

Dower, J, *War Without Mercy: Race and Power in the Pacific War* (Pantheon, New York 1993)

Dworzecki, M, *Jerušolaim de Lite in Kamf un Umkum: Zichroines fun Wilner Geṭo* (Union Populaire Juive, Paris 1948)

Earl, H, *The Nuremburg SS-Einsatzgruppen Trial 1945-1958* (Cambridge University Press, 2009)

Estonia 1940-1945: Reports of the Estonian International Commission for the Investigation of Crimes Against Humanity (Estonian Foundation for the Investigation of Crimes Against Humanity, Tallinn 2005)

Ezergailis, A, *The Holocaust in Latvia, 1941-1944: The Missing Center* (US Holocaust Memorial Museum, Washington DC 1996)

Finger, J, Keller, S, Wirsching, A (eds) *Von Recht zur Geschichte. Akten aus NS-Prozessen als Quellen der Zeitgeschichte* (Vandenhoeck & Ruprecht, Göttingen 2009)

Fleming, G, *Hitler and the Final Solution* (University of California Press, Berkeley CA 1987)

Friedman, P, *Their Brothers' Keepers* (Holocaust Library, New York 1979)

Ganor, S, *Light One Candle: A Survivor's Tale from Lithuania to Jerusalem* (Kodansha USA, New York 2003)

Gelpernus, D, Bargman, C, O'Neil, R (trans.) *Kovno Ghetto Diary* (Gosudarstvennoye Isdatelstvo, Moscow 1948)

Gentile, C, *Wehrmacht und Waffen-SS im Partisanenkrieg: Italien 1943-1945* (Ferdinand Schöningh, Paderborn 2012)

Gerwarth, R, *Hitler's Hangman: The Life of Heydrich* (Yale University Press, Newhaven CT 2011)

Gilbert, S, *Music in the Holocaust: Confronting Life in the Nazi Ghettos and Camps* (Oxford University Press, 2005)

Glantz, D, *When Titans Clashed: How the Red Army Stopped Hitler* (University Press of Kansas, Lawrence KS 1995)

Goebbels, J, Fröhlich, E (ed.) *Die Tagebücher von Joseph Goebbels* (Institut für Zeitgeschichte, Munich 1996)

Gold, A, *A Special Fate: Chiune Sugihara, Hero of the Holocaust* (TMI, Providence RI, 2014)

Gordon, H, *The Shadow of Death: The Holocaust in Lithuania* (University Press of Kentucky, Lexington KY 2001)

Grossman, H, *The Underground Army: Fighters of the Bialystok Ghetto* (Holocaust Library, New York 1988)

Grossmann, V, Ehrenburg, I, Lustiger, A (trans.), *Der Schwarzbuch: Der Genozid den Sowjetischen Juden* (Rowohlt, Reinbeck bei Hamburg 1994)

Halder, F, Burdick, C, Jacobsen, H-A (eds), *The Halder War Diary 1939-1942* (Greenhill, Novato CA 1988)

Hebert, V, *Hitler's Generals on Trial: The Last War Crimes Tribunal at Nuremberg* (University Press of Kansas, Lawrence KS 2010)

Hitler, A, Mannheim, R (trans.) *Mein Kampf* (Houghton Mifflin Harcourt, Boston MA1998) 2 volumes

Jacobs, B, Pool, E, *The 100-Year Secret: Britain's Hidden WWII Massacre* (Lyons, Guilford CT 2004)

Kaplan, J, *Prague: The Turbulent Century* (Kinemann, Cologne 1997)

Klee, E, Riess, V, Dressen, W, *Schöne Zeiten: Judenmord aus der Sicht der Täter und Gaffer* (Fischer, Frankfurt am Main 1998)

Klein, D (ed.) *Hidden History of the Kovno Ghetto* (Bullfinch, Boston 1997)

Knappman, E, *The Adolf Eichmann Trial 1961* (Gale Research, Detroit MI 1997)

Korchak, R, *Flames in Ash* (Merhavya Sifriat Poalim, Tel Aviv 1946)

Kowalski, I, *A Secret Press in Nazi Europe* (Central Guide, New York 1972)

Kruk, H, Harshav, B, Harshav, B, *The Last Days of the Jerusalem of Lithuania: Chronicles from the Vilna Ghetto and the Camps* (Yale University Press, New Haven CT 2002)

Lazar, C, *Hurban va-Mered* (Muze'on ha-lohamim Veha-Partizanim, Bet Z'abotinski, Tel Aviv 1988)

Levine, H, *In Search of Sugihara: The Elusive Japanese Diplomat who Risked his Life to Rescue 10,000 Jews from The Holocaust* (Free Press, New York 1996)

Longerich, P, *Politik der Vernichtung: Eine Gesamtdarstellung der Nationalsozialistischen Judenverfolgung* (Piper, Munich 1991)

Laosson, M, Päll, E, Saat, J, *Saksa Fašistlik Okupatsioon Eestis Aastail 1941-1944* (Poliitiline Kirjandus, Tallinn 1947)

Longerich, P, *Heinrich Himmler* (Oxford University Press, 2013)

Mallmann, K-M, Böhler, J, Matthäus, J, *Einsatzgruppen in Polen. Darstellung und Dokumentation* (WBG, Darmstadt 2008)

Mallmann, K, Angrick, A, Matthäus, J, Cüppers, M (eds.) *Ereignismeldung UdSSR 1941: Dokumente der Einsatzgruppen in der Sowjetunion* (WBG Academic, Darmstadt 2011)

Manstein, E von, Powell, G (trans.) *Lost Victories: The War Memoirs of Hitler's Most Brilliant General* (Presidio, Novato CA 1994)

Margolian, H, *Unauthorised Entry: The Truth About Nazi War Criminals in Canada 1946-1956* (University of Toronto Press, Toronto 2000)

Margolis, R, Tobias, J, *Die Geheimen Notizen des K Sakowicz: Dokumente zur Judenvernichtung in Ponary* (Antogo, Nuremburg 2004)

McDonough, F, *The Hitler Years. Volume II: Disaster 1940-1945* (Apollo, London 2020)

Megargee, G (ed.) *The United States Holocaust Memorial Museum Encyclopaedia of Camps and Ghettos* (Indiana University Press, Bloomington IND 2009, 3 vols.)

Melvin, M, *Manstein: Hitler's Greatest General* (Weidenfeld & Nicolson, London 2010)

Moczarski, K, Fitzpatrick, M, Stroop, J, *Conversations with an Executioner* (Prentice-Hall, Hoboken NJ 1981)

Morgenstern, M, *Martin Luther: Von der Juden und ihren Lügen* (Berlin University Press, 2016)

Oevermann, J, *Vilnius 1944: Spurensuche* (Self-published, 1995)

Olusoga, D, Erichsen, C, *The Kaiser's Holocaust: Germany's Forgotten Genocide and the Colonial Roots of Nazism* (Faber, London 2010)

Paldiel, M, *Saving the Jews: Men and Women who Defied the Final Solution* (Schreiber, Rockville MD 2000)

Paldiel, M, *Diplomat Heroes of the Holocaust* (Rabbi Arthur Schneier Center for International Affairs of Yeshiva University, New York 2007)

Paul, G, Mallmann, K-M, *Die Gestapo im Zweiten Weltkrieg. 'Heimatfront' und Besetztes Europa* (Primus, Darmstadt 2000)

Paul, G, *Die Täter der Shoah: Fanatische Natrionalsozialisten oder Ganz Normale Deutsche?* (Wallstein, Göttingen 2002)

Peterson, A, Smith, B, *Heinrich Himmler: Geheimreden 1933 bis 1945* (Propylaeen, Frankfurt am Main 1974)

Priemel, K, *Rettung durch Arbeit: Handlungsspielräume von Wehrmachtsangehörigen im Kontext des Holocausts am Beispiel von Vilnius, Litauen* (Masters thesis, Freiburg 2002)

Rhodes, R, *Masters of Death: The SS-Einsatzgruppen and the Invention of the Holocaust* (Vintage, New York 2003)

Rolnikaite, M, *Ich muss Erzählen* (Rowohlt, Reinbek bei Hamburg 2004)

Roth, A, *Aus der Kampfzeit des Deutschvölkischen Schutz- und Trutzbundes: Eine Erinnerungsschrift* (Schwitzke, Hamburg 1939)

Rotschild-Galerkin, S, *Walking, Running, Hiding: Memories of a Child in Vilna During the Second World War* (self-published, Toronto 2003)

Rudashevski, Y, Matenko, P, *The Diary of the Vilna Ghetto June 1941-April* 1943 (Ghetto Fighters' House, Tel Aviv 1973)

Sachslehner, J, *Rosen für den Mörder: Die Zwei Leben des NS-Täters Franz Murer* (Molden, Vienna 2017)

Sagel-Grande, I, Fuchs, H, Rüter, C, *Justiz und NS-Verbrechen. Sammlung Deutscher Strafurteile Wegen Natzionalsozialistischer Tötungsverbrechen 1945-1966* (University Press, Amsterdam 1977) 49 vols

Schur, G, Porudominskij, W *Die Juden von Vilna: die Aufzeichnungen* (DT Taschenbuch, Munich 1999)

Schwarz, G, *Eine Frau an seiner Seite: Ehefrauen in der 'SS-Sippengemeinschaft'* (Aufbau Taschenbuch, Berlin 2001)

Sebag Montefiore, S, *Stalin: The Court of the Red Tsar* (Vintage, London 2004)

Stang, K, *Kollaboration und Massenmord: die Litauische Hilfspolizei, das Rollkommando Hamann und die Ermordung der Litausichen Juden* (Lang, Frankfurt am Main 1996)

Stone, D, *The Liberation of the Camps: The End of the Holocaust and its Aftermath* (Yale University Press, New Haven CT 2015)

Sutzkewer, A, *Vilner Geto 1941-1944* (IKUF, Buenos Aires 1947)

Tauber, J, *Argeit als Hoffnung: Jüdische Ghettos in Litauen 1941-1944* (De Gruyter, Berlin 2015)

Tomaszewski, L, *Kronika Wileńska 1941-1945 z Dziejów Polskiego Państwa Podziemnego* (Oficyna Wydawnicza, Warsaw 1992)

Tory, A, Gilbert, M, Porat, D, *Surviving the Holocaust: The Kovno Ghetto Diary* (Pimlico, London 1990)

Urban, W, *The Teutonic Knights: A Military History* (Greenhill, London 2003)

Valentinas, B, *1941 m. Birželio Sukilimas: Dokumentų Rinkinys* (Lietuvos Gyventojų ir Rezistencijos Tyrimo Centras, Vilnius 2000)

Wette, W, *Karl Jäger: Mörder der Litauischen Juden* (Fischer, Frankfurt am Main 2011)

Wette, W, *Feldwebel Anton Schmid: Ein Held der Humanität* (Fischer, Frankfurt am Main 2013)

Wildt, M, *Generation des Unbedingten. Das Führungskorps des Reichssicherheitshauptamtes* (Hamburger Verlag, Hamburg 2002)

Williams, M, *Reinhard Heydrich: The Biography* (Ulric, Church Stretton 2002) – 2 volumes

Zuroff, E, Beruf: Nazijäger. *Die Suche nach dem Langen Atem: Die Jagd nach den Tätern des Völkermordes* (Ahriman, Freiburg 1996)

Index